Aesthetic Dining

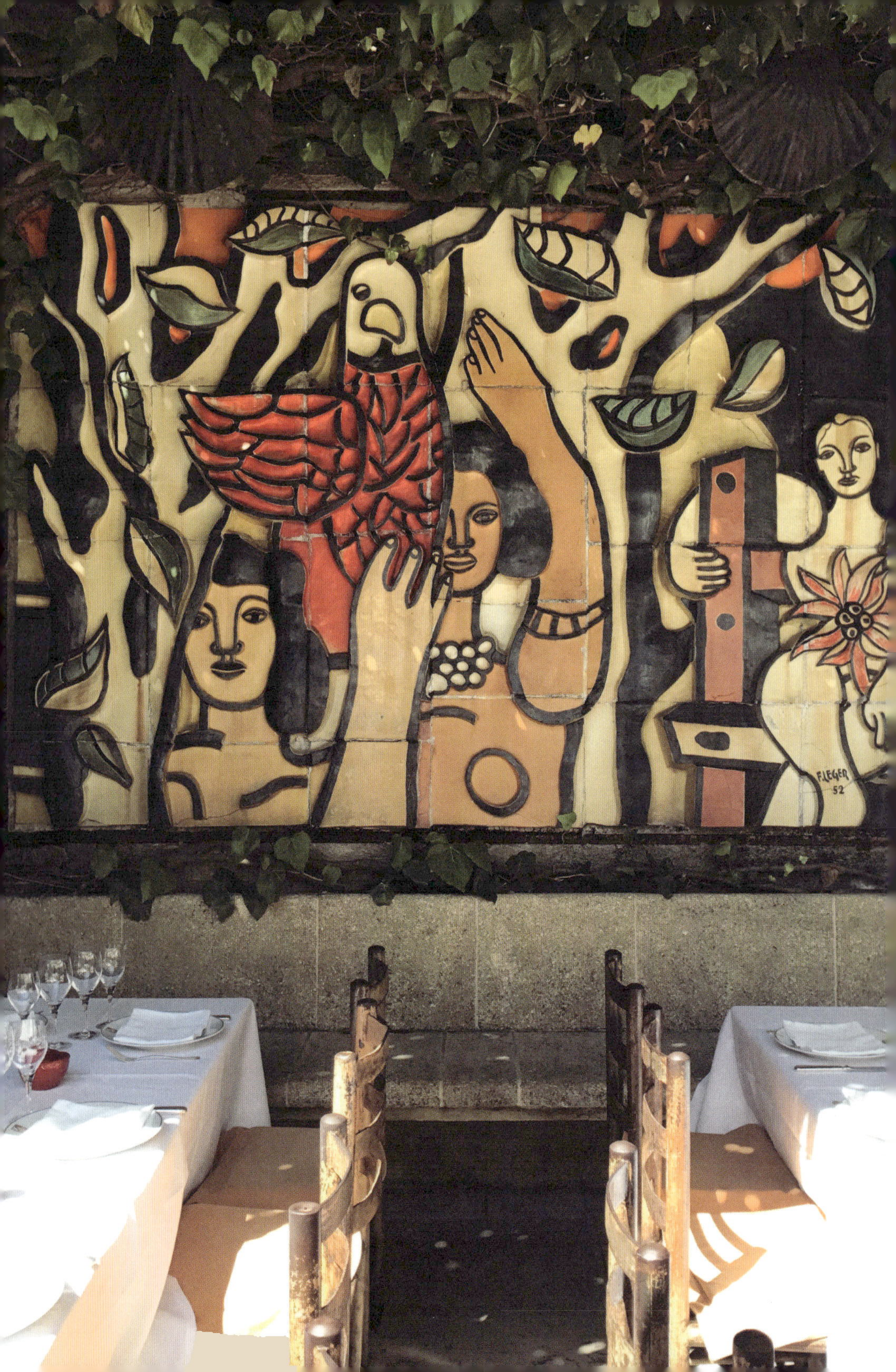
F. LEGER
52

Aesthetic Dining
The Art Restaurant Around the World

CHRISTINA MAKRIS

CULTURESHOCK

About the author

In pursuit of visual taste and aesthetic dining, Christina Makris has travelled to six continents, visited more than 100 cities, and sat at countless tables.

With a doctorate in philosophy, she has been involved with the arts as a collector, philanthropist and trustee, and with restaurants as an investor, consultant and sybarite.

Christina is currently writing on art and wine.

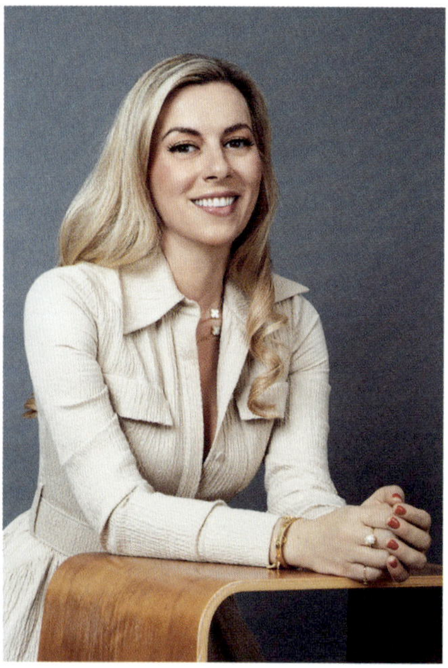

Published by Cultureshock
27B Tradescant Road
London SW8 1XD
www.cultureshockmedia.co.uk

Distributed by ACC Art Books
Sandy Lane
Old Martlesham
Woodbridge
Suffolk IP12 4SD
+44 (1394) 389950
www.accartbooks.com

ISBN 978-0-99-545465-1

Frontispiece: Ferdinand Leger's mural over the external dining space of the Colombe d'Or in Provence

Contents

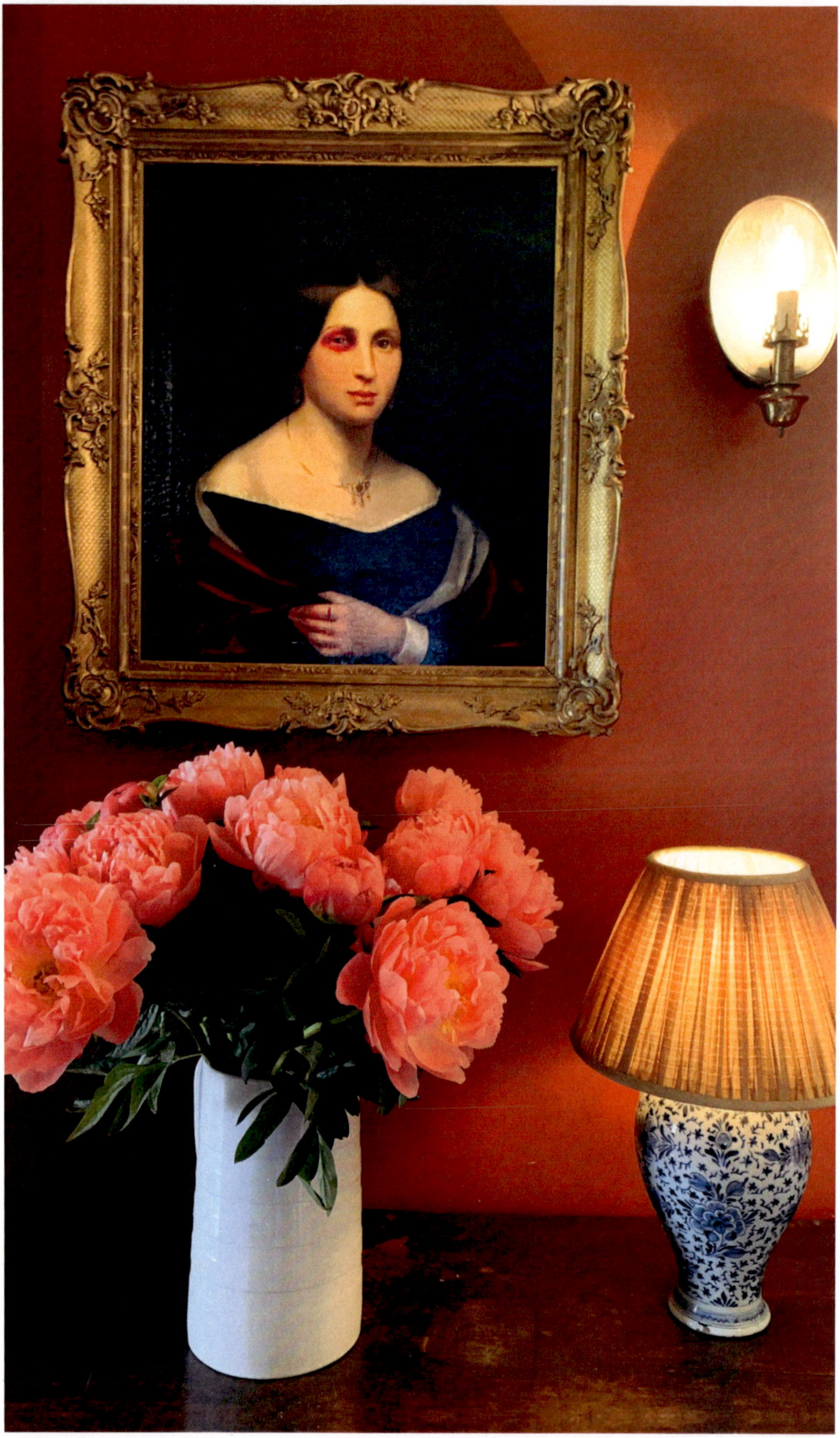

Introducing the Art Restaurant

"For the sake of making life as superlatively polished as the most sublime work of art, we ought to notice the Ordinary."
— Cynthia Ozick

Let's start with creative tension, or as Damien Hirst puts it: "Chefs are really very good at the cooking, or they're cunts." He should know, given that his involvement with restaurants, food and chefs spans over three decades. From the viscerally unappetising life cycle of flies and rotting meat in *A Thousand Years*, his first major sculpture in 1990, to *Cock and Bull*, the Hereford cow and cockerel in a tank of formaldehyde that hovered above the diners in chef Mark Hix's Tramshed restaurant from 2012 to 2020, Hirst has played provocatively with public taste. He's put his money where his mouth is too, with artistically immersive restaurants, notably Pharmacy One and Two, and is candid about their success and failure.

He is not the only artist with a strong view on chefs and dining. Brazilian Vik Muniz knows "enough chefs to know that a great many of them are real artists, they involve all your senses simultaneously. It takes some kind of knowledge of how you put these things together. It also has to do with a lot of imagination and creating scenarios." There is an undeniable affinity between artists and chefs. They just can't leave each other alone. They inspire and influence one another; they study their respective methods; they borrow from the other's practice for their own. British sculptor Conrad Shawcross is "very suspicious of artists who can't cook. If you are unsure about an artist, you should ask them to cook for you." There is something about the making, the fusing of ingredients, the taste of cooking, the possibilities of dining that binds the two professions together. Michael Craig-Martin says artists and the art business "are the most social of worlds"; dinners and dining together are important for enhancing careers and reputations. Artists and chefs circle each other, they befriend each other, and, as this book explores, they often celebrate these culinary and artistic relationships in art restaurants.

Aesthetic Dining: The Art Restaurant Around the World charts 24 restaurants that have art collections, chefs who collect art, restaurateurs who promote artists, and artists who make works for restaurants. The phenomenon of the restaurant orientated around visual taste has been in existence for over a century – Maxim's in Paris and Del Cambio in Turin were both established in the 19th century – and examples can be found internationally. This book documents for the first time their wide range of styles and cuisines, as well as their geographical and historical spread, while illustrating the fusion between visual and culinary taste through the recounting of the individual restaurants' histories and interviews with artists who have collaborated with chefs and hung works in their collections.

It examines the different models of art restaurants found throughout the world, ranging from historic venues where collections grew organically, such as the Kronenhalle or the Colombe d'Or, all the way to simulated or virtual experiences of aesthetic dining such as Vik Muniz and Daniel Boulud's decades-long collaboration. Every restaurant included is a testament to friendships, collaborations, sometimes competition, and the collective desires of their chefs and restaurateurs.

The book uses dining and chefs to unlock taste in art, and art to unlock taste, in the creation of a restaurant, from inspirations and concepts behind the cuisine to the vision for the interior design. Restaurants are important cultural hubs, and each in their own time and geography carry with them economic, social and even aesthetic truths. They are more complicated ecosystems than mere sites for an ephemeral meal that is quickly forgotten when the diner exits and continues with their everyday life. In fact, they often succeed in lifting an ordinary experience out of its normal context and making it *extraordinary*. The art restaurant highlights and uncovers facets of the quotidian events we take for granted, such as dining with those closest to us; it is a true celebration of the joyous activity that the global pandemic has made society pine for. In these everyday activities, the Australian artist John Beard says, "looking does not necessarily mean seeing, as eating and drinking do not necessarily mean tasting". This is where aesthetic dining comes in. Taste is the unifying factor in looking at art and dining – we use taste to explain both. Aesthetic taste and literal taste interact with one another implicitly and we know we are experiencing it when it is happening, even though we may not be able to explain it. The art restaurant shows rather than describes this phenomenon.

There have been important artistic involvements with cooking and restaurants throughout the 20th century. The Futurists had much to say about dining, writing a cookbook and replacing what they perceived as the gluten-induced lethargy of traditional, sentimental Italian cuisine with a high-octane-fuelled dining experience fit for a modern age of mechanical advancement. They were forebears of aesthetic dining in terms of conceiving the whole dining ritual as an instrument for revolution. The setting of the table, the cutlery and the room one dined in were as essential to the revolution as the ingredients on the plate. Mark Rothko undertook the Seagram Commission to paint murals for the Grill Restaurant of the Four Seasons Hotel in Manhattan in 1958, but famously pulled the work, returning the funds to his tycoon patrons, the Bronfman family, and donated the paintings to the Tate. He told his gallery assistant: "Anybody who will eat that kind of food for those kinds of prices will never look at a painting of mine." This is important for the history of art and restaurants because it raises the discomfiting spectre of how privilege and wealth are also part of the story.

There are paradoxical forces at work in restaurants. They require creativity – but also accounting. They produce an intense sensation of being in the moment, but they scale this up and replicate it multiple times during the day for multiple diners, making it both immediate and eternal. Christoph Ribbat, author of *In the Restaurant: Society in Four Courses*, calls modern diners "gastro-thinkers" who attach more meaning to dining out in all its forms than ever before. Food and dining culture has moved beyond being just about sustenance to become an expression of identity, community, history. And with the addition of serious art collections and commissions, it is loaded with richer, more complex and nuanced meanings.

This collection of establishments and their stories of collecting and promoting art is a plea to both visitors and restaurateurs. To the former, it demonstrates what artworks might be found in restaurants, and that this may serve as a marker for necessitating a more considered, heedful dining experience, given the diners are part of a system, a tradition, an aesthetic adventure. To the latter, it illustrates the importance of the environment for sharing meals, showing how a shared history is created and a community established by proprietors who understand that their passion for art collecting can be displayed for public benefit.

We behave differently when we look at art, we are more observant, we are more open to our senses being engaged to receive what is being presented on the wall. Likewise, when we go to a restaurant to eat, we may also be in a state of heightened sensual engagement. Art restaurants seek to provoke this sensation and play with the idea of considered aesthetic dining, as well as shifting the context in which we usually encounter art.

The Art Restaurant Today

The restaurant industry is one of the most competitive sectors in the world. Many experience its dynamism, development and evolution in our major cities and towns. Establishments come and go almost overnight. Even during the course of the research for this book and visits to the restaurants, the details, business practices, purpose and ownership of certain venues on the original list had changed, resulting in some no longer being included, such as Bibo in Hong Kong, Mark Hix's full London restaurant portfolio and Theaster Gates's Currency Exchange Café in Chicago.

The art restaurant emerged in what was a fragile ecology and sensitive economy even before the pandemic of 2020 pulverised so much of the global hospitality trade. There exists, therefore, an urgency to this project of documenting these establishments. Everybody knows or should know the feeling of sadness or disappointment when a favourite and regularly visited restaurant closes down. The staff lose their jobs, the kitchen becomes cold, the proprietor may face financial ruin and, selfishly, from the diners' perspective, they lose a connection to the backdrop of certain memories and milestones shared with others. When an earlier version of this project was conceived in 2012, Odin's off Marylebone High Street was still purveying a quiet, faded elegance, serving British comfort food in its art-filled interior, in its traditional, unassuming way. That was to be the last year of this historic venue, which was then occupied by a generic French brasserie brand in a neighbourhood that has turbo-charged its change regime to encompass a succession of multinational luxury chain outlets. And even that did not make an enduring impression on London's real estate palimpsest, as the pandemic took it out in May 2020. Inevitably, proprietors pass away, as Dooky Chase's Miss Leah Chase did in June 2019, and pieces from collections are sold off. Christie's, Bonhams and Sotheby's have held sales specifically for the collections of several restaurant art collectors. Langan's, the Kronenhalle, Paris Bar and The Ivy have all auctioned works. The next generation of owners often have different ideas about managing their parents' assets: Dooky Chase and Michael's have the children of the founders running the restaurants, while at the time of going to print, Lucio Galletto was planning his retirement and handing down the Lucio's business.

This volume is a celebration of specific art restaurants visited and appreciated, a love letter to restaurants in general, where we can share repasts with those close to us, and, finally, a call to action: go and visit these places, eat slowly, dine discernibly, observe the art and relish the immersive experience. Savour the delights of the cuisine, the company, the conversation. To be surrounded by art when you are dining is to be both enfolded in the sensory insights that may arise and to be receptive to the aesthetic experience of the *pleasures of the table.*

From Table to Tableau
Taste in Art Restaurants

"Beasts feed. Men eat. Only the man of intellect knows how to eat."
Jean Anthelme Brillat-Savarin

Restaurants that collect and display artworks and engage with artists are to be found internationally, in countries ranging from Egypt to China, in cities as contrasting as New Orleans and Zurich. Gourmands can feast with Matisse on the Côte d'Azur and Zeng Fanzhi in Hong Kong. Epicures can eat with Tracey Emin in London, Joseph Beuys in Modena or Faith Ringgold in Harlem. They can dine with Sidney Nolan pieces in Sydney and devour David Hockneys in Santa Monica. Gastronomes can even take a Michelangelo Pistoletto as a digestif in Piedmont or a Louise Bourgeois as a palate cleanser in Provence, with a Vik Muniz for dessert in Rio de Janeiro.

These art restaurants synthesise taste in food with taste in art, food and art being essential ingredients for gourmands or anyone interested in what taste means and what it does to us. We relish eating good food, we enjoy visiting unique restaurants, and we appreciate how art stimulates us. In these pursuits, there is something at work in the fusion, which the art restaurant enhances and revels in. In its most fundamental form, it exercises diners' abilities of taste, both at the level of literally tasting food, and on the aesthetic level of engaging our senses and processing our thoughts.

In these establishments the embodied and ritualistic experience of dining supports thinking about this activity and explores different interpretations of an art restaurant. What seems like a simple, straightforward act of eating in a setting enhanced by art not only engages all the senses but is also instrumental in creating memories and meaning by reinforcing context and evoking nostalgia – "hunger thinking", in Ernest Hemingway's words. Art restaurants provide opportunities to rethink the ordinary act of dining. Sensual engagement is brought into a process of social bonding in a commensurate environment. What begins as an individual, prosaic act of taking food into the body is replicated by others. This unfurls and multiplies, making memory and meaning, and also enhances the appreciation of what is refined, what is extraordinary, what is special, including the art in the space. When we combine the subjective experience of food and the subjective experience of art, a new element emerges that is somewhere between the gustatory, *literal* understanding of *taste*, and the predilection, the discrimination that constitutes *aesthetic taste*. It is "as much a matter of spirit as of body", as the renowned American food writer M.F.K. Fisher observed. At this moment of dining, "everything is right; nothing jars. There is a kind of harmony, with every sensation and emotion melting into one chord of wellbeing." These different uses of taste can come together in the art restaurant – in the most desirable situation – to create an experience of it. The restaurant may be "the gourmand's Eden", according to Jean Anthelme Brillat-Savarin, the French 18th-century magistrate, philosopher and founder of modern gourmandism, but the art restaurant ensures this paradise incorporates the same physical and intellectual pleasures involved in the appreciation of art.

There are many types of art restaurant in which to explore aesthetic dining. Some historic establishments may have ceased operating, but they have not ceased inspiring new models. From the 1980s onwards, Irish restaurateur Peter Langan's influence was notable in several London brasseries, including established venues such as Quaglino's, and more widely within the Chris Corbin and Jeremy King group that still hosts London's well-heeled diners today. Several contemporary art restaurants are examples of independent, innovative enterprises, combining art and food in a defined space. These vary from the invitation to dine in a restored Baroque hamlet surrounded by striking contemporary art (Castello di Ama), to being engulfed in plush pink velvet and thumped by existential slogans in drawings (Sketch). They may even be evolving experiences, such as how artist Vik Muniz collaborates with chef Daniel Boulud to produce picturesque feasts, creating an ethos of ritualistic binding for those involved. The possibilities of art restaurants and the range of international interpretations appeal to a discerning segment of the restaurant market. They signal an appreciation of the complexities of dining in an environment that will not stay static because adding artworks questions, provokes and, at the very least, delights the diner. Before the global pandemic ravaged the hospitality industry in 2020, there were an estimated 13,743 restaurants in Hong Kong, 18,110 in London, 26,697 in New York, even 1,216 in New Orleans, as well as a vast number of eateries in Cairo. Incorporating art into the dining space ensures the restaurant remains memorable – a gesture towards the complexity of taste – as well as offering a space for collector chefs to share their love of aesthetics.

Aesthetic Dining

The etymology of the word restaurant is the Latin, *restaurare* – to rebuild and restore. In the art restaurant, this connotation is enhanced because these establishments provide an experience for diners to exercise their aesthetic capabilities. In the presence of art, we are never passive observers, we contemplate, reflect, appreciate. In the midst of artworks, "a peculiar exchange takes place", in the words of architect and philosopher Juhani Pallasmaa. We "lend [our] emotions and associations to the space and the space lends [us] its aura, which entices and emancipates [our] perceptions and thoughts". This emancipation is fulfilling, physically and emotionally. It is appreciation, pleasure, and requires the senses to be actively engaged. The art restaurant encourages this sensory pleasure in its diners.

Art restaurants combine two of the most essential and pleasurable activities for those interested in matters of taste: the experience of looking at art and the

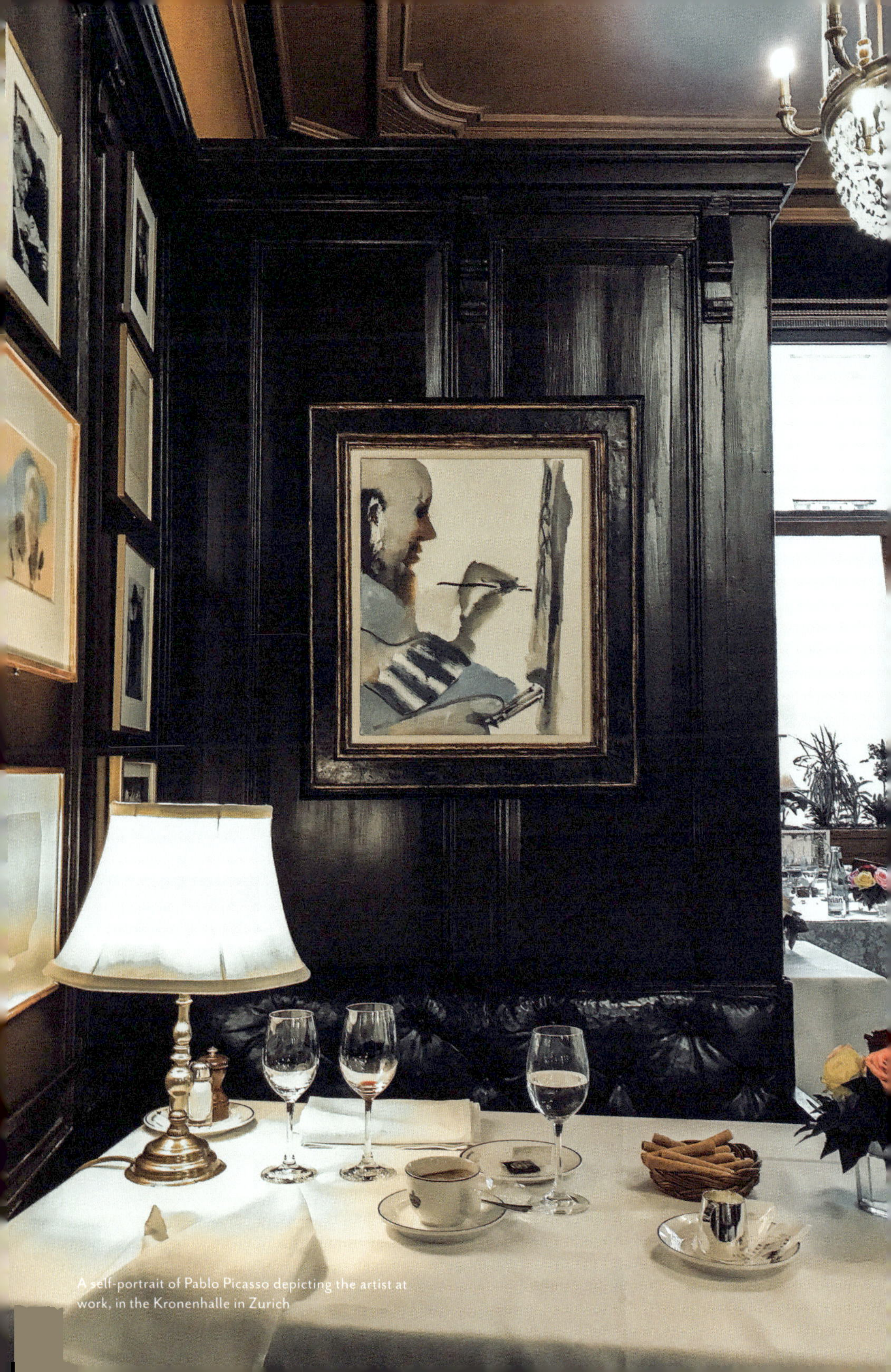

A self-portrait of Pablo Picasso depicting the artist at work, in the Kronenhalle in Zurich

experience of eating good food. The pursuit of this pleasure restores a sensual desire and need in us. We seek out these experiences like we quench our thirst; food restores, and art restores too. Something as quotidian as dining can be the basis for making sense of how we look and eat, as well as making memories through this aesthetic satiety. Brillat-Savarin argued "the pleasures of eating" begin with the "direct sensation of satisfying a need" but transform into the "pleasures of the table", as they become "a reflective sensation which is born from the various circumstances of place, time, things, and people who make up the surroundings of the meal". Eating in an art restaurant can accelerate this transformation. We know that looking at an artistic object is different from looking at something that is not art. Something as commonplace as dining – even more so in the company of others – suddenly enhances our abilities of judgement and discernment to appreciate art. Cynthia Ozick writes: "The Extraordinary can sometimes be a changeling, and can make its appearance in the cradle of the Ordinary; and then it is not until long afterward that we become aware of how the visitation was not, after all, an ordinary one." Pleasure is not superficial, not ephemeral, but instead builds into memory and meaning.

Thinking about taste as *aesthetic taste* also involves the way the body and its senses are brought to the experience, as they are in gustatory taste. Taste in the mind, just like taste in the mouth, uses analogy to explore a philosophical understanding. Embodied experiences of taste provide the framework to make aesthetic judgements and evaluations, and this can be heightened in the art restaurant. Even the most basic notion of taste, which implies corporeality and use of senses, has equipped aesthetics with some of its most exalted and abstract concepts used in art appreciation. Enlightenment philosophers including David Hume and Immanuel Kant took the notion of "taste" that was usually understood to be based in the body, and applied the critique of art. Although the body has traditionally been reviled by Western thinkers on a literal level, on an aesthetic level it has been essential to how we talk about taste and art. These considerations are present when dining in art restaurants: on the one hand they seem complicated, but on the other, peculiarly obvious. Fusing art and dining appears complicated because philosophical, aesthetic taste now becomes direct – as direct an act as taste in eating. Conversely, fusing art and dining is also obvious because physical taste is such a basic activity; we experience it multiple times a day, hardly reflecting on it, let alone ruminating on its significance.

Often art restaurants make as much of a feature of their art collections as their food, and some insist the art is taken as seriously as the dining. Massimo Bottura may have built one of the most distinctive restaurants in the world, serving fine caramelised pâté that dissolves on the tongue or subjecting aged parmesan cheese to a chemistry lab experiment, but he says contemporary art has been his "muse and his guide" in realising these culinary ideas. Lucio Galletto thought he had mastered traditional Ligurian cooking, until the celebrated Australian abstract artist John Olsen showed him how he could make his *aglio e olio* spaghetti even more mouth-watering (tip: fry the garlic). These chefs seem to be drawn to art collecting in a more fundamental way than other groups of professionals who collect, for instance, financiers, doctors or industrialists. The chefs are literal tastemakers for whom the collecting of visual art and cooking good food are inextricably linked to enhancing and heightening aesthetic taste, as they reinforce one another. There is an affinity between chefs and artists; both work by assembling ingredients and creating a greater whole for others to consume. As Vik Muniz observes, both chefs and artists are "between process" and both are concerned with "the technically impeccable". Both seek to interrogate the sensory in terms of what they make.

Throughout intellectual history, the concept of taste has been used to explain aesthetic appreciation. When diners experience aesthetic pleasure in an art restaurant, they use taste as a metaphor to make judgements and for the discernment required for aesthetic appreciation. Philosophers and cultural theorists have been drawn to this use of taste for centuries because it is relatively straightforward and so prevalent in daily activity – we eat every day, several times a day, very often in the company of others. Yet taste is inherently paradoxical, understood on two levels: the internal, subjective level of taste as it occurs in philosophical/psychological understandings of the self, and the external, objective level of taste in the social setting of restaurants. Taste begins internally on a bodily basis, and then refined in an external, social framework. Through the ritual of eating in restaurants that helps to create meaning in a cultural context, these art restaurants engineer the experience of aesthetic dining.

The artworks displayed in these establishments are an expression of each collector's personality and aesthetics, enabling them to stand out from their peers and clientele as being cultivated and discerning. There are many anecdotes about how Peter Langan of Langan's Brasserie or Michael Chow of the Mr Chow empire pursued and collected the actual artists as much as their works. Various friends of Langan, including Peter Blake and restaurateur Simon Parker Bowles, acknowledge the chef's eye for collecting unique works from artists ranging from Laura Knight to David Hockney. Chow's friendships with Andy Warhol, Jean-Michel Basquiat, Keith Haring and Ed Ruscha meant the artists continuously visited his restaurants throughout the 1970s and 1980s, enhancing the melting pot of tastemaking and cultural exchange, as well as creating mythologies of desirable and in-crowd eateries, where, at dinner, you just might be sitting next to a celebrity or literary giant, feeling like you are a part of the creative coterie in London or New York's intelligentsia.

In some of the art restaurants, the way art is acquired leads to and defines how the menu is created, and how the dining experience is engineered. Massimo Bottura says his Osteria Francescana menu, composed of dissonant and unexpected combinations of tastes, textures and presentation, is concocted in response to the contemporary art that he has had hanging on the walls of the restaurant through the years. A Maurizio Cattelan pigeon as a side order with your Po River eel – art encroaches upon the dining space by elevating the meal to an aesthetic experience, inviting in reveries, fantasies, pleasures. The "house shelters day-dreaming... protects the dreamer... allows one to dream in peace", the philosopher Gaston Bachelard wrote about architecturally enclosed spaces. Similarly, in the immersive environment of the art restaurant, its diners are in the space to conduct whatever conversation, create any exchange or fulfil any need they wish – to experience whatever seduction or fantasy in the pursuit of pleasure and satiety, greedy for the experience of life.

When taste is in the mind as well as in the mouth, and when identifying this experience with fellow diners, it touches upon fundamental tenets at the very core of our understanding of our place in the world. "Eating out has knowledge-expanding functions," as food historian Christoph Ribbat writes. "One dines in order to take in ideas and information about other cultures, new trends, new forms of creativity."

Filippo Marinetti, founder of the Futurist movement, identified the affinities between food and art when he said in 1932: "Every person has the sensation of eating not just good food but also works of art." He proposed the meal should be considered a ritual with all the elements of the table – cutlery, crockery, china, decoration, the dishes – working together, as would the diner's full sensations. In an art restaurant, one dines to continue the conversation with the artwork, its origins, the collector's intentions, and revel in its cultural symbolism. Suddenly a quick lunch in Scott's on a Wednesday afternoon can become something much more than a fleeting expense-account jolly.

The Meaning of Taste and the Taste of Meaning in the Art Restaurant

In the history of Western philosophy, taste has continually been relegated to the lowest position in the hierarchy of the senses. It was regarded as a servile function, a means to the end of satiating hunger, never experience in itself. The chasm grew when aesthetics chased perfection by privileging sight as the highest sense.

Anything based on the body was too animal and hence too irrational to apply to artistic appreciation. This negation of taste originated in Greek philosophy. Plato regarded the pleasures arising from the experience of taste as false pleasures. He believed taste was a means to pursue pleasure, which meant it was just relief from pain (its opposite). Hence taste was not its own, independent sensation, it was just not pain. Aristotle was marginally more generous in his explanation of taste. He argued since man aspired to achieve morality and temperance, he needed to exercise restraint. In order to succeed in this, man possesses the capacity for physical pleasure but then should actually suppress this pleasure. And since taste provides the capability to experience pleasure, holding it back achieves the moral state man sought in the Aristotelian version.

It was only from the Enlightenment onward that the notion of taste was used to explain aesthetic sensations and experiences. Critic and grammarian Dominique Bouhours used the term *la délicatesse* – with *taste* making an appearance in its etymology – in 1687 to single out the importance of emotion in aesthetic appreciation and the significance of individual responses to aesthetic objects over classical canons of correctness. Taste, although still bodily, is linked to the mental, the emotional, and is essential in appreciating art. The 18th-century Scottish philosopher, David Hume, argued that only the most experienced, rational observers of an aesthetic object could understand taste and be able to make the right judgements about the significance of the art. Despite the marginalisation of taste as bodily among Western philosophers, and the lasting influence of this view on thought and culture, they were all too ready to borrow the idea of taste and assign it to the highest form of creation: aesthetic taste. From that moment on, the discussion of taste in the philosophy of art traditionally pits it as a sensual, corporeal pleasure against aesthetic taste as the capability for discernment and making judgements.

For instance, the German philosopher Immanuel Kant's definition of taste has been prevalent since the 18th century, and dominant in modern philosophy of art. He defined it as the "appreciative sensibility of observers who experience delight when disinterestedly contemplating certain natural and artificial objects". Taste stands in as a description for the aesthetic, and is how we can experience the delight of art. Having this taste means you have a mental state of *disinterestedness* or *free play* for your mind to appreciate artistic objects. The form and content of the artwork come together to produce enjoyment. Kant believed art needs to engender this purity and pleasure, and puts the mind into a particular state – a mode of *disinterestedness*. Thus, we experience a notion of beauty that in turn is related to the good in a pure and unadulterated manner. The evocation of "beauty" may sound suspicious to contemporary ears. Nevertheless, it explains what goes on when we observe an artwork: we experience pleasure (related

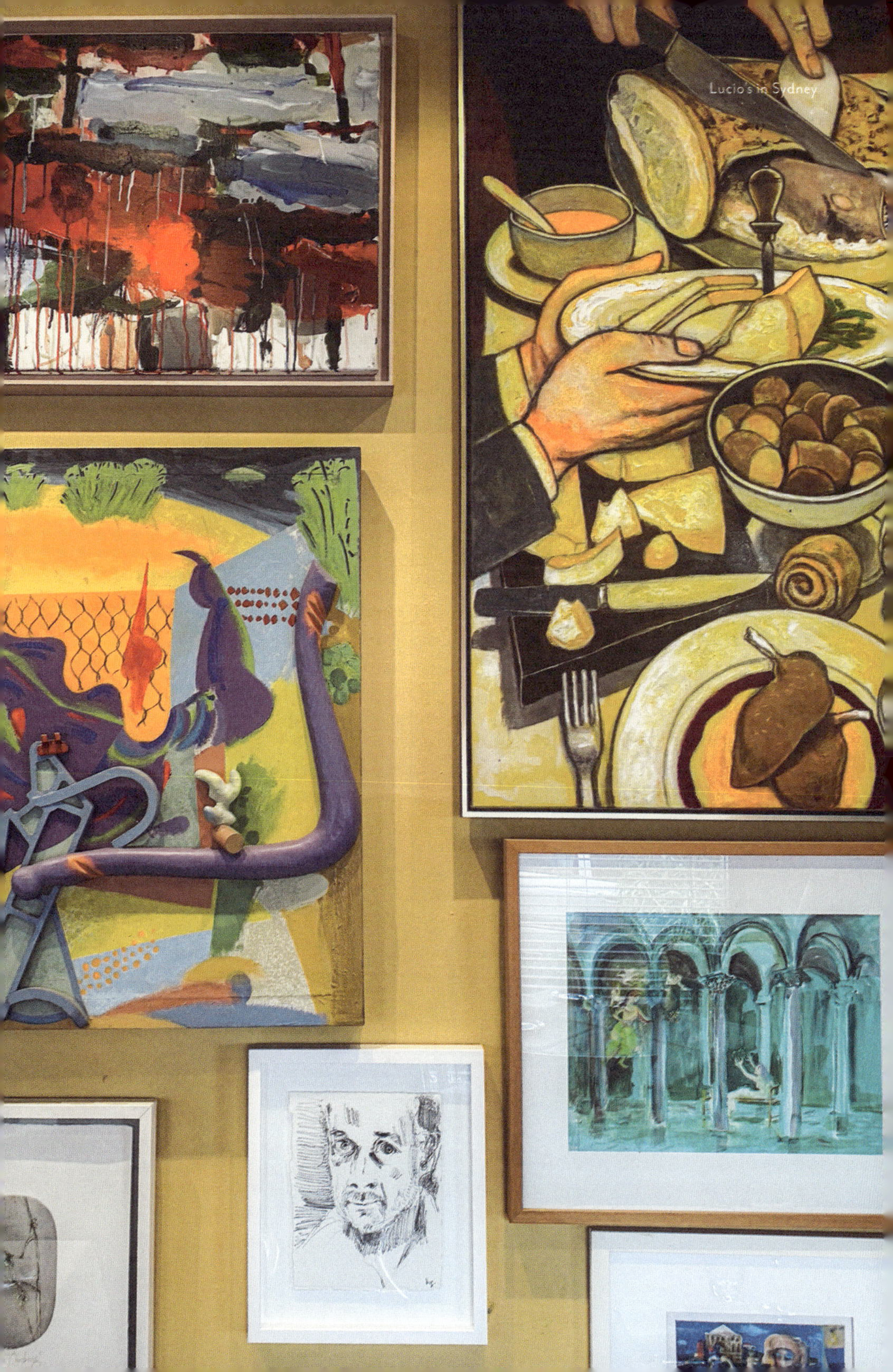

Lucio's in Sydney

to beauty) through our bodies. This requires discernment, which is based on judgement, and that requires the capacity to have aesthetic taste.

In the 20th century, aesthetic metaphor became a popular mode to explain taste and explore the hold it has over us. The philosopher Frank Sibley argued metaphors are essential to understanding and appreciating art, as they are pure representation and thus similar behaviours are required to understand them. All representation is interpretation. If taste now sits more comfortably in terms of appreciating art objects, the link to food should ostensibly be complementary. This raises a question on whether or not food should be considered an art form. Many chefs and artists believe it is, and many have an opinion on the matter. "Chefs want to be seen as painters," according to Damien Hirst, "but they never get the solidity... because the proof's always being eaten." The position relates to how we define food being a work of art, to deciding what is the artistic quality of food. Is it the object on the plate, the reaction to eating it, the total situation of preparation and presentation, or the chef's intention to make it an artwork? Restaurant designs and dishes are the only "art form" that change their content after reviews or feedback – most other traditional art forms remain fixed. The artistic relationship to food must be more than morsels laid out on a dish, or else any foaming froth or curlicue chocolate lines on a plate would be assigned unwarranted flights of aesthetic status. Food historian Margaret Visser argues a meal can be thought of as a work of art because it has "limits laid down, desires aroused and fulfilment, enticements, variety, patterning, and plot. As a work with art, not only the overall form but also the details matter intensely." Just like in an artwork, what the observer/audience brings to this is just as important as the ingredients. It necessitates the participation of the diner/viewer and dismantles passive appreciation of art. The art restaurants court this debate and interpret the meaning of food as an art form to various degrees; chefs collect and are inspired by art, placing it in their establishments because they know it enhances the dining experience, while also demonstrating that their practice is artistic.

Making the Ordinary Extraordinary in the Art Restaurant

Eating food and benefitting from the nourishment it provides may be an essential part of everyday life, but it is important to think about how food-related behaviours help to shape our perception of bodily experience. Studies in contemporary neuroscience, cognitive philosophy and food scholarship find strong links between food and mental states. Eating is not just ephemeral, without consequence. Instead, it provides basic building blocks for how we make meaning. Think about how mentioning a certain restaurant dish or recipe to somebody who has also eaten it instantly creates a common language and understanding of what it tastes and feels like – even beyond the words used to describe it. Our behaviours around food combine and connect the senses, emotions and perception. Eating is fundamentally linked to memory, to images, being and time; hardly surprising, given our survival depends on it. Food constructs and codifies meaning, becoming more than basic bodily nourishment, as the haptic and the emotional intertwine. A particular dish can serve as a unifying symbol of a particular time, place and state of being, as in this iconic account of morsel and memory in Marcel Proust's *In Search of Lost Time*:

> *"An exquisite pleasure had invaded my senses, but individual, detached, with no suggestion of its origin. And at once the vicissitudes of life had become indifferent to me, its disasters innocuous, its brevity illusory – this new sensation having had on me the effect which love has of filling me with a precious essence; or rather this essence was not in me, it was myself. I had ceased now to feel mediocre, accidental, mortal."*

Proust identifies the transformative power of taste, and this passage illustrates how a simple act of eating a piece of cake is bite-size metonymy worthy of carrying the fundamental understanding of our place in space and time. The quotidian becomes elevated to the eternal, just as the eternal, present in the grammar of the quotidian, is revealed in the moment.

Similarly, reflecting on environments for dining and looking at art, Damien Hirst says: "I sort of genuinely believe that anything done incredibly well is art. It takes it out of the ordinary and into this other realm... Occasionally you can have a bacon sandwich that you remember years later... while most things you forget about after a week. Even if you read a book, you can forget it, but somehow meals can last longer than a book sometimes. It just seems really odd to me that a meal can stick in your mind like that."

If food creates meaning through the memories individuals make by eating together, taste will further this by taking the direct embodied experience of the memory of the food and linking it to aesthetic taste through judgement. Taste, in both senses of the word, is directly relevant to food and to the sophisticated appreciation of cultivated, conscious eating; taste is also necessary in appreciating art. The art restaurant is the encounter of the two. Modern diners, says Christoph Ribatt, "seek sophistication, not satiation", and in an art restaurant they will look at art as they eat and exercise judgement of taste. Encountering an artwork when dining out is more than the pleasure of eating in a particular space, it is an exercise in the power of choice and uses the diner's capabilities of judgement. With the art refining it, the restaurant creates the environment for how patrons exercise their good taste and judgement. Tacitly, they signal this to each other, and it builds into a system of meaning, holding what is good and desirable, becoming the paragon of taste.

Modern diners "only have eyes for one another, not the plates", wrote the French gourmand Auguste Escoffier in the 19th century. What they eat in a restaurant is important, but we all know atmosphere and environment are just as significant. This is an enduring sentiment, possibly even a universal truth, if the contemporary dining scene is anything to go by. Consider how the works in art restaurants have been privy to conversations, dramas, gossip, declarations, deal-making, scheming, unions, celebrations, clandestine rendezvous, heartbreaks, as they have hung above tables and observed the patrons entering and exiting each sitting. This recalls the German Romantic poet Rainer Maria Rilke's concluding lines in *Archaic Torso of Apollo*, written from the perspective of the work of art, informing the reader: "For here there is no place that does not see you. You must change your life." Artworks observe us as much as we do them. In the presence of an artwork, the subject-object construction that has tyrannised intellectual and cultural conceptions of how we understand our place in the world breaks down if we really look at the work and let it take hold over us. The restaurant is now a heightened way to experience the extraordinary and to understand the effect taste has on our perception. The diners are also observed, and they will behave differently in the company of the artwork, even if only for the duration of the meal.

In addition to captivating the diner with the art, restaurants are also both microcosms and kingdoms, with their own hierarchies, rules, codes and behaviours between staff and patrons. Food historian David Beriss writes: "From the sensual and the local, to the symbolic and global, restaurants... constitute ideal total social phenomena for our postmodern world." When visitors enter the restaurant, they must surrender to the rules and order of that establishment. Stories abound of restaurateurs who mistreated important guests with irreverence and haughty dismissiveness. Peter Langan was as raucous and abusive towards his patrons as often as his famous spinach soufflé signature dish was served – from passing out drunk on Princess Margaret's table, to dropping his trousers at Mayfair's well-heeled passers-by on Stratton Street, to eventually coming to blows with his own business partner, actor Michael Caine. The non-traditional restaurant, the artists' restaurant, the art restaurant, can be a space to renegotiate interactions and hierarchies because it sets out to be different from the outset and offer a provocation and stimulating alternative.

Collecting Art for Art Restaurants

Art restaurants are infused with their take on history, social consciousness through the collaborations, commercial innovation, testaments to taste, and hospitality by their founders and chefs. The motivations for collecting art may be disparate, but the compulsion is inviolable. The philosopher Raymond Tallis argues collectors *collect possibilities*, implying a second-order desire and hunger – they collect for the experience of pleasure, "for a mode of seeing". This applies to the passion, the determination, the resolute fastidiousness of Peter Langan, Gustav Zumsteg, Marcus Samuelsson and the other restaurateurs. Gourmands, arbiters, connoisseurs, collectors, they not only savour the relationship with the artwork, but harmonise the artworks with the food. This in turn engineers the environment for the aesthetic judgement, *aesthetic taste* – that Kantian disinterested free play to be exercised. There is pleasure derived through the taste of food and there is pleasure produced in looking at art. By choosing to dine in a particular restaurant, sociologist Joanne Finkelstein writes, we suggest "an association between the elegance of the restaurant's atmosphere and one's own aesthetic sensibilities". The restaurant itself becomes a symbol of a place where a particular community with its honed-in aesthetic and *savoir faire* goes tastemaking and reaffirms its identity.

In these art restaurants, the orientation of the collection can be influenced by the establishment's location in a particular community, but the converse is also true. The reputation of the Paris Bar in 1990s Berlin attracted many international art students who went on to become global brands; Damien Hirst, Sarah Lucas… they all gave works to the bar to add to its collection and take their place among more established artists of the time, such as Martin Kippenberger. Furthermore, many of these art restaurant collections have been built on the basis of friendships and relationships developed between the chefs and artists who used the establishments as artists' restaurants and the art world entourage that went along with it. The Roux family of the Colombe d'Or befriended the art dealers Aimé and Marguerite Maeght, whose foundation is located a short walk uphill from the restaurant in Saint-Paul-de-Vence; the art critic Brian Sewell was a close friend of Peter Langan and was his collecting confidante. This also plays a key role in ensuring the art is localised – Michael's in Santa Monica has championed Californian artists and international artists who made California their home, Dooky Chase in New Orleans has promoted and displayed emerging Black artists from the southern US for the past five decades, and Lucio's in Sydney collects and exhibits only modern Australian artists, a practice initiated from the moment it served its first *bistecca* in 1983.

Displaying in this setting extends social bonding and invites participants to dine in an intimate, private environment of hospitality. An encounter with the

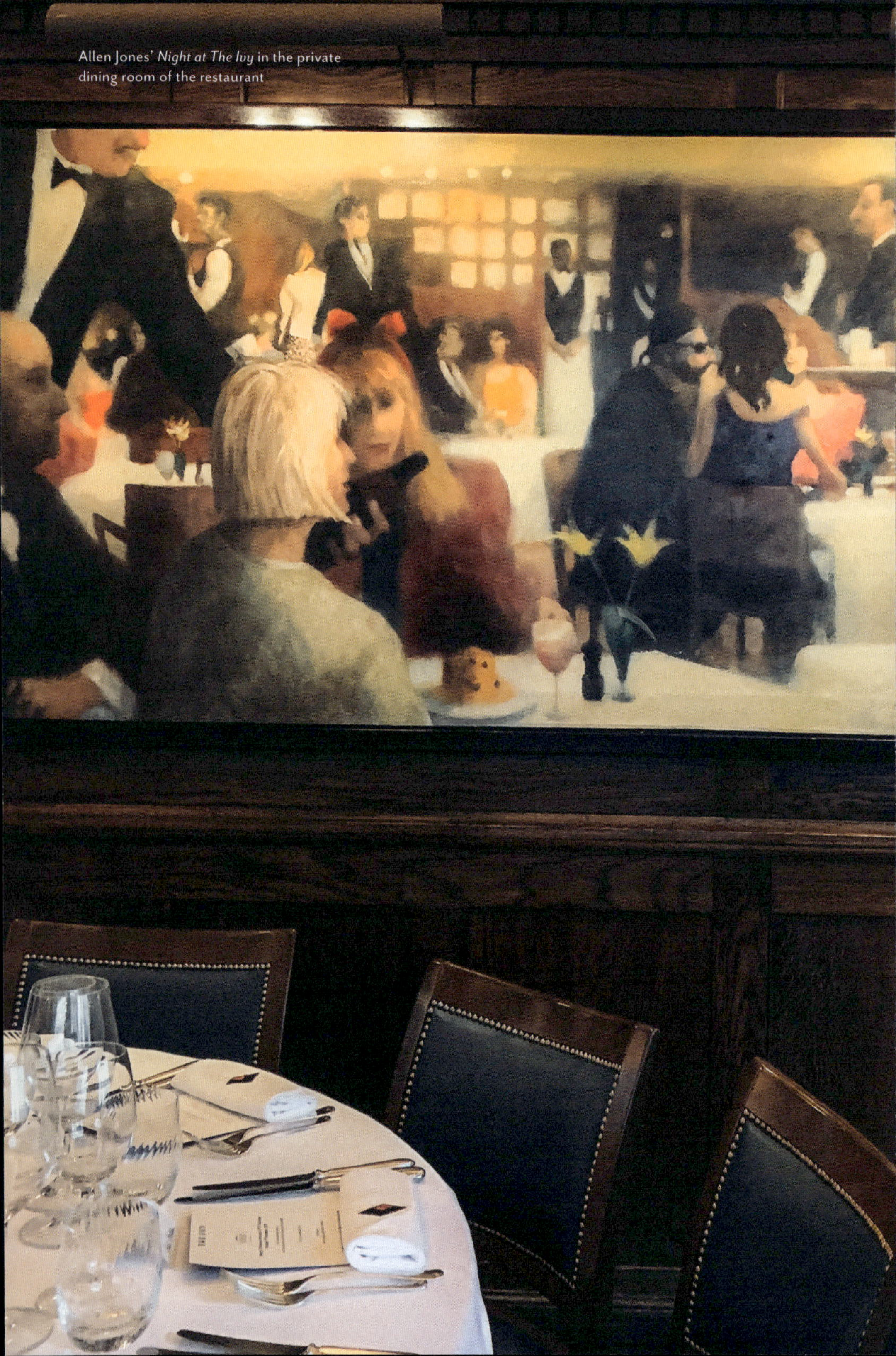

Allen Jones' *Night at The Ivy* in the private dining room of the restaurant

artworks in this paradoxically public yet intimate place allows the diner to feel the Matisse or the Soutine is *theirs*. Michael Craig-Martin believes it is like renting an artwork for the duration of the meal. For the artist who makes a work for the restaurant, too, it is a special experience; Gary Hume says art in a restaurant is "like a corner of a studio space with food and wine to sit and look at the work I've completed". From the moment the guest sits, eats and socialises at the table, the painting is solely their own – they have a unique connection to that work, even if they are replaced by the next diner at the same time the next day. This feeling is enhanced when they visit the restaurants to see particular works that remain in the same location for decades. They can ask for the Braque Table in the Kronenhalle or request to sit under Peter Blake's tribute to icons of the British stage at The Ivy. In turn, as a diner they participate in the ritual of patrons that came before them – whether they sit in Elizabeth Taylor and Richard Burton's banquette in Scott's or the corner table that was Lou Reed's preferred spot in Wallsé.

Art restaurants also use art in a socially conscious way – to support local communities and artists who are not in the mainstream and need the exposure. And they can be seen as public gallery spaces because they bring art to new audiences. By sharing it with their patrons, they contribute to the work's provenance, giving it an unusual twist of fate compared with the recognised private collectors' trajectory – for instance, when a museum-quality Matisse that once hung in a restaurant is now displayed in the Tate. Gustav Zumsteg's elegant Zurich apartment was overflowing with work by the time he inherited the Kronenhalle and moved most of it to the restaurant to share with diners. The art restaurant collections communicate with the past and build a reputation for both the collector and the establishment. Collections are models of worlds possessed, as Tallis writes. Art in restaurants offers a statement of cultural capital and identity for the owners, and for the institution itself. The restaurant is a backdrop and foundation for cultural exchange on a social level, and it also engages its diners on an aesthetic dining level and addresses conceptual and psychological moods of enjoyment and pleasure. Art historian Erin Thompson says: "The best way to understand the underlying drive of art collecting is as a means to create and strengthen social bonds, and as a way for collectors to communicate information about themselves and the world within these new networks." It is important for chefs and restaurateurs to demonstrate their friendships and bonds with artists. Collecting art differentiates a restaurant from competitors. However, the focus on art rather than music or furniture is significant and reveals the dual meaning of literal and metaphorical taste.

The restaurateurs and chefs are creative in the way they arrange flavour, texture and appearance of food to share their taste. Finkelstein believes the role of the chef "requires the talents of an architect, painter, chemist and diplomat" to construct gastronomy. The creativity extends to their dining environment. Chefs may be drawn to collecting in a particular way, differing from other communities of professions, such as doctors or financiers, because they deal in the currency of taste and control an environment for aesthetic dining. With some art restaurants, such as Wallsé, artists use the venue to dine and befriend the chefs, adopting it as an artists' restaurant. In other examples, the proprietors understand the significance of providing an environment to encourage artists and intellectuals to create a bohemian atmosphere. Michael Chow trained as an artist, as did Michel Würthle, hence they would surround themselves with like-minded people. These restaurateurs developed systems of exchange for the artists to *eat down* their bills and consequently *design up* – meaning the artists would be given food, drink, hospitality in exchange for artworks. This occurred regularly at the Colombe d'Or, the Kronenhalle and Langan's.

Through the art restaurant, the chef becomes an auteur and is able to deploy his creativity to exercise control over the totality of his environment. "It was a hoot!" veteran restaurateur Michael McCarty says, recalling a balmy night in June 1979 at the opening of his Santa Monica restaurant, "exactly like I wanted it to be: great food, great wine, great people, GREAT PARTY!!!" Chefs create this space for their patrons to experience the composite pleasures of eating and looking at art, both of which require the faculties of sensual observation and judgement. "In a practice where the construction of mood and atmosphere are crucial to success... nothing is accidental," writes Finkelstein. Patrons participate in the theatre of the restaurant with fellow diners, and along with purchasing a meal, they buy a *mood* – a lens to regard reality around them.

Dining Rituals in the Art Restaurant

Restaurants, when well-executed, are based on the undertaking and proliferation of ritual: the ritual of replicating the excellence of making the dishes, the ritual of seating and serving, the ritual of using dining objects, the ritual of selecting courses, which although may at times seem rushed, taken for granted or unconsidered by the participants, does not invalidate their being part of a greater whole of tradition and shared experience. In ancient Greece, *moira* literally meant "portion" as well as "fate". Serving food was the apportioning of fate; the outcome of a person's life was symbolised at the moment of communal dining. For the philosopher Karl Popper, "to eat together, to drink, to entrust oneself to others' care: this turns the restaurant into a place where the open society is both celebrated and lived out every day". Rituals in relation to food are as pervasive as they are rooted in the quotidian, contained in the commonplace act of eating within a community, and they also belong to celebrations and commemorations, extraordinary ways to mark time. For Brillat-Savarin, such traditions "consist of more than just norms and standards; [they] also consist of possibilities". On the one hand, the ritual is fixed because the gestures and actions remain the same and must be repeated. On the other hand, it is also dynamic because each participant brings their experience to, and takes on, the performance.

When we dine out, we undertake actions and behaviours, such as participating in ritual, playing a role in a theatre, partaking in ceremony, performing for the public. All are integral to eating in a restaurant. Medieval banquets incorporated dedicated audiences selected to watch kings and nobles eat. Religious ceremonies have always demanded the congregation observe and participate in the sacred rites. Similarly, in the restaurant, food and its consumption move beyond the physical and immediate, and become a performance. This metaphor of the restaurant as theatre has been experienced by all diners. Eating out is spectacle: sitting, watching the seating and serving performance unfold on the front-of-house stage, as the work of preparation and cooking occurs in the backstage area of the kitchen. Outstay your welcome in a restaurant during that familiar digestive lull after lunch, or before the dinner service hours begin, and you will feel the up-tempo as waiters, maître d', bus boys and other actors scuttle about and prepare the set-up for the evening's sitting, each responsible for their own role in the ritual, in the performance. The scene is set, the altar laid, and there is a feeling as if a spectacle is to occur. "It's all about theatre," Michael Chow says, "it's very important that you *cast* it like a theatre." It's all about "don't bore the audience", suggesting the need for keeping diners enthralled as captive. Michael Caine recalls the advice Peter Langan gave him when they first opened their brasserie: "Everybody must be able to see everybody else in the restaurant at all times… because you are not coming to our restaurant on the way to the show or after the show: you *are* the show. When you walk in, you are the star. When you sit down, you are the audience."

The restaurant as a theatre contains exchanges and hierarchies that are dynamic but still have a hold over participants for the duration of dining. The notion of the restaurant as a stage is a set to juxtapose bodies and images against each other, to examine what is projected and what is present. And to reproduce this at every sitting. Fashion structures the physical world, it "regulates public conduct as well as shaping private sensibilities", in the words of Finkelstein. Patrons perform and they also observe the performance of fellow diners, as well as interactions with the staff and between staff. Therefore, they willingly follow the restaurant's order, they participate in its traditions and rituals, arriving, being greeted, the selection of the food, exchanges with the staff, the display and presentation of the food, the consuming of the meal. All of these may seem commonplace, but they are at the core of our behaviours and social faculties.

Brillat-Savarin had already described the phenomenon of the restaurant as a microcosm as early as 1825 when he wrote: "The interior of a restaurant, examined in some detail, offers to the keen eye of the philosopher a spectacle well worth his interest, on account of the variety of situations contained in it." In this passage from his seminal *Physiologie du Goût*, he observes his fellow diners in a Parisian restaurant: "The family from the country"; "a husband and wife, Parisians, from the evidence of the hat and shawl hanging above their heads; it is clearly a long time since they had anything to say to each other"; "two lovers, judging by the attentions of one, the coquetry of the other, and the gourmandism of both. Pleasure shines in their eyes; and, from the choice that governs the composition of their meal, the present serves both to illuminate the past and foreshadow the future." Diners go to the restaurant to project desires and needs. This is bolstered by the observance of the fellow diners and the restaurant itself with its staff and servers. Here is a space where we go to reassert our status and identity. Brillat-Savarin continues:

> *"In the centre of the room is a table surrounded by regular patrons, who as a rule obtain special terms, and dine at a fixed price. They know the names of all the waiters, who let them into the secret of what is freshest and newest; they are like the stock-in-trade of a shop, like the centre of attraction, or to be more precise, like the decoys used in Brittany to attract wild duck.*
>
> *"There are also a number of those individuals whom everyone knows by sight, and no one by name. These people are as much at ease as if they were at home, and quite often try to strike up a conversation with their neighbours. They belong to a type only met with in Paris, which has neither property, capital, nor employment, but spends freely for all that.*
>
> *"Finally, there are one or two foreigners, usually Englishmen; these last stuff themselves with double portions, order all the most expensive dishes, drink the headiest wines, and do not always leave without assistance."*

The ways to describe the experience of dining have not changed for almost 200 years, with visiting a restaurant remaining a constant source of amusement, observation and sociology served on a plate. Everybody who has patronised restaurants has taken on various roles as actors, agents or protagonists in different dramas, plots and moments at different sittings. Brillat-Savarin's taxonomy of diners stands the test of time – on any day of the week, on any day of the year, over decades and centuries – and will continue to do so.

For the anthropologist Mary Douglas, food is a "boundary maker", it introduces binaries of what is experienced as outside/inside, exclusion/inclusion, the external/internal. Restaurants highlight these paradoxes by playing with the public and the private, the personal and the social. Desires and wants, appetites and sustenance, the base and animalistic are pursued in its public domain, with its rules of behaviour, conduct and manners. Here the body can be pleased in public, unlike other bodily needs, such as sleep, sex, washing, which are satisfied in private. Furthermore, in the company of fellow diners, we all observe interactions, cast aspersions, make judgements on those around us. Diners cannot help but be enwrapped in this. The gaze, which in other intellectual contexts usually violates the object observed, transcends this boundary. Here it becomes integral to the event, the staging involved in the restaurant, just as much as the ornamentation, appearance of the diners, their conversations and the seating arrangement, according to Finkelstein. In classic Turin restaurant Del Cambio, Pistoletto's artwork unleashes just this very phenomenon on diners, by encompassing them in its mirrored installation.

Taste and Cultural Memory Through the Art Restaurant

Restaurants are a relatively minor sector within food scholarship in social anthropology. David Beriss writes that they "bring together nearly all the characteristics of economic life studied by cultural anthropologists: forms of exchange, modes of production, and the symbolism behind consumption – all under one roof". Furthermore, in the context of this field it is not the food that defines the culture and civilisation that prepares and consumes it, the human side of the equation attributes meaning and assigns a culinary identity. Food is significant in a *phenomenological* sense: what it means at its very experiential level and at its essential core when we participate in it. Food is also important in an empirical, social sciences sense – what those individual participations amount to collectively, as they are inseparable from the signification of food and are enhanced in an art restaurant. The experience of food and sharing it builds a social and cultural configuration. Next, we build identities through communities, and this progresses to exhibiting status, emotions, associations, cultural patterns – culminating in civilisation. In the first instance, food is a symbol, and in the second, food is reference.

In the West, the restaurant industry has paradoxically been culprit and beneficiary of globalisation and development, yet it also has been a champion of the local, playing a significant role in terms of knitting together identities, ethnicities and communities in cities and towns. Star chef René Redzepi's *You and I Eat the Same* argues: "People should derive dignity and distinction – not to mention entrepreneurial opportunity – from family recipes and traditions." The progenitor of the restaurant, the communal gathering of the feast in ancient and medieval times, was also an opportunity to show off power and status, and even to procure political and financial gain. Brillat-Savarin writes: "Let one open any book of history, from Herodotus to our own days, and he will see that, without even expecting conspiracies, not a single great event has occurred which has not been conceived, prepared, and carried out at a feast." In France, a banquet by Olivier de la Marche in 1453 launched a crusade; Catherine de' Medici's fêtes in 16th-century France notoriously formed the backdrops to her family's political machinations and power advancement. In more modern times, political plots have been hatched in restaurants, business deals sealed and alliances sworn. Leah Chase in New Orleans offered a safe haven and platform for civil rights activists to meet and plan campaigns in her restaurant throughout the 1950s and early 1960s. Today, it has become a place to continuously renegotiate social and class boundaries in terms of who is in charge, who follows whom, what is fashionable, what is desirable. Fame and infamy have always been essential to the success of the greatest restaurants, and several of the art restaurants – Mr Chow, Langan's, Scott's – have been the setting for important moments and famous gatherings in cultural history. If to be in fashion means having mastery over history, to be placed out of time, to be in control of the present, then some of these art restaurants function as a time capsule or mausoleum of a particular social and cultural era. Here, diners are patrons in venues owned by and selected by individuals with taste, which ostensibly means they are privileged, are extraordinary, are important. Restaurants "require rumours and love, their mystique resides in the suspicion that somebody else was having a better dinner, a more titillating dalliance, a more exotic bottle of wine". When diners perform in a restaurant, the peering eyes, the eavesdropping, the heads following fellow guests as they enter and walk through the space – on one level these are ephemeral acts, just part of that moment, yet on another, they have occurred so much through history and memory they seem timeless, too.

Memories are active and dynamic. We do not possess a cache of memories to draw upon when we need them, as though it was a storage facility. Memories are interactions between the past and the present that are being constantly made (repetition) and refined (variation). This repetition-plus-variation also occurs in ritual, which is what creates narratives and meanings. Adding art to the blend means the simple process of eating in a restaurant becomes even more stimulating and ennobled individually and an act of fellowship as the experience

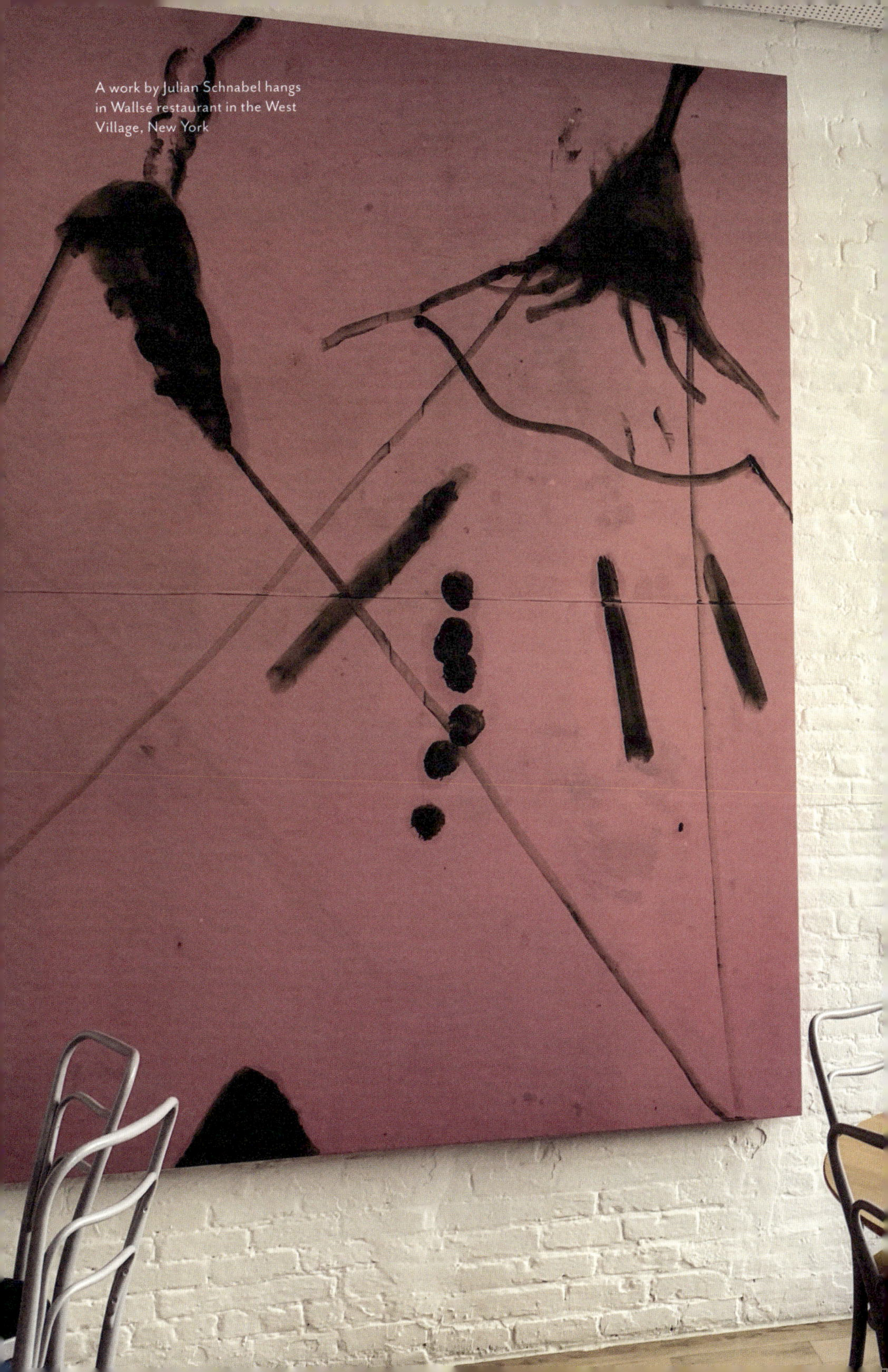

A work by Julian Schnabel hangs in Wallsé restaurant in the West Village, New York

is collective. In his seminal study *How Societies Remember*, the anthropologist Paul Connerton argued for a shift away from a visual memory based on static episodes that fit together, as in a narrative, towards adopting a non-visual memory – based on the experience, rather than the telling of the experience. It would be an "incorporating memory", more powerful as it "generates sensory and emotional experiences that sediments memory in the body". In other words, the *how*, not the *what*, in creating memories. Experience is complex, and even a visual memory will contain within it emotions and feelings that do not belong to the initial moment. We lace the aftermath of this with our memory.

This marks the art restaurant as a dynamic microcosm infused with social and symbolic exchanges to make memories, create identities and bolster community in the midst of sensory engagement. In the repetition and replication of the meal and the rituals of preparing and consuming it, diners create meaning and participate in the codification of each sitting, each act, each meal. This has a power to affect because it elicits emotions, and in turn contains aesthetic power, because as we structure qualities of food to understand them and evaluate them, we use the same processes of evaluation as when we judge beauty or when we show we can distinguish or demonstrate discernment between one object and the other.

Displaying Art in an Art Restaurant

Restaurants displaying art conflate gustatory taste and visual taste, shaping private sensibilities in the public space. Anybody who considers themselves a gourmand and connoisseur of food, and also appreciates aesthetic objects, may see how these places invite this enhanced dining experience. The art collections are both symbols of taste and residual proof of what it means to judge aesthetically when surrounded by artworks. Aesthetic experiences are *de facto* different from other activities and experiences; they require a different type of perception and analysis. Good-quality art in restaurants is a status-marker, it is a statement of participating in particular history, it is a connection between literal and metaphorical taste, and is ultimately a space and opportunity the venue offers for its patrons to explore and make aesthetic judgments. The artworks introduce what Walter Benjamin explained as an *aura* in the establishment, as the original artworks – many of museum-level quality – protect the experience from the repetition of the production of meals and sittings that is the commercial reality of the restaurant. They are indicators and reminders of a more discerning and aesthetic element of our existence, both individually and socially.

Perhaps part of the reason why the topic of art in restaurants is taken for granted, or has not been thoroughly examined, is because the pleasure of viewing art is inextricably bound up with the pleasure of eating, which in turn is indistinguishable from the pleasure of company, congeniality. Raymond Tallis calls this "the pleasure of an occasion". We so often eat hurriedly, too preoccupied or caught up in the social element of the experience to notice the act of eating. Brillat-Savarin distinguished between the "pleasures of eating" and the "pleasures of the table", suggesting the latter contained a more holistic and reflective component than the biological nourishment of the former. To the discerning patron, the experience of consuming high-end food, amongst consciously assembled decor with artworks, is a form of aesthetic dining. Roland Barthes claimed that food is a system of communication, because it deploys all the senses, is replicable, and is undertaken by a community. He found a *spirit of food* that is a system of signs. We eat the same food when we dine together and have the same experience at that particular moment, sharing this through language so that it becomes a system of meaning.

Gastronomy, "the seducer of virtuous monks", according to Balzac, from its very etymology carries with it notions of taste, distinction and refinement: both the bodily (*gastros*) and the laws or controls (*nomia*) that govern our ingestion. Similarly, taste applies as discrimination regarding art objects and standards for aesthetics. "Taste is construed as the ability to perceive beautiful qualities and to discriminate fine differences among the objects of perception, differences that might escape notice by someone without taste," according to the philosopher Carolyn Korsmeyer.

The chef-owners of art restaurants understand how their collections can offer something more to their patrons. In these establishments, art is a key ingredient to their success and transformative power. The artworks are reminders and opportunities to enjoy and engage in the aesthetic dining that registers the bombardment of the senses happening when we are surrounded by these stimuli. These are not passive moments, they require thought, judgement and taste to distinguish a Matisse hanging in a dining room from the lamp on the wall that illuminates it. This discrimination means we can focus on taste in an aesthetic sense, and that in turn suddenly means aesthetic dining is pleasurable, but it is also purposeful.

The Restaurants

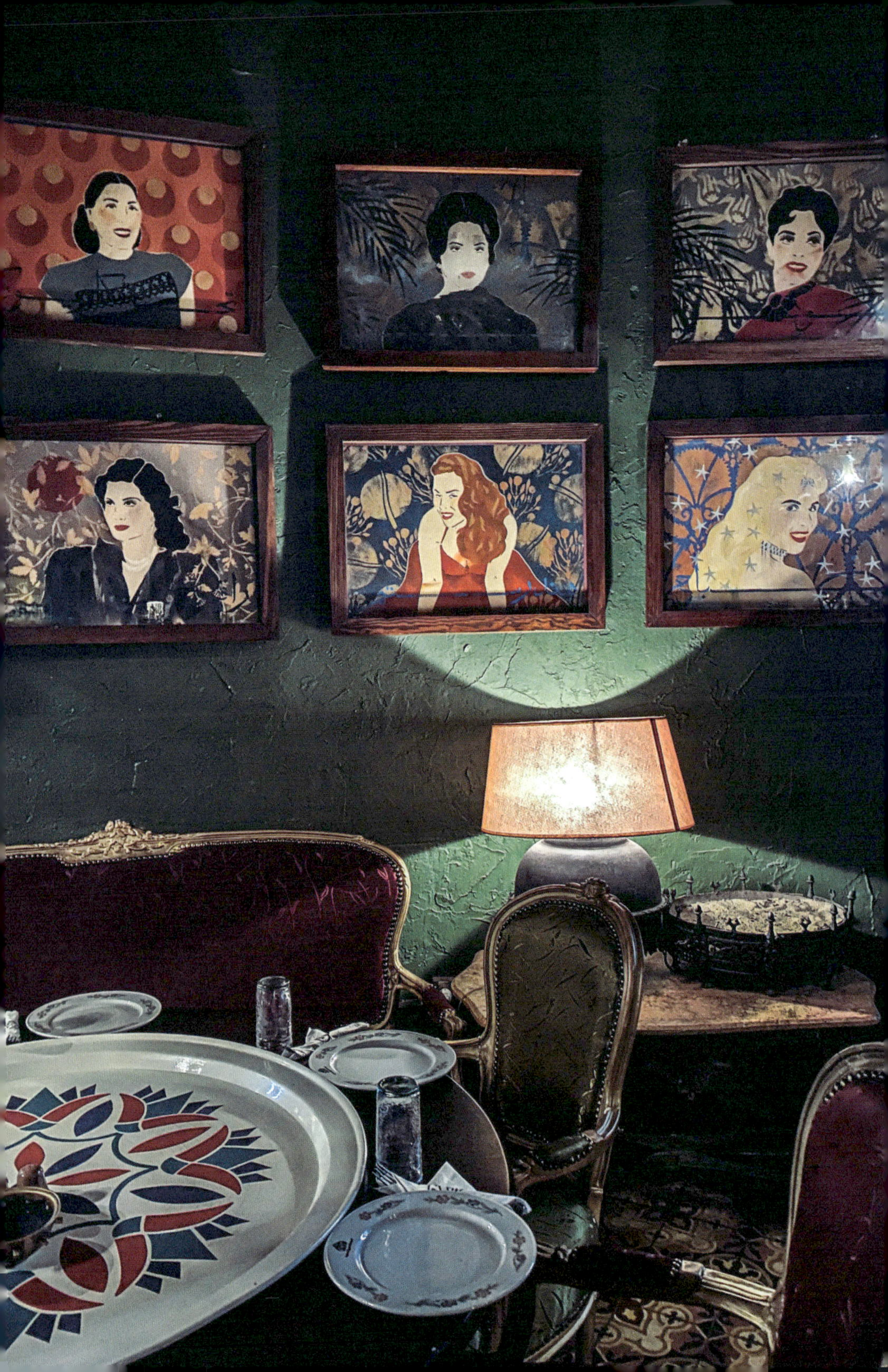

Abou el Sid

CAIRO

"I don't do art. I do fighting against influences. I paint, it's not political art, but it's an attitude."
— Chant Avedissian

Once upon a time in medieval Cairo, there was a cook from the poorest part of the city, Abou el Sid, whose recipes and preparation of simple dishes drew crowds of workers and servants far and wide to sample his nurturing and mouth-watering *fattah,* an ancient lamb dish used in feasts and celebrations. When word of Sid's culinary mastery reached the ears and stomach of the Sultan, he insisted on seizing the cook from his souk kitchen and imprisoning him in the palace to serve his new master and court exclusively. The chef became despondent in his golden cage and begged for his freedom every day, crying into his cauldron. Nobody knows how the story ends, but we do know Egyptian art collector and celebrity restaurateur Raouf Lotfi wants diners to come to this eponymous restaurant and find out.

Of course, what diners discover when they visit the prosperous district of Zamalek in the middle of the metropolis is that Abou el Sid never existed. It is a story the restaurateur made up, to set the scene, mesmerise and entertain his guests. This is all part of the importance of *hakawati*, or the tradition of storytelling in the Middle East, especially popular in Cairo's ancient souk cafés and food stalls. Stories are integral to captivating imaginations and binding communities, as captured in the *Arabian Nights*, where such tales – just like food stories – were essential to survival, as its storyteller, Scheherazade, found. In a similar manner, Abou el Sid as an art restaurant is cast in layers of stories and embedded narratives: the story of the cook, the story of the restaurant, the stories of each Egyptian dish's origins. *Mouckaya*, a slimy green jute leaf soup that was eaten by pharaohs to enhance potency and power in ancient Egypt. *Umm ali*, a milky bread pudding that was inspired by the breasts of a past Mamluk sultan Izz al-Din Aybak's third wife. Adding to this mixture is the story of Egyptian nationalism, mythology and symbolism through the presence of the late artist Chant Avedissian's artworks surrounding the dining rooms of Abou el Sid. The restaurant features pieces from Avedissian's well-known book *Cairo Stencils, Icons of the Nile*, a series he worked on between 1991 and 2013. The images depict the Egypt of the 1950s, with her "Hollywood of the Nile" figures from popular culture. The series ultimately explores the cultural values of creating a modern national identity. The stencils capture a very diverse period of modern Egyptian history, encompassing the last King Farouk's reign of Cairo – instrumental in transforming the city into "the Paris of the Middle East", a city of fervent excitement and cosmopolitanism. If restaurants and dining with others create food memories and foster nostalgia, then the experience of the Avedissian works becomes just as potent and captivates its patrons – just as the sultan wanted.

Chant Avedissian is one of the most recognised contemporary Arab artists, whose characteristic drawings and paintings depict Egyptian pop culture and political news content. He was born to Armenian parents, and studied in the West, developing his techniques and methods in Montreal and Paris. Becoming increasingly dismayed about being constantly represented and portrayed as a colonial, exotic artist, he eschewed the West and returned to Egypt to establish his artistic practice in the capital. Avedissian became the long-time assistant of the prominent Egyptian architect Hassan Fathy, whose landmark 1973 treatise *Architecture for the Poor* proposed and planned the regeneration of rural dwellings for the masses in the south of the country. Fathy suggested designers should use ancient materials in their buildings, including mud bricks and clay from the local land. "In modern Egypt there is no indigenous style," Fathy wrote. "The signature is missing; the houses of rich and poor alike are without character, without an Egyptian accent." It would be necessary to strip materiality back to its bare essentials in the search for a pure, Egyptian style. "The tradition is lost, and we have been cut off from our past ever since Muhammad Ali cut the throat of the last Mamluk." The architect argued for an aesthetics of tradition based on Egypt's own materials and construction methods. His was a search for "a lost *arabité*", implying the ingredients were always available to designers, architects and artists in the country; what was missing was the method and conviction to synthesise them.

This philosophy also influenced Avedissian in his search for a contemporary yet vernacular way to interpret the long and epic history of Egypt. The artist says: "Fathy was the best architect for me because he was building space… what influenced me was his research and his systematic insistence that every line you do has to come from the given geography of the land. He connected architecture to history." In response, Avedissian's art incorporated hieroglyphs, Islamic geometric patterns and Ottoman motifs, as well as magazine advertisements and celebrity publicity photos. The medium ranged from early textile pieces to later figurative paintings and the stencils he is best known for. Here he began to mix past tales of constructed fantasy with narratives of Egyptian 20th-century identity.

Chef Lotfi knew the artist and was an avid collector of his work. The two were friends for decades in Cairo and initially collaborated on casual, pop-up restaurants where the chef served simple *kosheri*-based Egyptian dishes and the artist made sketches and drawings for the walls. Both endeavours were executed in an off-the-cuff street-food style: the recipes using simple ingredients and the art using found images on found materials from market stalls such as discarded cardboard and metal. The collaboration was a prototype of Abou el Sid, an early version where the chef could demonstrate slight variations on national cuisine and the artist could display his work to the public. Several years later Lotfi established the current Abou el Sid in Zamalek, on an island in the middle of the Nile, admired for its neoclassical Western architecture and leafy streets. His intention was to integrate elements of oriental and occidental design in order to establish a restaurant reminiscent of a home, a mother's house from a certain prosperous, educated Cairene background. A Zamalek home of elegant taste incorporating French accents with the craftmanship of Egyptian labour: high ceilings, multicoloured tiles, narrow windows with arabesque carved shutters. The art would serve as a further reminder of mid-century Cairo in its Golden Age of cinema, culture and politics. All would be a mélange of flavours, colours, textures and sounds that evoke a sentimentality and longing for an elliptical past. Egyptian cuisine is not visually engaging, according to Lotfi, as it is often mixed and served in big bowls, making it difficult to present in an enhanced or aesthetically pleasing way. "It's something that we eat in homes. And only in the house of the family can you have this authentic experience." In the restaurant, the nostalgia it evokes through cuisine and the Avedissian works is both playful and comforting, as it suggests that everything was better in the past. Food and art transport the diner to a different time and place.

Egyptian cuisine is influenced just as much by its geographical location as by the many rulers and cultures that have existed in the country in its 2,000-year history: from Greek settlers in Alexandria to the Arab Mamluk Sultanate; from the Ottomans to Napoleon and the British. With over one-hundred-million mouths to feed, it is simple, inexpensive and democratic, based on grains, wheat and vegetables. And it is inextricably tied to the nation's identity from antiquity, with traditions of producing and preparing food that grows along the Nile evident in so many hieroglyphic figures and ornamental symbols found on papyrus scrolls. The flat motifs of the lily of the Nile, the sun and moon, the sacred lotus, as well as other abstract symbols, are consistent throughout Avedissian's practice.

The colour scheme of the restaurant is muted, earthy, in order to deal with the incessant and characteristic dust of Cairo, but also to provide cool shelter from the glaring sun and heat. The interiors contain fragments and tiles from neoclassical early 20th-century Alexandrian and Cairene bourgeois merchant houses; there are also reconfigured doors from previous incarnations of Egypt. At night it glows in the low light, as though guests were in a cabaret. Lotfi scoured old homes and markets for furniture and decoration – everything from chairs to wooden panels – to preserve the feeling of comfortable domesticity, but also literally to preserve the past in the restaurant. However, it is not an exact recreation of a vintage interior. It is constructed with bric-à-brac and mismatched pieces of furniture, giving it a new relevance in a bustling megalopolis.

"Abou el Sid is not about neatness and control," its founder maintains. It is "about a country, it is about healing the past, the romance and nostalgia of the '20s and '30s". It is not "about perfection, it's about *this* country".

In some respects, the restaurant is built both around the art collection and for it. Lotfi was responsible for giving Avedissian exposure from an early stage in his career by displaying his work before it was revealed to the art world and international commercial galleries. The artist created his works in a way that enhances their materiality. He used second-hand cardboard from fruit stalls, butcher's paper and packing materials. He then hand-painted multiple versions of the same stencilled images on the materials using pigments relating to Egyptian colours. Originally, they were not as much hung as nailed on to the walls (a technique Lotfi questioned) because Avedissian wanted them to age and degrade with time. He insisted they should not be framed. As a result, the pieces surrender themselves to the space, to the "imperfections" and conditions of a living restaurant. There is smoke, food, alcohol. It is not a pristine laboratory in which to examine them. They mix with the raucousness of the diners, becoming part of the experience, emphasised by their (seemingly) casual execution.

The stars depicted in the artworks are celebrities from the Golden Age of Egyptian music and cinema, and the politically active period between King Farouk's abdication and the election of the first president of the republic, Gamal Abdel Nasser, in the 1950s and 1960s. Egypt was one of the earliest nations to adopt and develop cinema: the first public screening in the world took place in 1896, and the first Egyptian film was made in 1912. The "seventh art" became the favoured medium to project the collective fantasies and desires of its people back to audiences, covering social structures, love stories, Bedouin mythologies and ancient history. Major figures of Egyptian cinema include the diva Umm Kulthum – "Our Mother" and the "Fourth Pyramid" of Egypt (Egyptian culture loves to assign both diminutive and superlative nicknames) – famous for her 90-minute songs and morose lyrics of longing, loss and sacrifice, and still the highest chart-topper in the Arab world. Avedissian's series featuring Kulthum contributed to him once breaking the record for being the biggest-selling living Arab artist at auction, in 2013. In the restaurant collection there is also a portrait of Samia Gamal, an accomplished belly dancer, nicknamed "the Genie Lady", and also crowned "The National Dancer of Egypt" by the president; Shadia, labelled "the Idol of the Masses", a crooner of nationalistic and love ballads such as *Egypt, My Love* and *Oh You, the Tanned One*; and Hind Rostom, an actress known for her seductive roles on the silver screen, dubbed "The Marilyn Monroe of the East", buxom and bottle-blonde.

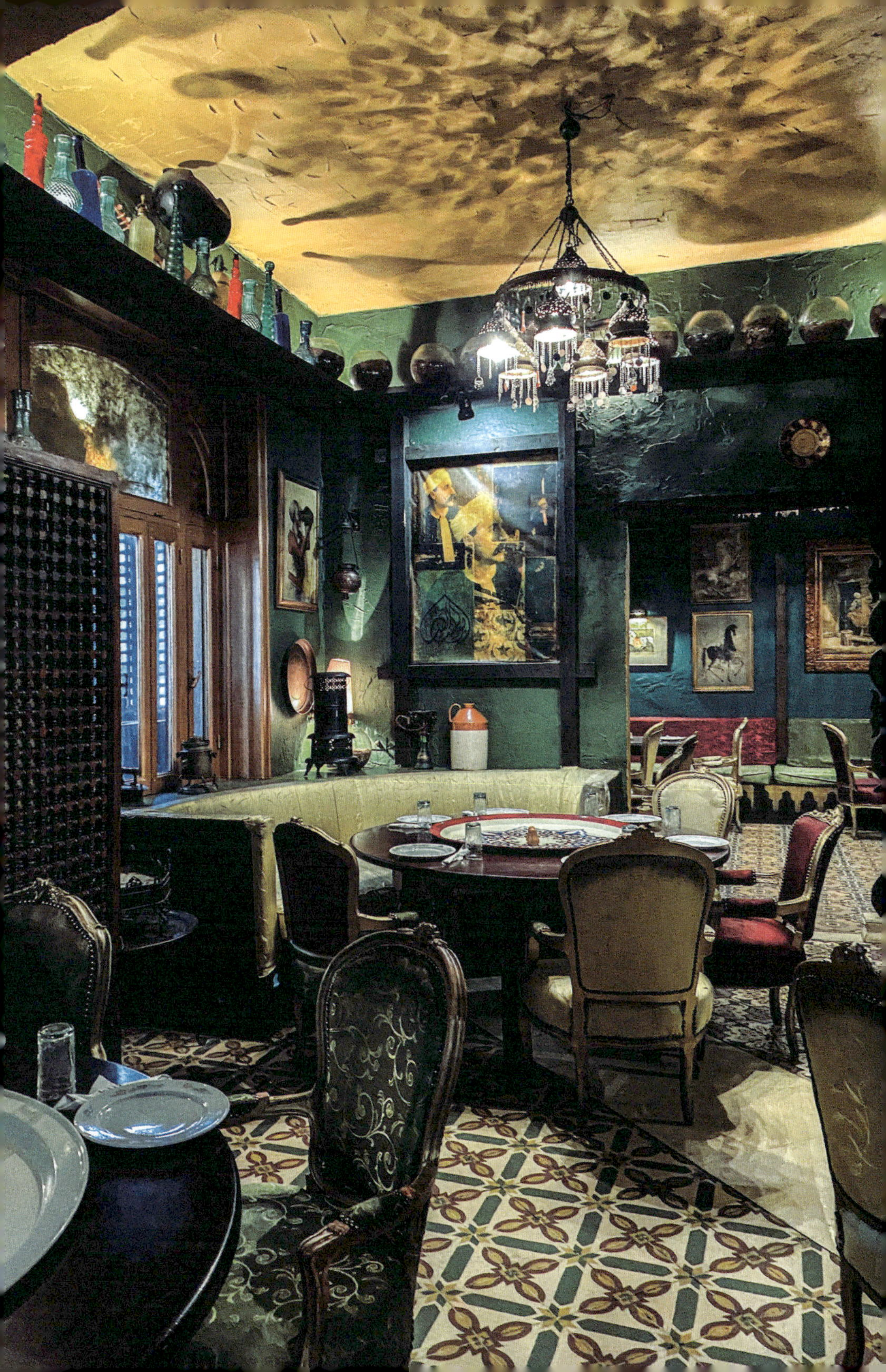

From the mid-1950s, Cairo was an optimistic, exciting city, economically thriving, outward-looking, full of potential and intention to modernise. Many of the cultural productions and projects were versions of Western models adapted for Egyptian audiences: cinema, cabaret performances, vibrant nightlife in bars and restaurants, and socialising with alcohol. King Farouk was deposed in 1954 and Nasser came to power to form the new republic, heralding an alternative radical socialism as its *modus operandi*, at a time when anti-colonial ideas and beliefs were spreading throughout the Middle East. The more Nasser accomplished during his term, including nationalising the Suez Canal and codifying major land reforms, the more his power and authoritarianism grew. As an artist working with chronicles and archival material, Avedissian's subject matter reflected the shift in presidential imagery presented in newspapers and magazines and on television – from what could be a politician in a Hollywood film with Brylcreemed hair and tortoiseshell sunglasses, to more militaristic scenes in a general's uniform flanked by guards.

Some of the cultural figures, such as Kulthum, reoccur throughout Avedissian's œuvre and the restaurant collection – just like images in popular culture multiply and are distributed through numerous channels and to varying audiences. In his *Cairo Stencils*, Avedissian sometimes changes the foreground, or alters the backgrounds, the floral decor, patterns and colours. The works are a facsimile, on one level, in terms of being copied from media images the artist finds in historic archives. However, on another level, the very origin of the actors', entertainers' and dancers' identities is constructed, too, as is often the case with individuals in the public eye. Delving – or even a cursory glance – into the biographies of most of the *Icons of the Nile* reveals complex and troubled upbringings and lives after fame in their older years. Yet the stencils are a reminder that this is also how social history is constructed: layers, like the stencil method, pieced together, reproduced with slight variations, but disseminated in a society and learned by all. They may be idealised and imagined, but they feel real. The artworks function in the same way as recipes: there are some constraints, in terms of ingredients and method, but ultimately they are passed down upon every retelling or remaking. In the restaurant setting, they contribute to the sense of nostalgia and experience of a time and place of the past. This establishment and its choice of artworks transports its diners to a period of an abounding, successful Egypt.

Arguably, the best dish Abou el Sid serves is sentimentality. The sentiment is an attitude towards a people and their traditions, but also a basis for *moral* attitudes. The restaurant is not simply a venue for escapism. It is a space to dine, enjoy and think about the past and one's place in the present. It is a token to visitors and outsiders of how nations present their story. Recipes bind communities

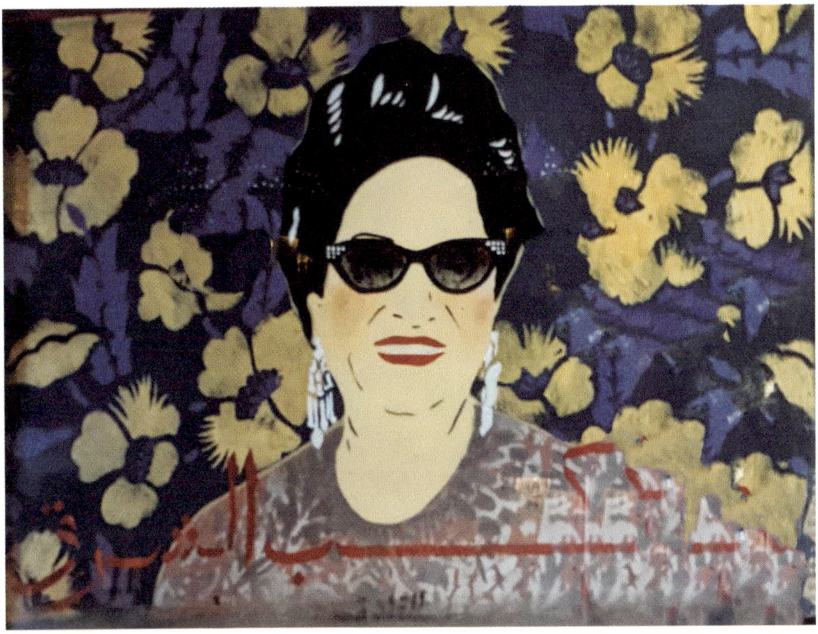

together. They are as much a social glue as Hassan Fathy's clay or Avedissian's stencils. Restaurants with their repetition of tradition also fold diners into the mixture through the dining ritual. The history of modern 20th-century Egypt is cyclical, tumultuous, and brings together religions, racial identities and political systems. It is a country that in just a century has experimented with colonialism, monarchy, socialism, military rule, populism, and continues to turbo-charge through history. Avedissian's works in Abou el Sid become a symbol of this Egypt old and new, illustrating to diners the good times of the past – irrespective of whether or not they even existed – by building bonds, by using memories, but also reminding them that they are part of living history and are contributing to the ever-evolving identity of a nation; just like Avedissian's stencilling method stages both the material image and its reproduction to keep its identity and meaning in a continuous, perpetual process of construction.

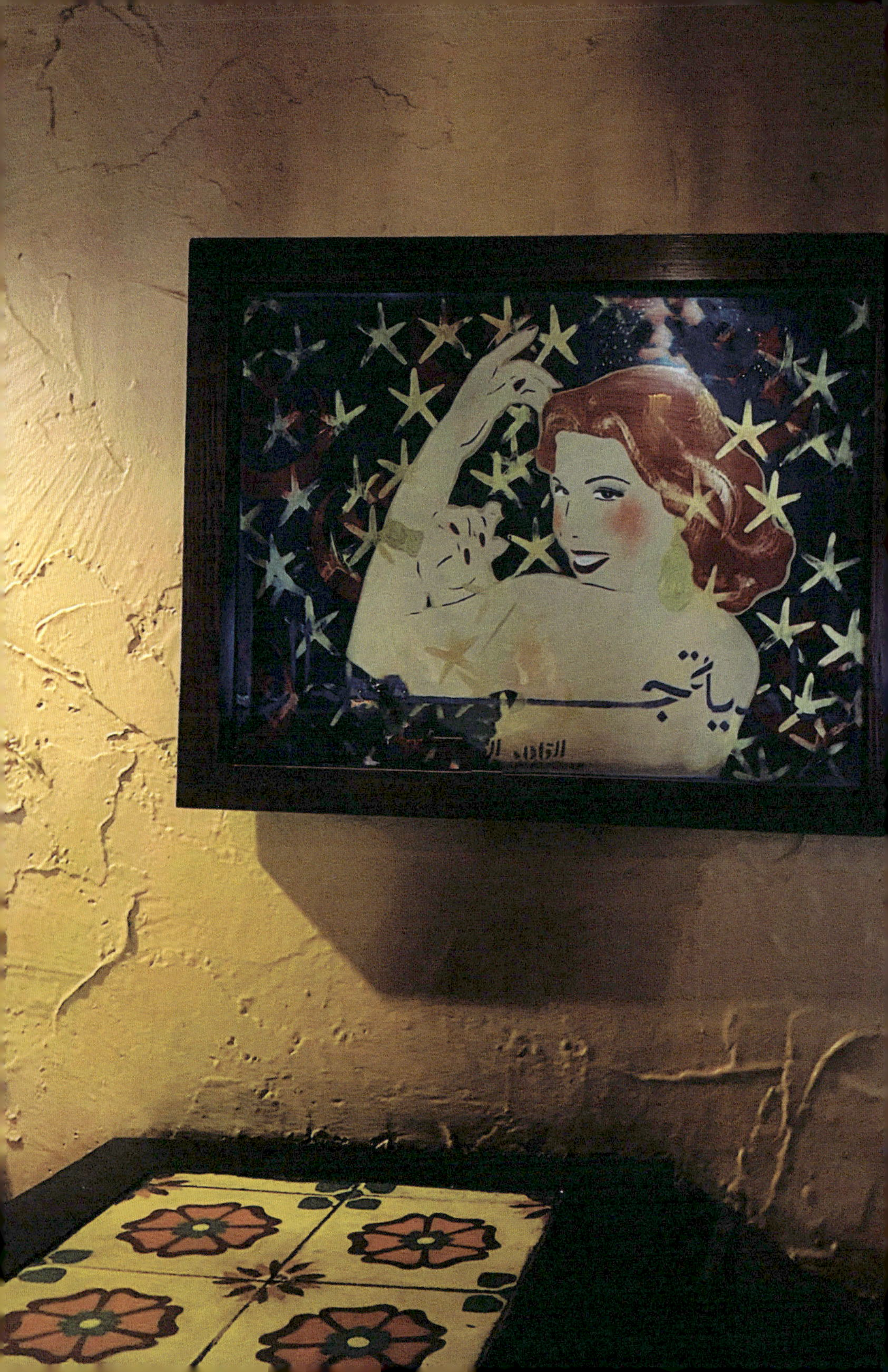

Works and artists in the Abou el Sid collection

—

A stencil of Tahia Carioca, the most renowned belly dancer that ever lived. She escaped a traumatic childhood, which included being orphaned and kept in chains at one point, to become a film star with 190 titles under her bejewelled belt. She was the boyhood crush of cultural critic Edward Said, who wrote in his tribute to her: "She embodied a very specific kind of sexiness, which she rendered as the most smooth and understated of dancers." She is depicted smiling with her head thrown back in hedonistic abandon.

—

Sabah, a songstress of the *belle epoque* Arab world, originally Lebanese, who made much of her career in Egypt, beams coquettishly over diners. The "Diva of Music" recorded more than 3,500 songs, acted in 98 films and married nine men in her lifetime.

—

Laila Mourad, a raven-haired beauty who was the official singer of the Egyptian Revolution in 1953, smoulders in one stencil. Born to Jewish parents, she also had a stage career as a serious thespian in Cairo.

—

In the midst of these glamorous and beautiful female entertainers is a stencil of a charmingly cantankerous Naguib el-Rihani. He was known for his comedic roles depicting the loveable underdog, but also established his own theatrical group, integrating French theatre with Egyptian dramas on stage during his lifetime. His mother disowned him because he brought shame on the family by choosing to become an actor. He is depicted wearing the *tarboosh* (fez), a symbol of an older Islamic Egypt, banned by Nasser in 1958.

—

Hidden away behind a souk lamp in the main dining room is a stencil of Zaki Rostom, one of the most significant Golden Age actors of Egyptian cinema. He would be placed in a less prominent position as his roles were always psychologically creepy villains, on the margins of society. He made landmark films, such as an Arab version of *Anna Karenina* in which he portrayed Karenin, and usually played the dominant and cruel husband. He ended up depressed and alone, dying of a heart attack at the age of 68.

The dining room of Abou el Sid, featuring antique tiles and furniture, and objects sourced from Alexandrine homes and Cairene flea markets; pieces from Chant Avedissian's Cairo Stencils including Umm Kulthum, Sabah and Tahia Carioca adorn the dining rooms

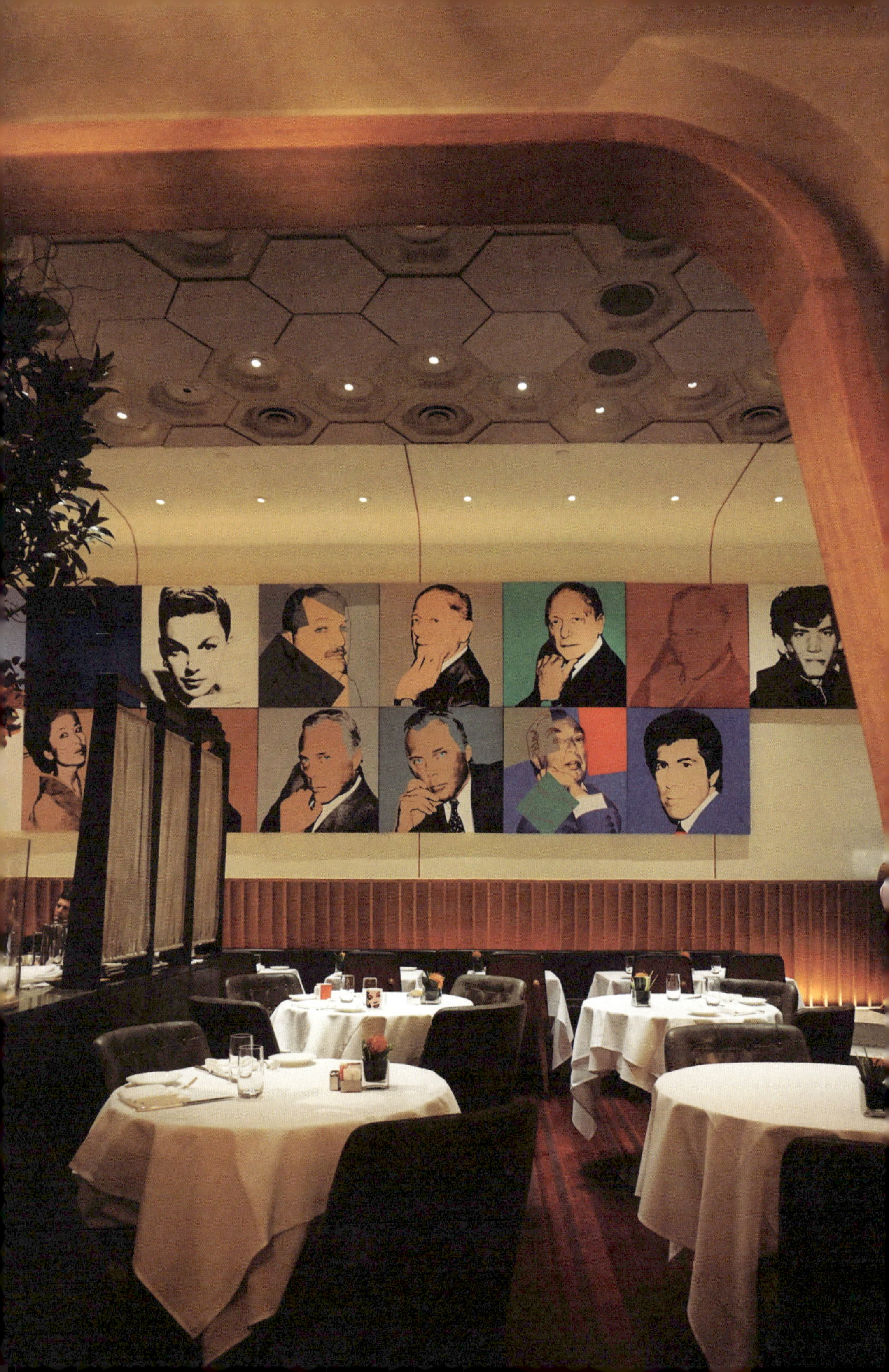

Casa Lever

"It's not what you are that counts, it's what they think you are."
— Andy Warhol

Imagine you are back in 1983 and asked who your fantasy dinner party guests would be. You probably *were* at a dinner party in 1983 when you were last asked this question. The answer would most likely list celebrities in the artworks on the long right-hand wall of New York City's Casa Lever: Aretha Franklin, Judy Garland, Muhammad Ali and, well, erm, the Shah of Iran... There are 36 Andy Warhol silkscreens of luminaries to choose from, and in this slick and swanky Midtown Milanese restaurant, they really do become dining companions. In the early days of their courtship, supermodel Jerry Hall took her then boyfriend now husband, media mogul Rupert Murdoch, and insisted on sitting under her own silkscreen, leaving her beau "exceptionally chuffed" on the night. Hall must have been pleased with herself, given she was discovered as a model at one of Warhol's famous *Interview* lunches at The Factory as a teenager in the mid-1970s, where the artist would play society god and invite a range of advertisers, collectors, emerging artists and models to spark opportunities and collaborations – and, of course, buy his art. From being just a guest at the table, to presiding over diners above the table in a screenprint, Hall is an example of how Warhol both makes and testifies to symbols of status and success. To include these works in the Casa Lever collection is to build on the significance of an art trophy for their owner, Aby Rosen, the New York real estate magnate and art collector who unabashedly displays the meaning of his power in business and art through them.

Casa Lever is located within Lever House on Park Avenue, north of Grand Central Station. The building was designed by American architects Gordon Bunshaft and Natalie de Blois in 1951. It was based on the modern aesthetic principles of the International Style. As a curtain wall building, it is an exercise in volume and mass, stripped of ornament, confidently symmetric. The restaurant itself is a neat and precise space. In the core of the mid-century property complex, what was once avant-garde and idealist in architectural mission and ambition is now a showpiece asset for its owner. The interior features booths inserted into a honeycomb structure on one side, updating the *cabinet de particulaire* of the restaurant progenitors in the 19th century, where diners could discreetly meet with their preferred companions, hidden away from the main entrance. This is past function and purpose, realised in a dynamic, retro-futurist setting. The cuisine is Milanese, but it is also prepared and presented in an equanimous yet sexy manner: small morsels of sleek veal and small servings of sinuous pasta.

The centrepiece is the succession of Warhol silkscreen prints, all uniform in size, on the white wall. They are part of Rosen's personal art collection and that of his foundation, the Lever House Collection, other works from which are displayed in the lobby of the main Lever House. In late 2014 he added 13 more Warhol Pop Art works, inviting portraits of philanthropists and art collectors such as Douglas S. Cramer, Ernesto Esposito and Gabrielle Navarra to the party. They joined the more familiar celebrity faces of Judy Garland, Russian ballet dancer Rudolf Nureyev and Aretha Franklin near the restaurant's entrance, Alfred Hitchcock above a leather-bound banquette with Giorgio Armani and Dennis Hopper. As with the full set of Warhol's silkscreens – an estimated 760 – they are, in the words of the critic Blake Gopnik, an "index of celebrity" for the artist. But in this art restaurant, and in the collection of Rosen, they are a compendium of successful, accomplished and wealthy individuals, acquired by a successful, accomplished, wealthy businessman. And, in turn, Casa Lever is frequented by diners on the same level of status as its owner – VIPs from finance, the media, entertainment and the arts. The power of this art restaurant is in how it caters to the myth of the self-made businessman, an American imperative towards material success. Even Warhol was conscripted to this cause as early as 1975 when he wrote: "Business art is the step that comes after art. I started as a commercial artist, and I want to finish as a business artist."

Rosen began collecting when he was 11 years old and bought a Robert Mapplethorpe in his native Frankfurt for $200, borrowed from his father. Eventually his collection grew to include heavyweight artists such as Basquiat and Bacon. He is rumoured to own over 100 Warhols, some in his private collection, others displayed in public spaces in other buildings in his property portfolio, including the Gramercy Park Hotel. In terms of power and its symbolism, Rosen and Warhol deserve each other in this art restaurant; one a property tycoon, the other a Pop Art tycoon. Warhol owns Rosen just as much as Rosen owns Warhol. Rosen buys a new work of art every time he "seals a deal", resulting in a collection of more than 850 pieces. Warhol wrote in his philosophical treatise: "Being good in business is the most fascinating kind of art... During the hippie era people put down the idea of business. They'd say 'money is bad' and 'working is bad'. Making money is art and working is art, and good business is the best art." The pair are complementary: Warhol was not materialistic *per se*, but he wanted power and influence; Rosen wanted to build an empire from materialism, and it brought him power and influence.

Celebrity Warhols belong in this type of New York restaurant setting: this is Big Business, and this is Big Art. Art Business even. An art restaurant such as Casa Lever in the centre of Manhattan is a statement on how the city is a focus for global power in real estate, art and entertainment. Rosen consistently blends space and decor to remind others that he uses taste as power, evidenced by his wider activities in acquiring property and art. His holding company, RFR, owns the Seagram Building, which housed the Four Seasons restaurant when Mark Rothko abandoned his commission on the grounds of not wanting to entertain "the idle rich". Rosen is a potent tastemaker. He buys heritage buildings such as the Seagram and Lever House and gives them a new lease of life. For instance, he controversially refurbished the Four Seasons in 2017, incorporating artworks from his collection made in 1958 as a snapshot of the cultural landscape of New York the year the building was completed. These included pieces by Franz Kline, Lee Krasner, Alexander Calder and Cy Twombly. There is collecting as an act of legacy-building in every property Rosen owns, contained in the sheer scale and ambition, yet equally detailed and considered.

On another level, the art in Casa Lever interprets how status is reinforced because Rosen chose Warhol, who, although he was highly critical of the celebrity system, actively participated in it and even generated it. The Warhol of the 1980s, when the public was growing tired of him, ironically was at his most commercial and business-minded, appearing in advertisements and collaborating with mainstream consumer brands, from airlines to burgers. As a result, the commodification of the fine-dining or "in-dining" restaurant experience is not just celebrated, but flaunted at Casa Lever, because it reveals patterns of behaviour that can be seen through the lens of sociology. As soon as one arrives in the establishment, the visual carnival begins. The tables in the main space are arranged in long lines, like a factory belt churning out stylish and wealthy Manhattanites, while the honeycomb booths at the side offer a vantage point to scrutinise both the other diners and the artworks – and, of course, to be observed oneself. Even a breakfast visit reverberates with energy and confidence. There is a reason the restaurant attracts superlatives for the successful and driven: "[One of the] best places to have a power lunch in New York City" (*Financial Times*) or "places to bag your next hedge fund husband" (*Town and Country*). It also evokes one of New York's most iconic eras: the Studio 54 parties and their association of fun, transgression and creativity with a coterie of glitterati, or attendance at The Factory happenings, which were "an international status symbol, like Rolex watches or Concorde". The silkscreens reproduce and reinforce the unmistakably glamorous fundamental tenets of dining out – the sensual pleasure of eating, drinking and conviviality amongst an in-crowd. They also reinforce who wields power in its different forms: money, beauty, status, talent and intellect. Casa Lever attracts a clientele that can have any combination of these attributes.

Everybody loves hearing stories and accounts of Muhammad Ali or Aretha Franklin. The celebrities are randomly arranged, no rhyme or reason but a jumble of biographies, accomplishments, fame levels, tragic endings. Each silkscreen has a story. There are two of Judy Garland, one in colour and the identical image in monochrome, as if one is the "on duty" Garland and the second unmade, unpainted, just like the sitter was prone to bouts of erratic behaviour. Warhol and Judy Garland were friends of a sort; he recalled a Factory party where he observed a "totally wasted" Garland fighting with Tennessee Williams ("Fuck you, Tennessee, how dare you say I can't act?... You've *gotta* write something for me"). The Shah of Iran silkscreen is contrarian, hence important, given Warhol's controversial 1975 visit to Tehran to create portraits of the emperor and empress – "Torture tastes better with Caviar", as one headline reported the story – where, according to his friend Bob Colacello, the artist grew to love the ease and luxury of staying in the Hilton and ordering caviar at any time of the day on room service "for *just* $10 *a pound*".

Casa Lever is also an experiment in how people behave around global blue-chip artists such as Warhol, the ultimate art world and auction house commodity. He is not short of critics, such as Clement Greenberg, who dismissed his mainstream and "cute" subject matter. However, his art market value and staying power deflect this. Located within an iconic property of a real estate magnate, displaying one of the most expensive artists in the world, attracting powerful and wealthy diners to its tables, this art restaurant endures and allures in how it tells a story of power and influence, seeing and being seen in the right circles, and this is emphasised by the Warhols. James A. Walker writes about "paracelebrities" – associates and auxiliaries of celebrities who benefit from how "celebrity can also rub off on those close to the stars". There are just as many – usually more – hangers-on around the famous, something Warhol toyed with too by playing to the audience. It is part of a system of meaning in terms of what the artworks placed in a restaurant like this represent. "There are so many people [in New York City] to compete with that changing your tastes to what other people don't want is your only hope of getting anything," he said. Warhol both loved and hated the celebrity machine but could not stay away from it. His polemics are present in this art restaurant, but not in a heavy-handed, didactic way, more in a deadpan and ironic manner.

Maxim's in Paris was the first restaurant to introduce mirrors into the dining space to acknowledge the activity that is as much a part of eating in restaurants as the actual food – seeing and being seen. They may not be literal mirrors – even when Jerry is in town – yet there is a statement about how the subjects of these portraits are so much a part of the restaurant experience. Warhol's legacy on fame and status remains and is an opportunity for Casa Lever to take people watching, to belonging to a coterie, to a new level. The artist was fascinated by mirrors; "I'll be your mirror; reflect what you are, in case you don't know," as Nico sang with The Velvet Underground, and Warhol loved the song. Mirrors

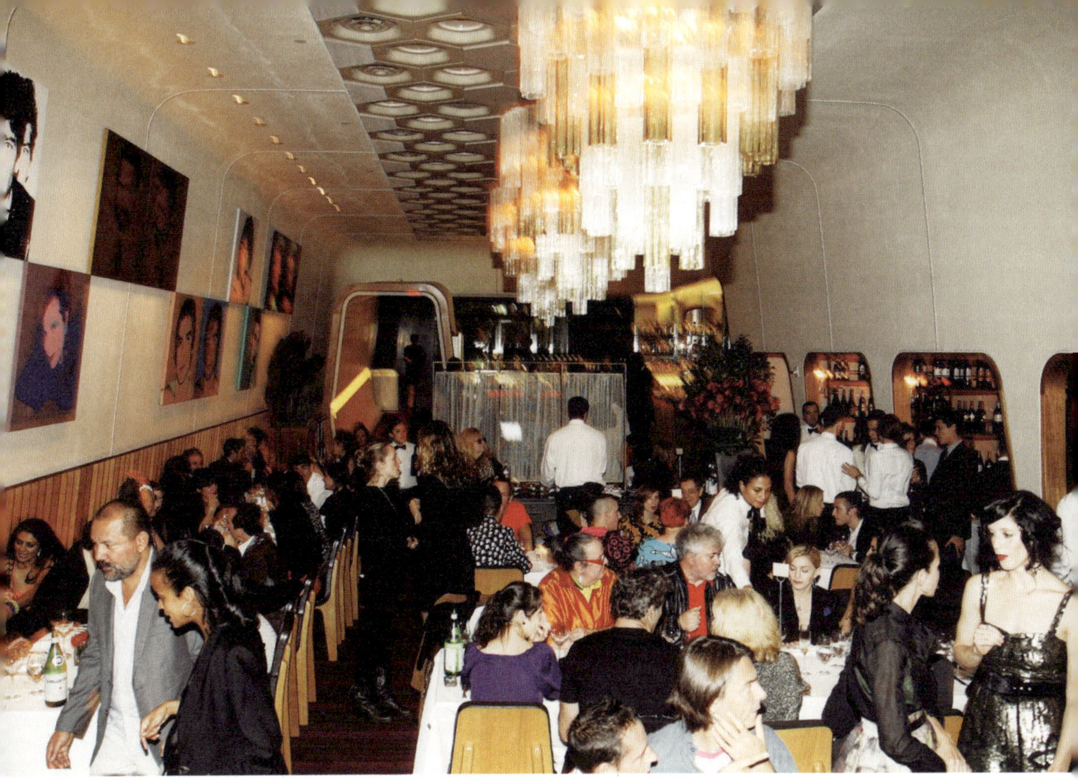

ignore the outside world – otherwise they would be windows – and turn the gaze back onto the internal space. Casa Lever as an art restaurant experience contains a tension between fashion, transience and the passing fad of who's who – core elements of Warhol's artistic philosophy, but also ironic in the pyramid-scale monuments to power and eternity of one of the largest property empires in the world. The discerning diner can sit and enjoy an *agnolotti del plin* with a glass of Barolo Riserva and watch the scenario unfold.

Warhol also enhances the restaurant context given his own contradictory and complicated relationship with food ("food is my great extravagance"), which was often depicted in his art. His religious upbringing would mean he associated dining with Christian rites and practices, an updating of the Last Supper along the restaurant wall. Meanwhile, his modest childhood gave him an understanding of food representing reward when things are good and scarcity when times are tough – although his success eventually enabled him to realise he could have whatever he wanted, from caviar to leftovers. His "New York City Diet" involved him going to a restaurant and ordering "everything that I don't want, so I have a lot to play around with while everyone else eats". This allowed him to keep trim and also to share the leftovers with homeless people. And it gave him an understanding of how the dining process is mundane, yet scalable and infused with cultural meaning. Restaurants in America are contradictory in a similar manner – on the one hand they try to project the mirage of a unique experience in that moment, in terms of service, catering and attention to the guest, while

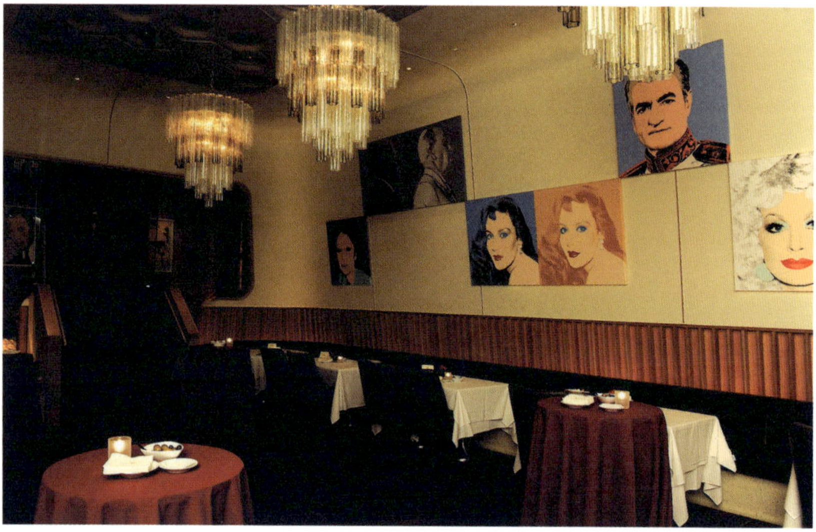

on the other hand this experience is replicated, repeated, churned out. There are also affinities between high and low culture, rich and poor: "What's great about this country is that America started the tradition where the richest consumers buy essentially the same things as the poorest. You can be watching TV and see Coca-Cola, and you know that the president drinks Coke, Liz Taylor drinks Coke, and, just think, you can drink Coke, too." There is an illusion of meritocracy – naturally the president and Liz Taylor are not like everybody else who drinks Coke. However, the consumerist foundation of American society also undermines the extraordinariness of the wealthy and privileged because they participate in the same system of consumption. "A Coke is a Coke, and no amount of money can get you a better Coke than the one the bum on the corner is drinking. All the Cokes are the same and all the Cokes are good. Liz Taylor knows it, the president knows it, the bum knows it, and you know it."

The silkscreens displayed on the Casa Lever walls contain this paradox. They are mass-produced off the back of mass-circulated images off the back of constructed celebrity identities. "You're recycling work and you're recycling people," Warhol proclaimed. Yet they are also artworks, with an informed practice and aesthetics. And they are placed in a high-end restaurant in the most expensive real estate in the world, as markers of global art trophies. Guests can enjoy this at literal face value, but they can also engage in the wider art restaurant experience of reflecting on what it means to dine with, and on, icons of consumption.

Works and artists in the Casa Lever collection

—

Douglas S. Cramer. The respected American television producer, whose programmes have included *The Brady Bunch* and *Dynasty*, is a significant art collector in the United States. He owns work by Ellsworth Kelly, Roy Lichtenstein, Richard Prince and Warhol, and has been a significant donor to MOCA and MoMA.

—

Dennis Hopper. The actor and his wife loved Warhol's early works from the *Campbell's Soup Cans* phase. They were responsible for throwing the artist a huge Hollywood party in 1962 before his first Ferus Gallery show and introduced him to the West Coast celebrity world.

—

Nan Kempner. An anorexic socialite – she was the "social X-ray" inspiration in Tom Wolfe's *The Bonfire of the Vanities* – and fashion collector. She only wore outfits by Bill Blass, Valentino, Halston and Yves Saint Laurent and reputedly attended 51 couture seasons in her life, bar one, due to being ill for one Fashion Week.

—

Giorgio Armani. The fashion designer and Warhol would hit New York's party scene in the early 1980s, even though, by his own admission, Armani could not speak English and Warhol did not understand Italian. The language of champagne, cocaine and disco needs no words, being universal in participation.

—

Muhammad Ali. This is part of Warhol's *Athletes* series, which began after a wealthy financier, Richard Weisman, suggested the idea and paid each sitter $15,000 to pose. The boxer has his fists raised high in gloves, with an intense stare. Warhol famously did not care for sports, but he did care about winning and success – just like its current owner – and this was a new arena of subject matter for Art Business. He once admitted the series was "a business deal".

Andy Warhol's silkscreens along the dining room with honeycomb-design dividers; the silkscreens of Alfred Hitchcock, Robert Mapplethorpe and Kimiko Powers watch over the diners; Jerry Hall, the Shah of Iran and Giorgio Armani feature among the collection

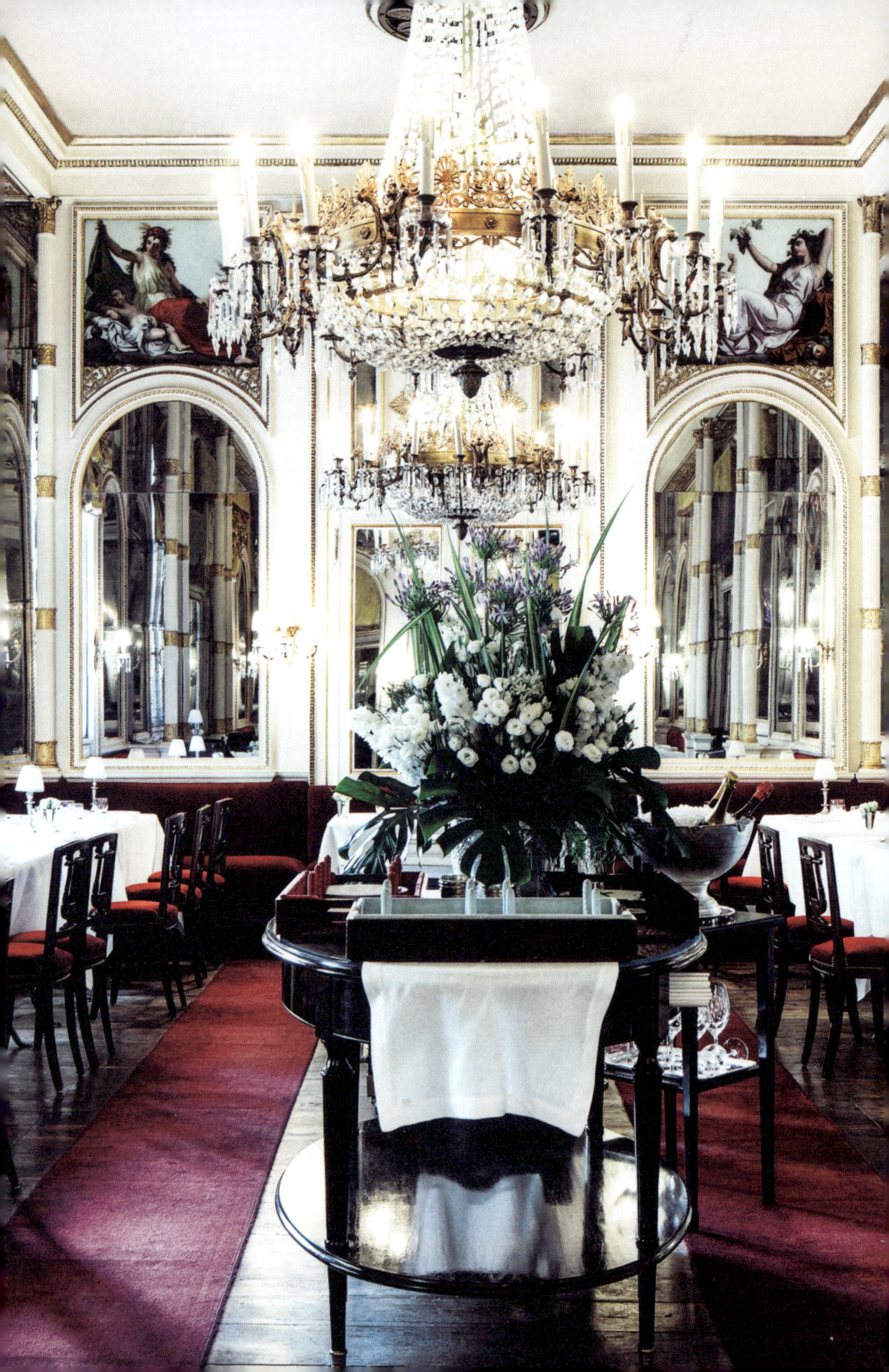

Del Cambio

TURIN

"Everything in my work has come from the mirror, and the idea that it reflects society and reality."
— Michelangelo Pistoletto

In the heart of Turin's Piazza Carlo Alberto, opposite the Palazzo Carignano, the first parliament building of Italy, the stage of Ristorante del Cambio has welcomed some of the most commanding and demanding patrons for over three centuries. Never has a dining room received such dramatic clientele as Mozart, Casanova, Nietzsche, Balzac, Verdi, Maria Callas and Audrey Hepburn feasting in its high-ceilinged, glimmering, mirrored spaces; enough personalities and melodramatics to satiate red-blooded heroes, to relieve divas' heaving bosoms, and provide sufficient plotlines between the composers to concoct a multitude of librettos. Now, just what to do with Nietzsche's fussy eating habits and preference for early Teutonic fad diets…

These figures, and countless other politicians, industrialists, celebrities, artists, writers and intellectuals, regularly dined under the gilded boiserie and shimmering chandeliers of the city's grandest historic restaurant, served by staff in impeccably tailored dinner jackets over pristine, crisp white linen tablecloths. Established in 1757, Del Cambio is one of the oldest restaurants in the world, and by upholding its rituals and traditions of classic Piedmontese dining, it becomes an artwork in itself. Long before modern patrons began to take for granted neoclassical details, and the aesthetic paradigm shifted to the Modernism that remains prevalent in contemporary times, the decorative arts in formal restaurants such as Del Cambio were enriched with meaning – in the articles on table settings, the girandole mirrors, in the shape and placement of the lighting, in the wall patterns and colours. This was the result of carefully constructed discrimination signifying good taste of a particular time and class, and a sense of belonging for those accustomed to the surroundings. Like all design, there was an intention behind what was sourced and placed in the dining setting, and in turn an expectation of behaviour and demeanour from diners. As food historian Margaret Visser says: "The extent to which we take everyday objects for granted is the precise extent to which they govern and inform our lives." This time capsule is one aspect of Del Cambio's enduring success as an art restaurant. However, in 2014 it was updated to incorporate contemporary art through a significant commission executed by the venerable Arte Povera artist, Michelangelo Pistoletto. The work, *Evento*, is a mirrored panel that encloses the second dining room and reflects guests in its construction and its content, dealing with levels of self-consciousness and self-reflection of the restaurant

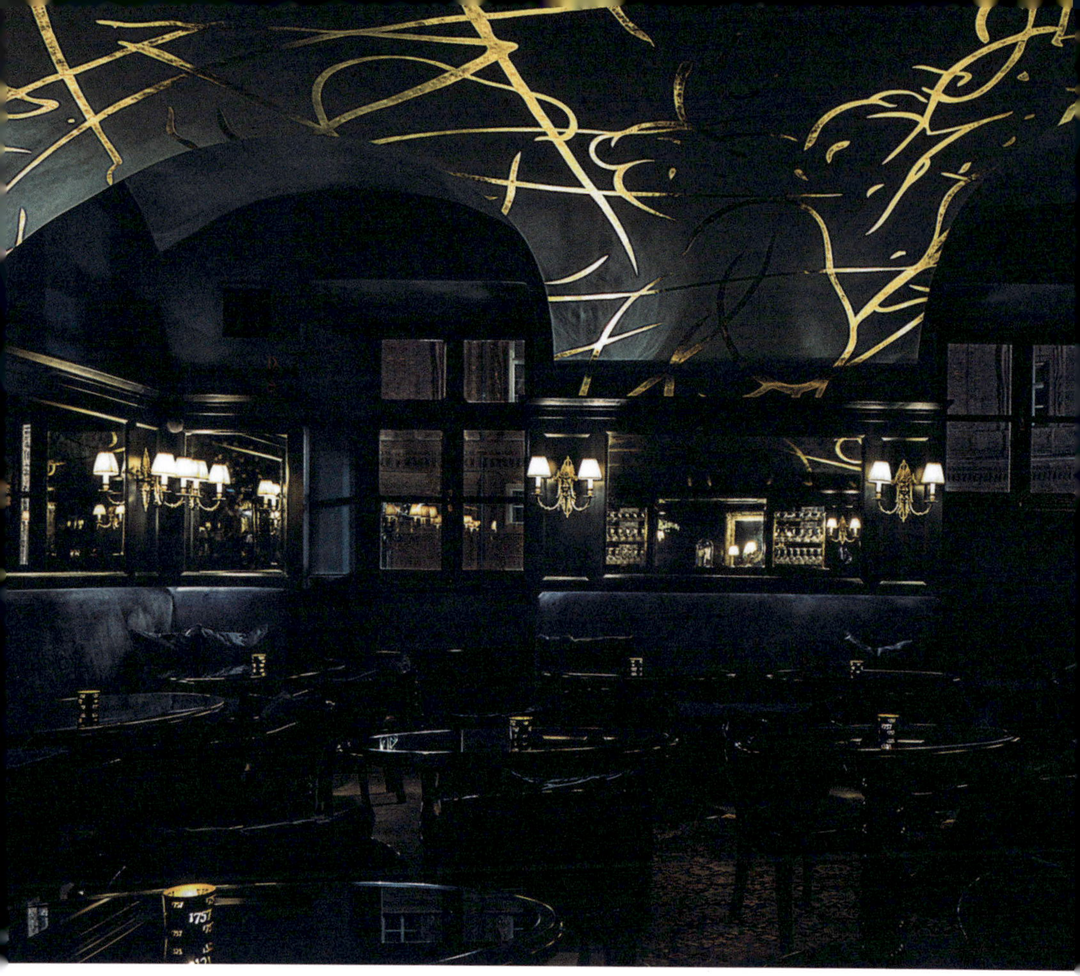

public space. With this site-specific piece, Del Cambio has been preserved as an historic art restaurant, reflecting its dining traditions in the mirrors, but is also refreshed in a contemporary sense, attracting audiences expecting immersive dining experiences. The Pistoletto work assists this paradox.

Del Cambio has served Piedmontese traditions, such as *vittelo tonnato* and *taglierini al truffo*, with a Barbera d'Asti or a Nebbiolo d'Alba, to Turin's high society from the outset. The truffle is the "diamond of gastronomy", according to Brillat-Savarin, and this restaurant is a fungal lapidary, weighing, shaving and presenting the delicacies with great precision and reverence. As a foodstuff it has never lost its significance as the epitome of literal good taste, and Del Cambio's cuisine grows from this grounding.

Turin, less fashionable than Milan and less grandiose than Rome, is a city slower in pace, quieter, more reflective, but uncompromising when it comes to the preservation of traditions and upholding socially agreed taste. Del Cambio has witnessed historic events, and even hosted its fair share. It is credited with the first use of *cambio* as the word for "exchange" in Italian. Napoleon III passed

through the city, changed the restaurant name to *Café du Change* in 1796, but could not leave behind his new-found obsession for *grissini*, the long crunchy bread-sticks locals eat, and established an express route to have them delivered to Paris on a regular basis. Nor could he leave behind other fixations: the Countess of Castiglione, Virginia Oldoini, who controversially became his long-standing mistress. Oldoini, who was an early pioneer of photography in her own right, and also cousin of one of the founders of Italian unification, Camillo Benso, the Count of Cavour, would regularly dine in the restaurant, probably justifying Brillat-Savarin's other observation on the Piedmontese truffle: "It is not so much a positive aphrodisiac, but it can upon occasion make women tenderer and men more attentive." By the time of the Italian Risorgimento in 1851, Del Cambio became the unofficial dining room of the first Italian Parliament, and its Bar Cavour remains a testament to that historic moment, honouring the count in the form of a grand portrait hanging over the bar. The space is as louche and dazzling as his reputed off-duty behaviour around fine meats and vintage wines. The statesman frequented the restaurant during his term, and right after signing the Treatise of Turin in 1860, is attributed as declaring: "We have made history, now let us go to lunch!"

Turin native restaurateur Michele Denegri acquired Del Cambio in 2012 with the intention of tapping into the recent culinary renaissance of the city, where the Slow Food movement was based, and the original Eataly established. The restaurant had to reconcile traditional cooking and being part of a respected industry with the need to innovate and remain relevant to new diners. Older patrons who belong to the affluent, industrialist classes of Turin have certain expectations of taste and *savoir faire*. Members of the Angelli family, interchangeably described both as the modern Medicis and Italy's answer to the Kennedy dynasty, are regularly seen at Del Cambio. Taste is socially constructed; people take their cues from those they admire and wish to emulate. Del Cambio trades on this psychosocial truth. There is a cachet to being observed dining in sophisticated or extraordinary restaurants. French sociologist Pierre Bourdieu argued eating out contains not just economic but cultural capital. Frequenting the right establishments marks one out as being financially well-endowed and socially privileged, displaying one's taste and abilities of discernment. Placing works of art in the dining area is evidence of the collectors "achieving their symbolic gratification of social distinction". This element of exclusivity and insider knowledge is also part of the appeal of art: it is important to know and demonstrate one knows good artists and artworks.

The interior of Del Cambio is an elegant interplay between light, mirrors and crystal – it is effervescent and delicate, despite the gilded design. It represents a time when restaurants confidently showed their patrons what high taste looked and felt like. The 19th-century frescoes in the large Sala Risorgimento are classic haute bourgeois decorations featuring pastel pudgy-yet-pretty cherubs and nubile, bare-breasted goddesses strewn across saccharine cloud formations. There is something enduringly titillating and amusing about the tables of older businessmen chewing through their deal-sealing lunches under these cloying murals. If taste is as much intentionality as it is form, as critic Stephen Bayley argues, then del Cambio constructs a dining environment to incorporate all visual and aesthetic elements – to maintain its historical origins but to give way to contemporary art, ensuring guests are also able to break the trance of the dining ritual, becoming aware of how they participate in it.

Pistoletto was the right choice for the 2014 commission as he would visit Del Cambio as a young man, drawn to its intellectual and historic pedigree. After the Second World War it became a significant gathering place for his artistic and academic peers to discuss politics and the evolving philosophies of post-modern times. The resulting piece is a signature Pistoletto *Quadri specchianti* work where he imposes photographs of human figures on a mirrored background along the four walls of the space. Groups of people in different positions, heights and crops gaze in one direction. They are a random mixture of ages and gender – children in bright playwear, ladies in pastel dresses, young men in stripy T-shirts, older men in grey suits. It invites the observer into the piece to complete it by sitting and being reflected in it.

Pistoletto describes *Evento* as depicting an event that does not occur in the work itself, but everybody in the piece and looking at it is waiting for this nebulous event to happen. He explains: "I make a sketch as a place to meet, the pleasure of getting together, the pleasure of living a moment of joy." The suggestion is the event *is* the dining experience, the conviviality, the gathering, the actual restaurant. The artwork – in that curious exchange between object and subject – observes the diners who in turn observe the artwork, but also see themselves in the mirrored panels. "Then every time you go to a restaurant, an event takes place. Especially if you come to a restaurant like this one, it will be an event." It is performance art in between courses, as the piece relies on the audience to complete it.

Evento signifies meaning on several levels. Historically, it is an honour for the restaurateur to have a piece by a renowned artist who also frequented the venue in his early career. It works in terms of what the mirror paintings mean in the artist's œuvre and his upbringing around Baroque art and the traditions of the Italian Renaissance. It is also a reminder of how important mirrors are in restaurants – they were one of the first features post-revolutionary establishments incorporated into their interior design, as opposed to their tavern and public house predecessors. The bourgeoisie have a strong taste for self-reflection and

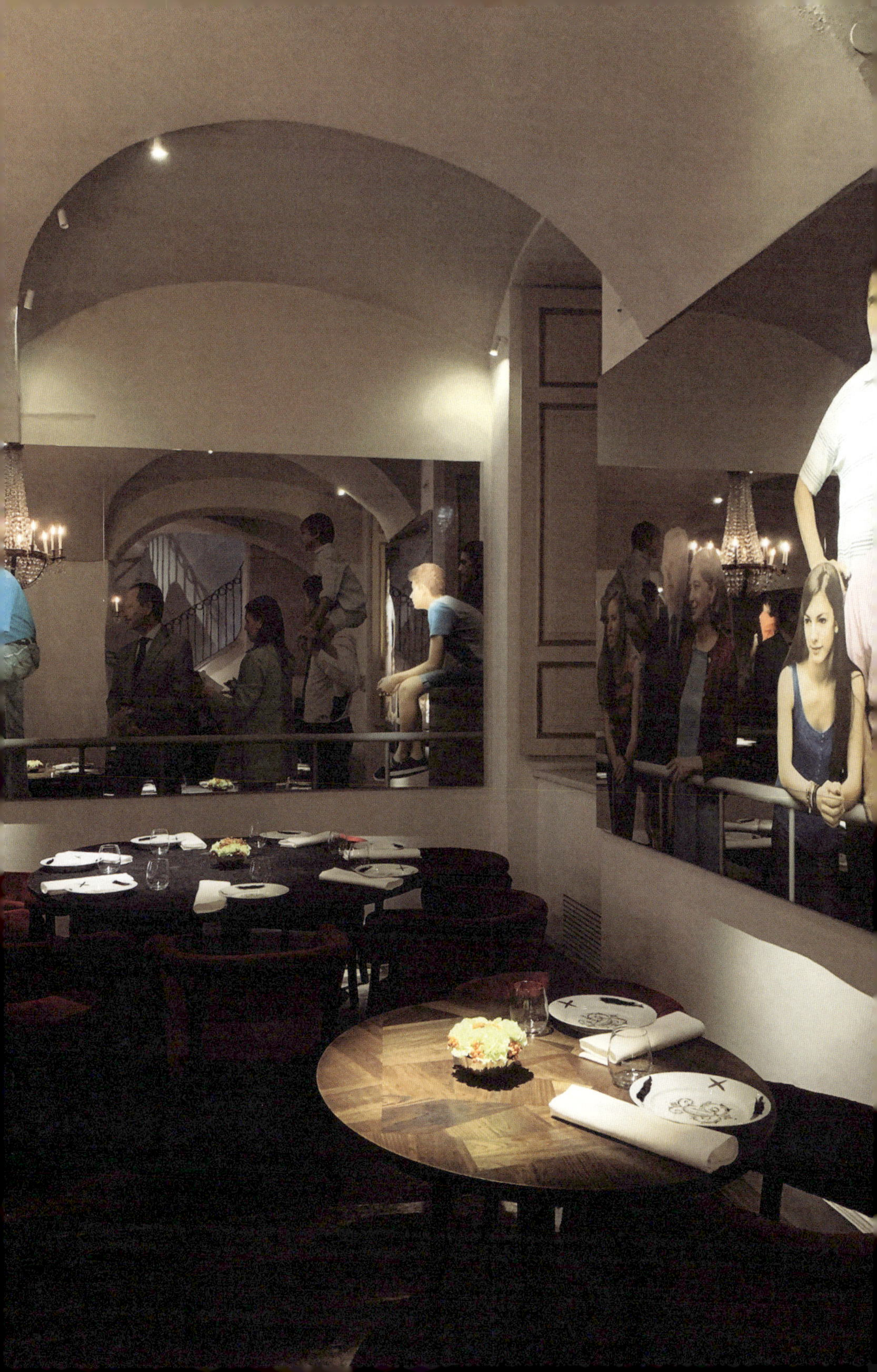

self-depiction in art too. Furthermore, at Del Cambio, the Pistoletto's significance is intensified by being placed in a dining space where mirrors were part of the original design, intended to enhance the performance of demonstrating high taste occurring in a restaurant. The meaning of *Evento* is enhanced by being created for a restaurant setting because it needs the diners to animate it. And Del Cambio's space is enhanced by the Pistoletto jolting an otherwise anachronistic haute bourgeois establishment into contemporary practices of art and aesthetics. This is a mutual reinforcement, not the same as encountering a Pistoletto mirror work in an art gallery. Pistoletto has argued: "Artists must not be only in art galleries or museums – they must be present in all possible activities. The artist must be the sponsor of thought in whatever endeavour people take on, at every level." His artistic practice and philosophy intended this completion by viewers, but placed in a museum or gallery his pieces acquire other connotations of art history and tradition. In a restaurant setting the work is demotic and lived on one level, but also becomes an instrument or object in the ritual of dining.

Del Cambio still wields a quiet, poised power as the dining room of Turin's high society. On a daily basis, it hosts good bone structure and strong politics, it heightens romance through feeding salacious mistresses and convivial rogues, it welcomes decency and propriety as the finish line for family *passeggiata* through Turin's thoroughfares. It is precisely what restaurants have always set out to do in terms of exciting diners and making them feel like they belong to a particular social stratum. It serves this exclusivity back to them on the plate but also in their own reflection in Pistoletto's artwork. The inclusion of contemporary art subtly makes the self-reflexivity of dining rituals apparent and celebrates it. It also documents how even the meaning of bourgeois taste will shift over time, hence the curiosity element of the restaurant's classic decor and cuisine, protected from becoming complacent by the Pistoletto installation, which makes the whole experience of Del Cambio an artwork in itself.

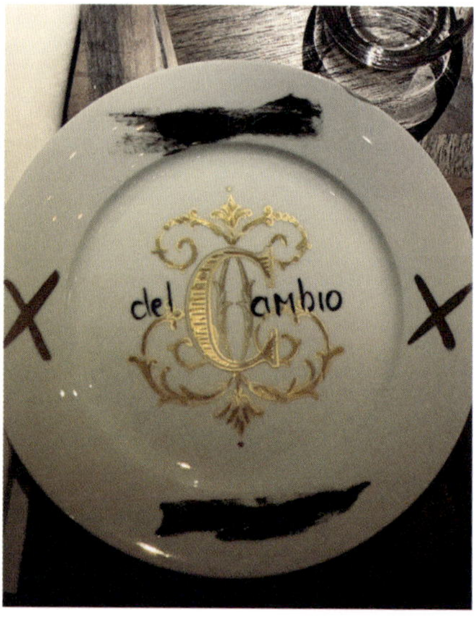

Works and artists in the Del Cambio collection

—

The Israeli artist Izhar Patkin reworked the classic Sèvres dinnerware to update the traditional design of the French porcelain factory, which was founded in 1756, one year almost to the day before Del Cambio was established. The artist wanted to preserve the perfection of the traditional design and methodology, until he discovered over 60 per cent of Sèvres plates produced do not meet the quality standards of the *Manufacture nationale de Sèvres*. This inspired him to work with the traditional high standards of production of the Vincennes porcelain, yet to update the decoration for a contemporary audience and re-evaluate what would be judged as perfection and imperfection. He stencilled over 300 pieces of the restaurant's dinnerware to incorporate the two arguments.

—

Del Cambio has furniture and chairs created by Martino Gamper, the renowned designer of chairs particularly known for his project, *100 Chairs in 100 Days and its 100 Ways*. He works with reclaimed wood and wanted to emphasise how in a restaurant the table and chairs are the most important objects, as they are "the meeting point for people to talk and eat". For him, the commission was the fusion of "function, form and behaviour". Turin has always been a design hub in Italy, with Fiat and Futurism securing its position as such in the early 20th century.

—

Arturo Herrera is a contemporary Venezuelan artist who works with popular culture imagery and reconfigures it to factor in Surrealism and Modernist abstraction. His mural – large lashings of abstract shapes and lines – takes over the whole ceiling upstairs at Del Cambio, as louche and haphazard as the behaviour of its patrons. He wanted to reference the gold leaf in the dining room downstairs, update it, and also ensure visitors would "be in dialogue with the architecture of the room". The gold leaf picks up the light and guides the visitor to the next line, changing throughout the day and glimmering above the candles by night.

The Sala Risorgimento in Del Cambio, from 1875; the Cavour bar; the second dining room in Del Cambio with Pistoletto's mirror work wrapped around it

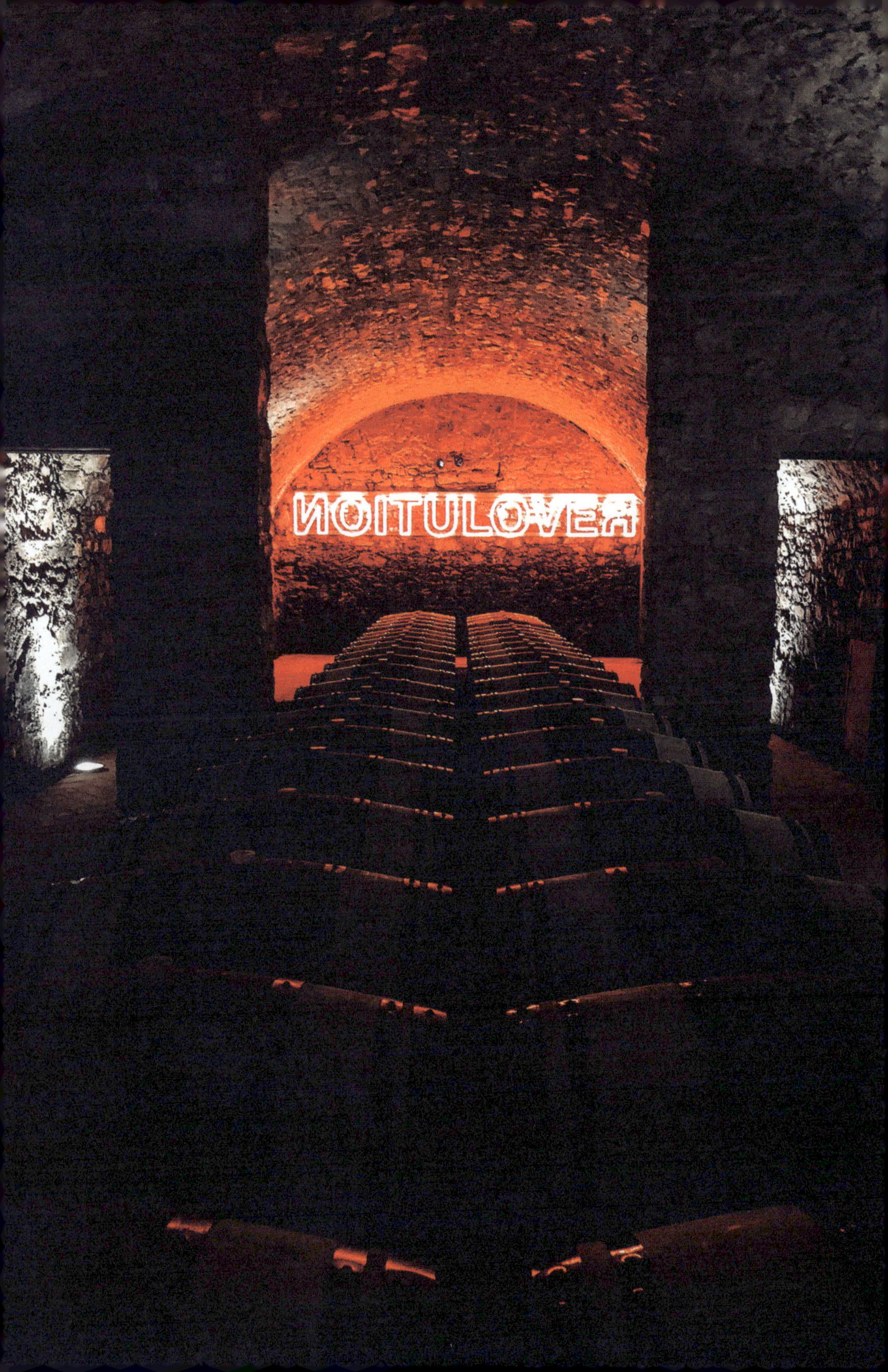
NOITULOVER

Castello di Ama

"Consult the genius of the place in all;
That tells the waters to rise, or fall;
Or helps th' ambitious hill the heav'ns to scale,
Or scoops in circling theatres the vale;
Calls in the country, catches opening glades,
Joins willing woods, and varies shades from shades,
Now breaks, or now directs, th' intending lines;
Paints as you plant, and, as you work, designs."
— Alexander Pope

"Lee Ufan? He drink *like a fish*... but Roni Horn doesn't drink a drop. Not a single drop," Vincenzo, the sommelier in the candlelit drawing room of the 18th-century country house declares with frisky derision, as he uncorks and pours a 2006 Vigneto Bellavista Chianti. "We opened this bottle when she came to inaugurate her piece in 2012... you see, it has this pattern of the number 7, just like her work, but she did not drink it, the rest of the party did." All of the artists who have passed through the gates of Castello di Ama have a link to one of its premium vintages, every bottle uncorked releasing the concoction that is the culmination of thinkers, artists and oenophiles who are compelled to respond to the land and its *genius loci* – the spirit of the place – that oversees it. This art restaurant is not confined to four walls, and, like a trellis, allows the landscape to climb and bloom into its experience, where all the senses, not merely the visual, work together.

A tiny medieval *borgo* situated between Siena and Florence, nestled in the heart of Chianti, Castello di Ama has been producing wine, its "nectar of the land", for four generations. Its Sangiovese grape finds its way into 300,000 bottles a year, with its San Lorenzo cru, in particular, attracting prestigious accolades over the past three decades. In 1992 its L'Apparita 1987 vintage was voted superior to the Pétrus 1988 at the Swiss Academie du Vin. The recent addition of the contemporary art and restaurant on the estate attracted a new audience of art collectors and gourmands. At Castello di Ama, art, wine and food form a synergy for exploring taste, "the mission of life", according to its owner, Lorenza Sebasti. The artists' responses are showcased in Ama's collection; "Artists are the greatest witnesses of what goes on here," she says.

For her business partner, Marco Pallanti, incorporating the artistic process and site-specific commissions on the land mirrors his own winemaking process and guides him in his contribution to Ama. He says for him the difference between a mere beverage and wine is the latter can only be created with one's own faith and belief – all he can do as a vintner is to produce the wine and release it into the world, while acknowledging "I have to understand that it may not be to everybody's taste." This is exactly how an artist would operate: following their convictions and risking work that may not appeal to all. His part in the drama is to make the wine, and, like an artwork, the reception and interpretation is up to the connoisseur.

The Sebastis are originally from a Roman family line who were early Chianti innovators in Tuscany, using the Lyre trellis method of training vines since 1982, which is a meticulous, rare and expensive technique to separate and space the vines for maximum sun penetration. Pallanti is heir to a landowning family in the region, and together, with a passion for exploring what the land can produce, the proprietors have cultivated the ideal conditions for the rituals of aesthetic dining. At Castello di Ama, aesthetic dining is both a science and an art. Taste is literal in the food and wine, but it is also aesthetic through the art collection. South African artist Kendell Geers, a friend of the proprietors and regular visitor, says: "Time is space between the vines and art can only be embodied through a holistic vision as the worlds of the imagination and the suprasensible multiverse weave their realities into our five senses of three dimensions." The cultivation is a reminder of man's endeavour to work with the land, as the art is a reminder of the artist's resistance to his materials. Here it is the exploration of taste in its literal and aesthetic meaning that organically binds the art and the land together.

For the past 16 years, Lorenza and Marco have commissioned a new work of contemporary art to be permanently exhibited in the grounds. They have invited international artists they collected at home to visit Ama, to eat and drink there, and spend time on the land in between meals. The artists are given free rein to decide whether or not the environment inspires them to plant a piece of art in the soil. "I cross my fingers the magic of the place will work on the artists and they will fall in love with the place," Lorenza explains.

Artists who have responded to the request include Pascale Marthine Tayou, Cristina Iglesias, Ilya Kabakov, Carlos Garaicoa and Hiroshi Sugimoto. They have created pieces ranging from installations in chapels and sculptures in the orchards to works in ancient cisterns, the cellars and the route leading up to the restaurant. The first of Anish Kapoor's now signature optical illusion works was made for the small Baroque chapel next to the restaurant, placed in front of the altar. There have been years, however, when artists did not accept a commission and no work was produced. This supports Pallanti's views on the similarities between the process of cultivation and winemaking, and that of producing art – certitude and belief are essential. For example, the vintners may decide not to create a vintage from a particular year because the soil and atmosphere do

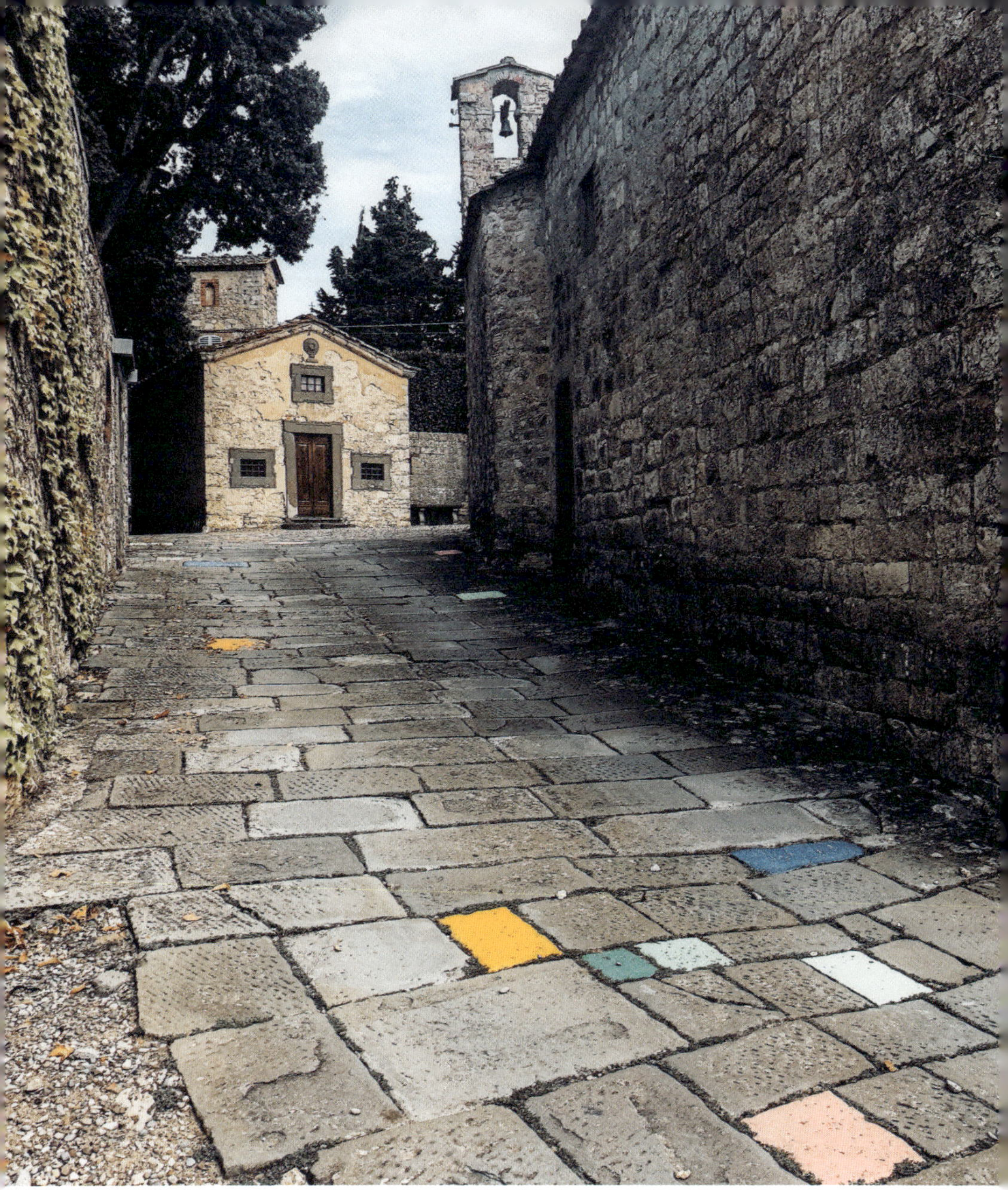

not enable it. Viticulture and the creation of art grow more entangled the more one looks at and co-exists with the works placed in the land.

The wine and the art led to Lorenza and Marco's most recent adventure in tastemaking: Il Ristoro di Ama, established in 2014. As Lorenza says: "First people came for the art, then they were asking about food." The restaurant is in the main villa of the estate, dating to the late 17th century, with views of the hills and Siena on the horizon. It is small, intimate and spread over three dining rooms and a stone terrace. The feeling of the art collector opening their home and sharing their interpretation of taste with visitors is enhanced by Lorenza inviting the family chef and head of household, Sicilian-born Giovani Bonavista, to run and operate the restaurant. The staff have been with the family for over two and a half decades. The fare is unpretentious, rustic and consistently, quietly good *cucina povera*. The art restaurant is intertwined: the land demands the art, and the art demands the cuisine to forge the synthesis.

The land of Castello di Ama's estate has an ancient history of wine production. The hills that crown Ama and its fertile soil have been cultivated since Roman times. Unusually, the hamlet and its surrounding vineyards sit 490 metres above sea level. In 1773, the Grand Duke Cosimo declared that the cru of this area was superior to all others. The unique blend of sedimentary rock and clay on top of the hills enables the growing of grapes and grains, but is also the bedrock for the artworks to come to fruition. There is a sense of stewardship for this land and the traditions and industry of winemaking, because the economic component of running the estate is essential to making the commissions possible. The context of production is rooted in the hills and wine-art-food form a territoriality that must be experienced as an immersive leap of faith – much like the artists do when they respond to the call of the land. "The artist drinks of the drunk vine called life in order to reconnect with their true nature, cutting the rational chords of logic in order to give birth to more than meets the eye," Kendell Geers says. "Sobriety is sacrificed in favour of vision." The art that interests these collectors is also firmly rooted in the land: they invite the artists to sleep, eat, drink and *just be* in the space for extended periods of time before they ask them to execute any work.

Lorenza believes Castello di Ama "works between revolution and tradition." They continue to produce and cultivate what they know best, the wine, but they also need to allow creativity and adaptation, whether it is in the business model or through the art collection they are building. The works they collect fit within this adaptively disruptive principle. For instance, Geers's *Revolution/Love* (2003) is a neon installation inside the working cellar. It is the only fully functional wine cellar that is also an artwork in a private collection. Two rows of barrels lead up to the sign, suggesting the work pays tribute to the wine production that enables it to be made, but conversely, the wine gestures towards the art in an affinity of man's endeavours of cultivation and creation. Geers illustrates the significance of Castello di Ama to his practice: "The wine I love to drink so much is a spirit no less, a spirit nurtured with time through the cycles of life. The spirit of wine, that Dionysiac divine intoxicating gift of the gods, depends on the sun, rain, earth, light, heat and the revolution of the four seasons through time. The grapes grow on ancient vines rooted in the earth, twisting between cracks in the rocks and turning through the soil, feeding on rainwater and sipping the early morning dew. When the Dog Star Sirius rises, the grapes sweat and fatten with the heat of summer, slowly ripening under the vintner's loving touch. The autumn harvest cannot be too soon, nor too late, because it has to be perfectly timed between the sun and the rain, between the seasons of growth and decay. The grapes are grown with love, only to be cut and fermented, distilled into wine, just as the midwife cuts the umbilical cord after the 10 lunar revolutions that grew from the seeds of carnate passionate love. Without love, there can be no revolution and therefore no life."

The art throughout the estate enriches and feeds the grounds. Lorenza believes the artworks are essential to the success of the land, what it grows and what it means. She will go as far as to claim the fate of the wine depends on the presence and aura of the works. Authenticity is pursued through an unshakeable sense of stewardship of both art and land, and as Lorenza states: "You cannot lie at the table." There is a stripping back to basics of nature, which the art then refashions and reframes for its visitors experiencing the aesthetic dining.

One such work is Daniel Buren's mirror installation (*Sulle Vigne: Punti di Vista*, 2001) that frames a quiet green space of the garden. It both reflects the viewer looking into it and is a window onto the acres of vineyards. The piece is mimetic in terms of reflecting nature that surrounds it and is also a careful construction as a three-dimensional landscape painting. "Daniel Buren opened my head," Lorenza says. "People can sit in front of the Buren and experience the same feeling in the sun, with the view of the hills." Unlike a fixed landscape work, it will change with the seasons, with the light; it will remain dynamic like the land it mirrors.

The production of the estate's wine is a result of climate, ground and know-how, according to its founders, and that *savoir faire* is creative. "Making wine is no different from coming up with a work of art," says Lorenza. "How to give the illusion of being able to perfect perfection: having an intangible gift, the shape of the grape, the colour of the vine leaves, and absurdly wanting to change it, to extract its nectar, to make seen what cannot be seen." The art is a demonstration of the know-how, as it also takes natural materials and fashions them into an object with wider meaning and symbolism for how we understand taste. The two are indistinguishable at Castello di Ama.

It was the realisation of a Louise Bourgeois commission that convinced Lorenza and Marco to open the estate to visitors who wanted to view their collection. The sculpture was one of the last pieces the artist made before her death in 2010. Its title, *Fountain*, refers to its location deep in the ancient cistern on the estate under the cellars – a spot chosen by the artist – and it is only visible through a small hole in the floor and barely accessible via a steep ladder. As a characteristically Bourgeois creation, the polysemous title and depiction prompts a slew of puns and interpretations. Made of pink Carrara marble – also an ancient material – it is the combined form of a seated figure of a woman with an upright torso that resembles a phallus. If that were insufficient symbolism for Freudians, the top section features floral sprouting leaves. And there is a perpetual contrast between the softness of the figure and hardness of marble. It is an enigmatic piece in a peculiar part of the estate, being both vulnerable and resilient; however, it complements the rest of what Castello di Ama means, as viticulture is also a contrast between the organic dynamism of the land and resistance and control of man's interventions to produce the wine. The sculpture marked a pivotal moment for Lorenza, and if Daniel Buren "opened [her] head", Louise Bourgeois "opened her heart". The work is an offering of love to the land in exchange for what the land offers back to its patrons.

Castello di Ama is a small-scale, boutique operation, and in its cultivation of taste it offers the visitor an environment to experience the exquisite details of wine, art and food. "We are guardians, not owners," says Lorenza. "This is the way we approach things. This art is not personal or exclusive, it is for the community, and for us it is a great privilege, but we also feel the responsibility to share this privilege and transmit it so it can grow with time." Placing the art throughout the grounds is done with the same care as planting and harvesting the Sangiovese rows. The result affirms "that what not even time can cancel is this *genius loci*", as the philosopher of architecture, Christian Norberg-Schulz, wrote. "Every place possesses its own particular identity and that it is the proper task of man to comprehend that identity and take care of it, through a process that evidently will never come to an end." The experience of aesthetic dining at Castello di Ama offers that dining ritual as its contribution to such stewardship; patrons and visitors participate and add their own version to the experience. And finally, the artists too add their mark to the caretaking process, as Geers states: "Art is my life, as the seasons of time and their revolutions of loving and dying are my faith. Art has no market other than the exchange of spirit and art has no value except as faith. What I eat and drink feeds my body, just as what I live and love feeds my soul, and what I create and destroy to become art is my spirit."

Works and artists in the Castello di Ama collection

—

The late Chinese artist Chen Zhen's *La lumière intérieur du corps humain* (2005) hangs glass symbols of human organs such as hearts, livers and lungs in the cellar in the centre of the barrels, making an offering, a sacrifice to the rituals of cultivation, production and consumption.

—

Roni Horn's *Untitled* (2017), one of her signature glass objects, has its own room in the Villa Ricucci. It looks as if it reflects water, but is solid and transparent, its purity contrasting with the soil on the floor.

—

Cristina Iglesias's *Towards the Ground* (2008) fills up slowly and hypnotically, and then gently drains after one hour. The work comes and goes and its placement in a secluded courtyard outside the main villa under heavy and fragrant fig trees means viewers can isolate how they use their senses to experience it.

—

Michelangelo Pistoletto's *L'Albero di Ama* (2000), in the cellar entrance, is a giant tree trunk split in two with a mirror inserted inside to produce an optical refraction.

—

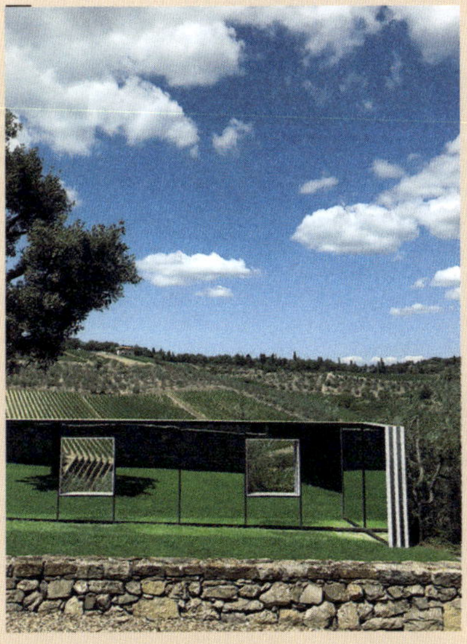

Kendell Geers' *Revolution/Love*; Pascal Marthine Tayoux's multicoloured stepping stones guide visitors to the restaurant; Daniel Buren's *Sulle Vigne: punti di vista* on the grounds of the vineyards

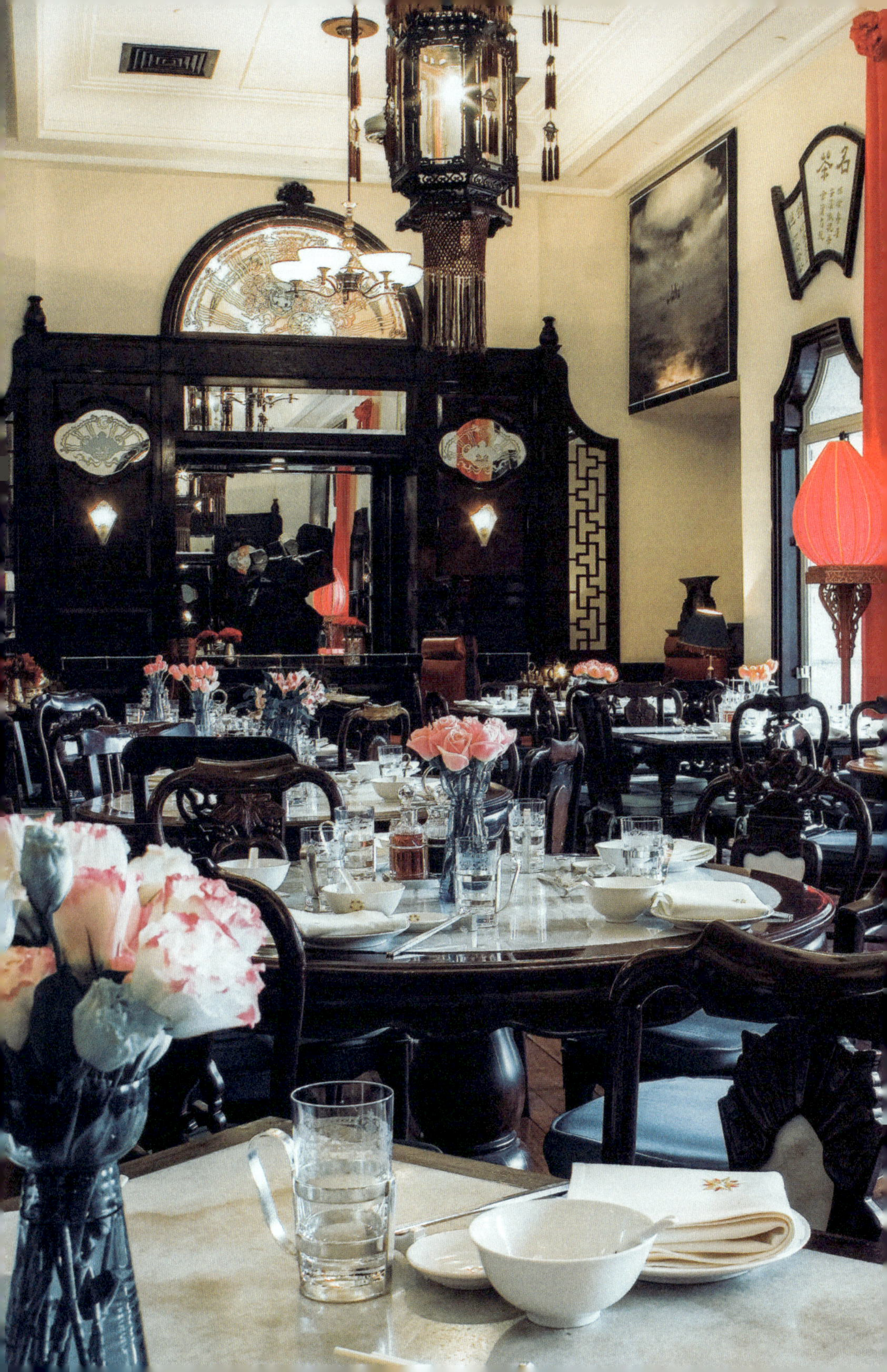

China Club

"Life is so brief that we should not glance either too far backwards or forwards... therefore study how to fix our happiness in our glass and on our plate."
— Grimod de La Reynière

In 1783, the French aristocrat and world's first restaurant critic, Alexandre Balthazar Grimod de La Reynière, hosted his own funeral dinner. A lifelong prankster, he decided to test the loyalty of his friends and family by gauging their reaction to his death. He had black-bordered memorial notices made announcing his demise, sent invitations for a pre-burial feast to those close to him, and instructed the hall be decorated with a coffin stand and a hearse outside. As the mourners assembled and settled around the table, he suddenly jumped out from behind a curtain. Shock gave way to laughter, and then a sumptuous banquet ensued. In 2017, the entrepreneur and art collector Sir David Tang, who was regarded as one of the most well-connected and affable raconteurs in the world, was planning his own decadent bash to celebrate his birthday. He would serve fine Cantonese cuisine, in the most opulent surroundings, with an international guest list ranging from top models to monarchs. However, less than a week before the date of this dinner, he unexpectedly died. Grimod was too early to his party; Tang was too late to his. Both figures will, however, go down in history for their reputations of being legendary tastemakers at the centre of the *beau monde* they created. In their respective times and social circles, they set and broke the rules, determining who was in and who was out of their worlds, judging peers by their manners and behaviour, often at the dining table.

The notion of *tastemaker* has meant different things throughout the history of art, design and aesthetics. The actual term was not coined until 1954 in the American press. Prior to this, courtiers, fops, Humean philosophers and gourmands have all been arbiters of good taste at one point or another. Tastemakers demonstrated their lifestyle *savoir faire*, influencing and holding power over their devotees' behaviours and spending choices. In the late 20th century this accolade was bestowed on David Tang. He possessed a talent for knowing how to turn any quotidian object or experience into an aesthetic experience, whether it was fashion or restaurants or writing, and also for that experience to be sought out by others who wanted to demonstrate that they understood the nuances of taste. As cultural figures, authentic tastemakers are never self-proclaimed. Their reach is measured by the reaction others have to how they fashion and assemble various facets of their lives – from shirt cuff typologies, to debating the virtues of door handles versus doorknobs in design, to the correct thank-you note etiquette, to the perils of alphabetical seating arrangements for dinner.

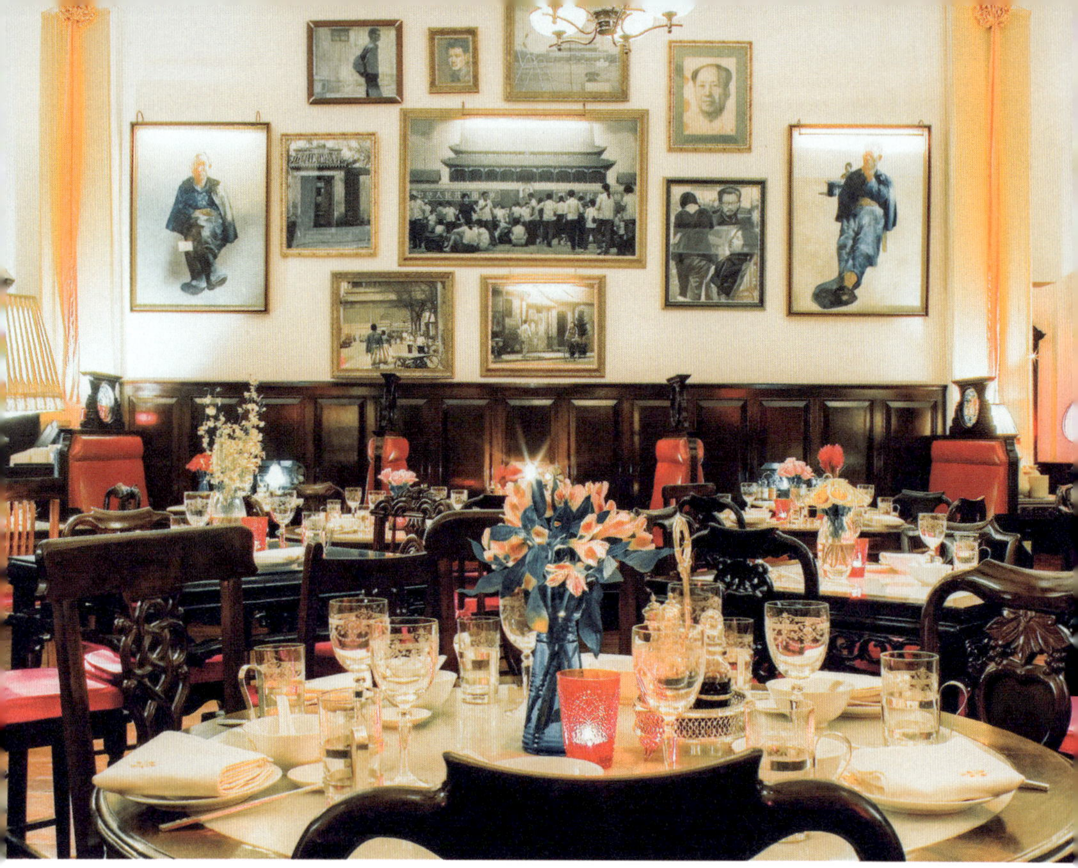

Like many good tastemakers, Tang also demonstrated his aesthetic discernment through collecting art, a substantial portion of which he displayed in his native city of Hong Kong in the China Club, the private members' club and restaurant he established in 1991. The extensive collection featuring more than 500 pieces is a survey of modern and contemporary Chinese art. This art restaurant is a synthesis of opulent yet understated interiors and high-quality cooking, with every wall, hallway and staircase filled with Tang's paintings from the multifaceted traditions of Chinese art, hung in picture gallery style. His son, Edward Tang, remembers that for his father, "art and food was a marriage and a meaningful union, certainly one that the China Club is about". Tang collaborated with the esteemed art historian, Johnson Chang, who was instrumental in setting the scene for Chinese modern and contemporary art being grouped together as a movement, and who also identified trends and styles to give the art its own scholarly and academic tradition. Even before the business successes that would make him a global icon, Tang was an enthusiast of Chinese culture, and began collecting art in the 1980s. Some of the works acquired came from Chang's seminal *China's New Art, Post-1989* exhibition, in which he showcased the significant contemporary practices of Zeng Fanzhi and Zhang Xiaogang. Along with 20th-century master Zhang Daqian, Tang sought out talents including Zhang Xiaogang, Liu Xiaodong, Yu Youhan and Duan Jianyu. He "also had a deep respect for history", hence the significance of the location he selected for the club.

The restaurant is in the former Bank of China headquarters, with views of the HSBC building and the Lippo Bank, standing firmly with other monuments of Hong Kong's financial and commercial power. The building itself is significant for stacking many layers of history, and Chang says especially the three floors in which the China Club is now housed hold "a sort of mystique for people of my generation". The Xinhua News Agency was located here and was "de facto the diplomatic arm of China", while during the Cultural Revolution in 1966, changes and policies for Hong Kong were effectively enacted from this space. David Tang then conducted his own counter-revolution by returning it to its colonial and Art Deco historical style. This revolution and renovation through tastemaking turned the clock back to a time of more organic progress and explorations of identity. Today, despite the turbo-charged pace of change in this city, the China Club offers a moment of respite and fantasy for diners seeking out fellowship of the like-minded – what escaping in a members' club restaurant is supposed to offer its patrons.

David Tang hailed from a shipping family in Hong Kong and established his Shanghai Tang fashion business in London to bring Eastern aesthetics and design to the West at a time when it was still just idealised and exotic. "As Chinese as he was," Edward says, "he was also unmistakeably an Anglophile." British society's upper-class manners and etiquette were both a minefield for him to navigate and a landscape to play in. Etiquette is "tribal" yet also arbitrary, he believed, and "when in doubt, choose the most light-hearted or funniest response" towards others. This caustic humour and irreverence laced many of his approaches to his creative projects. The charismatic businessman had a way with high-profile friends and acquaintances as well as the general public. He was comfortable dining with dictators or dustmen. He wrote a weekly agony uncle column in the *Financial Times*, which was acerbic, contrarian, but compellingly sagacious. Like all respectable tastemakers who possess a skill for making the right judgements, he would come out with unexpected pronouncements to ensure his followers could "lift themselves out of embourgeoisement".

Tastemakers are fascinating to others because their ability to synthesise the aesthetic is ineffable. You cannot easily put your finger on it, but you know when it is there. Tang wrote about the German philosopher Ludwig Wittgenstein, who explained those phenomena that are observed but cannot be explicated because they can only be shown, like a game with its rules. Similarly, Tang rationalised what taste meant to him: "I can't define good taste, just as I can't define a game. But when I see good taste, I am able to say that it is good taste, just as I can point

at a chessboard and its pieces and say that it is a game." This could be because good taste is ultimately physically pleasing on some level. "Equally, I am certain I can point out 'bad taste' when I see it," he said. "And I see an inordinate amount of it." Bad taste strikes a note of discord, good taste is harmony. He continued: "Bad taste mostly comes from those who do not possess an innate perception for visual satisfaction or are simply indolent." Taste is innate for the tastemaker; however, there is an option to follow their lead and explore aesthetic possibilities, or indeed aesthetic dining, through the art and interiors of the China Club.

In the early 1990s, Hong Kong lacked spaces, galleries and museums to display contemporary Chinese art. The renowned gallerist Pearl Lam explains: "What David did at the time in terms of displaying his art collection in such a space was like nothing else we'd seen in Hong Kong." Without a commercial art scene, the opportunity to encounter modern Chinese art did not exist. The China Club was able to show this contemporary art, and in many ways pioneered a model of a private collector placing their collection in a public space – a commercial venue – which influential Hong Kong philanthropist collectors and businessmen have since emulated. In many respects, the MK Lau Collection and KII Art Foundation, which showcase their works in hotels, restaurants, shopping malls and other public spaces in the city, owe their existence to David Tang and the China Club.

The club restaurant is a clash of historical eras and styles: fine, traditional Chinese cuisine housed in a heritage colonial building is merged with unruly, chaotic, contemporary art. The Art Deco *Indochine* salon was inspired by Luk Yu, a tea house and the oldest restaurant in Hong Kong, established in 1933. The interior features lacquered mahogany accents on the walls, elegant white tablecloths, ceiling fans and traditional Chinese calligraphy on scrolls. This tradition mixed with the concept of an English gentleman's club, which Tang was so fascinated by, was a pioneering proposition in the early 1990s in Hong Kong. It was also exceptional to design a dining environment that immersed patrons in a survey of 20th-century Chinese art. Tang worked with Johnson to use the club as a space to showcase first-wave modern Chinese art made when its practitioners first encountered Western art in the late 1970s, which was difficult to exhibit in cultural institutions. The curator recalls: "The interesting thing is the so-called avant-garde artists – the more cutting-edge artists of the time – were principally trained in the same art academies as the more classical academicians. So, basically, the club showed art from two sides of the same coin." The contradictory history of Chinese modern art is a reflection of utopian ideology that sought to educate the masses through art, and the more contemporary, individualistic and cynical pursuits of practice. Interior spaces and their design, for Tang, "should provoke our imagination so that we can fill

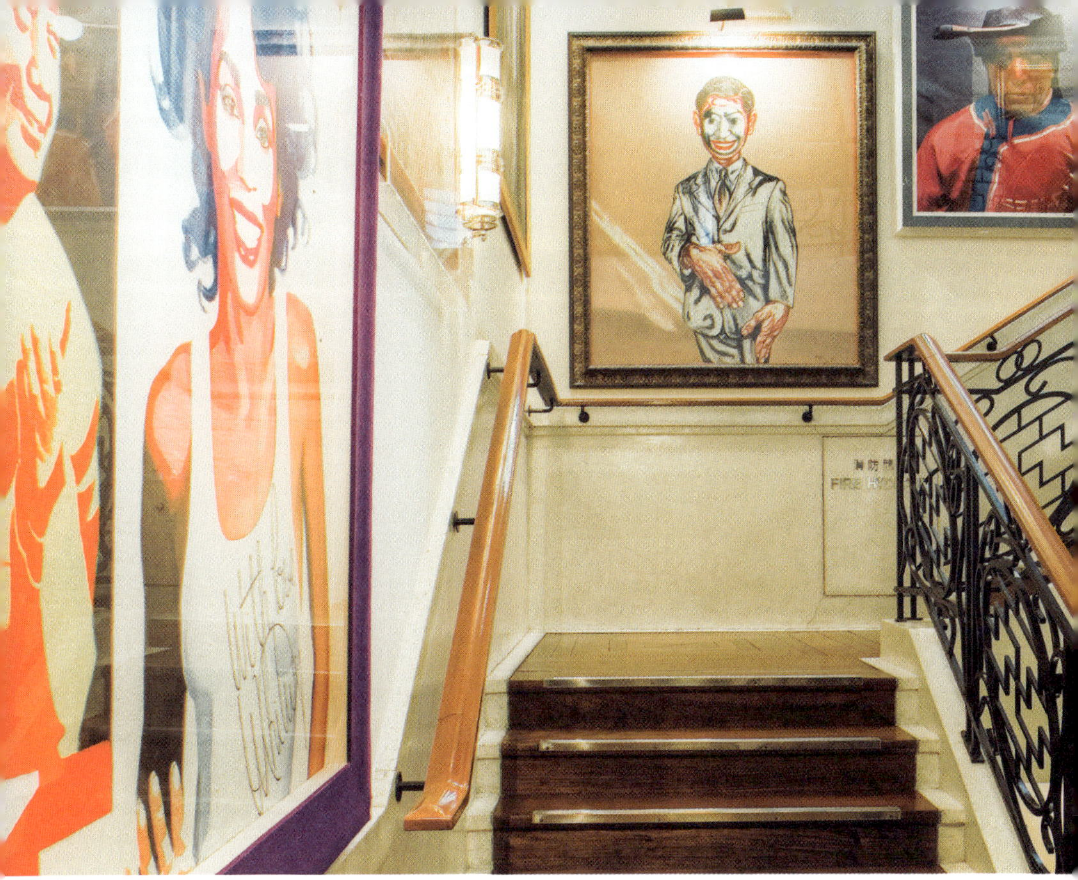

our surroundings with shifting images and streams of consciousness. Therefore, I am in full agreement that an air of history does create a depth to an interior." The details in the environment acquire a momentum and meaning beyond their function. They are not incidental, they are revered by patrons and observed as objects that transform the present into the past.

There is a section on the lower levels of the club of Chinese academic paintings: like many other non-Western art schools, the Western technique of fine oil painting was exported and there are still-lifes, portraits, landscapes and figurative works. There is also a section for post-1978 Tiananmen Square works, an important period in Chinese art for propelling the avant-garde as an expression of new social developments in China. These works are an array of iconoclasm and irreverence.

The collection also features a section of propaganda art, and the irony of an international entrepreneur collecting Communist art for a sophisticated members' club restaurant is not lost on diners. Tang as tastemaker was playful and entertaining, and part of his picaresque take on taste was to include these kitsch and sentimental works in his collection. If taste is related to discernment and free play involved in looking, the techniques and methods are then incorporated into the aesthetic of polemics and subversion. Provocation went

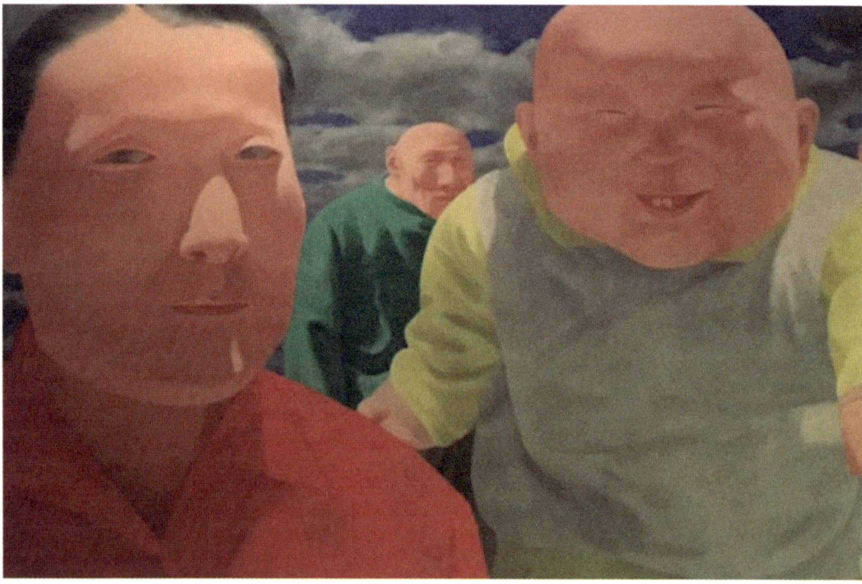

hand in hand with hospitality for Tang: "A real gent would take a practical joke in his stride, although occasionally it might not be ungentlemanly to resort to revenge." Urbanism comes into the refined space. Communist art starts outside, it is about the proletariat, the worker, the labourer. It is subversive by entering this sophisticated dining space, but equally subverted by being owned by a wealthy businessman.

The collection contains one of Liu Jianhua's enormous circular polychrome porcelain dishes. Inside it, five long-legged but headless and armless female figures clad in traditional Chinese silk *cheongsams* sit or lie prostrate. This stereotypical Chinese exoticism is served up with added humour: the piece is transformed into a fishbowl, and unheeding goldfish swim around the gleaming porcelain legs and torsos. There is also irony in the earlier contemporary works. A piece by Zeng Fanzhi initially provoked guests. Edward explains: "The mask painting, you know, people thought, that's a bit grotesque, or that's not really something that we want to be dining in front of." Fanzhi's signature mask works combine Western execution, being influenced by Expressionism and Francis Bacon, with Chinese opera costumes. The mask symbolism is part of the performance and theatricality of eating in a restaurant.

The club also features a library, which, according to Edward, is a very romantic space. Tang collected "thousands of books" and work from antiquarian booksellers in London. These objects inspire thoughts and musings, and as Tang wrote: "Great thinkers are always swimming in artefacts in their pools of writing. That is why the best rooms are always those replete with paintings and books, with content to fill a universe of memories and dreams."

The art collection in the China Club makes the experience simulacra and simulacrum: the mix of high and low pursuits, or the outcast and kitsch art now becoming mainstream and even leading in terms of being coveted by collectors is firmly a postmodern situation. The objective is still to pair iconographic urban art from the streets, from the workers, with traditional fine dining. The bombardment of senses and concepts through all of these stimuli makes it anything but a complacent restaurant experience.

Hong Kong is a place of such ideological contradictions played out on a global stage – old and new world orders, shifting economic realities and historical revisions form the imperfect but perfect backdrop of a sprawling, chaotic city for the art restaurant like the China Club, which, as refuge, signals a sense of community, dining and belonging. Members' clubs in colonial times were a derivative of those in Britain, originally created by landed gentry who needed a place to meet and stay when visiting London. The Reform Acts of the 19th century saw a proliferation of these as different groups of society gained suffrage and established their own select venues. This continued in the colonies. Tang's influence was the Shanghai clubs on the Bund in the 1920s and 1930s, set up as outposts by their members to stake their own claim in unfamiliar and changing surroundings. Edward says: "I think as we know, the concept of a club is obviously to be exclusive, but one of my father's philosophies was he didn't care who his members were, as long as the members paid."

The China Club invites those who want to share the same taste to belong to a tribe. The place of charm and manners in dining has a long history related to fundamental tenets of eating together. Dining manners, in addition to now being part of the ritual, had their origins in early feasting where trust and hospitality were connected. Manners are *de facto* superficial – literally going through the motions – but their origins play an important part in establishing trust by what is imbibed and put into the body. Even something as gestural as wine tasting in a restaurant comes from a tradition of serving wine at a banquet and demonstrating trust that a host will not poison their guests. Today these rituals may be deemed shallow and archaic, but the cumulative repetition through the centuries remains and builds the sense of belonging. Tang built his own fellowship in his club and, as he writes about setting dinners: "The best solution, I find, is to give the dinner party myself. Then I am in absolute control, and I will ensure the absence of droning bores and pretentious souffles. The first secret is to cram everyone as close together as possible, preferably so that we can all hear each other, and to ensure an array of beautiful or very attractive guests (or if ugly, then exceedingly accomplished, at least)."

Part of the amusement of eating in this art restaurant is keeping these contradictions and wittiness of the host perpetually in motion while diners relinquish control and leave themselves in the hands and aesthetics of the tastemaker. Discerning diners will continuously turn around in their heads the messages and arguments a restaurant in a club like this signifies, while being bombarded by the art and taste stimuli. Debates that include opinions on high-end dining, political protests, the commodification of art, are of course enhanced by good wine – and that is what a good art restaurant should do to ensure a more significant dining experience. The continuous paradoxes of commodification undoing the objectives of the Communist art, the contemporary art aesthetic polemics undermining the refined dining experience. All the while the workings of the aesthetic dining are quietly present in the background of eating and drinking in the presence of art. The arguments remain inconclusive, nobody comes out on top. However, that is part of the appeal of the experience, to provoke, tease and keep in motion. And as our host once wrote, musing on what his ideal dinner gathering would be: "Wouldn't this be the kind of dinner party everyone dreams of? If it does not sound the stuff of dreams to you, I can only take this as meaning that you are unimaginative, insular and of the bourgeoisie, for whom the dinner party represents the social summit of their *jejune* lives."

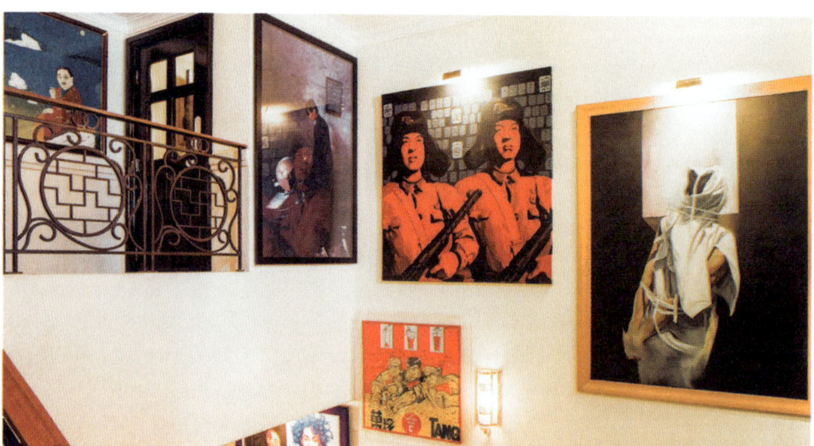

Works and artists in the China Club collection

—

The Long March Bar in the club features socialist art from the 1970s, woodcut prints depicting revolutionary scenes and fighters. Chang notes these were part of an historically important series, and some have gone to the British Museum.

—

A portrait by Zhang Xiaogang, a Surrealist painter known for integrating symbolism and the uncanny in his work. Chang curated a show for the São Paulo Biennial and included this work.

—

The Fang Lijun is very important, according to Chang, because it was a part of the 1989 exhibition of New Chinese Art and featured in the catalogue. The artist was a key proponent of the Cynical Realism movement of the 1990s.

—

A small Liu Wei piece that was a gift to Edward from Chang. Liu Wei works in multimedia to simulate the chaos and aggression of contemporary politics and society in China.

—

A Wang Guangyi depicting a late 1970s worker soldier and the word, TANG, which is a mass-produced orange juice in the US. The painting was a gift from Chang to Tang, for obvious reasons. Guangyi is one of the more recognised artists of modern times, as he manipulates images of propaganda to criticise authoritarianism and dispel its grip and seriousness on the people. He combines Cultural Revolution propaganda with Western consumerist advertisements to mock both extremes.

—

Feng Mengbo, a multimedia artist with dexterity and application in video, draughtsmanship and painting.

—

Works by Qiu Zhijie incorporate cartography, diagrammatic systems of information and poetic mysticism to address the individual's struggle against destiny and forces larger than themselves.

Interior of one dining room in the China Club paying homage to traditional noodle houses in the city; dining area with Communist-era works hanging above; Yu Youhan's *With Love, Whitney*; Fang Lijun's *Series 2 No 7*; Guangyi's *Great Criticism: Tang* hangs over the staircase

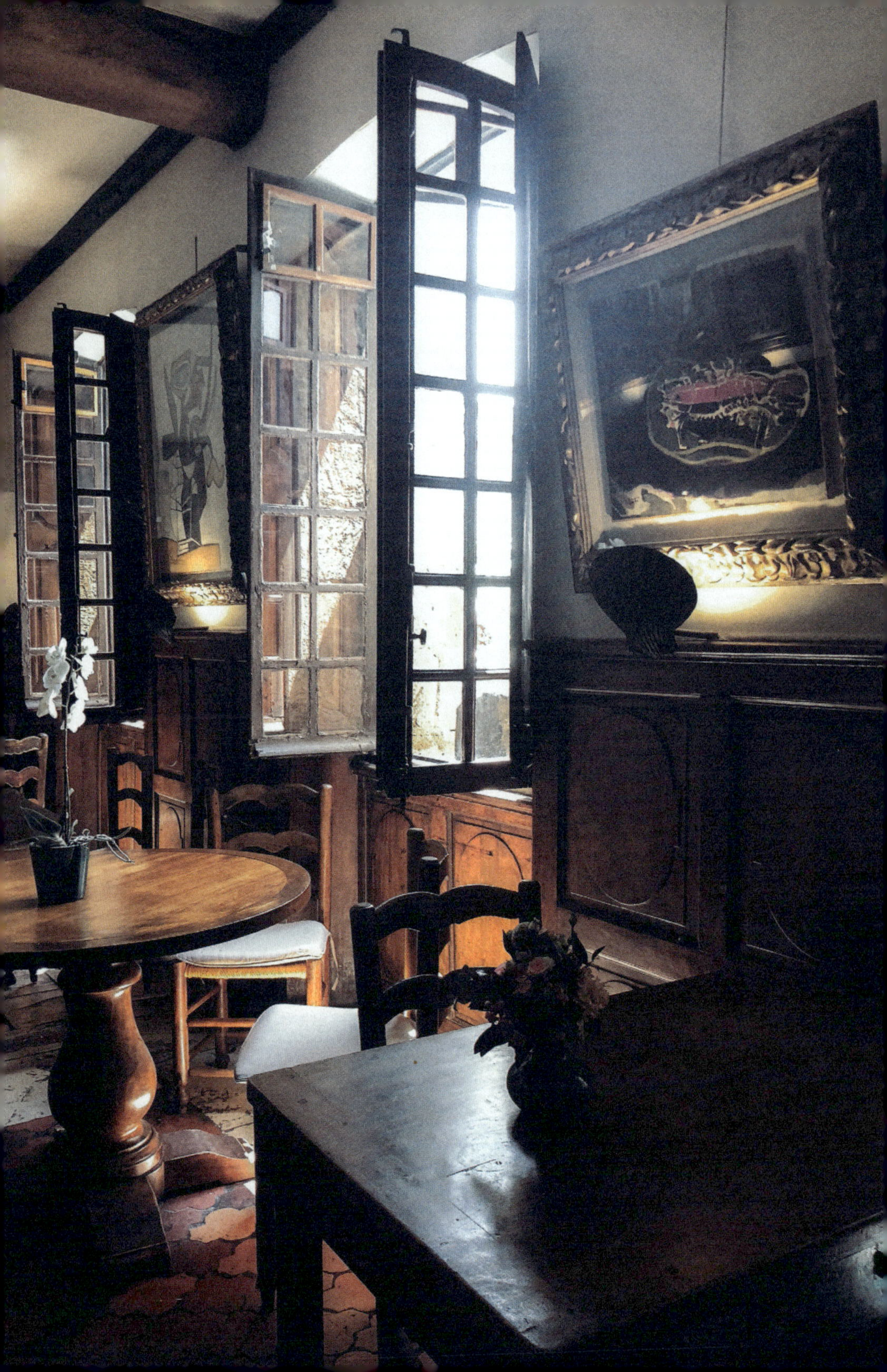

Colombe d'Or

"All the Secrets are in these walls."
— Danièle Roux

Picasso strode into the courtyard as if it was a scene from a Western; by that point in 1951, he would have completed *Smoke over Vallauris* and *Massacre in Korea*, meaning he would have been widely recognised, and diners would turn their heads to stare. Matisse first pulled up in a chauffeur-driven limousine for lunch. For over a century the Colombe d'Or has been steeped in such anecdotes and mythologies of what the archetype of an artists' restaurant is, and where the greatest names of modern European art congregated to drink rosé, play *pétanque* and eat down their bills. The Colombe d'Or is continually cited as an inspiration and the perfect restaurant experience for many restaurateurs – whether they aspire to run art restaurants or not. The accolades are deserved, the stories are accurate to the extent they are repeated and passed down by the Colombe d'Or's community of perennial guests, devotees and admirers. The tales about the place and the visitors it attracted are enjoyed and revered as they become consecrated artefacts in themselves, recited with care, presented with love from one mouth to another ear. It is difficult not to smile in reaction to hearing these stories for the first time. A visit to the Colombe d'Or instils this same sense of joyous reverence and reverie when one arrives today, and this is due to the pivotal role the art and artists played there.

The original story begins in 1920, when a local man, Paul Roux, returned to his medieval hilltop village from the First World War and opened Chez Robinson, a simple Provençal tavern in a 15th-century coach house building. In its inaugural decade, it functioned as a *guinguette* at the weekends, a drinking establishment with music and dancing to accompany the al fresco feasts and gatherings of local villagers. By 1930 it had expanded into an inn, with three bedrooms above the kitchen to house dedicated visitors and revellers for whom returning to their own homes after the late nights and early mornings would be too much of an undertaking. The Alpes-Maritimes was always an attractive region of France for artists, given the intoxicating blend of Mediterranean colours, the winds, the mountainous terrain, the sensual, outdoor lifestyle. The proximity of villages such as Vence, Mougins, Vallauris, Le Cannet along the Riviera fostered collaboration and the exchange of ideas and influences among creative and cultural individuals. During the Second World War, the South of France was a free zone, attracting more intellectuals and artists fleeing Paris and other European capitals.

In the 1950s the Colombe d'Or, as it was now named, became the go-to for glamorous bohemian and convivial gatherings, as did the whole village of

Saint-Paul-de-Vence, which attracted cultural and creative visitors from film, art and literature. Jacques Prévert, the celebrated poet and screenwriter, lived in the village and would dine daily at the inn. He was instrumental in inviting critics, writers, filmmakers and artists to the restaurant for *grandes fêtes*, discussions, debates and debauchery. Then in 1964 Aimé Maeght created his Foundation Maeght, a short walk uphill, and this established the village as a pilgrimage destination for anyone involved in cultural production or harbouring artistic aspirations. In the 1960s, the notion of culture went mainstream. Everybody wanted to paint, create ceramics, write poems, and even more so in the Côte d'Azur's bright, temperate climate and enchanting terrain. When they needed to eat, the array of 15 small dishes of Provençal *hors d'oeuvres* awaited them at the Colombe alongside its *Cuvée de la Colombe d'Or*, produced by winemakers from Pierrefeu.

Paul Roux, "a peasant with genius inside him, who was full of diplomacy and grace", as described by Danièle, the latest generation of Roux family owners, had a personal interest in art and dabbled with painting on the side while running his restaurant. The artists became his friends and encouraged him to take up the paintbrush and make his own works, which are now interspersed among the known artists. He also created the design for his prized menu in 1951, and the image is still used today. The bright, rainbow colours of the penmanship are reminiscent of a clown sketch Picasso made in the inn's guest book in the same year. Roux and the artist became close in the 1950s, with the former declaring: "I watched him until I learnt." His self-taught floral still lifes, village scenes and other bourgeois pleasantries and fancies – *art naif* – do what the established modern artists experimented with in attempting to unlearn form and tradition, and paint naïvely on the terracotta walls.

Roux had innate taste and knew the importance of beauty and painting, and how this enhanced the dining and living space. He used the art he collected to differentiate the restaurant, while also signalling to the cultural community that he had taste and associated with these artists and cultural figures. He changed the signage outside the restaurant with the following statement of intent: "*Ici on loge a cheval, a pied ou en peinture* [Here we accommodate those on horse, on foot, and with paintings]." A restaurateur could host internationally renowned art dealers, directors, actors, poets, artists. The collection is not themed, more an organic selection of works that the Rouxs have a close relationship with. This was based on the friendships with the artists and the importance placed on hospitality and gifting that makes it more solid than a gesture or obligation. In this art restaurant collection, the works offered by the artists are taken out of their œuvre or context and surrendered to the timeless microcosmic universe of the Colombe d'Or's walls.

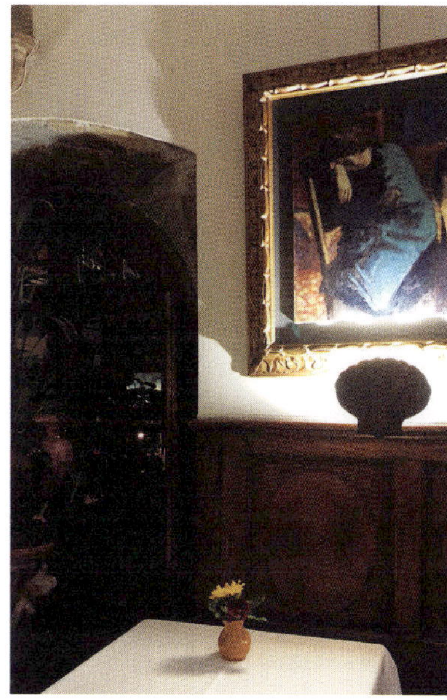

The art displayed in the main dining room would make many museum curators and insurers nervous, given its proximity to oft-inebriated diners, cigarette smoke and large open windows at street level. These fears were realised when most of the paintings were stolen one summer night in 1959. Paul Roux spent six months involved in the police investigation – playing his part in the art caper – and they were found at the eleventh hour at Cagnes-sur-Mer train station, set to be smuggled abroad. The family's Chagall was too large for the thieves to lift, and when the artist came to see the damage at the inn the morning after, he angrily exclaimed: "Why not steal my painting? Am I not a big painter too!"

The artworks are testaments – the afterglow – of the artists who came and went, a body of proof of the cultural exchange of ideas between disciplines and genres, especially in the culturally fruitful 1950s, when the Cannes Film Festival was established and the reputation of the village went global, thanks in part to the tabloid coverage of film stars such as Brigitte Bardot and Alain Delon, who were regular patrons. The Bonnard and the Braque that hang in the main dining room were purchased from the Maeghts at this time. The Braque painting is a brash still life of a lobster on a platter, but here with the correct number of legs, unlike other lobsters with missing legs in the body of work of an artist who preferred painting from memory rather than models. Memorable too, based on the message in the guest book: "*Souvenir du meilleur accueil* [souvenir of the best welcome]" (27 April 1948). The Bonnard is a depiction of a wistful downcast woman, dreamy and aloof, an Emma Bovary provincial heroine disinterested in the dining scene before her, a contrast to the conviviality and company in the room. Bonnard made his last painting in December 1946 before he died in the nearby village of Le Cannet in early January; the guest book timestamps his last visit on 6 April 1946.

The second Madame Roux, "Titine", shared her husband's interest in gathering creative and cultural figures at the inn. They collected the art from artists they knew well, and one day it occurred to her that they should have a Picasso piece, given the artist's regular visits. Titine went to his studio in Vaullaris, and

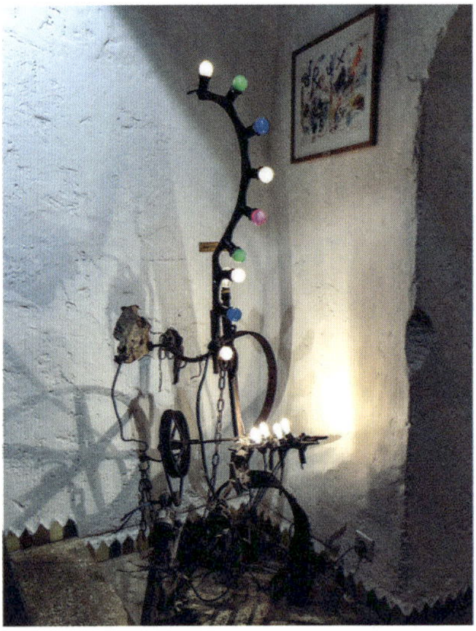
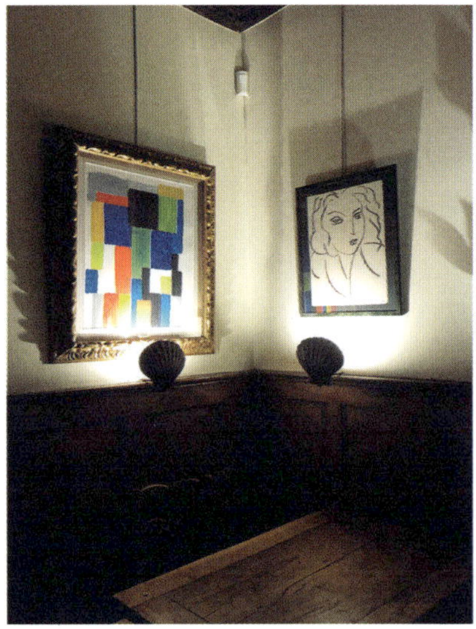

declared: "Look here, you are the only artist that has not given us a painting, the Colombe d'Or should have one of your paintings!" The artist looked over at three recently completed works against the wall and asked her to choose one. This is how the still life with flowers that hangs in the main dining room was acquired, giving new meaning to *qui ne tente rien, n'a rien* [nothing ventured, nothing gained].

The art collecting continued in an organic, haphazard way for the Rouxs. From the first moment Alexander Calder visited the Colombe d'Or, he was taken with Yvonne Roux, believing she was one of the most beautiful women he had ever seen. After each sojourn at the inn, he would send her artworks throughout the year, for several years. Hence the large number of whimsical, primary-coloured gouaches, drawings and maquettes, in addition to the iconic mascot dove mobile above the pool. The Rouxs were not driven by the market nor even collecting fashions and imperatives. The works are of museum quality, yet the family have not lent to exhibitions, save for the Miró that was shown in a retrospective at the Grand Palais in 2018, now hanging back in the main dining room.

It can be difficult for an historian to reconcile the impulse for isolating exact dates of who came when and how with the floating timelessness the Colombe d'Or radiates, but the prized guest book contains some of the information. Sketches, drawings and messages range from "La Colombe d'Or est un petit paradis" (Matisse, 5 May 1948), to a Miró abstract rainbow sketch from 1962. The pedigree of artist visitors does not disappoint and includes Raoul Dufy,

Chaïm Soutine, Georges Braque, Fernand Léger, Joan Miró, Marc Chagall, Francis Picabia, César and Jean Tinguely. They meld into a creative fraternity that nourishes the mythology of the restaurant as a place that both feeds and inspires artists – and any other guests hankering after this history.

Extraordinary, temporal things happen in the Colombe d'Or. Happenings more complicated than just time stopping through escapism or romantic daydreams. Rather, the diner's own moment of experience joins other diners' series of moments, and within those art-laden walls, seeped with history, secrets, gossip, intrigue, happiness, desire and joy, he or she becomes a part of the restaurant's mechanism of memory. The philosopher Gaston Bachelard, who tried to capture this grammar of internal spaces, writes: "For a knowledge of intimacy, localisation in the spaces of our intimacy is more urgent than determination of dates." It is the experience over the exact details of the time that matters most. Unlike any other art restaurant, it is perhaps the Colombe d'Or that most mysteriously makes time a supple mediation but also grounds it in the present. It collects patrons' memories and experiences through its gatherings, locks them in its terracotta walls and throws away the key.

All diners have to do is look at black-and-white guest photographs of the past four decades depicting languid lunches under the dappled sunlight, friends laughing as they toast and smoke, dinner parties under summer skies on the terrace, and it is not a cliché to feel like they belong there too. They can sit on the exact same stool at the bar as Picasso is pictured sitting on; the artist's portrait now hangs on the wall next to the spot. The colour of the walls, the tablecloths, the artworks, the table settings with their gas lamps, ceramic ashtrays and heavy crockery, are familiar and tangible. Every visitor can be sitting with François Truffaut, after the Cannes Film Festival, or take a spritz at the bar with Sophia Loren before supper. With friends, with lovers, with peers, it is all part of the motions that coalesce and present the dining as ritual at its best. The artworks preside over the exchange of tastes, the sensorial flourishes, the creation of memories, and this is also enhanced by the food.

Visiting the Colombe d'Or, dining and ideally staying in the inn to take the time to have all three meals there, to observe how staff with military precision prepare, execute, clean up and repeat the sittings, guests are reminded of the fundamental arguments about restaurants being about ritual, and the experience being a performance. The Colombe d'Or demands participation in these rites of dining. It is like church, except it is tied to tangible, real happenings and activity between diners, between staff and visitors, between the art history and everybody. There is also a responsibility for the diner who visits and participates in this ritual. They must understand their part in the service – ordering from the menu that has remained unchanged for just under a decade, taking what they are given, and how they are given it (as gluten-free American tourists find out). Staff pour the diner's rosé, they debone their *loup de mer* as they have for decades. Manu, the head bartender, has been mixing the aperitifs for more than 40 years. Guests must abide by the social hierarchy of the place in terms of who gets which table (there is a system, but the author is sworn to secrecy), who sits next to whom, and who is served by whom.

The Colombe d'Or caters to the fantasy of the restaurant as escape, a place to fulfil desire, as being part of the continuum of patrons and diners who visited before you in a carefree, sheltered space, like Boccaccio's garden, and the artworks enrich this. Food and art are enchanting and satisfying in that moment, but always leave the diner wanting more. Colette's pleading summation in the guest book speaks for every diner: "Wait for me, Colombe, I am coming back!" The art scattered around the Colombe d'Or is an enticement to aesthetic dining, the works exist gently, exuberantly, reinforcing how senses are engaged and how discernment works. The collection is authentic and subtly places these world-class works alongside normal, paysan dining. It is the art-collection equivalent of breaking and dipping thick crusted bread in the Bourgogne sauce of the *cassolette d'escargots*. Rustic art collecting.

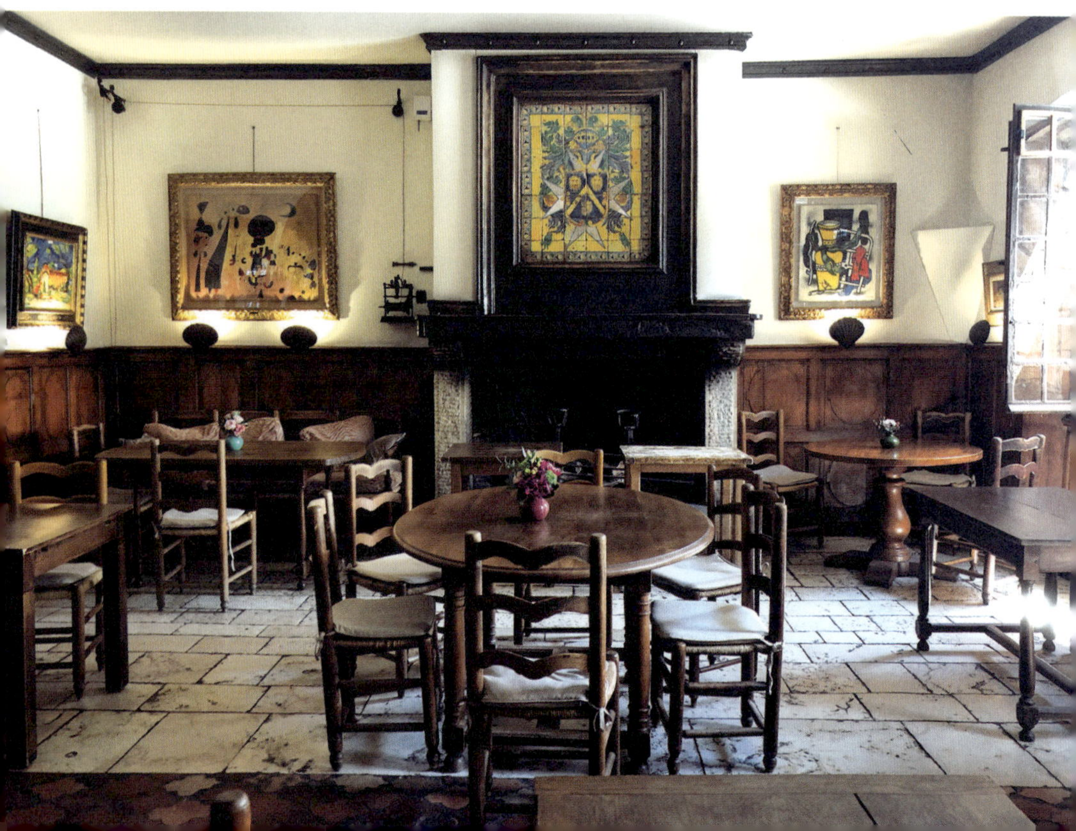

Works and artists in the Colombe d'Or collection

—

A giant marble César thumb (*le Pouce*) in the courtyard dining area, slightly quirky, but completely giving its approval over the diners as they come and go; it is the first piece guests encounter, and also the last one they see as they wait for a valet to bring their cars around.

—

The iconic Léger mosaic of female forms commissioned by Roux in 1952 to preside over al fresco diners and lend a feeling of sensuality to the gatherings. The nudes hold flowers and plants and blend into the ivy on the wall that frames them. The work is significant not only for its monumental size. For the artist himself, this later work was his turning off the engine of his hyper-mechanic aesthetic for something more organic; even the machine needs a lunch break and a glass of rosé.

—

A Matisse line portrait of a woman's face, a dreamy work rooted in classicism. In the cold light of a museum context, the work is an isolated specimen; hung in this corner of the art restaurant it symbolises the elegance of dining *a deux*, candlelight and romance.

—

Sonia Delaunay left Paris for the South of France during the war and moved with the Riviera set of artists that included Matisse. This small canvas is an abstract of rectangular shapes in bright colours. It is cheery and animates the corner of the dining room above the heavy wooden panel.

—

A Jean Tinguely métamatic sculpture in the collection from the period the sculptor would visit the French Riviera to work on commissions for foundations and public spaces.

—

There are several Alexander Calder gouaches in the dining rooms, gifted to Titine. The artist began painting in gouache in 1953 when he moved to Aix-en-Provence and these works characterise that period of his life when his kinetic sculptures moved back to the page in the form of sculptural paintings. They are rendered in bold, brash black line and primary colours – playful and naïve but enigmatic and cosmic.

Internal dining area depicted off-duty with Georges Braque lobster hanging above the table; a portrait of a downcast woman by Pierre Bonnard; a Jean Tinguely sculpture sits next to a drawing by Yves Tanguy dedicated to the Colombe d'Or's proprietors; an abstract painting by Sonia Delaunay hangs alongside Henri Matisse's untitled drawing of a woman; works by Joan Miró and Fernand Léger hang on either side of the fireplace in the dining room

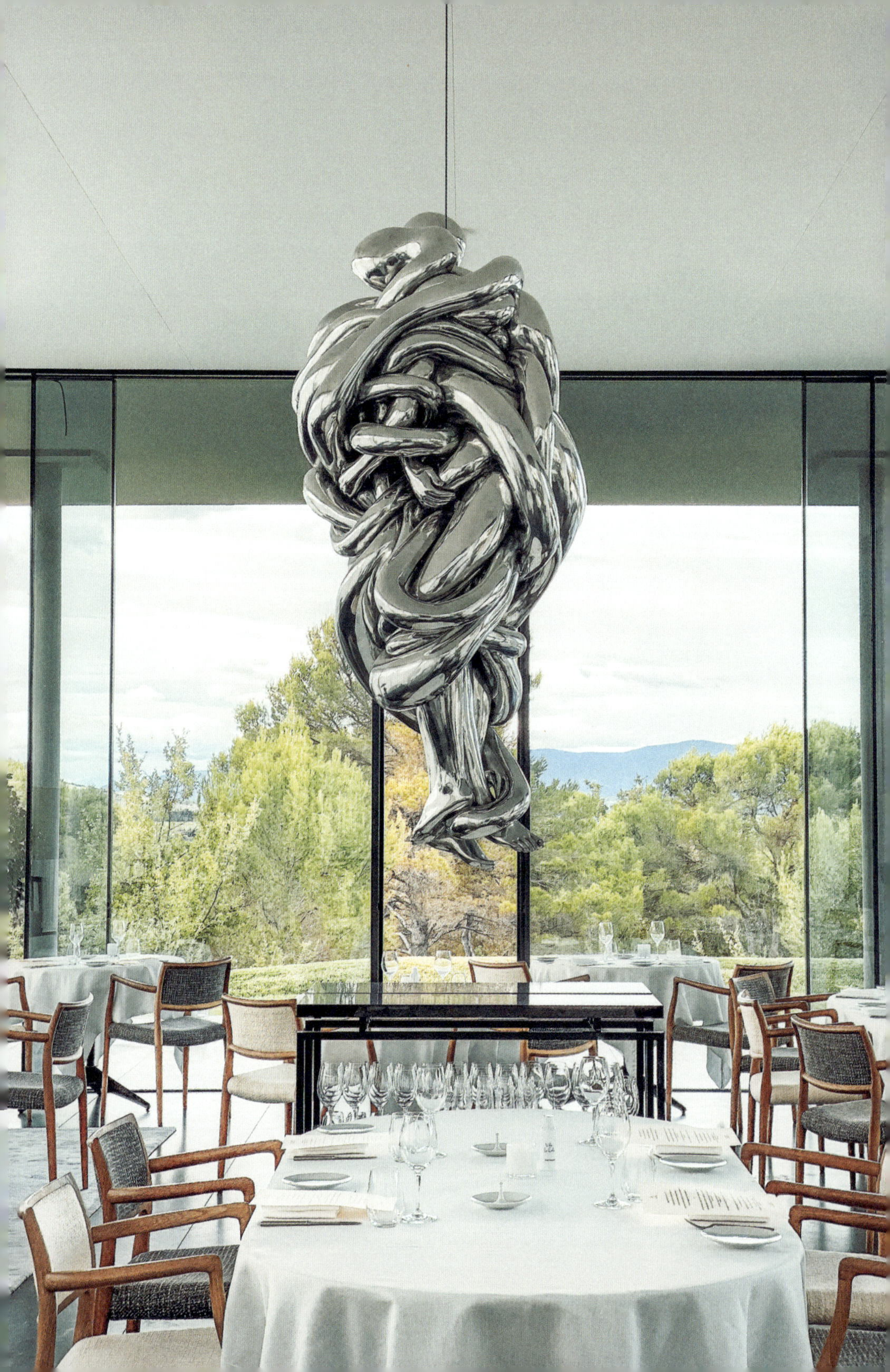

Château la Coste

"You pile up associations the way you pile up bricks. Memory itself is a form of architecture."
— Louise Bourgeois

Since the 17th century, the notion of *terroir* as it relates to French land and the grapes produced has been tied to regional identity and intellectual history. "Soil is a focus of all of France's thoughts and emotions," writes the geologist Armand Frémont. *Terroir* suggests such a grounding and place, but it is a concept not exclusively fixed. In winemaking, transplants and grafting produce new varieties and tastes, adapting and continuing a region's history in a new direction. Similarly, wine is both natural and artificial. It rises from the earth, grows in the soil but also requires man's input to come to fruition. This synthesis of the organic and the man-made is what Irish businessman Patrick McKillen fabricates in his 1,200-acre Provençal estate, Château la Coste, by dotting the vineyards on the hills with sculpture and architecture commissions by world-renowned and intellectually formidable artists and architects. The pieces culminate in the villa's restaurant, Louison, a glass pavilion designed around a Louise Bourgeois work on the highest part of the estate overlooking the rest of the vineyards and artworks. This ancient site of winemaking built on tradition is both technological and natural. Dispensing the art throughout the land and creating a restaurant around an artwork becomes the expression of this quest.

Taking on such ancient land was a new departure for McKillen, previously more familiar with navigating the luxury terrain of London's Mayfair district. British artist Conrad Shawcross, who installed the latest sculpture, *Escalations,* up on a rocky hill overlooking the vineyards in June 2020, was moved by how "extraordinarily courageous" the collector's endeavour is. McKillen became captivated by the Luberon, as this region stretching from the Rhône river to the Italian border displays evidence of winemaking by Phoenician and Anatolian sailors dating back to 600BC, when Greek settlers founded Marseille. Its own geological saga produced Syrah, Cabernet Sauvignon and Vermentino wines, and the resultant *Appellation d'Origine Contrôlée* distinction. McKillen recalls the moment of discovery: "We looked at many, many places... And then, one morning, I drove into Château la Coste. I didn't even drive 20 metres – I decided to buy it right there, because it had a magical feel." The current vineyard was the hook, but then having researched how the land was farmed by the Romans to harvest grapes for biodynamic wine production, McKillen found his place to develop this vinicultural tradition. He would cultivate and steward this *terroir,* but add his own ingredient to the mixture to share his taste: his art collecting.

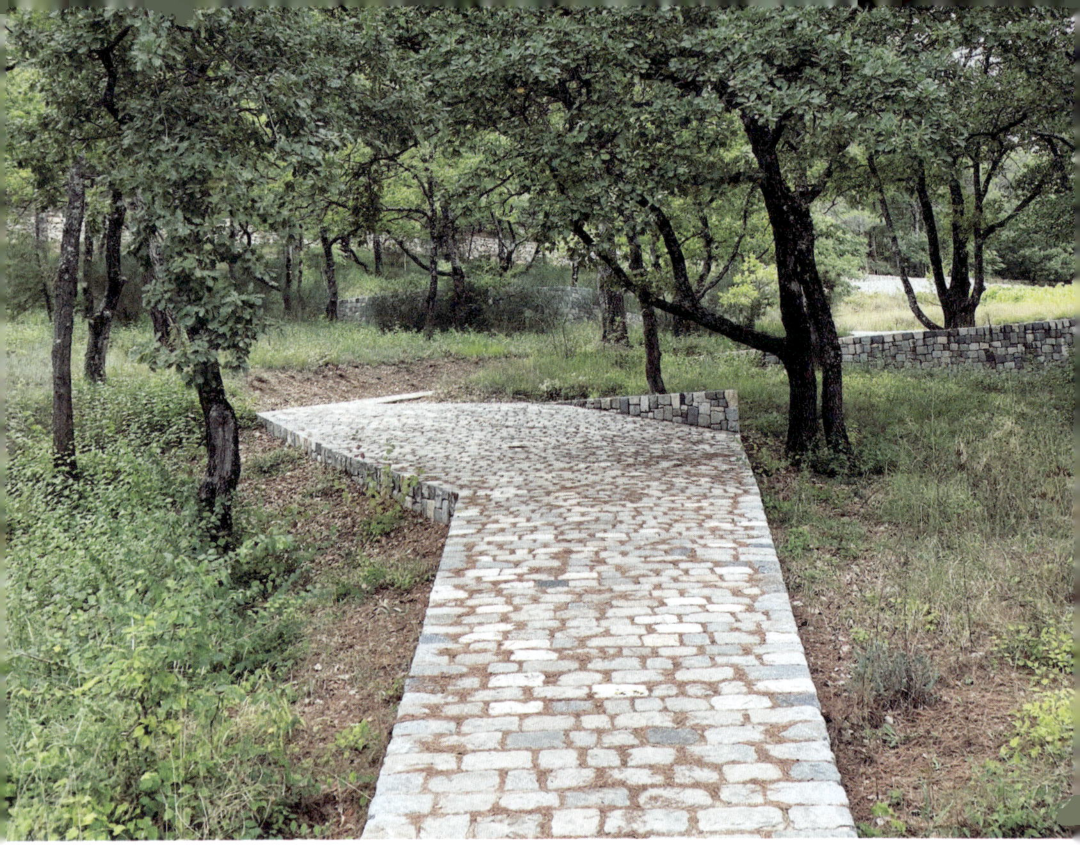

The result, for diners, is la Coste's sequencing of architectural pavilions, sculptures, horticultural spaces, aiding their procession through what is a pleasure ground dedicated to exploring the meaning of taste. The location, the art and architecture are in dialogue to provide a framing for aesthetic eating and sensual satiety.

There is a dexterity in terms of sculptural works that are made on an architectural scale and architectural structures that are artistic in terms of imagery and form. The boundaries of disciplines do not matter as much as the experience these enhance for the visitor. McKillen recalls how he asked his artists to "come and become an architect for the day". Throughout the past decade of his stewardship, the artists have come, scouted the grounds, walked the pathways and woven between the vineyards to find the location on which to build their pieces. Shawcross explains how he "enjoyed being like a coal miner" when he worked on his piece. He lifted 250kg iron planks "in the June heat" with Argentinian kitchen workers from the estate's restaurant, Diego and Marco (his team was unable to travel due to the pandemic), who he "trained up… some of them quit after a few days; they said they valued their hands too much". This particular art restaurant has expanded its walls to encompass the entire estate. The dissolution of these disciplines is what the architect Juhani Pallasmaa calls "architectural images", which have the power to "move our emotions" because "they are grounded in our unconscious reactions and biological historicity". Walking in the grounds of la Coste, and dining in the Louison restaurant, requires all senses to engage, and the intellect is required to appreciate how the gastronomy contributes to the aesthetic experience. "Buildings are always essentially invitations and verbs" for this. The composition of the Luberon landscape and its history are fixed; McKillen's design of the space to include the art is cradled by this location but finds new significance with all the works being integrated in the specific environment.

There are 37 such architectural structures and land sculptures spread among the grounds. McKillen asked most of the architects on his property portfolio to contribute to la Coste. There is a Renzo Piano-designed pavilion that features a multi-folded origami-like roof; an Oscar Niemeyer pavilion – the last piece the architect signed off before he died in 2012 (the second swansong work of a significant artist at la Coste, the other being by Louise Bourgeois); and Frank Gehry's *Pavilion De Musique*, both interactive and imposing, which was originally unveiled at the Serpentine Gallery in 2003, the year it was installed at the estate. The wine cellar is designed by Jean Nouvel in an industrial hangar style to indicate power and presence. These structures are not follies, but shrines; they mark the landscape, organise space, and although they are secular, visitors trek to them as if on a pilgrimage. It may not be a religious pilgrimage, but there is still something sacred about the full aesthetic experience at la Coste.

Art restaurants and aesthetic dining encourage slow eating to take in and allow the fabric of the art the meaning of taste to be discovered by diners. In Château la Coste, the diners have no choice in the matter, given the time and physical commitment it takes to visit, to walk through the grounds to encounter the artworks, to hike to Louison. Like traditional pilgrimages, this too is a "transitional rite of passage in order to approach, enter and experience the sacred" through dining in the midst of artworks. The restaurant is placed in a floating minimalist pavilion designed by André Fu. Three of the four walls are glass, ensuring the landscape and other artworks are never out of view, or even out of the dining company. This structure furthers the reach of the art restaurant walls.

Bourgeois' *The Couple* (2007-09) is the main work in the restaurant, and was a piece McKillen acquired to place in the landscape of la Coste, and specifically to build a restaurant around. Two intertwined figures in aluminium hang suspended in the central dining space above the largest table by a thin wire. The piece is both delicate and momentous, the lovers cling on to each other for dear life. Bourgeois writes on her practice: "Horizontality is a desire to give up, to sleep. Verticality is an attempt to escape. Hanging and floating are states of ambivalence." The work casts this vacillation on many levels – do the figures embrace, do they fight, are they trying to blend into each other, but something holds them back? Are they dropping into the space or are they trying to leave the world behind? There is an implication of the conflict present in having feelings for another person when it entails loss of self. The material furthers the complexity: the wire looks taught and tough, but it is still thread-like; the shape of the figures is fleshy and round, but it is made of cold, hard steel. Placing a work like this in a dining space isolates these intricacies and gives diners the opportunity to revel in the interlaced meaning of the piece. Given the role of wine on sacred occasions and in religious rituals, the restaurant also becomes an altar to Bourgeois' art. And Michelin-starred chef Gérald Passédat is its priest, creating modern provincial dishes based on Mediterranean seafood and using local ingredients.

The vineyard and the landscape that carries it feed into the art restaurant because the architecture encourages light, incorporates pools of water and includes views of the other artworks over the hills. There is an aesthetic system and structure at la Coste that contains the Bourgeois at its core, as an inner sanctum. Louison is literally in the centre of the experience, a web that draws the diner in. It is a nest or even cradle that implies caring and nurturing, just as the restorative origins of restaurants would do.

With the addition of these artworks, McKillen developed the land to realise its potential in terms of purveying varying interpretations of taste. Each artwork, or "architectural image" to use Pallasmaa's phrase, is in dialogue with the landscape and in a relationship with the other works around it. These works are an "organising image" and "genuine architectural structures strengthen our experience of the real, as well as horizontally and vertically, above and below, distant and near". The diner is immersed in how *terroir* is alive, active and contributes to a full understanding of how the senses constitute taste in the pursuit of pleasure. The art and the land are in dialogue, granted, but the art also moves the land by stimulating the imagination needed to experience the two together. To build is to dwell, as the philosopher Martin Heidegger argued, and it was the additive details of architecture and art onto the landscape that, after long negotiations, persuaded Louise Bourgeois and her estate to sell her largest work, *I Do, I Undo, I Redo* – the three nine-metre-tall towers viewers can climb, produced for the inaugural Tate Turbine Hall Commission in 2000 and which was in storage. The artist always intended the piece to go to a museum or cultural institution. McKillen wanted it and approached Nouvel to suggest building a specific structure to encase the towers. The architect proposed carving into one of the hills on the edge of the estate and rebuilding the hill with a retractable roof of concrete. This, coupled with the fact the sculpture would be in the collection open to the public, piqued Bourgeois' interest, hence la Coste won her consent. It was one of the last works she oversaw being installed before she died, aged 98, in 2010.

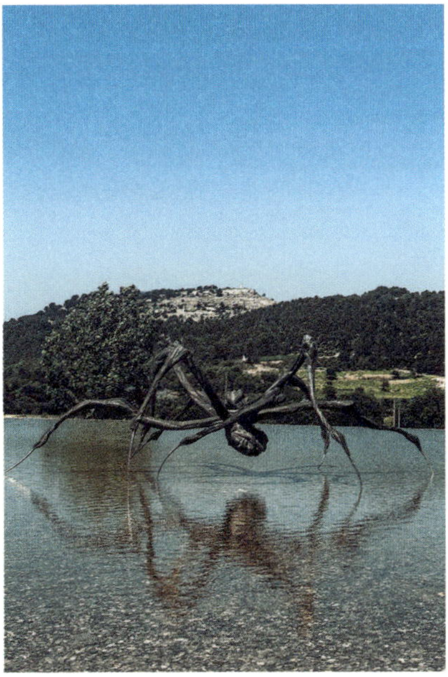

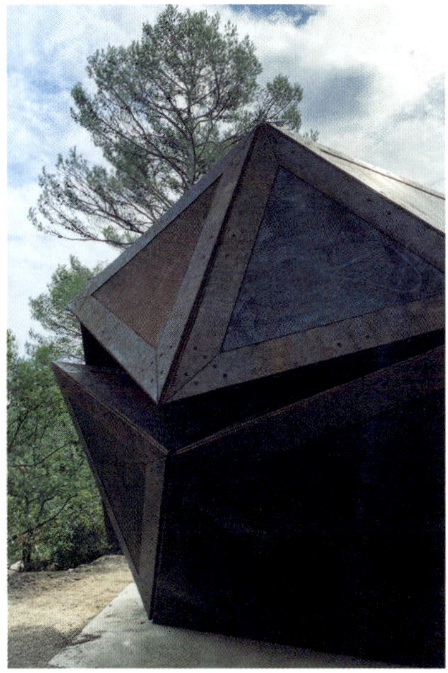

McKillen's interest in Bourgeois began when he purchased the first of her series of six spiders, *Crouching Spider*, in 2003, the only one on display in France. The cast-iron sculpture is suspended over a flat plane of still water and can be viewed from different angles and heights from the Tadao Ando art space. The artist interrogated the collector on why he wanted one of her pieces and how he intended to display it. He told her about the water and "her eyes lit up". She was pleased with the fact he wanted to take the work back to her birthplace, where, because of the combination of the light and water, it would appear anything but solid. McKillen already owned the Calder mobile *Small Crinkly*, from 1976, but he didn't want it to languish in a basement or storage, so he released it to the landscape – and as the Colombe d'Or can attest, Calder's works thrive in the Mediterranean light and breeze.

The artworks, being man-made and often in artificial materials, may on one level seem a contradiction to the natural landscape in which they are placed. For instance, Tom Shannon's *The Drop* (2009) is a cold, metallic oval shape that contrasts with the greenery of the grass and oak trees. However, the piece also works with the land as a sign to understanding the scientific element of cultivating the grapes. Irrespective of the rolling landscape of Aix, with its wild shrubbery and rocky red soil, nothing is left to chance at Château la Coste. Its proprietor is considered and instinctive in the design of the grounds and the restaurant,

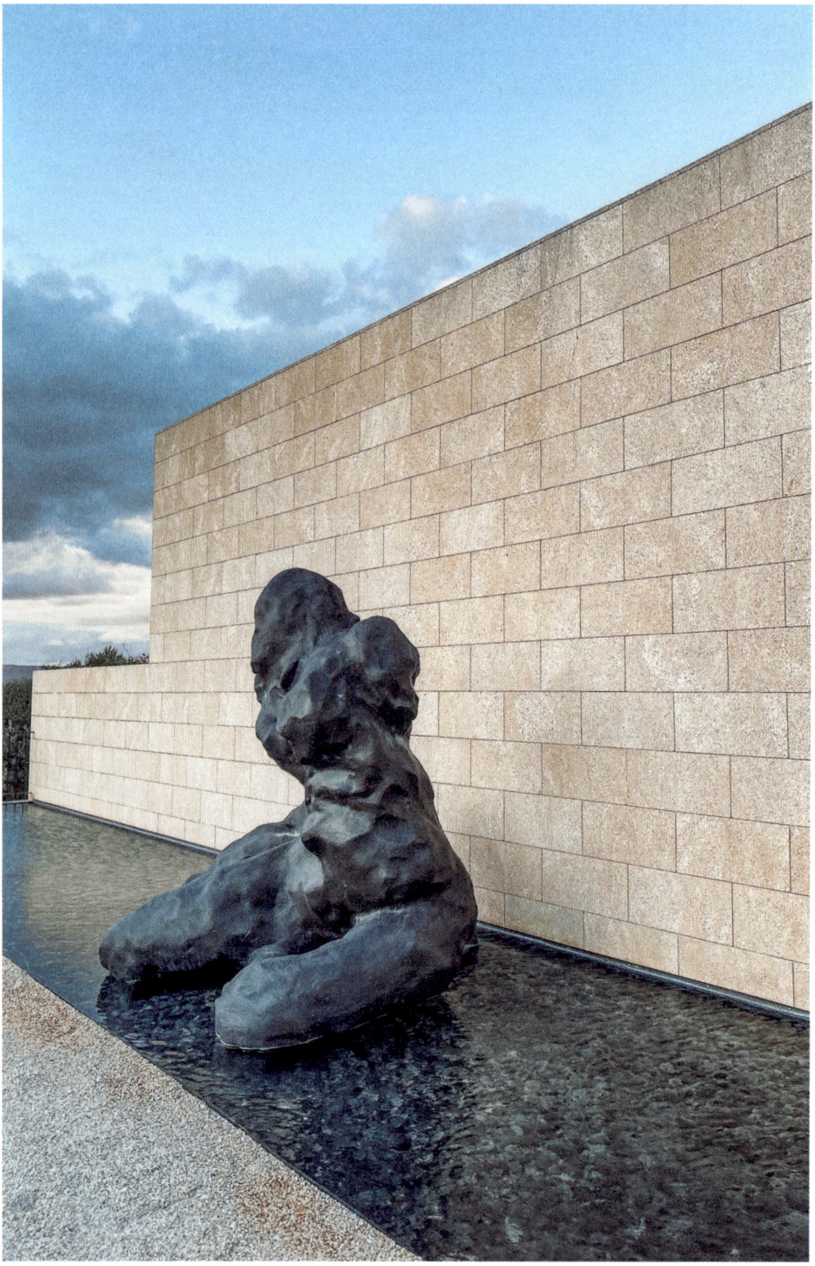

and engineering the conditions for aesthetic eating. This is more than an outdoor sculpture park or theme park for artworks. He says: "There is a science to where the pieces are located. I'd studied the land and done the walks." Design by embodied practice. *Terroir* does not merely manifest in the fruits of the earth, it also affects the designer, the maker, who adapts his œuvre from feedback he receives. The walk requires three hours to explore the full range of site-specific commissions. There are immersive installations and full-blown land art. Sean Scully's *Wall of Light Cubed* (2007) is a 1,000-tonne cuboid of multicoloured limestone blocks, Andy Goldsworthy's *Oak Room* (2009) is a huge underground dome and Richard Serra's metallic rectangles, planted in the soil, jut out to interrupt the visitor's vantage point. Some, such as Gehry's Music Pavilion, are in full view. Others, such as the Tracey Emin self-portrait – the first architectural piece the artist made – require a trek, a climb and a solitary walk down what is effectively a suspended gangplank or sky bridge over a 30-metre cliff to peer into a barrel and see a depiction of Docket, her late tabby and one-time companion. The Château la Coste experience is convivial, but it is not complacent.

The location and its agricultural framing work with the art. Because of the cradling in the landscape of the Puy-Sainte-Réparade valley, the artistic, architectural, sculptural and design boundaries are dissolved, while the sensual indulgence and swirling round the tongue is enhanced in this aesthetic dining experience. Just like farmers and wine producers harvested the land, to repurpose yet further the offering, la Coste includes the creations of some of the most considered and cerebral contemporary artists, architects and sculptors. These architectural images are promises and invitations to the visitor to participate in aesthetic dining that engages all senses. They also function as farmhands, contributing to the land and its production. McKillen explains they are in the service of the grapes, and thus honouring the fruit with the gift of the art and architecture. "The winemakers are the first artists and the rest of us are visitors and guests, including the artists," he says. This is a respect and offering of the art to the wine, or a respect and offering of the wine to the art, restoring anybody who encounters it. To build and dwell also means to "cherish and protect, to care for, specifically to till the soil, to cultivate the vine", wrote Heidegger. Through this care man nurtures and strengthens his relationship with nature and his place in the world. La Coste offers this fundamental reflection through its synthesis of the different meanings of taste.

Works and artists in the Château la Coste collection

—

A Tadao Ando work is the literal gatekeeper of the estate, the grey concrete structure having been created in 2011 to seal it off from the main road. He also designed the dedicated art gallery that is half immersed in the soil. It is rare to find works of the Japanese designer in Europe, yet la Coste has three, the other being the pavilion on "Four Cubes to Contemplate our Environment" (2008-11). His structures imply a preciseness and finality, but also an escape into poetic ideas. "After having secured the functional basis of a building, I search how far it can be detached from function. Architecture lies in the distance between it and function," says Ando

—

Tracey Emin's oversize bronze sculpture of a female nude is the first large-scale work the artist has made. The influence of Bourgeois is apparent, and McKillen recalls how she felt unconstrained and free in the grounds to experiment. "By the way, who of us isn't inspired by Louise Bourgeois, those of us that build?"

—

Ai Weiwei's *Ruyi Path* (2017) uses repurposed stones from Marseille port to build a zigzagging pathway, which connects the modern part of the estate to an old Roman road that was in the grounds. The artist's father came through Marseille docks on his first visit to the West in 1929 and Weiwei wanted to pay tribute to him by grafting his story into the landscape and history of la Coste.

—

Hiroshi Sugimoto's *Mathematical Model 012* (2010) is a precise sculpture that tapers from a wide base to a needlepoint reaching for the sky. The work, like his series, is inspired by Isaac Newton and the notion of natural science – where the forms that occur in nature are controlled by geometry and mathematics.

—

Paul Matisse's mechanised *Meditation Bell* (2012), constructed with disused aircraft aluminium, is a bell that rings at a pitch that is so deep yet so subtle it is lost in the sounds of the French countryside.

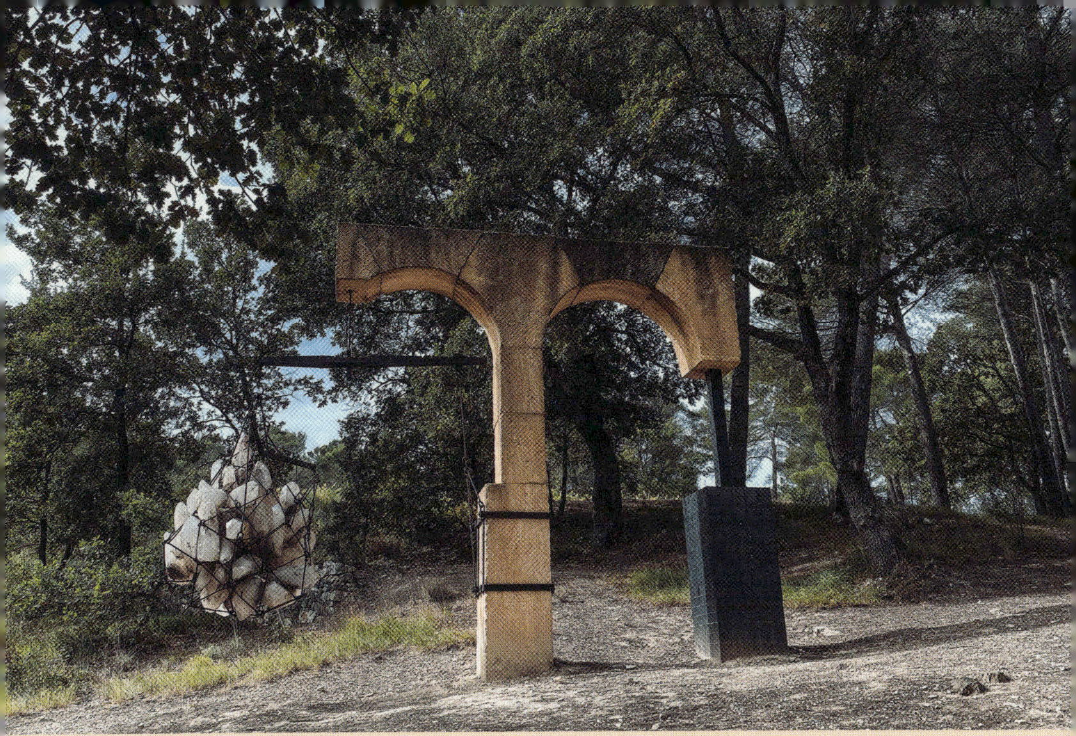

—

Lee Ufan's *House of Air* (2014) is a quaint stone hut that displays the South Korean artist's minimalist paintings. He says the work only comes to life when it is in contact and context with the natural environment: "My artwork gets its live, existential meaning only when it can harmonise with the surrounding space and thus transform the space into a new one."

—

Psicopompo (2011), by Brazilian artist Tunga, is a sculptural allegory in steel and quartz named after a mythical Greek scale used to measure a man's soul. Alchemy and transforming objects from one form to another is wine as much as it is art.

—

The restaurant lobby at la Coste contains an eclectic mix of artworks from McKillen's pre-existing collection plus design pieces he personally selected: Giacometti figurative sketches that were in storage for 40 years, a Charlotte Perriand low walnut table, a Warhol dollar-sign silkscreen, Ron Arad reclining chairs, a David Douglas Duncan photograph of Picasso in Native American dress – McKillen owns the rights to the Duncan estate – a Bourgeois *Ode à la Bièvre* embroidered book commemorating her childhood and playing on the riverbank. Each piece has a special meaning in the history of each artist and designer's œuvre, which is why they appeal to McKillen – and why he shares them with his diners and visitors.

Louise Bourgeois' *Couple* suspended above the dining table in David Fu's pavilion housing Louison restaurant; Ai Weiwei's *Rui Path* among the vineyards; Bourgeois' *Crouching Spider* at the Tadao Ando-designed art centre; Conrad Shawcross' Schism; a sculpture by Tracey Emin; Tunga's *Psicombo* on the hills of the grounds

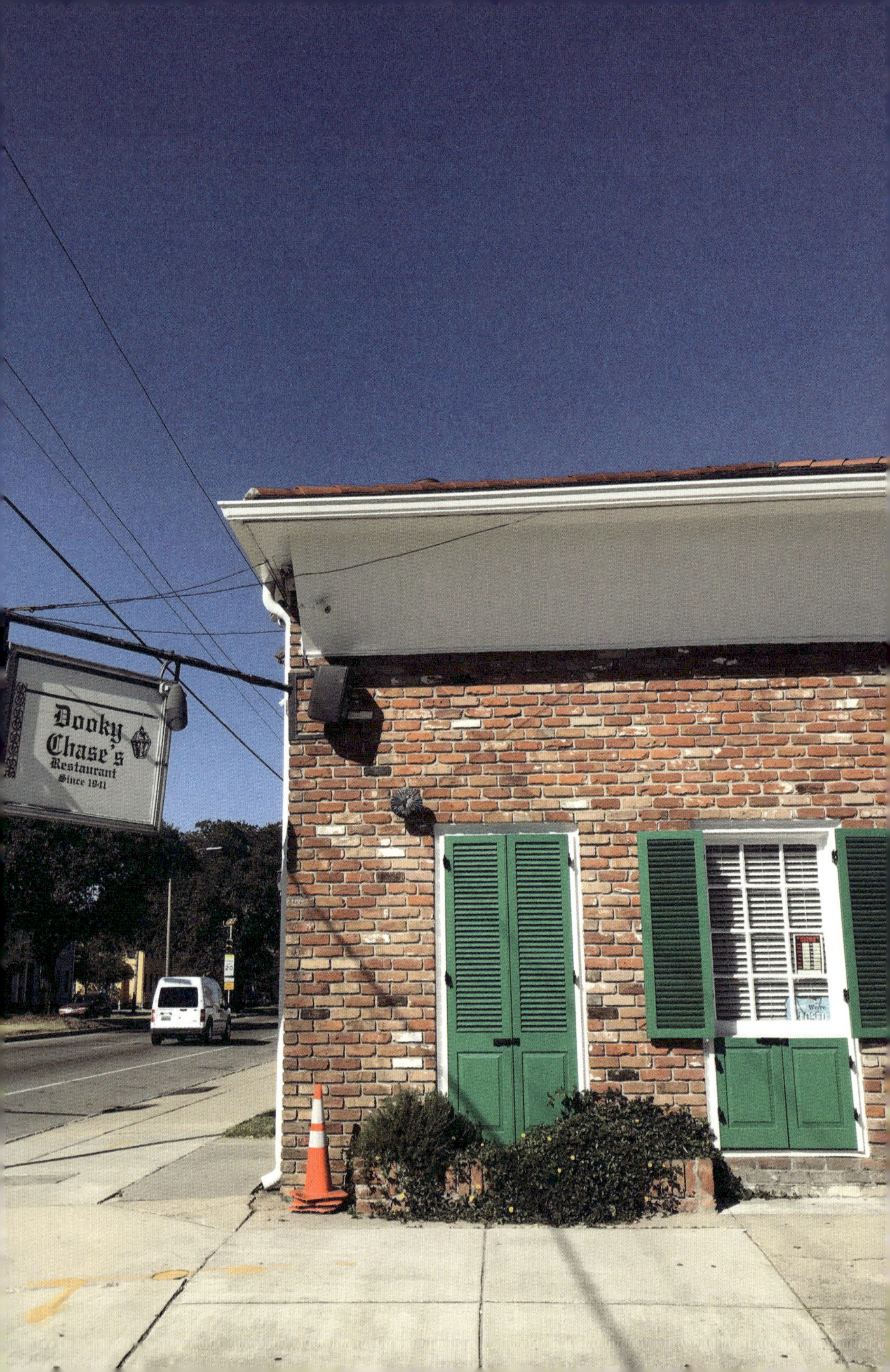
Dooky
Chase's
Restaurant
Since 1941

Dooky Chase

"When the subject is strong, simplicity is the only way to treat it."
— Jacob Lawrence

"I fed them all – all of 'em!" Miss Leah exclaimed with a thump of her fist on her usual table in the Gold Room. "I fed Elizabeth Catlett... I fed John Biggers... I fed Jake Lawrence... I fed Mel Edwards... I fed Raymond Saunders." And up until her death in 2019, the 96-year-old Leah Chase, matriarch of New Orleans's historic dining institution, Dooky Chase, could be found in her kitchen every day in her trademark fuchsia pink apron directing her staff on preparing and serving its Creole-cuisine comfort food. From this kitchen she transformed a modest, humble family restaurant into a cultural landmark, which served as a setting for significant moments of southern American history. "I feel like the course of history has been changed over a bowl of gumbo," she stated, with added ingredients of pride and defiance. Her sagacious and practical optimism made her an American folk hero, and she is a reminder of how the domestic and carer classes of the United States wielded a quiet power and influence over the lives in their communities, but often remained unacknowledged and unnoticed on the wider world stage.

In addition to the political and historical role the restaurant has played in New Orleans, it is also an art restaurant, given Chase's chance exposure to modern art through encountering the work of Jacob Lawrence. Once she saw this, the connection between art and food became automatic and natural: "Food and art make you happy. Those things feed off each other [and make people] simply feel important and useful." This attitude led Chase to become a pioneer in building a collection of 20th-century African American artists, nourishing them literally and in other ways, nurturing their art careers by exhibiting their works on her restaurant walls. The artists joined the list of patrons from political, social and entertainment spheres that repeatedly came for Miss Leah's compassion, wisdom and love. Dooky Chase is an art restaurant that plays a wider role in the cultural and social history of New Orleans and the United States. The art collection was a further statement and tactic Miss Leah used to entice and bind her diners into a community composed of different races, classes and cultures.

The story begins in 1939, in the New Orleans back-of-town residential area of the Tremé, where Edgar Dooky Chase Snr established a small sandwich shop and lottery ticket outlet, which traded well in this historic neighbourhood where, traditionally, the *gens de couleur libre* lived. The shop evolved into a bar by 1941, attracting blue-collar workers from the New Orleans Black community, mainly rivermen who had few places to cash their Friday pay cheques. There were no

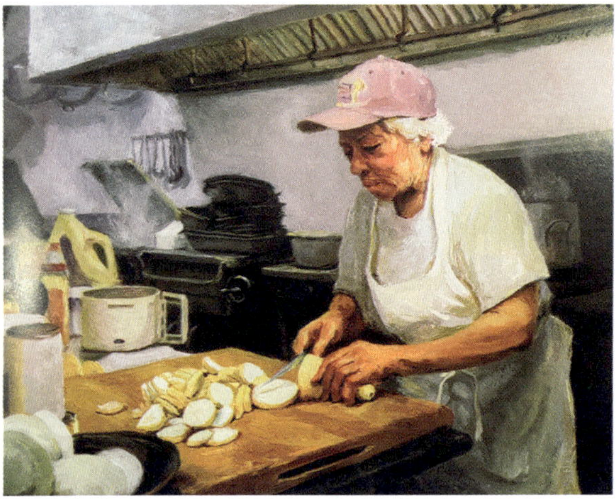

Black-owned banks then, but there were Black-owned catering establishments, like Dooky's, with the necessary cash flow and trust of patrons. At the end of each week, Dooky's bar was packed with men drinking beer and eating po'boy sandwiches. Friday nights were roaring good times where beer and whiskey competed with the Mississippi on flow. After a few years, Edgar Snr decided to expand the menu and it became Dooky Chase's family restaurant. In 1944, he persuaded his son, Dooky Jnr, who had been orchestrating his own successful 16-piece jazz band, Dooky's Band, to assist him in the restaurant, which he joined with his wife, Leah Lang.

Leah worked in fine-dining establishments from the age of 17 in the French Quarter, and had a vision for embellishing Dooky's with the same haute-cuisine flourish while retaining its own character in terms of cooking home food. The restaurant for her was "an extension of the home" – her mother or grandmother's home – where families and communities would come together, undertaking dining rituals. Growing up in the South, "they didn't want us taking food outside to eat, they wanted us to sit down at the table and show a certain respect for the table". Chase added white linen tablecloths and quality china and cutlery to her signature Creole cuisine – traditional, unaltered recipes she learned to prepare in her youth. Dishes such as shrimp gumbo and Clemenceau were concocted, perfected and served with a typical southern flair for warm hospitality. Dooky's quickly became one of the first African American fine-dining establishments in the United States, without the snobbery and exclusivity that often accompanies formal restaurants. On the contrary, it brandished radical inclusivity, at times functioning as a community centre or voter-registration headquarters, and then in the 1960s, Dooky Chase became a meeting place for key figures of the Civil Rights Movement to plan campaigns. Upholding segregation laws was never on the cards for Dooky Jnr and Leah, even throughout years of regular hate mail from opposers – and once even a pipe bomb.

The list of political diners who passed through the restaurant doors includes Martin Luther King Jnr; members of the Freedom Riders, the activists who rode interstate buses in protest against segregation, such as Reverend A.L. Davis and Reverend Avery Alexander; figures from the law, such as A.P. Tureaud, the NAACP attorney for New Orleans; Ernst "Dutch" Morial Revius, who went on to become the first African American Mayor of New Orleans; O. Ortique, the first African American Justice of the Louisiana Supreme Court; and other prominent Freedom Riders and activists such as Oretha Castle Haley, Jerome Smith, Rudy Lombard and Virginia Durr. They all ate there and held strategy sessions and discussions in the back room. Years before the United States Supreme Court reversed its *Plessy v. Ferguson* ruling of 1896, which up to that time upheld apartheid in public spaces, including museums and restaurants, Dooky's used hospitality as an act of disobedience and protest by offering jambalaya and Dixie beer to the Civil Rights Movement.

Dooky Chase also appealed to significant figures in the music industry, and patrons from the jazz and blues scenes who dined there regularly included Sarah Vaughan, Count Basie, Lena Horne, Nat King Cole, Louis Armstrong and Quincy Jones, and more recently Beyoncé and Jay Z. Ray Charles went further and referenced the restaurant in his *Early Morning Blues*: "*I went to Dooky Chase's to get something to eat, the waitress said, 'Ray you sure look beat' / Now it's early in the morning / And I ain't got nothing but the blues.*" Dooky's became a go-to place for touring musicians too, emphasising its widespread cultural reputation.

Leah's involvement with the visual arts began in the early 1970s when her friend Celestine Strode Cook, a formidable, wealthy businesswoman and Civil Rights figure in her own right, was elected to the board of the New Orleans Museum of Art, inviting Chase to join. Reluctant at first, partially because the segregation laws meant museum visits by African Americans were not permitted until 1964, this was an unknown and intimidating domain for her. Finally, she relented and went to the museum to view an exhibition and listen to a lecture by Jacob Lawrence, the notable Harlem painter who was the first Black artist to have a show at NOMA. In her own words: "I thought, oh my god, I'm going to sit here and look how stupid I was. I thought you had to dress up to go to the museum. I put on the best things I had. I dressed up nicely and went and sat in the museum." Dressing in her Sunday best to go to a museum as a sign of respect and reverence should not be lost on today's visitors. She sat in the front row, worried: "I am not going to know one earthly thing this man is talking about because I won't understand it, but he spoke about his art, and he came from where I came from..." Both Lawrence and Chase were part of the Works Progress Administration programme, both plying their respective trades (artist and cook), and this resonated with Chase. "His work was learning art to sell, so you see I could relate to him because I knew what WPA was all about... I knew what the Depression was all about, so I could relate to him." He spoke about his *Migration Series*, 60 panels depicting African American migration from the South to find opportunities in urban centres in the North, made in 1941 and funded by the WPA. Chase recalls: "That was my life in art; I could relate to that."

Celestine had fundraised and lobbied for the Lawrence show to be displayed in New Orleans and she introduced the artist to the chef. They became fast friends. Through Lawrence she met a number of other important African American artists, such as Elizabeth Catlett and John Biggers – "the finest artists and all they had for me to learn from" – who she invited to the restaurant. Chase's first work in her collection was Lawrence's *Confrontation on the Bridge at Selma, Alabama* (1975). It depicts a group of African Americans held back by a white policeman with a dog. The more she looked at the works, the more she was convinced "they spoke to me", and they were "like a prayer of thanks" to God in terms of artists repeating and replicating a gift given to them by a higher force. She started to acquire more pieces and hang them in the restaurant, turning the dining rooms into the first art gallery for Black artists in New Orleans.

Chase realised these artists and their younger counterparts lacked opportunities to exhibit their work, because galleries in New Orleans did not show Black artists. She decided to start buying to support them, one of the earliest being an Elizabeth Catlett for $350, *Two Generations*, a double portrait of a Black mother and young daughter. Catlett was one of the most significant African American female artists of the 20th century in the United States, whose works referencing social justice and family ties engaged a broad public. She was influenced by African and Mexican art, and their bold shapes and figures, arguing for a practice that serves a social purpose and speaks for its people. Miss Leah remembers: "When E would come, she would love her fried oysters. I would fix E all the oysters she liked. Her husband liked lobster. I would fix lobster for him, so I got about five pieces by EC. It was a good exchange." Catlett went on to become a highly respected teacher and mentor, in addition to developing an artistic practice that spanned painting, sculpture and woodcuts.

Leah decided to fill the whole restaurant and its three dining rooms with art. She hosted dinners after exhibition openings at NOMA because food binds communities together and there is "respect for the table", as her grandmother instilled in her. Just as she hosted Civil Rights activists, she would build a movement around the artists, using Dooky Chase to address social problems. Her

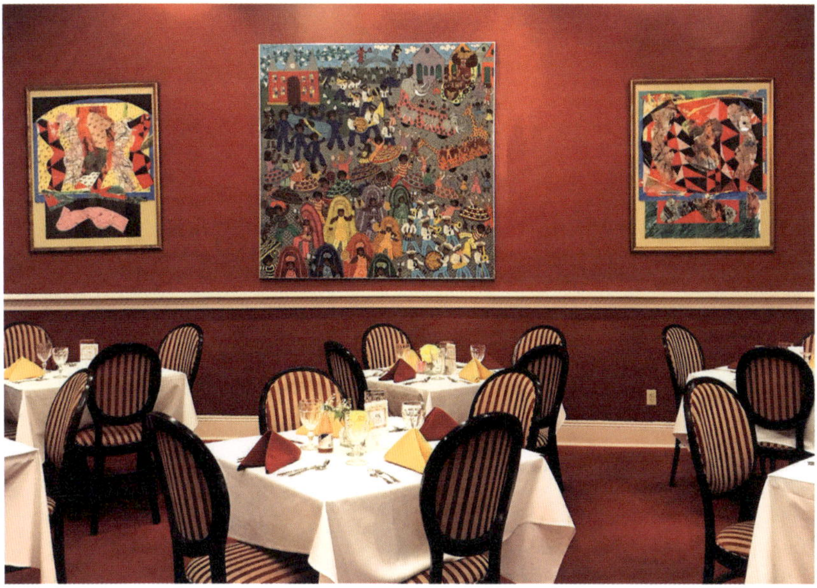

husband was sceptical of her patronage and often called her a "bankruptcy centre". She remained defiant, disregarding whether or not the public would like the art or her mixing levels and abilities. "It's just wonderful to have works by those people you get to know as friends, artists who not even that long ago didn't have plenty of places to sell and a lot of money. So what I would do would be to feed them and they would send me art. They liked gumbo, I gave them gumbo, and I said, 'Now you send me a piece of art.'" The result over the years is a personal collection ranging from naïve folk art depictions of agricultural life to hard-hitting political contemporary art. Creole mothers share the wall space with hip-hop poets.

The young African American artist, Gustave Blache III, painted a series portraying Leah Chase in the kitchen. He spent three years observing the chef. She gratefully commented, "you paint the way I like to look at paintings," meaning they are simple and impactful, appealing to those without an art history background. Blache believes Chase's interest in art was "another layer of community support", given her Civil Rights background. The 36 pieces are firmly in the tradition of realist art that celebrates the dignity of work, influenced by Daumier and Degas (the latter had a connection to New Orleans and was the only Impressionist to visit the United States). One of the portraits in the series was acquired by the Smithsonian's National Portrait Gallery – an honour for the artist who was in his mid-thirties, and for Miss Leah, who now hangs with the greatest figures in American history.

This art restaurant became "an anchor for the neighbourhood"; even the public housing units surrounding the establishment are kept tidy and neat, and there is no graffiti because the residents feel "we can't have people coming into the neighbourhood to Dooky Chase's seeing writing all over the walls". Leah became a philanthropist and volunteer in the city. There is a delicate and faithful pencil drawing of rapper Tupac Shakur on the wall of her Gold Room, which she acquired after visiting an art class in a local school where the students were asked to bring in something that was of significance to them. A pupil brought poetry written by Shakur, and it was the first time she'd heard of the rapper. She commissioned a drawing by an unknown artist depicting Shakur to symbolise those failed by society and misrepresented by bad deeds and the crime they commit, which overlooks their humanity and talent. "And I keep that up there to remind me: Leah, pay attention. Pay attention to people because you never know. We write people off. Why couldn't he be saved? Because nobody paid attention. That gets to me every time." She learned the plurality of perspectives on experiences and history from art, and in turn she ensures the local community learns from her art collection.

Miss Leah was a pillar of New Orleans and the local community. She used her art collection as a missionary would, for teaching and to bring hope and a different experience to new, uninitiated audiences. She became a lifetime trustee of NOMA, having testified to Congress for access funding for the arts, and she fed three presidents of the US – once admonishing Barack Obama for adding chilli sauce to her gumbo dish. Her sense of responsibility towards the city meant she was committed to using art to open the eyes and minds of members of her community. Dooky Chase's uniqueness as an art restaurant lies in its combination of location, arts, identity and the history of the southern United States for all of its issues and frustrations. Leah Chase accepted the effects of history and made history, and the art collection is a testament of what she lived through. As she stated the year before she died: "I got lots more pieces to put up. But I'm getting older now and slower and I can't get it done like I want to get it done."

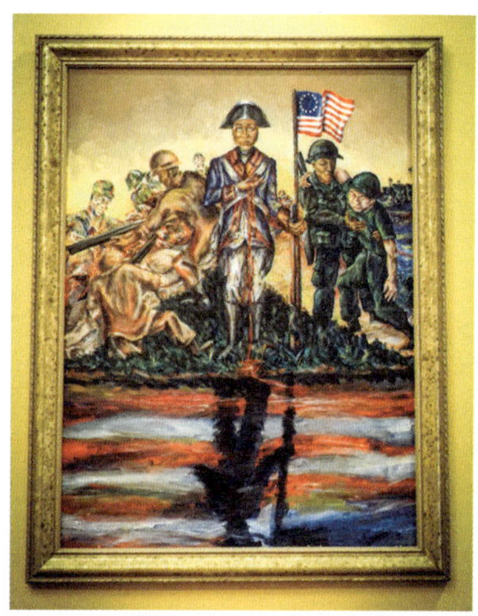

Works and artists in the Dooky Chase collection

—

John T. Biggers was one of the founding members of the Negro Art Movement, which grew out of the Harlem Renaissance. His work was concerned with social justice, but also the role of myth and ritual in communities after his UNESCO-sponsored trip as the first Black artist from the US to visit Africa. "Then I met John Biggers," Miss Leah said. "What I liked about John was that he had a lot of respect for women. You can see it if you look at his work around these walls; if you look at the painting *Upper Room* that is hanging here in the restaurant. We know the upper room was where the Apostles waited for Christ to come. And the upper room is where Christ appeared after he rose from the dead. John Biggers painted women holding up that room. He wanted to show the strength and the power of women."

—

An Elizabeth Catlett woodcut depicts a statuesque, classically proportioned Black woman pointing forwards and leading a group of women, some carrying children. Miss Leah said: "That's my favourite Elizabeth Catlett – so strong. She's just telling the sisters, 'Come on. We're moving. We're gone.'"

—

Melvin Edwards, a pioneer of contemporary African American art known for his metalwork sculptures, features in the collection. He is also a draughtsman whose work is characterised by angular, geometric lines and compositions that convey political content.

—

The Fisherman, by Ron Adams, shows a larger than life, muscular barefoot man in overalls on his boat on the Mississippi – a riverman – fishing for crayfish. Miss Leah mused on modern men who lift weights today to attain those muscles, whereas this "man never lifted a weight in his life. He just lifted up his boat when he got ready to move; lifted everything around him to survive and get his work done. That face says, 'I'm just a simple man, doing what I do.' And I like that."

—

"I was good friends with the artist John Scott," Miss Leah said. "He was just like my child. He used to come over here all the time. I'm old-school and I believe you should go to church on Sunday. I used to preach this to him. When he died, I went to the memorial ceremony and realised the spirituality that was present in his work. His work was his prayer."

Dooky Chase restaurant in the Tremé area of New Orleans; Gustave Blache III's portrait of Miss Leah Chase; the main dining room of the restaurant with works by Elizabeth Catlett; work by Ulrick Jean Pierre

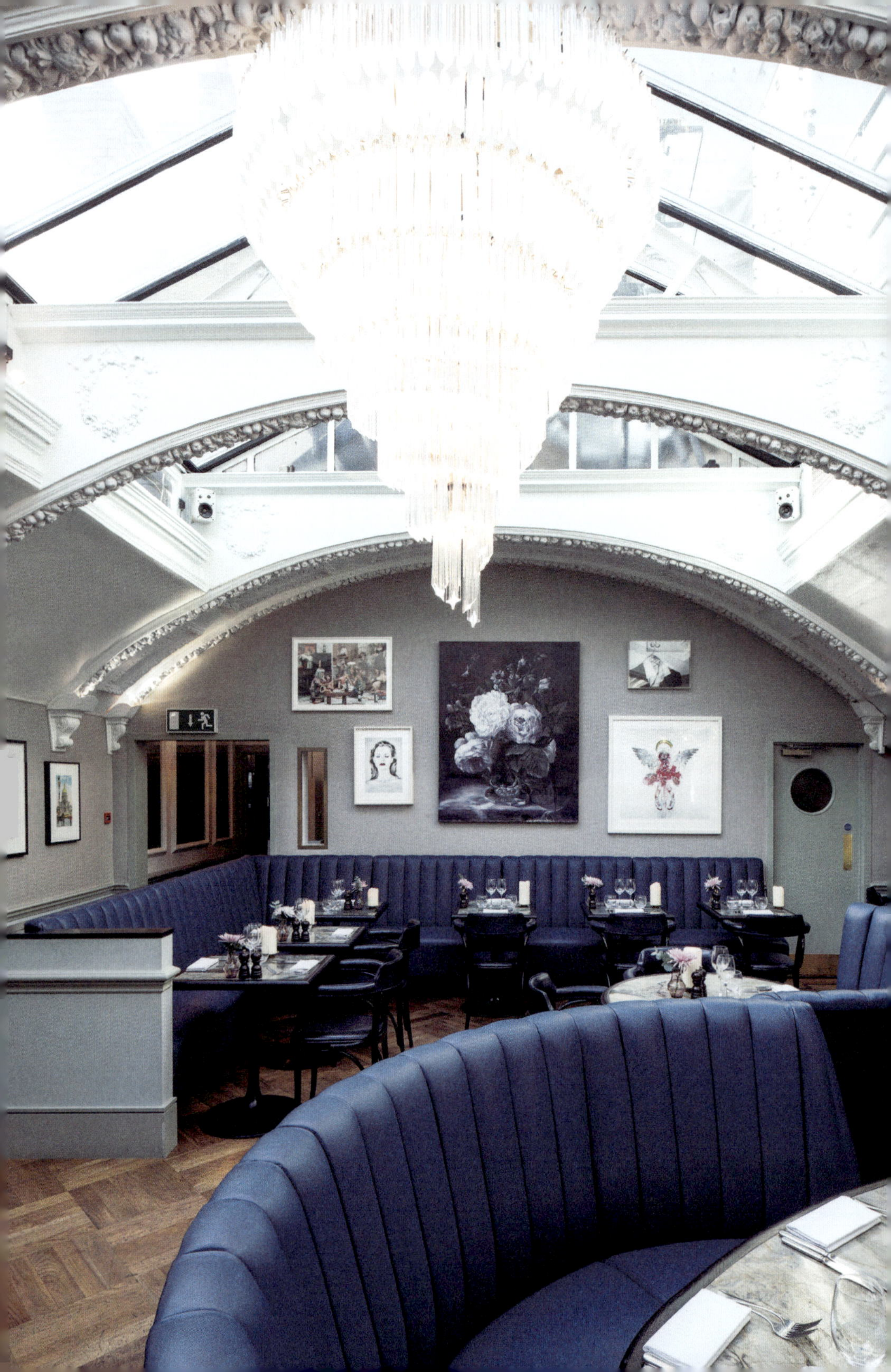

The Groucho Club

LONDON

"All celebrated clubs are founded upon eating and drinking, which are points where most men agree, and in which the learned and the illiterate, dull and the airy, the philosopher and the buffoon, can all of them bear a part."
— John Timbs

"Hencoop hospitalities for Amazons of *ton*," wrote P.G. Wodehouse in 1930, in response to the growth of private members' clubs for women that began in the late 19th century. Institutions such as the Lyceum, the Empress and the Pioneer accommodated upper-class society women. They were a by-product of the wider proliferation of the 19th-century clubs that catered to the growing middle classes, with their members' aspirations to belong to particular cliques, offering, according to another journalist, "gossip, guzzle and gamble". Almost a century later, the Groucho Club hijacked the idea of the members' club, setting out to be inclusive of, and for, outsiders, and from the outset the antithesis of the examples in St. James's, which were male and very much the Establishment. The Groucho both challenged and continued the tradition of the English members' club, because its development is more multifaceted and complicated than the anecdotes surrounding it: the stories of artists behaving badly and their myriad inebriated antics. It is also an art restaurant because of its inclusion of British art and the strategic building of an historical collection. And it is the scene for the constantly shifting dominance of literary versus visual culture in Britain. Although visual art was traditionally sidelined by literature, in the late 20th and early 21st century it became the pre-eminent form of cultural output. In this context, too, the Groucho subverts the members' club blueprint, but also follows it, as these venues always attracted intellectuals and creatives to joust and play, be that on the page or on the canvas.

Members' clubs originated in 17th-century City of London where at first, they were more a stomping ground for writers, critics and journalists. "A *clubbe*," wrote John Aubrey in 1659, was "solidarity in a tavern". Soon after, Sir Walter Raleigh founded *The Mermaid*, a tavern next to St Paul's Cathedral, which became a members' club by attracting writers and wits of the time, such as Donne, Beaumont, Bacon and Fletcher. Shakespeare also frequented it. Ben Jonson founded the first organised literary dining club, The Apollo Club, in 1616, in the Devil Tavern near Temple Bar; its fraternity included Swift, Pope and Dr Johnson. From early on, the taverns were intellectual watering holes, offering commensality and a respite from the solitary life of the writer. By the late 17th century, setting up a club became a means of gathering together those who held the same ideologies and politics, often in coffee houses, which Charles II attempted but

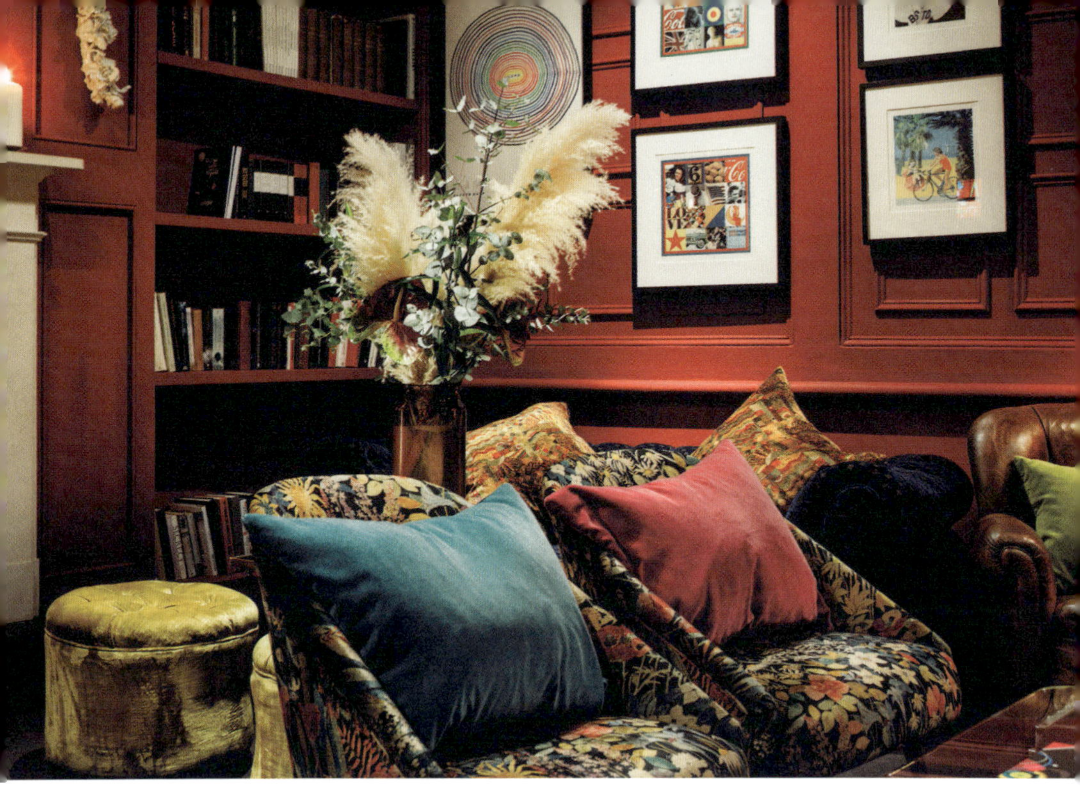

failed to close down. In 1693 Francesco Bianco founded his Chocolate House in St James's in opposition to the coffee houses in the City of London. Today, this is the most elite and status quo-upholding club in British society – known as White's to contemporary patrons – and its immigrant founder's name was subsequently Anglicised and de-catholicised to Francis White. By 1886 there were more than 100 clubs with a total of 60,000 members in Central London. Each one had its hierarchy within its four walls and was its own microcosm, organised by political belief and profession, catering to people who required a discreet venue to dine after or during meetings with peers. This period set the model for the snobbism and exclusivity of the members' club known today.

In contrast to this, the Groucho was co-founded by Liz Calder and Carmen Callil, significant figures in the UK publishing industry, the former having established Bloomsbury Press and the Orange Prize, and the latter Virago Press, among many other accomplishments between them. They chose Soho, which had been the nexus of the publishing and literary industry in London, rather than Mayfair or the City of London, where members' clubs catering to financial and political interests were traditionally located.

There are, however, constants and parallels between Establishment social clubs and outsider establishments such as the Groucho. Members' clubs have historically drawn a distinction between those that belonged and those excluded. The Duke of Devonshire once proclaimed: "You can, to a very considerable extent, judge a man's tastes, possibly even his character, by the club to which he belongs." Similarly, there is a bohemian conceit and hierarchy among the existential drunkards of Soho entertainment venues that had existed since the end of the Second World War. Places documented in Daniel Farson's seminal study, *Soho in the Fifties,* which included the Coach and Horses and the French House, were already challenged for the bohemian crown by the arrival of The Colony Room. They all competed for the district's *habitués*, but many cultural figures had the insatiable thirsts and deep pockets to patronise most of them. According to writer and artist Molly Parkin, she would live and work in the Chelsea Arts Club but go to Soho to "meet kindred spirits". Francis Bacon would do the rounds and buy champagne for everybody in sight, ensuring he was always surrounded by many fair-weather friends. By the time the Groucho came along in 1985, opening next to The Colony Room on Dean Street, it was considered an interloper, with its membership of media and publishing professionals regarded as *arriviste* and too engineered to be authentically bohemian like its dank and disorderly predecessors. Considering all of these venues were created in opposition to the class-conscious and hierarchical Establishment members' clubs of St James's, Mayfair and the City, the irony is not lost. However, the psychology of collective behaviour and belonging to a group is such that it brings out the best and worst in individuals. In some ways the Groucho had the fortune of hindsight to mix the right elements of location, atmosphere and members – to curate them – into an exemplary *alternative* alternative members' club.

The Groucho was initially patronised by writers, publishers and journalists – in other words, it continued the British tradition of the literary dominance in culture and media. The artists that grew up against the backdrop of economic downturn, civil unrest and escalating inequality in mid-1980s Britain fulfilled the role of observers of, and commentators on, the disintegrating social conditions. However, this coexisted with realising the pecuniary potential of their work and their artistic brands to collectors and institutions on the other side of the divide. By the early 1990s, with the advent of Cool Britannia, visual British culture became a leading currency, and suddenly its practitioners were famous, sought-after and revered by collectors, the media and the public, internationally. The artists were clubbable in all senses of the word, and through the social bonds and commercial affinities, the Groucho became well-known as the requisite artists' club with the walls beginning to be covered in works by the members. The food and drink added to an environment that fostered kinship, ensuring it also functioned as an art restaurant. When Damien Hirst set up his Pharmacy restaurant in 1997, he convinced most of the kitchen staff to leave the Groucho and join him there.

The Young British Artists became the Groucho clan, while the slightly older generation, such as Francis Bacon, Barry Flanagan, James Birch and Martin Fuller, who were patrons of more established Soho and West End venues, especially The Colony Room, would also drop in. Peter Blake was a founder member of the Groucho and would visit for a nightcap on his way home from dinner (presumably via another art restaurant where he had a tab), but it was of course never just one drink: "Impossible. You cannot get out of there before 2am." The collection features eight pieces by Blake, ranging from *Sources of Pop Art 2*, a fountainhead chart consisting of Elvis, pin-ups, a Coca-Cola logo, the American flag and so on, to *Fag Packet* (2004), which is exactly that – a taped-up cigarette packet of Fifth Avenue cigarettes. His contemporary, David Remfry, gave the club collection an image of a high-heeled woman walking her dog, leaning over as if she were about to fall over; she is "off-kilter", according to the artist, because "everybody falls over when they go to the Groucho".

When the club began, it had innocuous paintings by the wives of members: florals, landscapes, wallpaper. Nicky Carter, who would become the Groucho's curator, was an art student at Goldsmiths and started working there as a waitress in 1989. The general manager, Liam Carson, asked her if she had classmates who would like to show works in the club. She did – and they happened to be Damien Hirst, Angus Fairhurst and Mat Collishaw. Carson had studied Langan's model and wanted to create the same buzz and atmosphere, and art was integral to that. Julia Hobsbawm was one of the original members and recalls how at the start, the club was about being seen: "That was 'the scene', if you like: who was hanging out with whom. But over the past two decades, thanks to some amazing curation by Nicky Carter, the art became more and more visible, and it was as if the walls were watching and being watched too." Carter set out to acquire 10 new pieces a year in the most systematised eating down model in terms of exchanging art for membership. She is effectively an archivist with a collection of more than 200 works that reflect trends, innovations and ideas in the British cultural landscape. She patronises graduate shows. She includes female artists. This varies from other clubs that tend to acquire high-value, high-status artworks from blue-chip artists. Some of these artists are here, their works donations from early in their careers, convivial and much in the spirit of a gift.

The first work Carter acquired was an Angus Fairhurst piece from 1992, *When I Woke Up in the Morning the Feeling was Still There* – a title that resonates with many members after a late-night visit. It takes on a poignant meaning given the artist's untimely death and is a reminder of what the writer Christopher Howse documents as the often-problematic side of Soho excesses of drink and the need to step up to the bohemian role – yet also part of its allure and enduring mythology.

The Groucho Club collection is irreverent, playful, ironic and humorous – all hallmarks of British art from the Pop era to the present, and evidence of the relatively comfortable and socially manageable nature of Britishness. Other members' clubs in Pall Mall or St. James's may display images of horseback battle

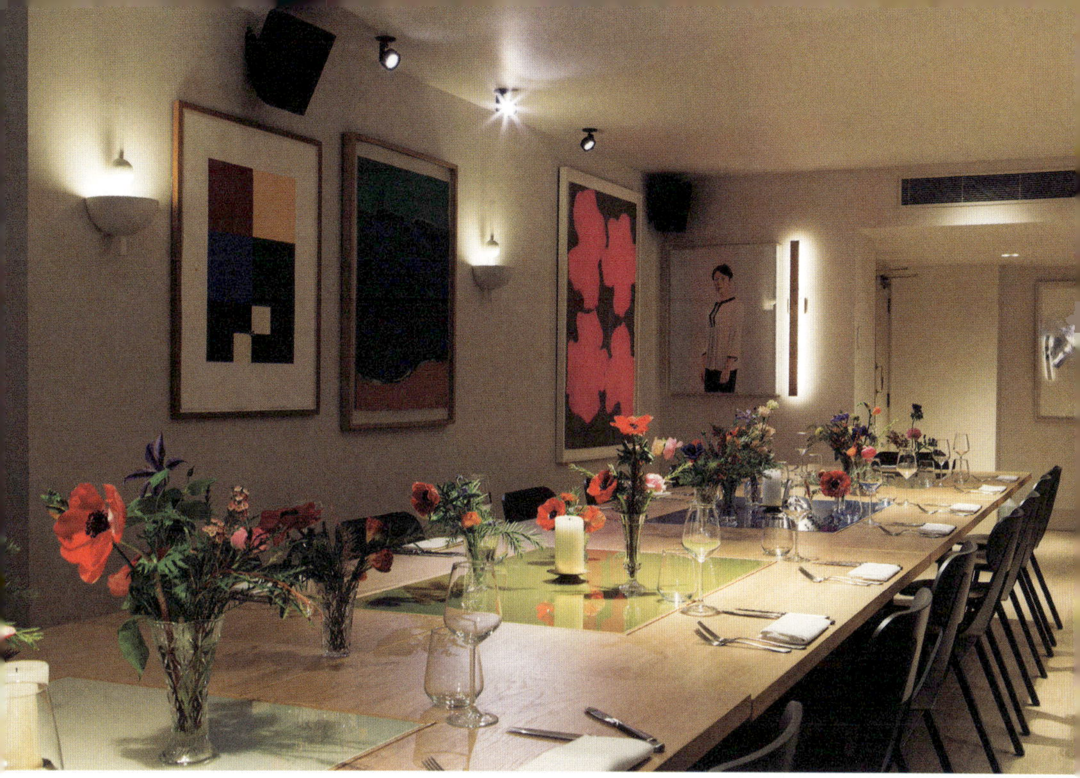

scenes throughout the Empire (Cavalry Club) or industrial triumphs of automobiles and airplanes (RAC) to immortalise past glories and conquests, or puffed-up portraits of illustrious patrons (East India Club), but the Groucho gives visitors a painting of scotch eggs, portraits of fictionalised drug dealers – vols. 1 and 2 – a penis-with-a-cat drawing and a photograph of an Ann Summers sex-toy party.

The stories of debauchery that gossip columnists depict and paparazzi photos show can often keep the Groucho's important art collection in the background. Damien Hirst reputedly put his £25,000 Turner Prize cheque behind the bar in 1995 to pay for his tab on the night, because he "knew [he] was going to spend it. But you can't pay a bill with a cheque made out in your own name. It doesn't make any sense." Despite the lore of the gesture, he settled the bill a few days later – "boring". Alcohol and dining are not an unusual combination, but an array of works ranging from Blake and Hockney to recent discoveries such as Oliver Beer and Polly Morgan is remarkable. Morgan says for artists to be invited to produce a work for the club is "a natural progression from being a regular to being an exhibitor", and it is "thrilling" to see her work alongside artists she admires. "There must be ascetic artists out there who can't be characterised by their overindulgence, but I haven't known one. Restaurants and bars have always nourished artists, so they are natural places to display their work. Galleries are mostly quiet places of reverence, restaurants and bars the opposite."

In some cases, the artworks were certainly not static, stuck to the walls, collecting smoke and dust. Gavin Turk made a parody English Heritage blue plaque

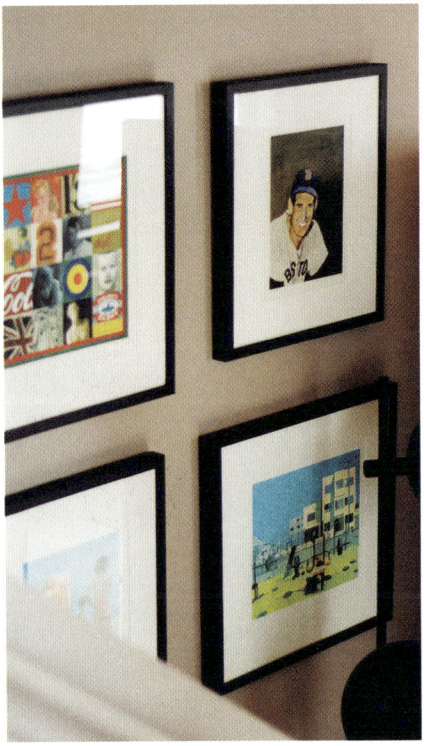

to declare "Gavin Turk, Sculptor, worked here, 1989–91". The piece was repeatedly toyed with by guests, according to the artist, used as a frisbee, scribbled on, hurled out of the window. It was eventually stolen, and he had to offer a replacement which is now firmly screwed on – "no touchy, touchy". For Turk, it was amusing that his work was "appropriated by everyone in the club". He recalls how he went to the US and asked his hosts if they could go to "a place where artists have their pictures up, and I was told that if you're a really good artist, you don't have your art hanging in restaurants or bars. Oops." The artists may have grown up in an era of economic uncertainty, but the "spirit of Hogarth prevailed, and the artists themselves led the revival". They were Laocoön sent in as a canary in the mine, but their warnings were delivered like a court jester. They enjoyed legitimacy in society, the media and the popular imagination at the height of their fame, but there was a problematic disappearance of the avant-garde's purpose that, as Richard Humphreys says, "paralleled the end of the revolution that it had been assumed by many would come, and young artists now occupied a strange, dystopian but quite comfortable landscape with no maps to get them there". The club may have been a laugh, but there was an anxious and even morose undertone to the art.

The Groucho came into its own in the 1990s when those members of society who were previously considered successful in London – bankers, stockbrokers, politicians – were surpassed in influence by media and publishing figures, as well as the artists and writers. This new segment of society may not have been as conventionally prosperous as old society, but they were wittier, more intellectual, and had more fun. And their products – especially those of the artists – were now sought-after commodities. The art collection post-1990s, from YBA onwards, is characterised by deadpan humour, irony and general irreverence. The behaviour

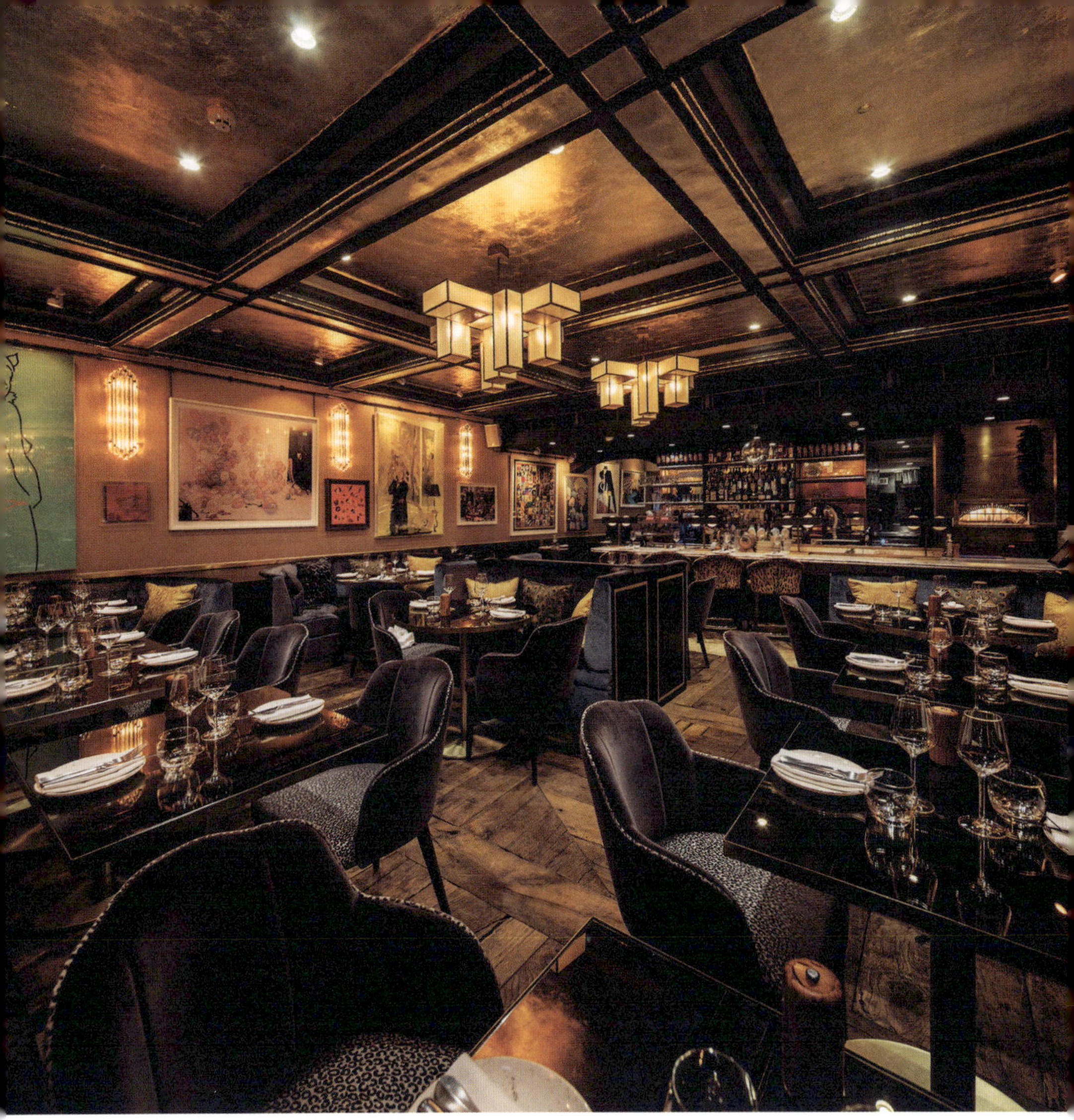

of the artists accompanying the works suggests the same provocation and disdain for any authority, convention or structure. As a result, it has been dismissed in the past as gimmicky and ultimately devoid of meaning.

Yet there is a "curiously Victorian quality" to the art from the 1990s and 2000s, which Richard Humphries writes can be seen in how the YBA art is concerned with Victorian subject matter such as love, sex, family: "A slightly sentimental concern with poverty or exclusion, a nervy promiscuity with past styles in art [and] a rapid Pre-Raphaelite-type move from outsider to insider status." In short, an affinity with the Victorian aesthetics and design the club set out to counter. However, the work was also laced with the requisite arguments of 20th-century aesthetics and fascination with artistic manqué: Duchamp's

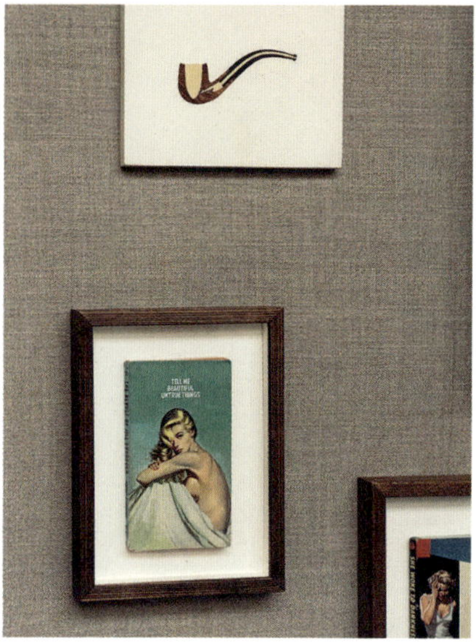

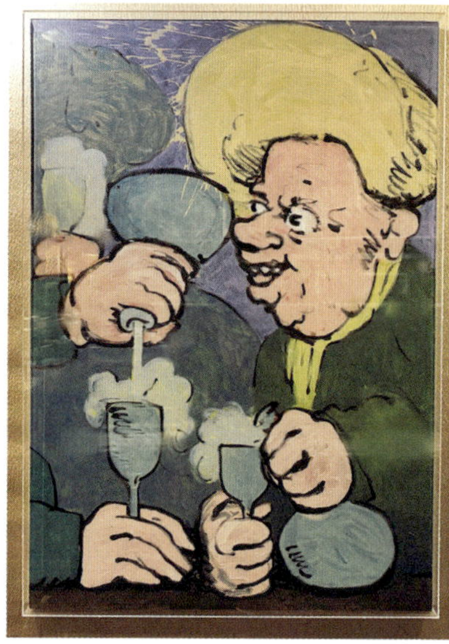

readymades, Situationism's happenings, the postmodern philosophy of Michel Foucault and Jean Baudrillard.

The Groucho Club's art collection is testament to how it is a place for artists to play at their own hierarchy and tradition of belonging, and also disrupting that order. To obtain access, to belong, the artist must give up a piece of work, surrender it to the collection and let it take its place among more established artists. Morgan says: "There is such a long history of artists eating and drinking in Soho and in the Groucho especially in recent history. Being able to leave work behind is like marking time; leaving relics of a time gone." The art collection is its own club, and it contains its own anti-Establishment, established rules. The contemporary artist Oliver Beer explains: "Whether it's the Met or a rowdy members' club, an art collection is like the portrait of the collector – and it's fascinating to think about how and why a work becomes part of that collection." There is a fraternity of the members and diners who belonged to the club – their career trajectories, fame, life happenings may change, some become more successful, some fail, but for those years they frequent the Groucho, they hold an understanding and affinity that may supersede schools attended, workplaces, relationships. This is reflected in the collection, which Oliver Clegg says is different "because it represents the artists as well as their work. It's about the people who come to the club as opposed to their work serving a purely decorative function within a club environment." The Groucho is a stage for bawdy theatrics and inebriated joviality, but the presence of the collection makes it an intergenerational art restaurant that houses generations of artists, all of whom want to belong to the same mythology and yet equally want to surpass and challenge Cronus, through homage.

Works and artists in the Groucho Club collection

—

Michael Craig-Martin, *Going* (2006). A trademark multicoloured work depicting digital tools such as a laptop, mobile phone and BlackBerry contrasted with traditional tools – a compass, a watch and prosaic office furniture. Perhaps a reminder that despite the late nights, the day jobs beckon in the morning for the media patrons.

—

Jim Lambie, *My Eyes Adored You* (2007). A large mirror collage made of broken fragments and cut-outs of eyes. The significance for a gregarious venue where image is everything is not lost.

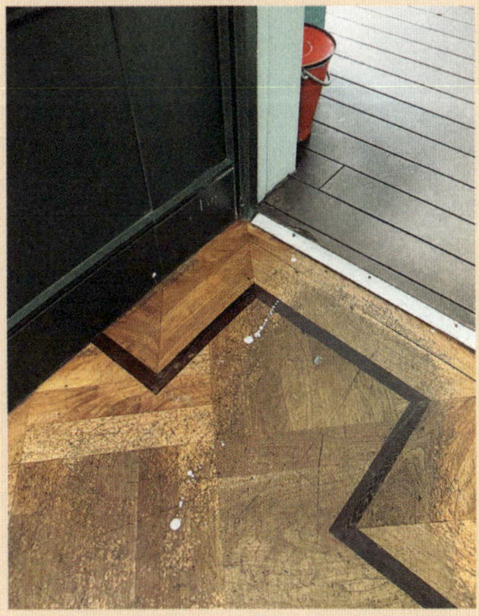

—

A trail of mother-of-pearl droplets inlayed into the wooden floor in the dining room is Susan Collis's *Low Down Dirty Mother* (2012). It looks messy and slippery, yet is made of semi-precious material.

—

Tracey Emin's drawing *Me Owe* (1997) features a penis and a cat face. Her tabby, Docket, was once her companion, but the pun in the title also suggests the eating down exchange.

—

Dan Baldwin's *Love* (2012) is a psychedelic multicoloured work with children, flowers and rainbows. It's serene, and the artist says: "Magic happens within those walls – hard to define. Always there will be some spontaneous meetings, drinks with people unplanned – it's a magnet, it's addictive. I'm proud to be in there."

—

Marcus Harvey, *Ann Summers Party* (2001). The photograph is of a suburban home setting, spewed with bottles, dildos and other sex toys. Two women are seen comparing the wares.

The club's top-floor dining area; works by Peter Blake in the lounge; Alessandro Raho's *Louise* hangs alongside Sam McEwan's *Four Flowers Night Version* and *Q is for Quarters* by Sir Peter Blake in The Gennaro Room; works by Sir Peter Blake; the dining room in the Groucho Club's restaurant; Oliver Beer's *Brighter Ideas II (part of diptych)*; *Happy Hour* by Charlie Billingham; *Low Down Dirty Mother* by Susan Collis inlaid in the floor of the dining room

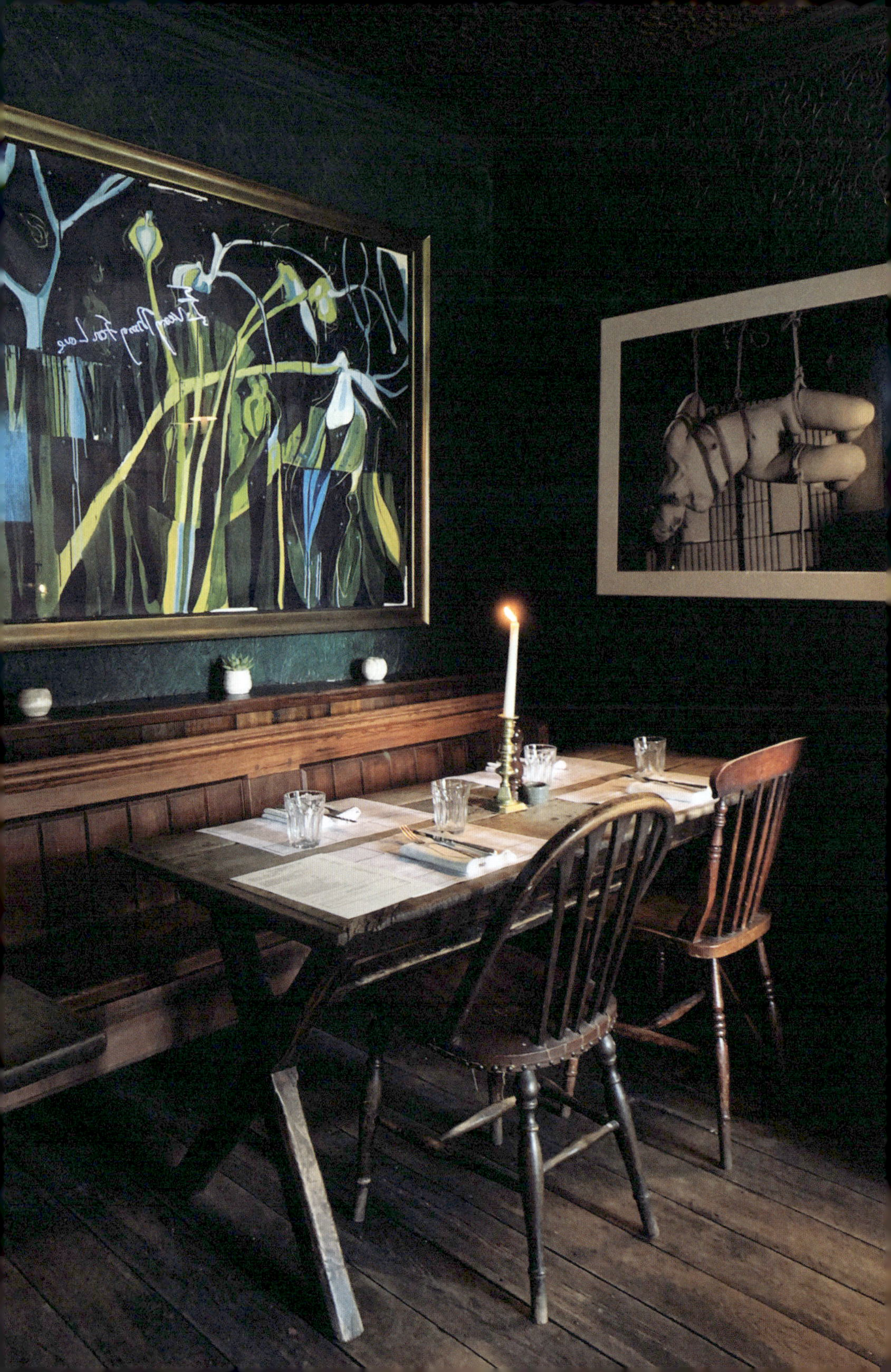

The Gunton Arms

NORFOLK

"Anyone who limits her vision to memories of yesterday is already dead."
— Lillie Langtry

Upon entering Norfolk's Gunton Arms, the diner is greeted by a 19th-century-style portrait of a woman. She is encased in a gold frame, wearing a green silk dress, dark hair in an updo, wistfully looking at the viewer who meets her gaze, as sitters in these sentimental types of portraits often do. Except she has a black eye. A marked, bruised left eye. The painting is by contemporary German artist Hans-Peter Feldmann, known for reappropriating European bourgeois imagery on antique canvases. This subtle inversion and slight absurdity in the guise of a traditional setting is characteristic of the Gunton experience and unfolds throughout the pub's three dining rooms. At first glance it seems like a conventional, rural hostelry – wooden panels and furniture, crackling fires and cosy ambience – but on closer inspection the interior is interrupted by incongruous contemporary artworks along the walls. For Ivor Braka, the art-collector-turned-restaurateur, if one cannot find the right art restaurant experience – to entice, to perform in and to satiate – one creates it oneself. He proclaims: "A restaurant should be somewhere you take someone you want to sleep with!" In his view, the purpose of a restaurant has been lost in contemporary times, having become too conceptual and too ascetic, rather than remaining sensual and aesthetic. His antidote is his Norfolk pub, dishing out rural fantasy and play, alongside traditional rustic British fare. All this against a backdrop of sexual innuendo and rowdy puns contained throughout his vast art collection on display. Braka delivers his own shiner to his patrons.

The Gunton Arms is a 19th-century former shooting lodge in Gunton Hall Park, owned by the Suffield family, which accommodated the furtive and the illicit from the outset. The Prince of Wales, King Edward VII, would stay at Gunton Hall and rendezvous with his mistress, Lillie Langtry, a socialite and actress of the 1800s, whom he kept in the rooms upstairs, now a bed and breakfast. Braka wanted to honour this aristocratic and salacious pedigree. Restaurants have historically encouraged mystery and intrigue among patrons, an opportunity to leave the domestic sphere and enact fantasy in a public space, where senses are heightened due to food and drink, and the audience awaits. Braka bemoans the modern dining environment and interiors, where guests, the kitchen and overall aesthetic are revealed at once in a minimalist setting. "There used to be a romantic side to eating out. Restaurants were originally designed so you could have a *tête-à-tête*, with private booths where you could draw the curtain, with candlelight which would make even the ugliest partner, male or female, seem sexually desirable at the end of the evening," he says. "Now they're designed by people who are only thinking of their own design, who show you everything in the room immediately." The Gunton Arms revels in this secrecy of the dimmed environment. One such space, the Waverly Room, is an alcove off the side of the main dining room, complete with candles, a curtain and a series of Beatriz Milhazes works around the table. Braka maintains this private room is constantly in demand by his diners, as the drawing of the curtains affords them privacy and they can continuously "talk about sex". For Milhazes, her pieces placed in the restaurant are about the vivacity and sensuality that living with art can reveal. "There is a strange but good communication between my work and the architecture of the building," she says.

Braka's childhood and upbringing instilled a tension around food and eating which he resolved through designing his own restaurant. His father, a Jewish-Syrian textile merchant, "hated eating out", and always insisted on having the same dish at home on a daily basis. Whereas his mother, English and social, adored visiting and being seen in restaurants. She would take young Ivor along with her in London every week and knew many of the staff and other diners in venues such as the Enzo Apicella-designed Meridiana, Le Caprice, and his favourite, La Popote, because it captured his imagination by being "gay-owned, gay waiters, Bacon in the upstairs bar". The interiors were wondrous to him because they featured "dark lighting, purple velvet banquettes in booths with curtains to draw for privacy, dark green walls and pink woodwork. Butterfly prawns, *duck a l'orange, foie gras*". The overall effect was "decadence in a 19th-century bordello" and clearly left a lasting impression on him when designing the Gunton Arms. Meanwhile, Braka's love of art began when a friend of his father's, Andras Kalman, a Hungarian-born refugee who became an art dealer, introduced him to the myriad forms of modern painting, primarily simple, representative works that appealed to emotions and senses, rather than the academic eye and mind. Kalman was a dealer of L.S. Lowry, a painter outside of mainstream art at the time, collected by his father. He was an inspiration to the young Braka, as the émigré assimilated English life and adopted his new homeland's norms of "fair play, modesty, church-going and the traditional English public houses". This instilled an interest in the same principles in his mentee – and ignited his fascination with the English pub. The two forces came together to form his version of hospitality and dining in a playful and intimate environment that would be enhanced by the art from his personal collection. The Gunton Arms features more than 100 works in a succession of visual and verbal games along the oak-panelled walls, and diners can follow the associations and wordplay throughout the lodge.

In the Emin Room, Braka believes a series of neon works by Tracey Emin "directly conveys a need for sincerity, for total emotional commitment and a huge fear of the possibility of the lack of it". The impact of the phrases "Trust Me", "I said

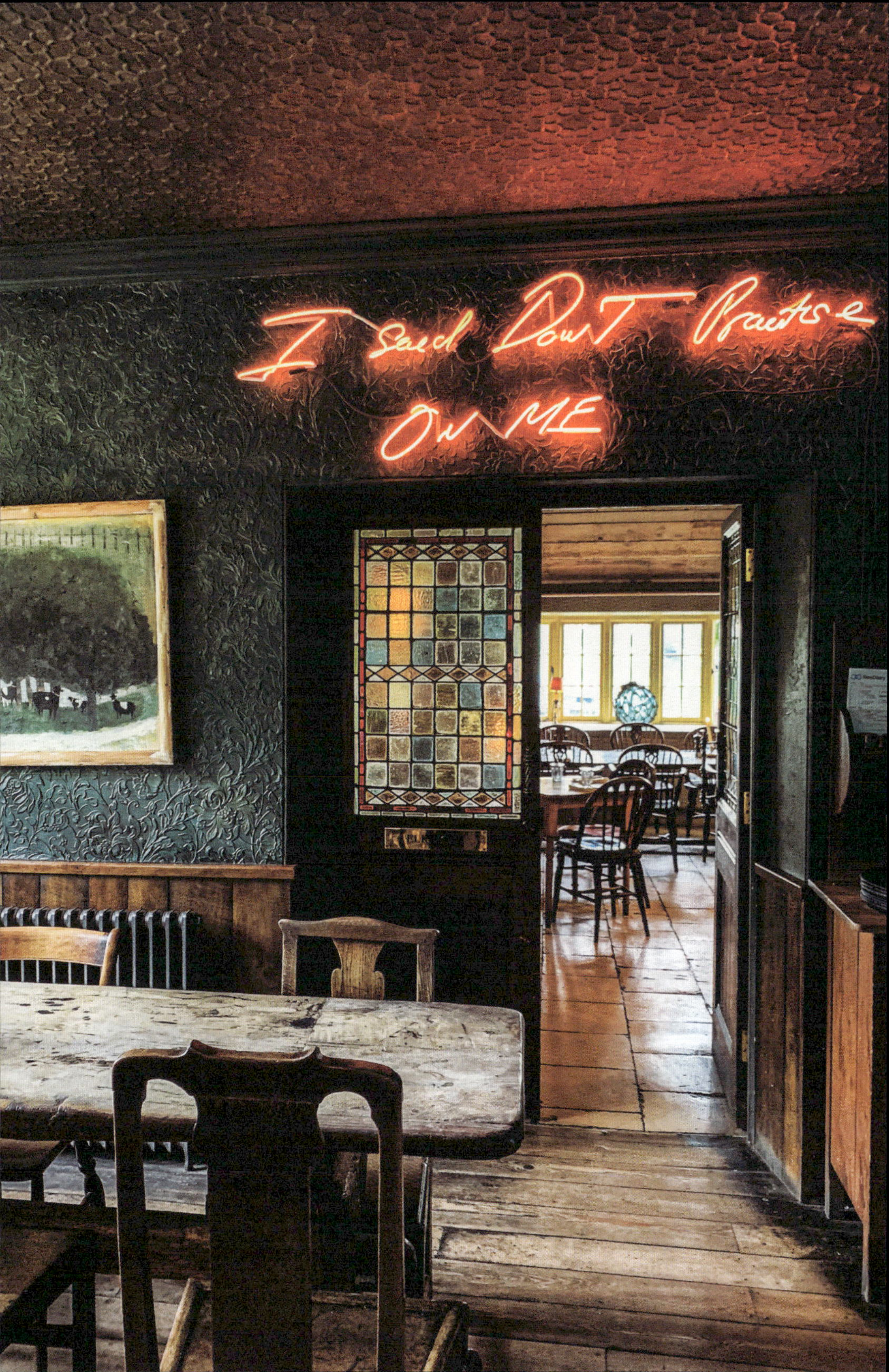

Don't Practise on Me" and "Everything for Love" are enhanced in a setting where people will visit for a traditional Sunday lunch with friends and family. If neon can be needy and neurotic, it unsettles such a prosaic dining experience on one level, but on another, what better way is there to comfort-eat away our maladaptive emotions and feelings than under these electric pleas? The room also displays a pair of dinosaurs locked in an embrace by an American photorealist painter, Alexis Rockman, a work that has personal appeal for Braka, as he collected PG Tips tea cards of animals, illustrated by Peter Scott, as a child. They "bring back my early scientific interest as to whether these Jurassic or Cretaceous creatures had sex in the usual way, were they viviparous or oviparous, I wonder". Restaurants exist so their patrons can satiate basic bodily needs and further their survival; an image of copulating extinct creatures is wryly contradictory. Also in the room, a woman, her body tied, is suspended above a dining table. In perfect black and white, it is unmistakably an Araki. It has BDSM undertones, but also highlights the satisfaction and sensuality of a body suspended, abstracted, hung. Not unlike what happens in the kitchen next door: preparing the meat for cooking, tying the legs of a bird to broil, stringing up a rump of beef for roasting. These are contortions of the body that usurp the usual way it is configured in a dining context – we eat meat, but we *are* meat. The artworks are visual and linguistic puns: in this "sex room" the Araki is placed opposite a Joana Vasconcelos crab covered in intricate Azores lacework. Araki had female models "queuing around the block" to be photographed by the artist, according to Braka, and Vasconcelos's crab also refers to restriction and bondage, albeit with hand-embroidered white silk threads. And for those diners not that way inclined, the Vasconcelos work can just appeal on a literal level, as Norfolk Cromer crab is offered on the menu.

Braka's taste in art is not without its detractors; local diners have formally complained to the police about offensive imagery. A lithograph series by Paula Rego depicts alcoholic mothers and their children. One image features a woman vomiting into a toilet, with a red colour and shape all around it, another shows a man and woman locked in a physical fight. The works issue a stark, moralistic warning about the hazards of addiction and abuse, but they are also comic and spicy, a reflection on the perils of drinking to lose inhibitions and moral behaviour. This is also a reference to Hogarth's *Gin Lane* infused with the Latin Catholic flair of Goya's cartoons. The lithographs were a response to a request from a wine producer for the artist to create labels for his bottles. Rego interpreted this as an invitation to comment on the plight of lonely mothers who turn to drink to alleviate isolation and boredom.

The Gunton Arms is Braka's grand statement of irreverence that has come to define him as an art dealer, a cultural figure and a restaurateur. He exclaims: "I don't want regulations, I want anarchy!" Gunton appeals to his fantasies of

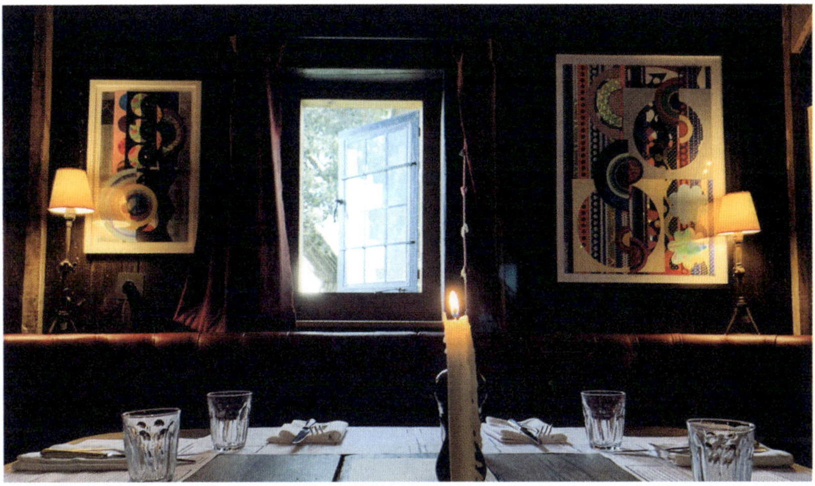

aristocratic, landed gentry escapism on an immediate level. Its aesthetic is charged with these caprices, from its dark oak wooden panels, the imposing fireplaces, its taxidermy crows and elks, and the historic furniture (including the 18th-century coffin stools used to rest a bier in a wake) to the sterling silver three-pronged cocktail forks and an antique riding crop he bought with Jerry Hall in a Soho sex shop. Braka respects the Gunton Arms's history as a royal hunting lodge. On another level, the restaurant refers to the tradition of the rural public house in Anglo-Saxon heritage, a venue for ordinary folk and locals to congregate, drink and be merry. Gunton Arms goes high, Gunton Arms goes low.

What binds both of these philosophies together, however, is the notion of the corporeal, which is communicated through the art collection. The pieces are sexual, sensual, animal. They are bawdy and lewd rather than just being controversial or offensive. They are comical too. This ties in with the dual purpose of the pub for Braka. Diners can visit Gunton and have a pale ale and steak, play billiards, watch football. They can also come to look at art by internationally renowned artists, and discuss Jim Crow laws and the place of Black rage in contemporary art. Ideally, they will do both.

The art collection is a mental map of the proprietor and snapshot of his motives for collecting, which ensure some of the global names in his collection, such as Tracey Emin and Paula Rego, are acquired and integrated as part of Braka's thesis on Gunton as a haven for the quirky and the irreverent. The wordplay and verbal puns fit a restaurant which serves sturdy, meat-based dishes. The menu was created by Mark Hix, and blessed by him lending Stuart Tattersall, the longest-standing chef of his restaurant empire, to Gunton, which became a permanent loan. This is English comfort food poked, prodded and swallowed in a mock-brothel setting. Braka's restaurant force-feeds a bourgeois dining sensibility into siding with the witty humour of the aristocratic classes or the drunken antics of the working classes. Meat is visceral and animalistic – this relates to the hunting lodge – while stags permanently traverse the grounds outside. And the pieces in the restaurant are in turn selected by Braka to acknowledge the fantasy world he creates, combining both high and low elements of culture and entertainment, but always with a sense of humour, never taking it too seriously, as the consummate provocateur. This carnivalesque irreverence of the ribald country pub is a traditional function of the place. Braka plays with the high and low history of the aristocratic hunting lodge, worthy of bedding the prince regent's mistress, and the local pub for the labouring classes to be badly behaved. He wants to maintain this "philosophical ruralism" in terms of combining two spheres of experience and be deliberately demotic in terms of bringing international contemporary art to the locals. "I wanted the contrast between the rather traditional room and the kitsch statue of a naïve boy with the riding crop, and then I have a real riding crop that I got from a fetish shop and placed it in the restaurant." It is a self-serving endeavour because it is a look into his "own mental landscape", but he is "introducing more challenging art than fishing boats or windmills... I am introducing them to international contemporary art. I enjoy having a response from a farmer or bricklayer who would not normally come in, and it's not shoved in their face, it's natural... what I am doing here is political."

Braka creates a willing suspension of disbelief, as Dr Johnson argued about Shakespeare's plays. This only works if "you use clever pastiche, otherwise you fuck the experience. You are drawing attention to the modernity of certain experiences. I want people to feel that even though it doesn't look exactly right, the experience is a continuity, a plausible alternative reality." If the diner trusts the experience, he subverts the orderly conduct of the restaurant. On one level it works, it serves, it is a country pub; on another level the art is having its own conversation and progression though literal wordplay, as with the Tracey Emin and Glenn Ligon neons. There is also much double-take visual play, such as the Jonathan Yeo images of autumn leaves that are actually made of cut-outs from pornographic magazines of vulvas and clitorises. The art collection – not just ornament or decor – should provoke thought, evoking baser emotions, be they of pain or pleasure. Diners need this playful disorientation and probing as much as they need refined and lofty resolutions and conclusions to formulate a sense of how taste works.

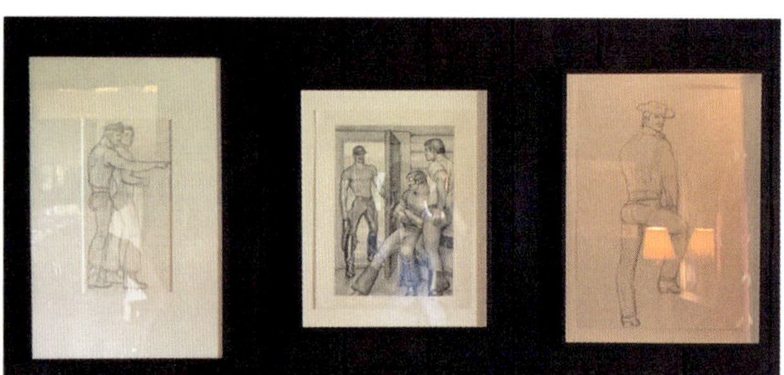

Works and artists in The Gunton Arms collection

—

A metal plaque by Jenny Holzer (*THE MOUTH IS INTERESTING BECAUSE IT IS ONE OF THOSE PLACES WHERE THE DRY OUTSIDE MOVES TOWARD THE SLIPPERY INSIDE.*) points out the intersection of the mucus membranes, such as the interior of the mouth, and the outside spaces. As is characteristic of her work, it is an officious looking sign, harsh and stern, but the content undermines the form by signalling to an internal, intimate place in the human body.

—

Tom of Finland is on display in an anterior dining room because Braka argues the artist Laaksonen is so often misunderstood as a pornographer, but in his view is an accomplished draughtsman of homoerotic desire. The contrast of the heft and strength of the visceral subject matter with the soft execution of the pencil is straightforward.

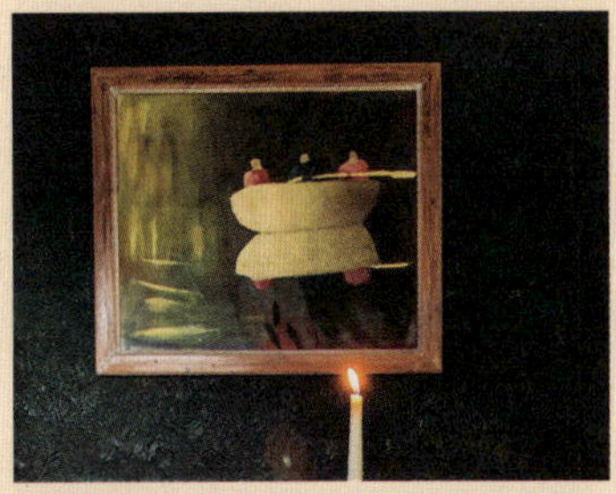

—

Other works that divide opinion include a Glenn Ligon sign, using neon, for Gertrude Stein's phrase, "Negro sunshine". Braka argues he wanted to display a provocative and subversive piece, as the artist is African American and homosexual, and takes polite dinner party conversation on to matters of race and identity, bringing them into the open. Underneath this is a painting by the artist, a reference to Warhol in composition and a joke from Richard Pryor, also controversial.

—

In the midst of the sex, emotion and contortion, Braka throws in a straightforward painterly work of local Norfolk artist Mary Newcomb, who he knew from Kalman and had seen in the dealer's home as a child. *Three Men in a Boat* is a simple, harmonious and peaceful way of being in the English countryside – a "more tea vicar" work in contrast to all the copulation and genitalia in the rest of the collection.

—

The art collection extends to the grounds outside, with several pieces of sculpture, including a Sol LeWitt ziggurat pyramid, an Anthony Caro sculpture of a red figure and an Antony Gormley figure in the field, minded by the deer that graze around it.

Nobuyoshi Araki's photograph of a woman tied up, over a dining table; Tracey Emin's neon light sculpture over a stained-glass door; works by Beatriz Milhazes; a series of Tom of Finland's erotic illustrations; *Three Men in a Boat* by Mary Newcomb

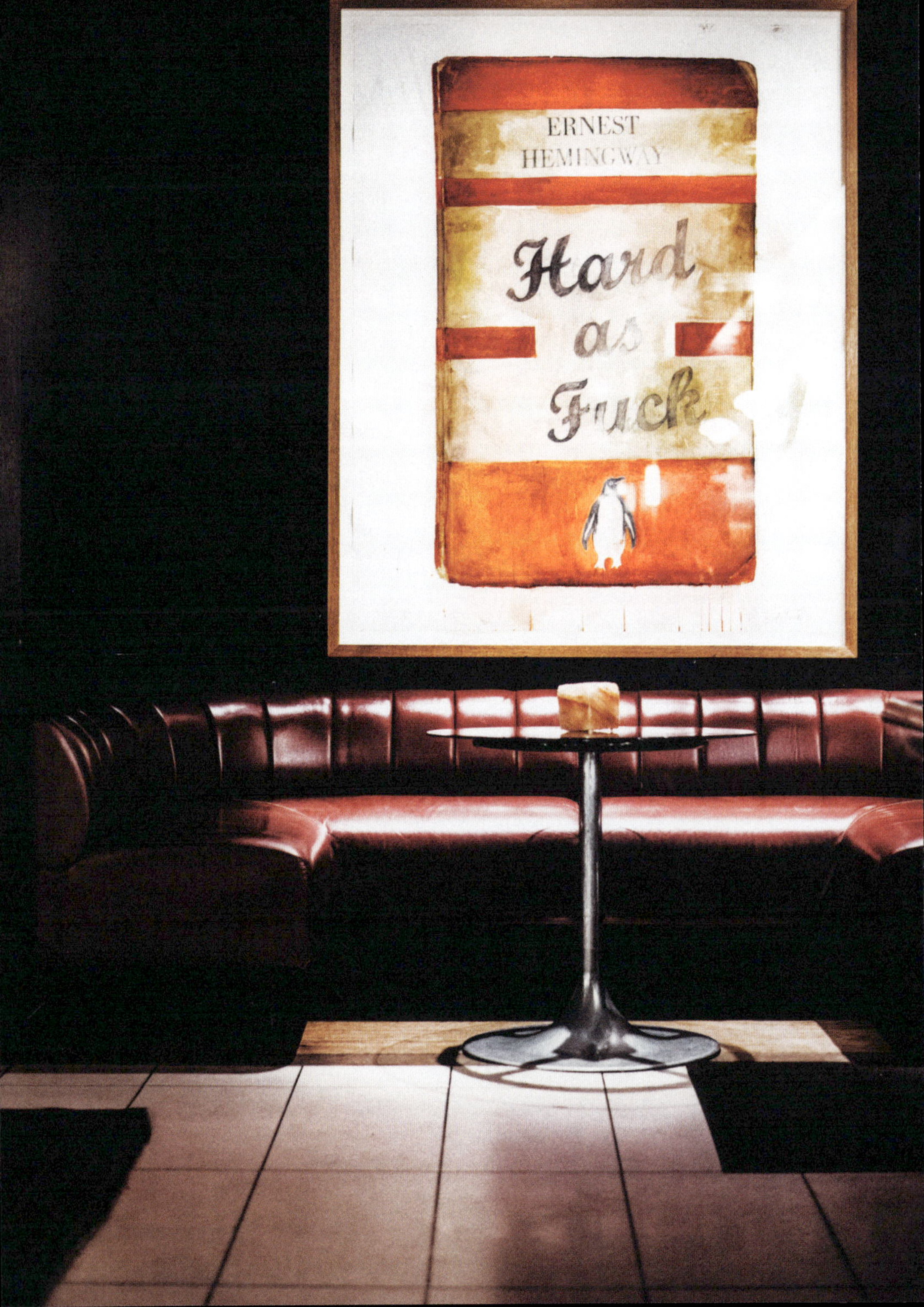
ERNEST
HEMINGWAY
Hard
as
Fuck

Hix

"If anything is good for pounding humility into you permanently, it's the restaurant business."
— Anthony Bourdain

If Tracey Emin can cook, legend has it that it's thanks to Mark Hix's tutelage: "I taught her, yes." Over the past two decades, Hix's reputation as a restaurateur in London, sourcing, preparing and serving classic, rustic British fare, became inextricably associated with collecting, commissioning and displaying British art. He was responsible for devising the most talked-about dining experiences in the capital in the noughties and 2010s. Hix invented modern nursery food, reheating simple British favourites, such as fish and chips and sausage and mash, and serving them back to the cool crowd at premium prices for their time. This suited his diners just fine, because they were the It-crowd of London's party scene: artists, journalists, musicians who grew up in the bleak and austere 1970s and 1980s, and had now made it, wanted to flaunt it, but never, ever took it too seriously. His patrons grew up scoffing fish fingers in their council homes, then, many years and successes later, grazed on their equivalents with champagne and cocaine in Soho. The chef's iconic historic restaurants such as the Rivington Grill (2006) in Hoxton and the Oyster & Chop House (2008) in Farringdon ostensibly served as the Young British Artist generation's canteens, as a result of Hix's close friendships with, and support of, significant artists, including Michael Landy, Tim Noble and Sue Webster, Mat Collishaw and Sarah Lucas, from their early days on London's art scene of the 1990s. Hix became a permanent fixture on the city's dining and gallery circuit. His bonhomie and barfly personality complemented the way he approached his art collecting. His affable hospitality welcomed the nouveau art world into his restaurants and he set the stage for many parties, dinners and events that are just as much a part of this generation's mythology as the works of carcasses, cigarettes, genitals and linguistic puns.

Even if his portfolio of restaurants – HIX Soho (2009), Hixter Bankside (2017) and the Chop House – were early victims of the coronavirus global pandemic in April 2020, Mark Hix as an art collector, chef and entrepreneur nevertheless takes his place in the lineage of restaurateurs concerned with the design of their interiors, such as Maxime Gaillard of Maxim's, Paul Roux of Le Gavroche, Lionel Poilâne and his French bakery, Peter Langan of Langan's Brasserie and Chris Corbin and Jeremy King of the Caprice Group. For this reason, Hix is the most postmodern art restaurant chef. His establishments have all been amalgamations of a century of the art restaurant tradition and its various models: he reinterpreted the French tradition of trading food for art; he worked in Le Caprice under Corbin and King, who operated a similar *modus operandi* (Corbin having been head waiter at Langan's and picked it up from Peter Langan); he is a peer of now globally recognised British artists who adore him; and he supports younger, emerging artists through prize-giving and collecting. The chef has had ample examples from other art restaurants to select and assemble what would work in his own endeavours. He understands his place in this history as a restaurateur who is a patron of the arts too, commissioning work, granting tabs for artists to eat down, inviting artists, gallerists and their collectors to parties following exhibition openings – all contributions to an important ritual for artists in their career progression.

Displaying art in the dining space has always been intentional for Hix, as he tells a story of how early on in his career he met Poilâne, who invited him into a back room of his famed Saint-Germain-des-Prés Left Bank bakery to show him walls completely covered with artists' drawings and sketches of bread and other foodstuffs that were exchanged for loaves of bread through the years. This piqued Hix's interest in testing the exchange system in London. At the time he was chef director of Caprice Holdings, specifically Scott's and The Ivy, where he learned from seasoned restaurateurs King and Corbin how art collections could transform formal humdrum restaurants into something more elevated and discerning, and instil a sense of occasion. The pair knew artists including Howard Hodgkin and Peter Blake, and commissioned them to create pieces for their venues. What they did "with the older generation", Hix did "with the next generation". He became so close to these artists that when he left Scott's to set up his eponymous Chop House in Farringdon, some of them, such as Michael Landy and Gary Hume, offered to remove their pieces and follow him in solidarity. He declined the offer, opting to strike out and create the art restaurant project afresh.

His first establishment in Clerkenwell capitalised on the energy and possibility of Cool Britannia East London. The food was proudly British, based on red meat and shellfish, all locally sourced, as was the art – products of London's finest art schools and courses such as Goldsmiths, the RCA, the Slade. This mixture stood him in good stead to befriend artists that became strictly and loosely associated with the YBAs, and Hix became part of the scene. "One party leads to another, and you end up feeding them all and it becomes a bit like a club, which occasionally spirals out of control," he recalls. This means absinthe jelly parties, tumbling out of doorways, endless champagne and lager, passing out on the streets in the East End.

Hix has collected art from his early career and has always enjoyed the "unknowns and knowns" – the artists who make it and those who don't. He also

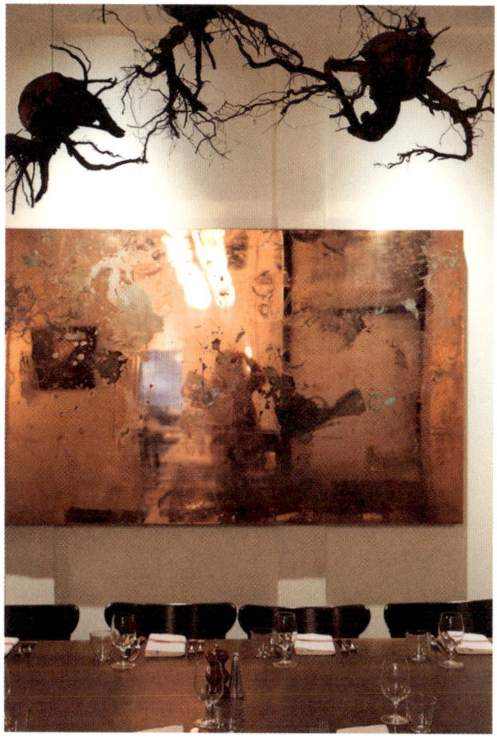

collected vintage cooking paraphernalia, furniture and old cookbooks. Living in the East End of London in the 1990s meant he was in the right place to benefit from the gentrification of the area and the relocation of galleries such as White Cube: "I remember when I used to sit at the bar at Rivington alone – a bit like a *Cheers* bar – and phone my mates to come around. Back then in Shoreditch, it's where artists hung out and lived." He began hosting gallery dinners at his restaurant after exhibition openings and offered meals to artists in exchange for artworks. The East End had an energy for radical art and artists. He recalls: "Even the bigger artists would go to the smaller, emerging galleries and support the projects. There was a divide then when West End gallerists wore suits and East End gallerists like Stuart Shave were grungy, underground. But during Frieze Week, they would go to the East End to galleries like Maureen Paley, but of course the [car] engine would still be running outside so they could escape back to the West End at any given moment."

The chef collaborated with Damien Hirst in 1998 to open the Pharmacy in Notting Hill. The artist designed the interior and offered works from his *Molecular*

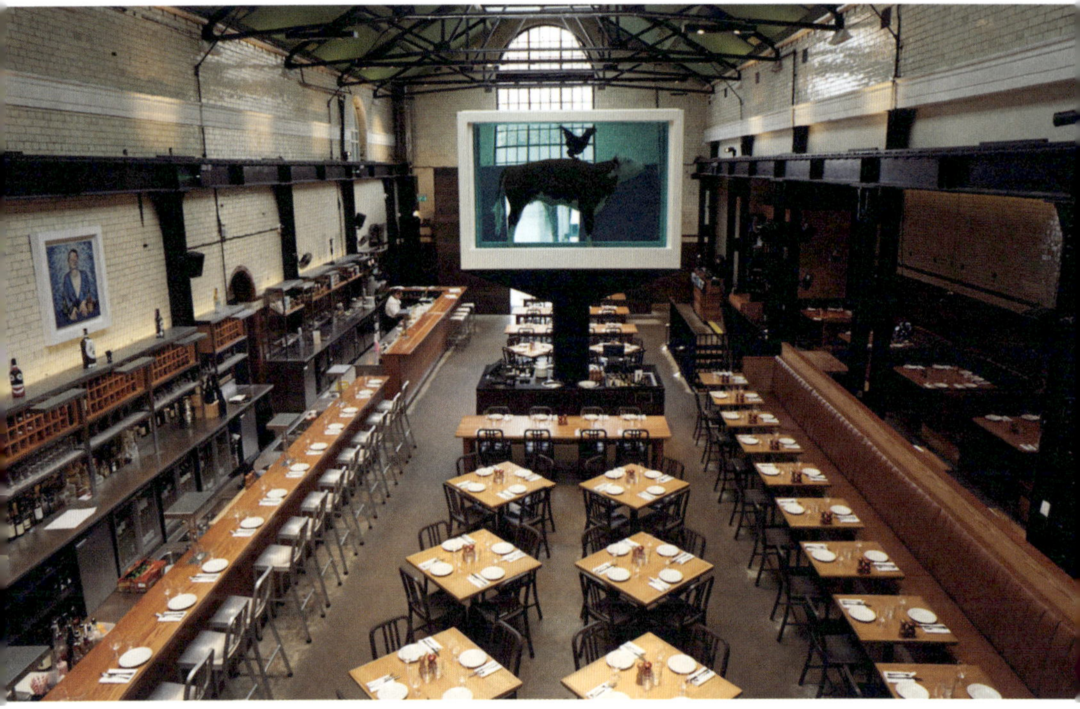

Structure series of 1997-98, which resembled an exact pharmacy interior with boxes of pills and other medicines. This was so lifelike, the Royal Pharmaceutical Society warned the owners the displays risked misleading visitors. The restaurant, although equally popular with the creative set and the West End yuppies in its five years of operation, closed in 2003. Most of the contents, including the fixtures, the furniture and crockery, were auctioned at Sotheby's, netting the artist £11m. Hirst, whose artistic practice ranges from found objects to high and low culture, to commodification and ultimately British art history, used a restaurant as a canvas in the development of his aesthetics.

After Notting Hill, Hix had his sights set on Soho, where he established the bijoux HIX, moving on to more projects such as Hixter Bankside. He treated his restaurants like he treats his recipes – experimenting with different ways to prepare the same main ingredient. A topside of beef can be grilled, stewed, roasted. His venues catered to artists, bankers and tourists. He is energetic, optimistic and "irrepressible", as artist Polly Morgan says, trying different combinations of what works in a restaurant: location, be it the South Bank or Farringdon; food, from meat to fish; and style, from the Tramshed warehouse to cosy Rivington candles and intrigue. If they don't work or taste right, he discards them and starts again. So far, he has set up more than 12 restaurants throughout his career. The two constants are good meat and good art. Food and art are connected, but not just in terms of what's on the plate: "I remember many years ago doing a talk with Bridget Riley and Michael Craig-Martin, who likened his work to how I cook. I have a hard and fast rule that there should be no more than three ingredients on the plate. And if you look at Michael's work, there are never more than three colours. Bridget Riley is a bit like that too." There is a totality of what the restaurant experience is in terms of aesthetic taste and unity, and there is a methodology to it. It is about "*How* you involve the artists, *how* you include art in the look and feel of the restaurant. What an artist's idea of art in a restaurant is, for example." When Hix speaks about the link between food and art, the terminology is natural, obvious and automatic – there is no hyperbole, no tenuous connections. It's as if the space of dining and the space of experiencing art are one continuum, because the pleasure for the diner is the same. "The way I've done restaurants over the years has been through collaborations and exchanges – it's a nice way to do it. I've not had to work too hard on it: it fits in with the day-to-day stuff, and it makes the whole thing a bit more interesting."

Every piece of art featured in his restaurants has a story, an anecdote, or a history behind its creation and inclusion in his collection. The works are daring reminders of the entrepreneurialism and shock factor of the YBA. However, this is offset by the comfort of Hix's cuisine. The food neutralises the artwork, but paradoxically the straightforward cuisine Hix has promoted through the years was shocking in its simplicity compared with what was fashionable in London's restaurants – fusion and fussy dishes. The work collected and displayed is as disparate, as open to formats and materials, as the YBA movement's ethos was. There are found objects, sculptures, photographs, paintings and installations. The subject matter ranges from animalistic and satiety – echoing sex and eating – to nostalgic: immaterial memories of time and place. Eating food is a memory-making cultural activity, and, for Hix, it contributes to the art history-making of the YBA artists. Dining surrounded by British contemporary art provides an alternative to the white cube space and, as the chef maintains, it becomes more accessible for visitors to experience art that can seem out of reach or esoteric due to its aesthetic challenges.

HIX Soho was inspired by the Colombe d'Or because the chef saw the Alexander Calder mobile in the pool area of the inn on a visit. Furthermore, because the Soho venue had minimal wall space, Hix decided to use the ceilings to display art. So in the main restaurant space, an array of tin cans, stuffed animals, plastic fish and mock biscuits dangled over the heads of diners. He asked each of his artist friends to make a mobile: "Some of them had never made a mobile in their life, as was blatantly obvious. A couple were static and fixed to the ceiling – a static mobile!" Each had a brief to interpret the mobile form. "So then other artists, like Antony Gormley, asked to make one. Then Michael Craig-Martin did one of his little pills works. They all found out their contemporaries were making mobiles and wanted to join in. I don't think there's been a mobile art project in a restaurant since the Colombe d'Or." Shezad Dawood offered a stuffed flamingo suspended in mid-flight through a neon circle, preserving the bird's pink elegance in electrified perpetuity. Sarah Lucas's *Pies Mobile* floated tinned pies – a piece of London post-war history, executed with wry nostalgia. Damien Hirst contributed by reducing his signature animals-in-formaldehyde into hanging goldfish preserved in small Perspex boxes. There were other artistic details in the restaurant, for example, Angus Fairhurst's wallpaper (*Underdone/Overdone*), to lose its diners in abstracted forest scenes.

The need to display art in a restaurant is demotic, as Hix believes that arguably more people are exposed to art in restaurants than galleries. In terms of the connection between art and food, patrons and art connoisseurs constantly "want to be stimulated" and thus the juxtaposition of the two enables this. Also, "You don't have to like the whole menu to enjoy one dish. I like art that I like, it doesn't have to be part of a larger thing." An understatement from a collector whose collection and actions have functioned like a shadow gallery system for the past decade. He encouraged new audiences not to be self-conscious about being in a white cube gallery environment. He wanted his diners to look at the art with a beer in hand, nibbling on pork scratchings.

All of the pieces in his restaurants have been site specific and created with each venue's location and identity in mind. When he opened the Tramshed in Shoreditch, he transformed a grade II-listed building designed in 1905 by the public space architect, Vincent Harris, to generate electricity for trams. High above the fast, buzzing atmosphere, the spacious interior was dominated by Damien Hirst's commissioned piece, *Cock and Bull*, on a plinth. It is one of the artist's *Natural History* series, a whole Hereford cow, symmetrically sliced in half, with a cockerel standing erect above it, all perfectly preserved, laboratory-like, in formaldehyde. On the one hand it served as a silent ironic spectre, on the other, it was a summary of the menu. The Tramshed combined the casual eating style of Hix venues with a library displaying the chef's personal collection of cookbooks and the HIX ART space in the basement housing regularly changing exhibitions of both emerging and established artists: Tim Noble and Sue Webster's anatomical photographs, or Sarah Lucas's chicken photographs, which formed the staff uniforms.

In 2014 Hix and Hirst partnered again to create Pharmacy 2 in the artist's Newport Street Gallery. The restaurant was effectively a continuation of the

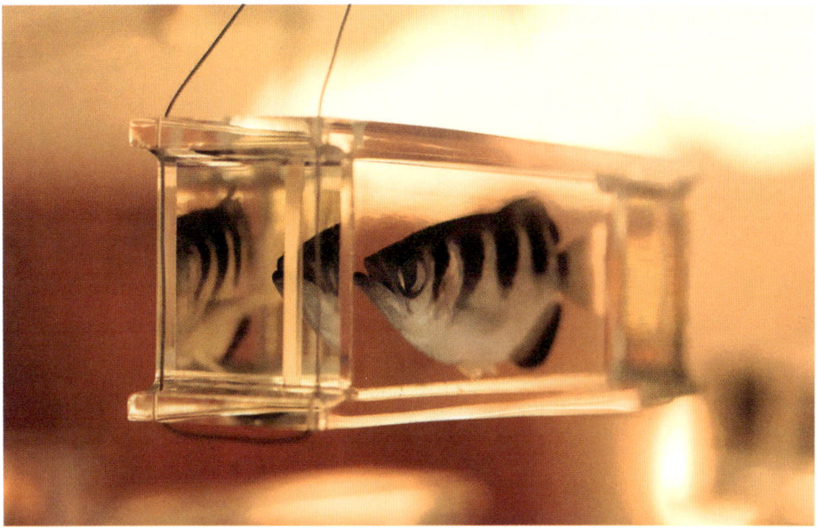

art gallery below, allowing diners to eat in an installation setting. It referenced Hirst's *Medicine Cabinets* and *Butterflies* series of the early 1990s, featuring kaleidoscopic butterfly pieces, medicine cabinets, pill displays, and surgical detritus and wastage in display cabinets. The artist-designed round lozenge-themed bar stools ensured diners were exposed at every angle to something medical and invited to self-medicate through food, drink and art.

Hix's approach to collecting art was based on "friendship and enjoyment of life" – friendships evident in works from Antony Gormley, Harland Miller, Michael Landy and Polly Morgan. The restaurants and their cuisine have been ironic, like the more than 300 YBA works he has collected for decades – constantly acquiring, never selling. Tongue-in-cheek and irreverent on the surface but concerned with humanity and emotional truths when you scratch below it.

In contemporary food culture, celebrity chefs became a fixture in the media. They were usually men, taking cooking out of the realm of women and the household. They propelled the profession of the chef out of the margins and into a phenomenon that made a great impact on people's everyday lives. Over the past 20 years, Hix became this type of chef, writing cookbooks, speaking in the press, appearing on television – however, he is the only celebrity chef that used the art restaurant to attain this status.

Hard as Fuck by Harland Miller; a dining table at Hix; Damien Hirst's *Cock and Bull* commissioned for The Tramshed; a fish preserved in formaldehyde solution by Damient Hirst

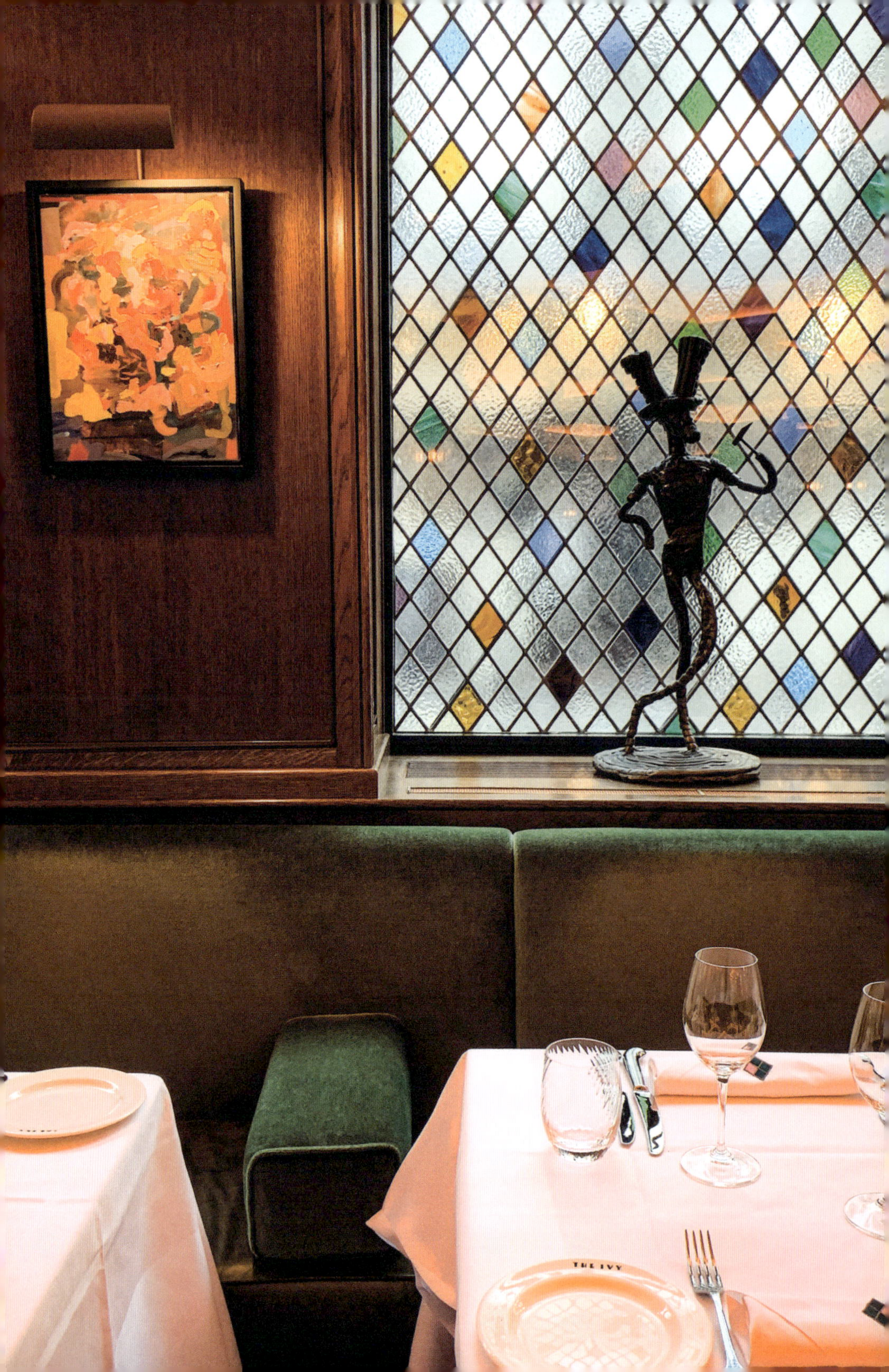
THE IVY

The Ivy

"The theatre is a wonderful place, a house of strange enchantment, a temple of illusion."
— Noël Coward

The Ivy in London's West End combines all the ingredients of a successful, enduring "It-restaurant": the hospitality and vision of Italian immigrants, a location in the centre of the metropolis, a gregarious and loyal clientele, and staff devoted to maintaining an atmosphere of spectacle and celebration. This recipe has worked for over a century, and just as much as The Ivy is a physical space, filled with devotees who revere the restaurant and its endless cavorting and joviality, they also ensure it is preserved as a state of mind. All of its patrons – no matter what field or background they have been drawn from – have played their part in creating and sustaining its magic and glamour. And, in exchange, The Ivy, physically and in abstract, has sustained their personas by holding up a mirror to London's high society, business figures, artists and other creatives, celebrities from A-to-Z lists, and all of their fans and wannabes. The Ivy as an art restaurant reflects changing fashions, economics, politics, cliques and shifts in cultural significance. Its location off Cambridge Circus, in the heart of London's Theatreland, its triangular space and its history of being a storage area for theatrical sets, costumes and props gives it a backstage feel, extending the theatre of reality. A subtle triangulation between the theatre, art and social class is ritually and continually enacted inside The Ivy. In recent decades, it also became an artists' restaurant, with the same artists hanging on its walls regularly frequenting the restaurant and very often dining under their own works. For British artist Michael Craig-Martin, the art collection "adds a level of indication that you are in a glamorous place" and that diners sit on the same social level as artists and other creative figures drawn from the literary and theatrical as well as visual arts. A stage is an organising device and conducts behaviours and the sensorial in its own way, and at The Ivy, this is enhanced by the display of its art collection as diners are drawn to behaving differently in the presence of artworks and amidst a creative community.

In 1917, decades before paparazzi tip-offs and photographers' flashing bulbs, the restaurant began trading as a modest café, with wobbly linoleum floors, wood panelled walls and cheap paper napkins. It was overseen by a Lombardian émigré, Abel Giandolini. The wedge-shaped space, on the corner of West and Litchfield Streets, surrounded by some of London's best theatres, quickly became popular with theatregoers and staff alike. It remained open until 1am, and attracted actors, musicians, playwrights and audience members nightly after productions

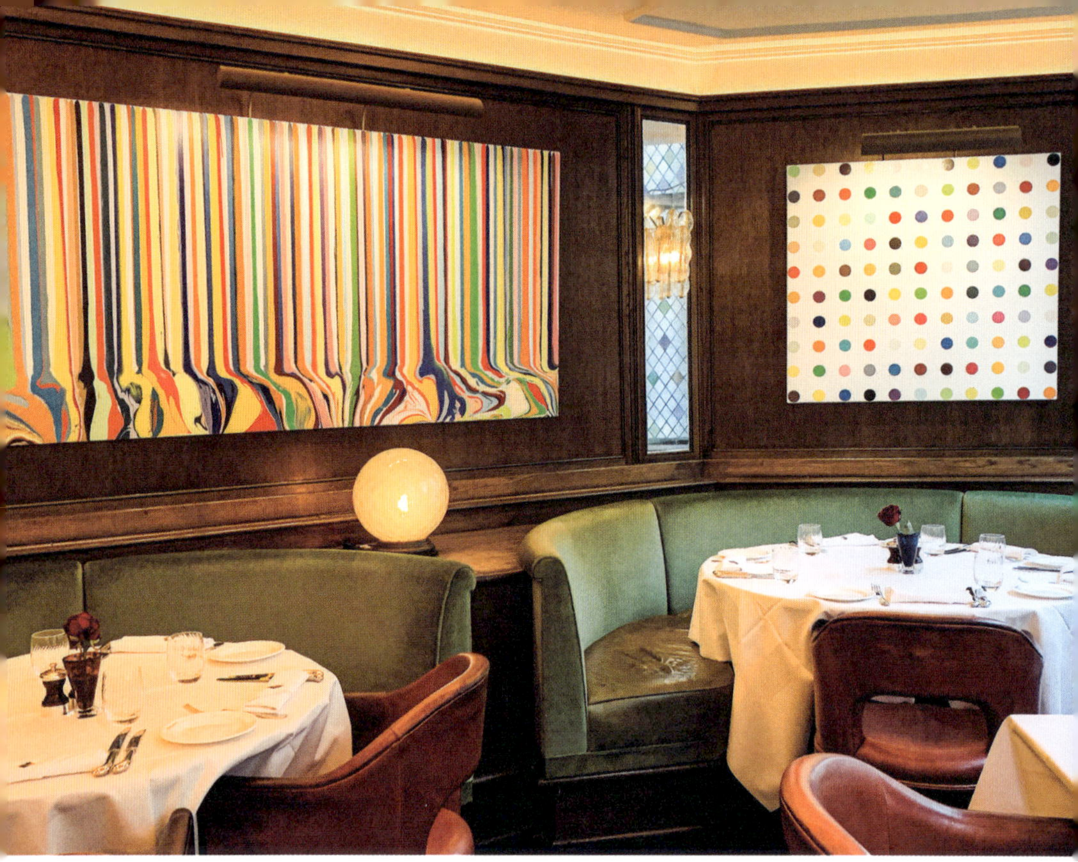

and shows. In what has now become restaurant lore, it was christened by the starlet Alice Delysia, quoting a line from a musical, "we will cling together like the ivy", and swearing her allegiance as a lifelong devoted diner. Giandolini gradually added the requisite touches to transform the once functional café into a refined space: a French chef, an Italian wine cellar, Irish linen napkins and an alcohol licence – the last petitioned for by patron Winston Churchill.

Successful restaurants revolve around personalities who operate and develop them to suit their vision of generosity and hospitality. In the early period of its history, The Ivy had Mario Gallati, its legendary maître d', who understood the need to enhance the feeling of conviviality to attract and retain the right clientele. Soon enough, the restaurant drew in patrons from creative and political circles. Waiters would deliver meals to actors' and actresses' dressing rooms for interval breaks, and cultural figures including critics and journalists began to visit in between shows. John Betjeman, the poet and TV personality of today, was a frequent patron, as well as Edward Sackville-West, David Cecil, Cyril Connolly and Raymond Mortimer. They were young and intellectual, but they were "not-so-angry", Gallati wrote in his autobiography of 1960. The Ivy became a place for beautiful, glamorous and creative people to cavort and play in, generating much gossip, which is an accompaniment or side dish at The Ivy to this day. Gordon Selfridge would use the restaurant to seduce showgirls and Edwardian It-girls. He regularly dined at The Ivy for oysters, champagne and romance, and would waver between behaving like "a gauche schoolboy" or "pathetic old man", depending on luck and outcome with the ladies. The staff would be there to discreetly note all of these episodes, but to keep pouring the wine. "So many distinguished people came to The Ivy during my 28 years there that I find it difficult to write about them all. Probably it would be easier to say that everybody who was anybody in London between the wars dined at the restaurant," wrote Gallati. He was instrumental in the social engineering of the restaurant space, ensuring the right – or often wrong – patrons sat next to each other, being discreet when necessary, and *outré* when not. This was continued by Fernando Peire in contemporary times, who began as a maître d' and is now on the board of Caprice Holdings, and is the custodian of the restaurant and its culture.

From 1950 onwards, The Ivy dawdled along, falling into the hands of other owners, among them the Wheeler family of fishmonger fame, who then lost the restaurant in a card game. The Ivy was saved by restaurateur luminaries Jeremy King and Chris Corbin, who acquired it in 1990 and wanted to preserve The Ivy's history and heritage for contemporary times. Jeremy King ran Joe Allen's, a casual American grill and haunt for the auxiliary and technical workers of theatre productions, as well as a plethora of showgirls. Chris Corbin had been head waiter in Peter Langan's eponymous eatery. They had collaborated on restaurants in the past by creating Le Caprice in 1981, with the fashion designer Joseph Ettedgui also investing in their vision of hospitality and business nous. The combined histories and business experiences of Corbin and King infused The Ivy with the lineage and spirit of their previous establishments, but by the late 1990s also forged a new interpretation of the celebrity restaurant in the era of New Labour and Cool Britannia. According to Michael Craig-Martin, The Ivy and what it set out to achieve in terms of new forms of pleasure and entertainment was part of the shift away from "a deep Puritanism in Britain". In 1990s London, "there was a sense of overcoming certain reservations on how to behave, eat, live, a feeling that it was all right to eat and live voluptuously".

Art was essential to this project. Corbin and King asked architect MJ Long to design the interior space – a recommendation from Peter Blake, whose studio she designed. Long, who later went on to design the British Library and the Keeper's House at the Royal Academy, specialised in creating purpose-built studio spaces for artists including Blake, Frank Auerbach and RB Kitaj. Corbin had seen the value of placing art in restaurants from Peter Langan in terms of signalling an atmosphere to artists and celebrities, and he and King commissioned renowned British artists to make works for The Ivy, including Peter Blake, Howard Hodgkin, Bridget Riley, Allen Jones, Joe Tilson, Patrick Caulfield and

Michael Craig-Martin. They offered an eating down model, and this credit helped to attract more artists and create the scene around The Ivy. Artist Liz Rideal believes it "was certainly unusual to have an art collection hanging in a British restaurant when Jeremy King and Chris Corbin put theirs together". The initial group of artists, celebrities in their own right and appropriate for a restaurant that purveyed the best of British in terms of cuisine and patrons, became part of the nightly celebrations, not just because they had tabs there, but because they were on a par with the other diners.

British artist Bill Jacklin's large mural, *A Night at The Ivy*, captures this time and hangs in the private dining room. It depicts a scene with Allen Jones's work in the background and a number of the artist's friends, his dealer Pierre Levai, the photographer Abe Frajndlich, Jeremy King and Jesus Adorno, the waiter, who later became a director of Caprice Holdings (he left in late 2020). Jacklin explains: "Everybody that knows my work from New York or London knows that I like to paint people in places, in situ, especially collections of people doing one activity. I like collectives of motley groups." He made the piece from sketches in the restaurant, visiting every night and drawing people directly as they ate and drank or sometimes through the reflection in the mirrors, thereby introducing a reminder of the optical self-reflexivity that is part of the restaurant experience to his artistic practice.

When the entrepreneur Richard Caring took over the restaurant in 2013, he auctioned off half of the art collection to support a London homelessness charity. He then commissioned what he believed were the updated, new generation of artists that signalled contemporary success and at times even the excess that accompanies *having made it*. Artists including Marc Quinn, Tracey Emin and Damien Hirst made works in exchange for a tab. The collection lost a Bridget Riley piece created in 1990 for a wall in between stained-glass windows and a Joe Tilson mural of vineyards with a "Dionysus" inscription, but gained an Ian Davenport line drawing and Hirst spot painting in their place. The restaurant offers an alternative context to appreciate the art. As Craig-Martin says: "I like the idea of people seeing art in a public place where they haven't made a special effort to see it. You go to a museum, you decide to go to a museum. I think it's nice to put art in a park, in a public space, or in a restaurant where people who would not normally seek that context find themselves in it." According to Maggi Hambling, this makes The Ivy art restaurant "a public collection", and from an artist's perspective, to "walk in and see one's painting hanging" is a joyous feeling because of the pleasure it gives other diners. "I like the unexpected setting of a restaurant for art. You go to The Ivy to eat, so the art is a surprise. And if you're sitting beside great art, eating great food and drinking great wine, it is a voluptuous experience, [essential] for a great evening."

Several of the original works, such as Peter Blake's, remain. His monochrome montage pays homage to many of The Ivy's past patrons, including Vivien Leigh, Giacomo Puccini and Noël Coward. It is also a tribute to 1980s date nights and the magic of dining with a lover. According to Blake, it contains "a little shelf in the front to place a red rose that you would give to your lady as you went to dinner and a box of Black Magic chocolates, which you would also give to her, and a bottle of wine called Olivieri". Olivieri was one of the early Chiantis introduced to Britain in the 1980s, which matured and shed its wicker sleeve to become the preferred choice for London's top wine lists at the time, while Black Magic chocolates were marketed as sexy and seductive, with the whispered strapline: "Who knows the secret of the Black Magic box?" Blake also made a series of three Marilyn Monroe works mixing photographs of the starlet at the top and postcards at the bottom with diagonal blocks of red, yellow, blue and green colour combinations. His Pop Art, executed with exquisite, tender care, is at home in The Ivy because it serves both celebrities and their fans and acolytes the same fare, and the same promise that their particular dining experience will be special and extraordinary – even if it is replicated and consumed again and again. The artist still visits the restaurant with his wife Chrissy to this day.

In this triangular space, all tables are equal in terms of single row placement, all focusing towards the bar area. If the restaurant is a stage, then it organises how images are projected and observed and how bodies behave. Within these private walls, without windows or light from the outside world, access is mediated through the multicoloured diamond-shaped stained-glass panels – art is the gateway. The external macrocosm of celebrities, politicians and journalists distils into its own microcosm of conviviality, celebration and pleasure,

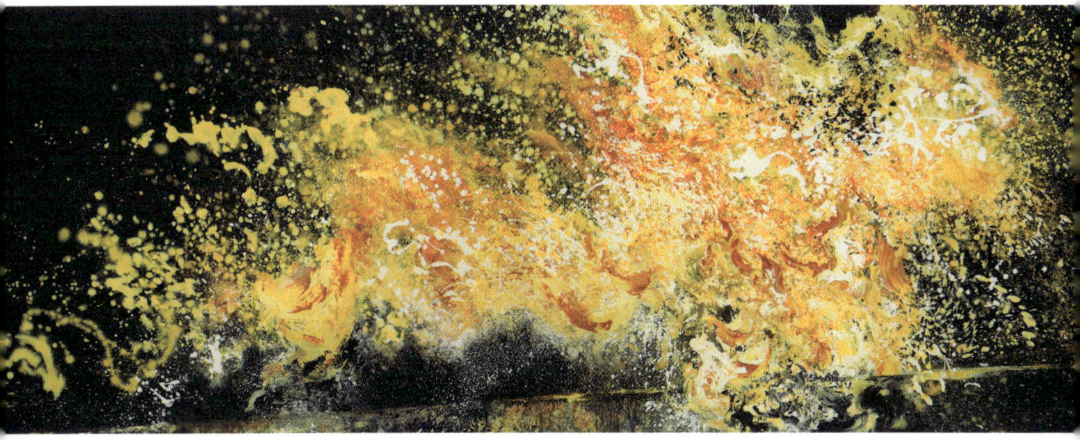

where politicians, businessmen, publicists, journalists, musicians, artists and actors all intermingle. The Ivy was never straightforwardly elitist; it upholds the bourgeois reality that anybody who can afford to eat here can come here – it combines high and low-rent clientele. A Hollywood actress or international pop star can sit next to a prosaic marriage proposal, a mundane family day out, an extravagant meal on business expenses. This is referenced in Tom Phillips's *The Professionals*, whose 10 panels depict artistic and literary figures, including T.S. Eliot, Franz Kafka and Henri Rousseau, who had day jobs – professions – but were also significant artists. Half of this is possibly true for today's business-lunch professional clientele. The work is an acknowledgement of, and welcome to, these diners, as The Ivy is a place that attracts people successful in one field but often very creative in another. According to Peire: "There are clubs in London where they don't like certain types of professions, but for us, if you are, say, a banker, and you like supporting media or arts through finance, then you are a creative type." All diners here are aspirational and performative, not just in the way that any guest performs the ritual of dining, but because they want to be a part of the creative class and come to The Ivy as a restaurant for artists, actors and creatives. If art is the theatre of the possible, in The Ivy, this performance becomes reality for its diners.

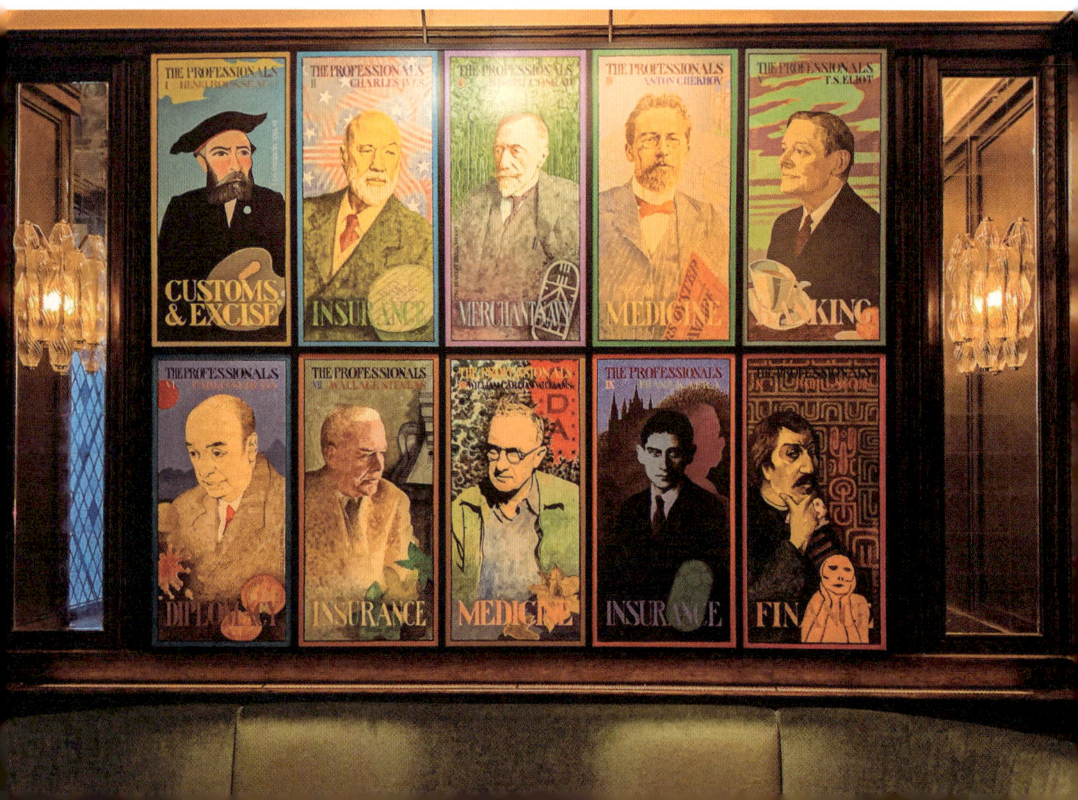

Works and artists in The Ivy collection

—

A rainbow spot painting by Damien Hirst hangs next to a Davenport of signature lines melting at the bottom of the canvas. The two attended Goldsmiths at the same time and shared a studio when they graduated. Now they share a wall in the restaurant. Hirst came in to dine one day and was seated under his painting, something he explicitly requested never to happen again due to his meal being interrupted by guests ogling him. He states: "I can't sit under my work. It's a bit like being at your own degree show and people walking by and looking at the work and looking at you."

—

Two Tracey Emin nudes hang behind the maître d's podium. The artist cut the composition and canvas in two to fit the wall. There is something reassuring and promising about the first work seen being a female nude and also the last work observed on the way home.

—

The entrance still contains Eduardo Paolozzi's tribute to an Art Nouveau brass staircase. He once said: "I like to make use of anything. I can't bear to throw things out, a bottle of wine, a nice box."

—

Maggi Hambling is the artist most associated with The Ivy today, as she is there on a regular basis – either visiting her friend George Melly, deceased but now in portrait form in the restaurant, or eating under her *Wall of Champagne*. She had been working on a *Wall of Water* series and adapted it to respond to the restaurant's invitation to make a work for its largest wall.

—

Barry Flanagan's anthropomorphic hare sculpture – part of the original Ivy collection – stands upright with human characteristics, a signature of many of the Welsh artist's works. The shape-shifting cast in bronze prevents it from being just a schmaltzy, dated work.

A harlequin stained-glass window and the sculpture *Stage Door Johnny* by Barry Flanagan; Ian Davenport and Damien Hirst's pieces over the corner dining area of The Ivy; Maggi Hambling's *Wall of Champagne*; Tom Philips, *The Professionals*, 1990

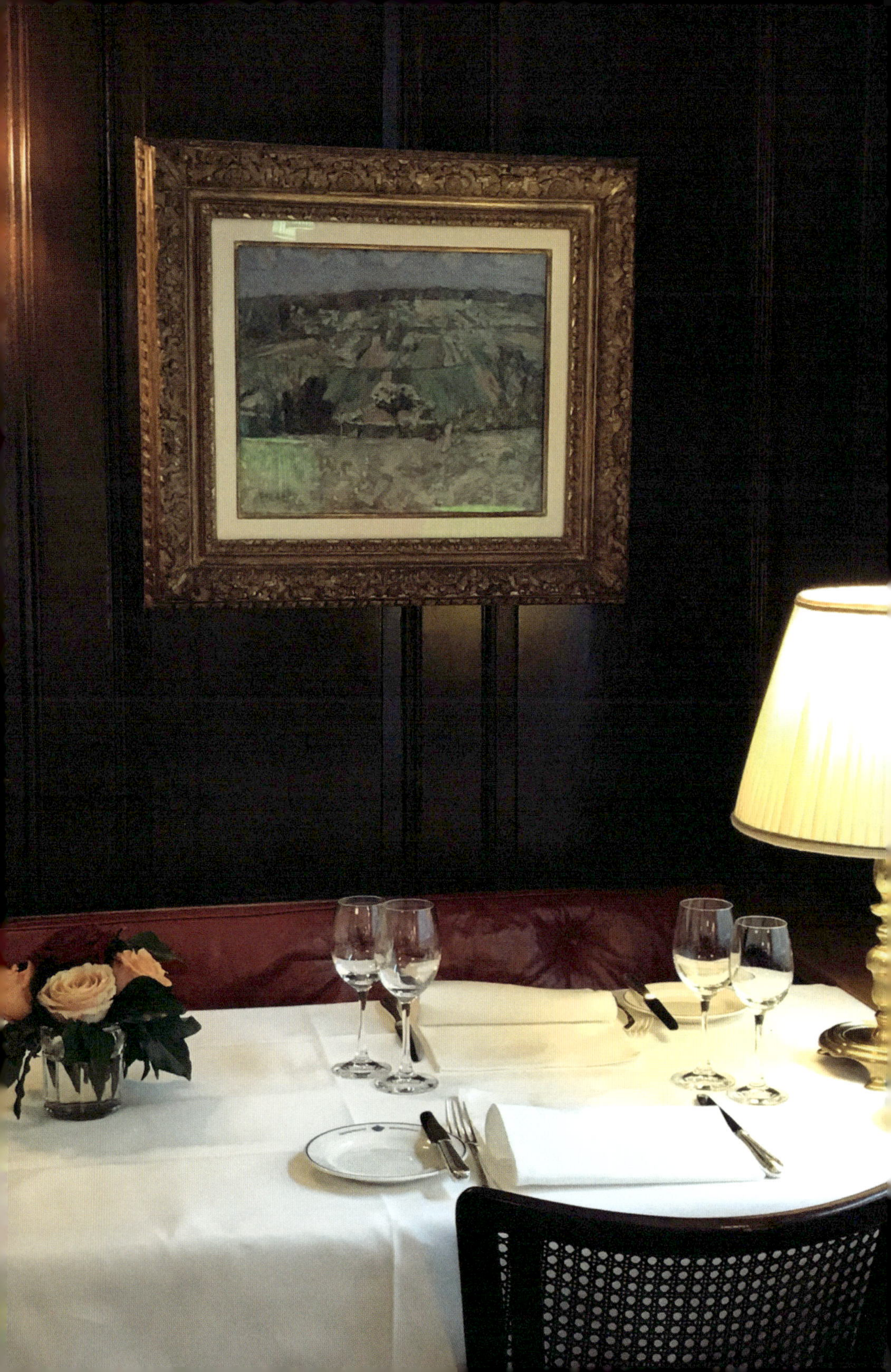

Kronenhalle

"Once I saw the village butcher slice the neck of a bird and drain the blood out of it. I wanted to cry out, but his joyful expression caught the sound in my throat. This cry, I always feel it there. When, as I drew a crude portrait of my professor, I tried to rid myself of this cry, but in vain. When I painted the beef carcass it was still this cry that I wanted to liberate. I have still not succeeded."
— Chaïm Soutine

The Kronenhalle has been serving its diners in the same quietly refined manner for almost a century. Based on an average of 195 covers over the day for lunch and dinner, that is an estimate of 13,628,160 guests during its 98 years of hospitality. If repetition creates dining ritual, these rites at the Kronenhalle are impervious. In the vacillating and temperamental restaurant industry, it is a great achievement for an establishment not to alter a single detail in all its years of operation. Even when it underwent a full refurbishment in 1981, it was updated with exactly the same materials, fixtures and interior layout to look identical to its previous state. Such exactitude feels postmodern for a classic restaurant. The Kronenhalle is a *gesamtkunstwerk* of an art restaurant, a Valhalla of an art restaurant, combining all the required ingredients: art-collecting proprietors, eating down exchanges, renowned artist patrons, preservation of dining traditions and diners who come to participate in this ritual. Even when only one or two of these ingredients are present in other art restaurants, it can lead to an aesthetic dining experience, but at the Kronenhalle they carouse and whirl at once. It is no wonder it is consistently cited as the inspiration for other art restaurateurs – Michael Chow believes it is "the most perfect restaurant in the world". The Kronenhalle's owners, its staff, its patrons, and even its artistic community contribute to the preservation of its status as the consummate art restaurant.

The Kronenhalle occupies an elegant Biedermeier building on Rämistrasse 4 in central Zurich. The space is divided into three dining rooms, with an adjacent bijoux bar designed by famed Swiss architects Trix and Robert Haussmann. All are completely filled with art, ranging from museum-quality artists, such as Picasso and Chagall, in the main rooms, to lesser-known local practitioners that hang in the Swiss Room upstairs, including Marino Marini and Germaine Richter, as well as works by Diego Giacometti. This Swiss Room is where "those who don't necessarily want to be seen – or seen together – dine", according to one of the managers. In normally reserved Zurich this is as appealing as the boisterous gregariousness of the main hall, which has the feel of a medieval tavern, albeit with pristine, starched tablecloths and delicate, blush Chasselas. For the Fluxus artist John Armleder, the Kronenhalle is "a gallery and museum,

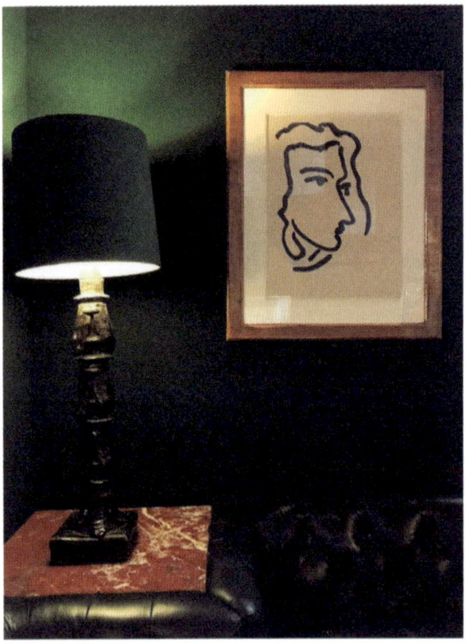

without the downsides of either, and has the food to boot". The artworks can be admired in a slower-paced, convivial environment, with the food and drink to assist the experience by engaging the full range of senses. Curator and native Zuricher Hans Ulrich Obrist says he has "a real relationship with some of the pieces in the Kronenhalle, because under some of them I have eaten 20, 30, 40 times". He estimates he may have spent 100 hours with the Miró: "But it's not about ownership, because of course you don't own the work. It's also not about visiting, it's more a sense of belonging." Everybody passing through the restaurant contributes to its greater whole and becomes part of the community, because admiring art always makes people think they have their own particular relationship with the works – which of course they do, on an immediate, experiential basis, but they are one of many in totality. This duality is part of what the Kronenhalle offers its patrons.

The kitchen of the Kronenhalle is just as much a museum of Swiss cuisine, as the walls are of 20th-century European art, given how little has changed. The menus are still offered without listed prices for the fairer sex, the *rösti* is presented with the precise level of flourish by two servers, the men wear monochrome uniforms and the women French maid half-aprons. The staff are militarily exacting: it takes them three years to train before they can work front of house, and then they often stay at the restaurant for their whole working lives. They are naturally attentive to the diner's needs, but also expect guests to fit into the historic dining rituals. This often-intimidating exactitude was not lost on the Modernist Swiss author and Kronenhalle regular, Friedrich Dürrenmatt, who wrote about how the composition of the hall had a daunting effect on his geeky Greek accountant in his 1955 novel *Grieche sucht Griechin* (*Greek Man Seeks Greek Woman*). Or more recently in Andrew O'Hagan's 2020 *Mayflies*, when his protagonists dine at the end of the story and encounter the waiters who seem "like they too had been painted in oils", the whole effect of "the restaurant of the 1920s" causing them to wonder "about the patrons who had come before us, those historic eaters of oysters and clear soup".

The space was originally the Hotel de la Couronne, built in the 1880s. Gottlieb Zumsteg turned the ground-floor stables into a basic tavern in 1921. The large dining room was designed in the style of a medieval beer hall with 14 heraldic coats of arms drawings representing each of the *zünfte*, the city's trade guilds, adorning the highest point of the walls. Zumsteg's wife, Madame Hulda, had an eye for aesthetics, adding fine-dining touches of heavy handicraft tablecloths, ornamented cutlery and all the finishes associated with respectable, bourgeois eateries. Hulda's commercial nous meant she understood what a captivating hold a location can have on desirable clientele. With her characteristic grandness, she welcomed diners from all levels of social strata, including Zurich's bohemians. Art restaurants today owe their existence to the restaurant ecumenicalism of then.

Zurich was a refuge for intellectuals and creatives from the First World War at the time and the Kronenhalle benefited from this intellectual migration to the city. James Joyce would write at Table 17, under the Bonnard drawing of a washerwoman, where he worked on parts of *Finnegans Wake*. Bertolt Brecht, Thomas Mann (who preferred the red room downstairs because it reputedly reminded him of a German luxury cruise ship) and Richard Strauss were all regular visitors. The Kronenhalle's interior was even recreated by the composer for a production of *Ariadne auf Naxos* in the neighbouring opera house, a stage setting which continued in productions on tour until recently, arguably an innovative way to franchise a restaurant.

Madame Hulda would serve *vorig vo de rüche*, reworked leftover morsels from wealthy patrons' dishes, and offer them to impecunious artists, intellectuals and students. Many gifted drawings and paintings in gratitude. She disapproved of how much the young men drank and would insist on filling them with meat soup to line their stomachs. Fortunately, "many of them grew up to become men of status and authority", she later recalled. Hulda also encouraged several artists to display their work on the walls of the restaurant as a way of exposing them to potential collectors and members of the art establishment from the museums such as the Kunsthaus and galleries in the vicinity. She was a natural landlady and patron, attaining mythical status, like Madame Roux at the Colombe d'Or or Muriel Belcher at The Colony Room. She took an interest in her guests' lives, regardless of their background or profession. Her staff called her "*Mutter*" and she created an environment that was a second home for them, as most stayed for decades. When Marc Chagall lived in Zurich in the 1960s to work on five stained-glass windows for the 9th-century Fraumünster Abbey, he would visit the Kronenhalle daily. He called Madame Zumsteg "*ma soeur*" and her son Gustav was "*mon fils spirituel*". The artist returned to the restaurant every year for Madame's birthday until he died, drawing greetings cards and personalised sketches for her, now part of the collection.

Today, Madame Zumsteg can be found in the main dining room hanging in the form of a portrait painted by Swiss artist Varlin. She peers through her monocle, regally posed in her sparkling jewellery and Balenciaga gown crafted in (naturally) Abraham thick black silk. She could equally be at home in the Tonhalle or Opernhaus Zürich, but instead oversees a different set of theatrical proceedings from the canvas. Upon entering the restaurant, diners must ascend the corridor towards the painting and suffer her gaze after verifying their table reservation with the maître d'.

Gustav Zumsteg took over the restaurant from his parents in 1957. He had a background in textile design and owned a factory, Abraham Silk, which supplied the prestigious fashion houses of the time: Yves Saint Laurent, Givenchy, Chanel and Dior. He built friendships with Cristóbal Balenciaga, Yves Saint Laurent and Pierre Bergé, the last of these escalating his interest in art collecting. As an aesthete and gourmand, he sought out pleasure and beauty, irrespective of art form. He saw natural connections between beautiful objects and environments, and richly decorated his living quarters. His personal collection had more than 100 pieces and when he took over the Kronenhalle, he transferred works to share with the public and to create more space at home for new acquisitions.

Gustav lived in Paris before the First World War, and met Picasso, Matisse and Chagall, among other artists. He also travelled to the South of France, where he picked up two more things that proved a lasting influence on the Kronenhalle: a love of Provençal cooking and a meeting with the gallerists Aimé and Marguerite Maeght, who were instrumental in introductions to artists and enhanced his collecting activities. The "Maeght Équipe" included the likes of Jean Tinguely, Juan Miró, Georges Braque and Chagall. He formed friendships with the artists, the evidence of which can be found in the large number of dedications on the works on the restaurant walls. His lifelong interest in design and links with artists, designers and art world professionals meant he was active in building his identity as a collector, bolstering his intellectual capital, expressed through the restaurant as a place to display his taste and a venue to attract individuals from the creative spheres.

For the Kronenhalle specifically, he commissioned Diego Giacometti to design the marble tables and brass lamps in the bar. The latter include whimsical owls, curved lines and bone-like chains for the chandeliers. The bar itself was redesigned in the mid-1960s by the Haussmanns to resemble a gothic science-fiction chamber of dark walnut furniture with green leather accents. It is heavy and monied, and naturally attracts financiers as well as creatives, while being another extension for the Kronenhalle as a platform for the art collection. For the main restaurant, Zumsteg asked Augusto Giacometti to create a stained-glass window, which is church window and abstraction of light and colour in equal parts. He also convinced Picasso to donate a self-portrait, *Painter at Work* (1965), depicting the artist deep in thought, focusing on his canvas and disregarding the viewers in the room.

Gustav would follow and buy from auctions in London, Paris and New York. In London, he purchased Chaïm Soutine's *Nature morte au canard* (1923), which still hangs in the main brasserie. It depicts a plate of agitated red tomatoes and a decapitated duck with urgent and aggressive execution. The plate tips precariously, as though the food will tumble forwards, probably onto a Zürcherin's silk blouse dining underneath. Soutine's fascination with the essence of food, both fleshy and ethereal, also suggests its ritualist aspect: how the everyday dish gains a religious status by elevating it out of its ordinary context. At times Zumsteg also became a benefactor of artists, not just collecting their work, but funding their development. *Large Letter Drawing from Jean Tinguely* (1990) is a receipt of this investment, a rainbow-coloured, multi-line composition moving in many directions with the following message: *Cher GUSTAVE: Merci pour MOCKBA Jevient a Zurich Mercedi Je telephonerai Avant Salutioan & a Bientot: Jean le 8.4.90* [original spelling]. Tinguely, famed for his large Meta Harmony works combining kinetics, machinery and art, had not been widely shown in his native Switzerland. As a board member of the Kunstfreunde in Zurich, Zumsteg influenced the acquisition of pieces through the foundation to place in Zurich and Geneva. He also personally funded Tinguely's solo exhibition in Moscow in 1990. Their friendship lasted until the artist's death in 1991, and a kinetic sculpture of Gustav now hangs in the Kunsthaus.

Zumsteg collected art that appealed to him, ranging from figurative paintings to pieces acquired from artist friends. His motivation was to share his taste with his diners: he called it "hospitality art". He was shy and retiring in person, but a confident, bold tastemaker through his art and running the Kronenhalle. He extended the reach of the restaurant by donating pieces to cultural institutions and auctioning off work that found new homes in museums. Matisse's *Still Life with Oysters* from 1940 swapped the dining hall wall for the gallery wall of Kunsthalle Basel. Zurich's Kunsthalle also benefited: a Braque still life from 1926 (*Plate with Fruit, Pitcher and Knife*), Matisse's *Branch of Ivy* from 1916 and Bonnard's *Landscape on a Sunset* from 1927 are displayed in the museum today. He once owned a Vuillard interior and sold it to the Musée d'Orsay, while Léger's *Nature morte à la chope* from 1921 was acquired by Tate, and is still in the institution's permanent collection today. Despite what he acquired and dispensed with during his lifetime, his final will explicitly forbade any selling of works, meaning the current interior arrangement and hang is exactly as it was during his time at the restaurant. And there is not a detail out of place in the Kronenhalle: once a year they take all the works down to deep clean the walls and everything goes back in the same place. Although there is one small Miró work on paper that is the fly in the ointment: the managing director explains how it was taken down for its first routine clean and when they tried to re-hang it, nobody could remember the right side – mother and son continuously disagreed on the orientation. Nobody knows to this day if its present hang is correct.

At the very least, Hulda and Gustav were agreed on the significance of the art to the restaurant and how inviting in the artistic community would contribute to the greater whole of the Kronenhalle as a place to experience art in a pleasurable environment with friends, with lovers, with family. They were aligned on making it "the world's most culinary museum". The Zumstegs were unorthodox collectors and restaurateurs in equal measure. Through their vision and lifelong purpose, the Kronenhalle also functioned as an alternative or shadow survey of Modernist European art, mirroring displays in cultural institutions. Hans Ulrich Obrist says encountering an artwork where you least expect it is a powerful thing, citing philosophical writer Robert Musil's statement: "If there is still art, it is where we expect it least." Art outside of the gallery "can have a transformative experience in a different way from the institution". Diners are transformed because the art in the Kronenhalle means the quotidian of dining becomes ritualistic and thus elevated. In this way, they join the ranks of those who came before them – from Madame Hulda, to Gustav, to the full hierarchy of the staff, to the artistic and intellectual patrons.

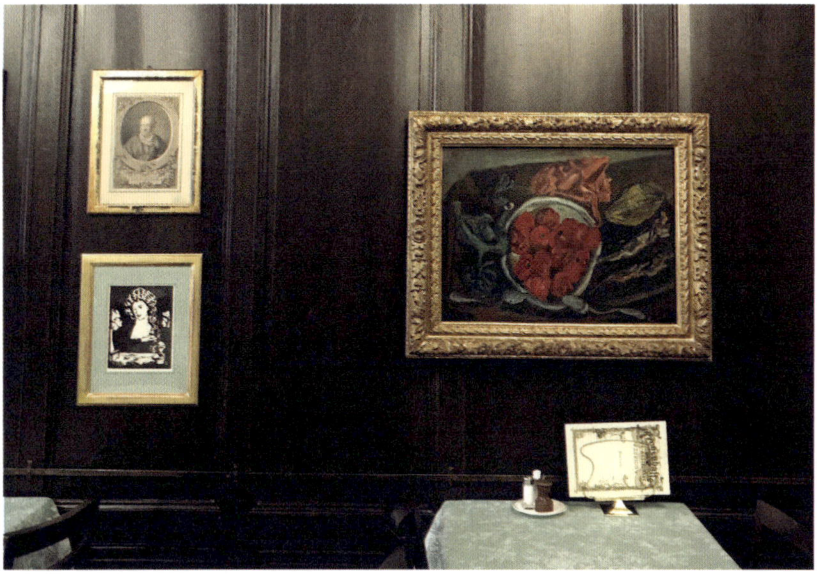

Works and artists in the Kronenhalle collection

—

The restaurant displays two Picasso works: a late head drawing from 1972 that hangs in the bar above a corner table, regular diner Fellini's favourite piece; and a large head drawn in chalk and ink.

—

Chagall's *la coucher du soleil*, executed in 1974, a work very different from the customary rabbis, goats and floating lovers that defined the artist's œuvre. A solitary figure stands on the margins in a sea of blue, with a red-orange sun half immersed in the blueness, a triangular shape of a sailboat, and green shapes for earth. For Chagall, this is a minimalist piece composed of just three bold colours (blue, red and green), while offering an expansive, meditative composition that teeters on the edge of abstraction but makes shorthand concessions to representation.

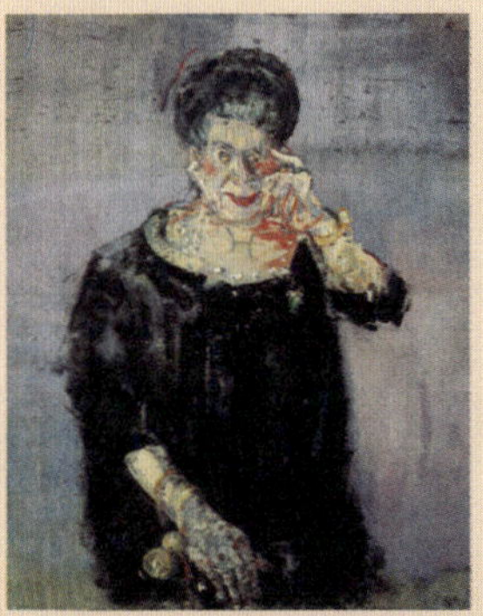

—

Miró's *Les éclats du soleil blessent l'étoile tardive* (1951), a jubilant piece that is a tribute to stars and nightlife.

—

Ferdinand Hodler, *Kirschbäume* (1901). The artist painted the same scene over and over again, because it was "enlarged, simplified nature". The flatness of the landscape contrasts with the busy method of execution and brushstrokes, reminding the viewer that even a seemingly straightforward scene contains complexities of the quotidian.

—

A Rodin watercolour nude of Isadora Duncan from 1918 in the Red Room, the most date-appropriate space in the restaurant, with *tables a deux*, velvet banquettes and soft lighting. The dancer is draped in a silk robe, open to reveal her elongated body.

—

Robert Rauschenberg's *Jungle Funnel (Borealis)* from 1989 is a green floral pattern overlay printed on silkscreen, which appealed to the silk-company owner in Zumsteg. The piece was created when the artist visited and lived in Zurich as part of his ROCI (Rauschenberg Overseas Cultural Initiative) exchange in the 1980s.

Landscape painting by Pierre Bonnard; Pablo Picasso's *Peintre au travail*; an ink work by Henri Matisse and a Diego Giacometti lamp; Soutine's still life over a dining table; a Picasso drawing in the bar; a portrait of Madame Zumsteg painted by Varlin (Willy Guggenheim)

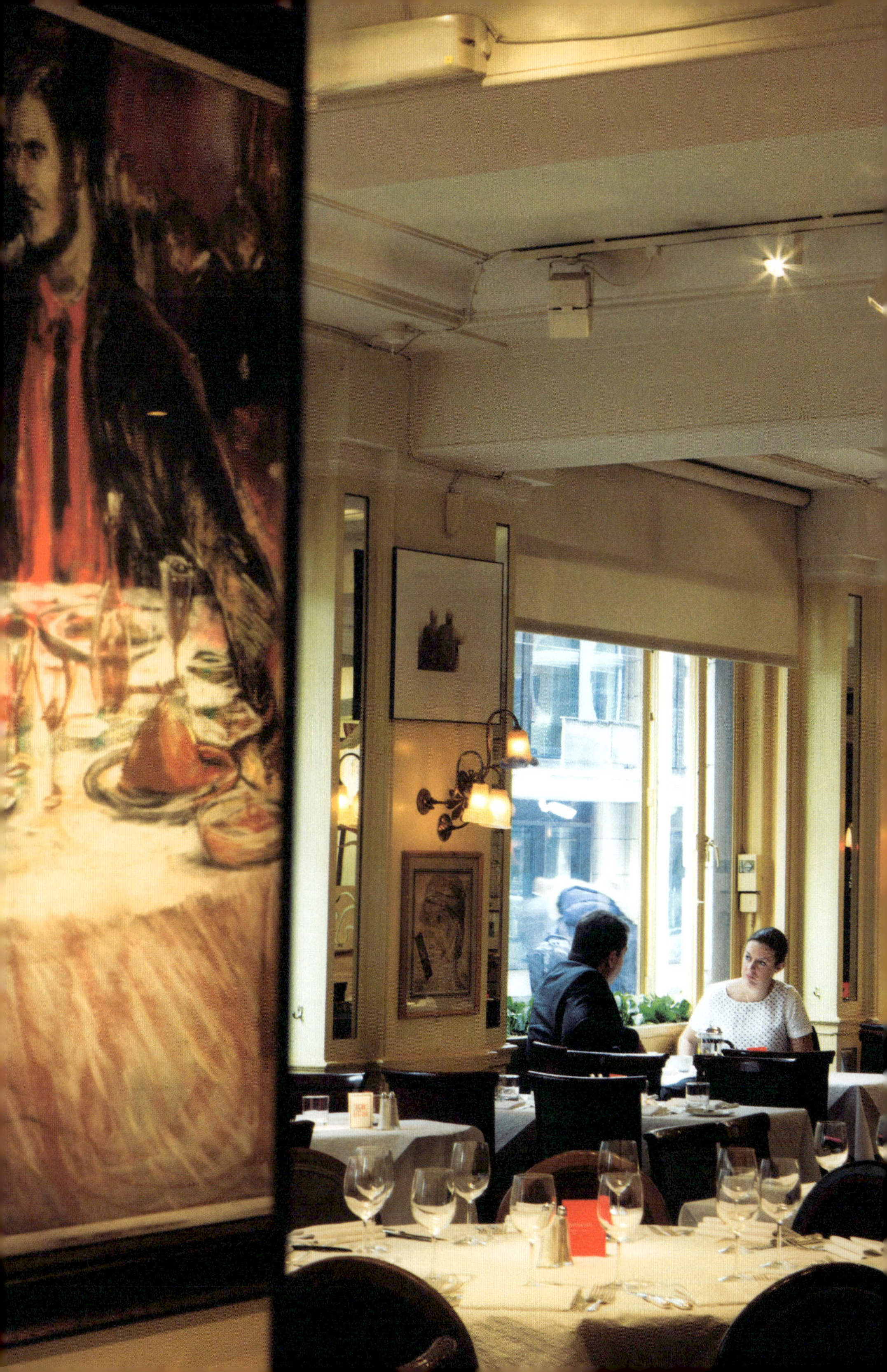

Langan's Brasserie

LONDON

"The charcoal kills us, but what does it matter?
The shorter our lives, the greater our glory."
— Antoine Carême

Many who were in London in the 1970s and early 1980s in Mayfair have a Peter Langan story. The most repeated anecdotes are grotesque, repulsive, and test genteel notions of good taste in a restaurant experience. One such story tells of a Saturday night when there was a scream from the ladies' bathroom of Langan's Brasserie. The proprietor rushed to investigate and found a female patron standing disgusted at the sight of an upturned cockroach in the stall and demanding an explanation. Langan angerly quipped: "Well that cannot be *our* cockroach, *Madame... our* cockroaches are fresh!" And then proceeded to put it in his mouth and wash it down with a coupé of his staple tipple, vintage Krug. "His behaviour and utterances were always colourful, and artists warmed to him, as did taxi drivers, policemen and women," wrote the London School artist and lifelong friend, Patrick Procktor. Langan did not make it to his sixth decade, but his legacy far outlasts his lifespan and continues in many of London's most popular contemporary restaurants, having influenced the establishments of Corbin and King, Mark Hix and Richard Caring. Peter Langan wrote the rules of the modern British art restaurant experience and aesthetic dining, and several of these restaurants follow them to this day.

He was a magnetic force on the London scene in the 1970s and 1980s, which not only drew a socially diverse crowd to himself and his restaurants, but also created a cultish following composed of artists and intellectuals. Even if one did not know Langan would die so young at the age of 47, the antics and behaviour were extreme and erratic enough to indicate it would all come to a head eventually. Before the hullabaloo of celebrity that infused Langan's in the second half of the 1970s, which included escapades with Joan Collins, Princess Margaret and Marlon Brando, there were quieter moments of charming and intimate restaurant experiences. The art in his establishments was a backdrop, but also signalled an emerging sense of good taste. This was what artists such as Howard Hodgkin and David Hockney identified in him and in his restaurants. Before he took that twinkling magic of going out to eat and amplified it in flickering neon at Langan's Brasserie, he turned a small Marylebone bistro, Odin's, into the consummate artists' restaurant in the earlier part of the decade.

Langan moved to London in 1966 as an Aer Lingus salesman and began working in the small Devonshire Place restaurant Odin's by accident rather than by design. The bistro's owner died in a car crash, and his wife Kirsten Benson married Patrick Procktor, who had begun to provide watercolours for Odin's walls, and encouraged other artists including Lucian Freud, Francis Bacon, R.B. Kitaj and Hockney to offer works too, as well as holding regular dinner parties in its cosy, oxblood walled, red carpeted 20-table space. Procktor and Benson lived at 26 Manchester Street in Marylebone, in a flat previously occupied by William Coldstream, who was Procktor's mentor at the Slade. Langan lived at number 32, and "the influence of chance, the part played by geography, by the arrangement of flats in close proximity", resulted in friendship. Langan came to Odin's for all of his meals. One day he saw Kirsten crying and unable to start the day's work, took off his jacket and went into the kitchen to start cooking the lunch service. Soon after, she gave him the restaurant.

Brian Sewell, the acerbic critic whose sharp pen kept the London art scene on a knife edge in his weekly reviews in the *Evening Standard* for four decades, also began visiting Odin's and found himself captivated by Langan. He and Procktor fought over Peter, his memory and the reportage of accounts of his life, by both writing memoirs exposing stories about him. This is entertaining, as Sewell and Langan met as a result of Procktor's works, which the critic detested. Langan purchased the artist's watercolours from Nicholas Vilag, who ran a gallery next door to Odin's – a "gallery" that was more like a jumble sale, a "dark, impenetrable confusion of frames, canvases and bulky folders", according to Sewell. The dealer had a Royal Academician friend who had "fallen on hard times" and resorted to forging signatures on oil paintings in a bid to upgrade poor-quality works into Old Masters. Langan asked Sewell what he thought of the Procktor watercolours, and the critic's response elicited from the chef "indrawn breath and muttered obscenities of a kind that I hadn't heard since my years in the Army". After this, Sewell became one of Langan's closest friends, and was uncharacteristically emotional over his friend's loss – betraying himself "as affectionate for the first time", according to Procktor. This affection lasted until the end of the critic's life: even a decade after Langan's death in 1988, he admitted he was constantly reminded of him in small details of the quotidian, for instance in "bubble and squeak, ripe figs and mature women with black hair". He also maintained Langan was an intellectual with spiritual depths, who, had he lived longer, could have become the director or a trustee of Tate. Simon Parker Bowles, the proprietor of the respected St James's establishment restaurant, Green's, said the greatest thing about Peter was his ability to size people up: "He used to say, 'You're looking at me, kid, the best shrink in the business.'"

Langan performed for his patrons, but naturally the question as to how much was real and what was feigned arises. Chris Corbin, once owner of The Ivy and now proprietor of The Wolseley, began his catering career in Langan's as a waiter and recalls how his former boss "could be a very cruel trickster. He could fool you by making you think he lost control. But he was in control".

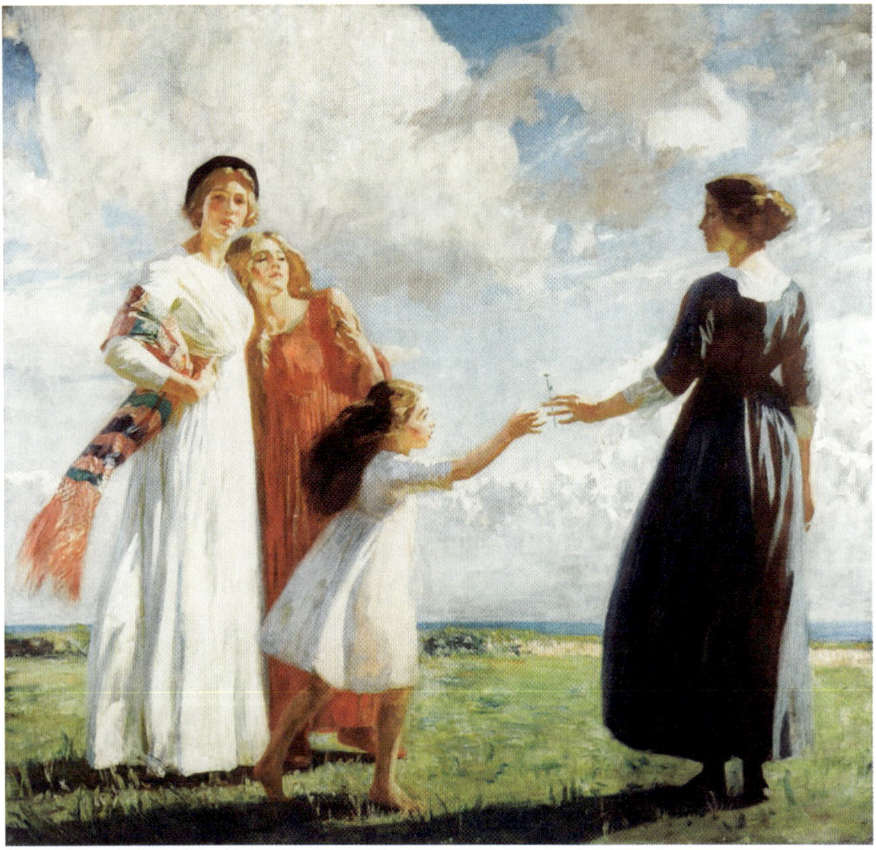

Peter had his sights set on creating a London version of La Coupole in Paris, the historic Art Deco brasserie in Montparnasse frequented by artists and intellectuals in the early 20th century. In 1976, he secured the former site of the Coq d'Or on Stratton Street in Mayfair and opened his restaurant. The actor Michael Caine had been a patron of Odin's and Langan convinced him to partner on the venture. With Caine came Hollywood, and then they convinced Richard Shepherd, a rising-star chef who cut his teeth at the Capital Hotel with its haute cuisine, to join. Shepherd was the first chef to be awarded a Michelin star in Britain. The ingredients were in place to make Britain's first restaurant with its own ready-made scene attached.

Langan's animated and inebriated antics in the 1970s and 1980s included shouting at patrons, crawling on the floor between tables and biting ladies' ankles, resplendently plopping onto random tables and falling asleep on the spot – a talent he could demonstrate in any doorway, under any table, even one time in Sotheby's when he went to view works for sale. The staff phoned the restaurant to request they come and collect their owner ("please send two men"). When he moved to a penthouse flat in Harley Street, he would often return home after the restaurant shut, fall asleep on the building doorstep as he tried to open the door, only to have the doctors step over him in the morning when they entered their surgeries.

However, in among the jests and rumbustious behaviour it is an undeniable fact that Langan had an unmistakable talent for aesthetic dining; a magnetic conviviality ensured his restaurants were always full and the places to be seen in 1970s and 1980s London. He was discerning in his taste in cooking and in art, but it was executed in a clumsy way, as he swivelled and splashed his version of aesthetic taste across the walls. He had an eye for what Hockney called "the poetry and sentimentality of representation". He would mix high and low – purchasing Victorian bric-à-brac from Portobello Road and Belle Époque reproductions, and pairing them with Laura Knight and other romantic British paintings, including a "yard long" Sickert he bought for just £300, and sober London School works from the artists who were his friends and patrons.

Michael Caine, despite his continuous disdain and eventual contempt for his business partner, admired his panache and skill for creating the ideal restaurant experience. Caine muses on the time Langan explained to him: "Everybody in the restaurant must be able to see everybody else at all times." He asked Peter why. "Because you are not coming to our restaurant on the way to the show or after the show: you *are* the show." Furthermore, it was not sufficient to have a buzzing floor of diners at all times, it was also essential that "the walls must talk". And judging by how crowded they were with drawings, prints and paintings – two floors' worth – the walls would not shut up.

In the 1970s, restaurants in London tended to be small and intimate affairs, having developed from trattorias and cafés. There was also a burgeoning homosexual scene associated with the catering industry, where Michael Smith and the fraternity of the English house garden restaurant began to shift from casual-labour cooks to professional, career chefs. This contributed to the gay subculture forming in the capital, with other chefs like Fergus Provan joining artists such as Bacon and Hockney in bars and restaurants to explore the new possibilities of nightlife. Restaurants now offered an alternative setting to dining being just about the conventional and domestic, dominated by an ideal of the heterosexual nuclear family. These establishments became a new version of home for their particular patrons, many of whom chose more unconventional lifestyles.

People may prefer to recall the unruly escapades of Peter Langan, but there are accounts of his mastery of hospitality and the restaurant experience in equal measure. One way to understand this is through his friendships with artists, and in particular David Hockney, whom he met in 1967 when the artist painted Procktor in his lodgings on Manchester Street (*The Room*). They remained close friends from the early days when Hockney drew Marinka Watts, a waitress at Odin's and Langan's – one of only two women he depicted, the other being his muse Celia Birtwell – to the later part of the decade when the artist was in Los Angeles. Unable to attend Langan's 40th birthday dinner – which the chef was convinced would be his last, given his liver damage – Hockney sent a portrait instead. In fact, he drew and painted several portraits of Peter throughout the 1970s and designed menus for Odin's and Langan's. These show the restaurateur's physical decline as alcohol and lifestyle eventually took their toll on his health. There is not a complete record of how many were made, since some were on simple and disposable paper, but they have become coveted trophies in the catering industry – chef Sally Clarke, who trained in Michael's Santa Monica, displays one in her eponymous Kensington restaurant.

Key moments in Langan's life and career intersected with those of the artists. Procktor recalls how he made the artists feel so welcome they would dine weekly, sometimes daily: "Peter had developed the only partly conscious idea that Odin's would become the Café des Artistes of London. Hitherto, through the 1960s, apart from the few meals we cooked at home, people like myself and David had dined out almost every night. We had favourite places all over London, such as the Greek Taverna in Charlotte Street, Oats in Hollywood Road, and The Hungry Horse, but to find a restaurant close at hand which was not only welcoming but extremely good, and, to boot, that bought one's paintings in exchange for food, was a thrill both for David and for me."

It was Peter Langan who initiated the exchange of art for food in London restaurants. He called it "eating it down". This was what he could offer the artists

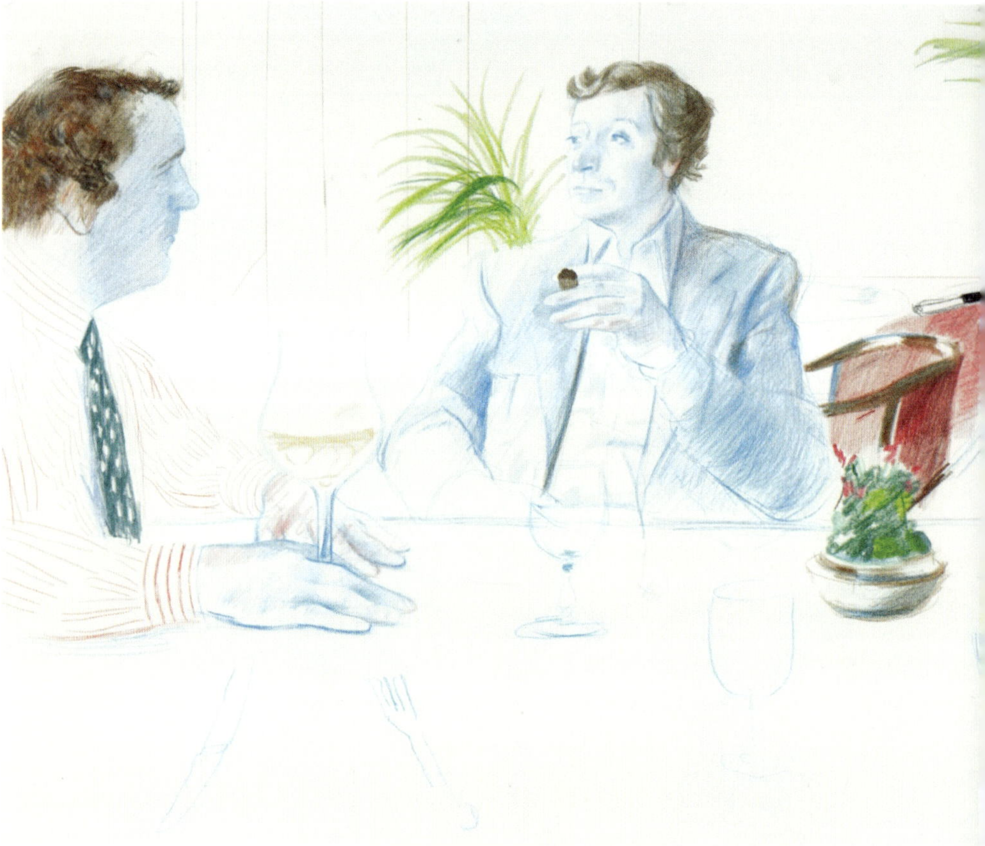

in return for their representations of life. Kitaj gave him two erotic drawings – one of a *ménage à trois* scene inscribed with "For Peter and Food", which he placed in the entrance of Odin's behind the maître d's stand, and the second of a sailor fondling the breast of a prostitute, inscribed "For Peter and Love", which he hung in the dining area. Hockney made a drawing of this latter scene in the 1970s which he gave to Langan. The chef extended this system of trading meals for artworks to gallerists, including the Fine Art Society, where he purchased many of his early Modern British pieces.

Meanwhile, his artist friends, Procktor, Kitaj and Hockney, could recognise the restaurateur had a respect for painting. In Procktor's words: "I had never met until Peter a man for whom painting and drawing never lost their magic. Although he did not draw, images had a force for him." For Langan, painting

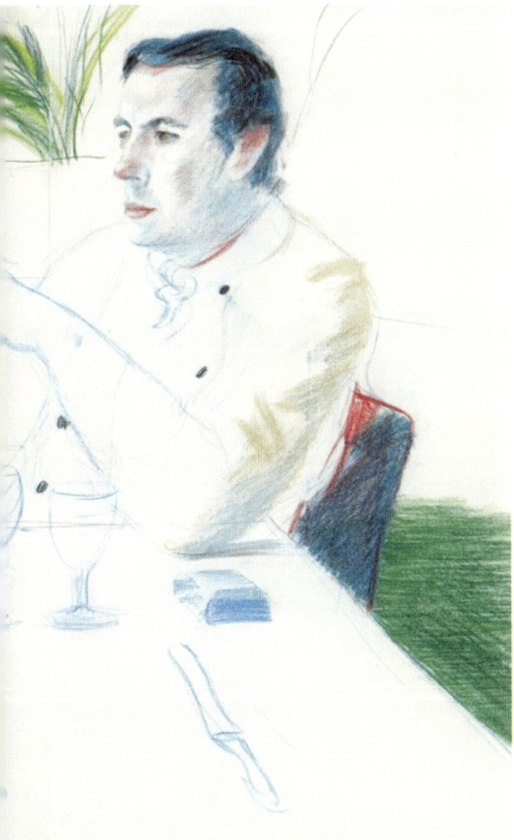

captured those "special days" where memories are made, memories of love, celebration and conviviality. This mirrors the defence of figurative painting and the human form Hockney and Kitaj were making at the time, arguing the artist could be both representational and poetic.

The restaurateur's unpredictability could at times work in his favour as those around him were both repelled and compelled by his behaviour. Hockney remained unfazed by his volatility and would repeatedly eat at Langan's when he moved back to London from Los Angeles. Beth Coventry, Langan's ex-girlfriend and head chef at Green's, recalls the moment when Hockney made the iconic menu drawing of the three proprietors in an impromptu moment in the restaurant, ordered by Langan with a thump on the table: "Now, just do it now!" The artist dutifully responded – one wonders if with a roll of the eyes – and insisted Caine take off his glasses. A quick drawing created at a restaurant table that sold at auction in 2018 for £850,000.

Today, Langan's Brasserie survives on these memories and legacy of the past; even a mausoleum to its founder. It may serve as a memento mori to newer establishments of their eventual decline and demise. Langan had a morose streak to him, as alcoholics often do, and it seems had a premonition about his short life and wanted to use the restaurant to scar time. "Special days are also sad ones when someone you have loved is dead. Even when it's expected, it's still a moment of surprise, the tears of relief and sadness – the worst sorrow is when your brain cries and the tears never reach your eyes... My special times have been all of these emotions, some I don't want to remember, those are the dry tears of darkness and depression," he wrote.

Langan was drawn to figurative painting from the 20th century. Some of the pieces in his restaurant may seem gauche and sentimental now, but they were often scenes and stories of escapism and punctuations of an otherworldliness in the dining space. Some were, of course, just bargains, as Sewell likes to remind us in Peter's autobiography, in which the critic overwrote his own take on events. But there was a parallel for Langan between the dining experiences and artworks – memory making and something paradoxically homely but extraordinary. This is the enchantment other restaurateurs since then have often remarked about and have tried to emulate. According to Corbin, Langan "had a magic about him, he's one of those people you were drawn to because of charisma, irreverence and because of his taste. Wonderful taste. Not just taste in the food. In atmosphere, in aesthetics, in all those things that surround you. Whether it be the knives or forks, or how you cut the bread." In the restaurateur's own words, he plied his diners with his trade, the eating and drinking, "so my moments were often memories of good times in the restaurants, where people meet, go home and make love all night, then I feel I have done my job". The restaurant would be a sensual space, a space to indulge the sensorial, almost prandial foreplay for his diners, nothing else would do for the self-proclaimed "culinary pimp".

Works and artists in the Langan's collection

—

Some of the artworks Langan purchased were more successful than others, some museum-quality. A Harold Gilman (*Portrait of a Black Gardener*, 1905) was loaned to the Royal Academy for a retrospective in 1982. A Richard Westall (*Faust and Lilith*, 1831) was also exhibited at the RA that year – it appealed to its owner because of the heroine's breasts.

—

The first floor of the brasserie featured a commissioned mural of a generic Venetian scene, *Gondola and Salute*, by Patrick Procktor, which the artist delivered as a cool, wintry view. Langan had insisted on a Serenissima summer image and promptly coated it with tobacco-coloured varnish to warm it up. They fell out over this.

—

Laura Knight's *The Gift* (1910), a large-scale piece bought at Sotheby's in 1971, depicts three young women in a Cornish meadow by the sea – a lyrical fantasy. Langan paid £190 for it; a similar painting sold in 1988 for £78,000.

—

Langan wasn't concerned just with well-known artists. He owned work by more obscure painters such as Alfred Hayward, Graham Robertson and Steven Spurrier, as well as Sims, Sickert and Connard. Sewell introduced him to Eliot Hodgkin, cousin of Howard, for smaller still lifes, but the two quarrelled and the artist sold him a selection of his less successful works.

—

The cocktail menus feature a drawing Procktor made of Langan in 1974. Sewell tells us this was during the oil crisis of 1973-74 when patronage was down and Langan had no funds to purchase more art, and even had to sell his Bentley. It depicts a morose, reflective proprietor, with dishevelled hair and bags under his eyes, the "cruellest portrait" of Langan. Exercise caution when selecting your cocktail.

—

Guy Gladwell's *Farewell to Peter Langan* was drawn towards the end, when alcohol abuse consumed the subject's daily life. He is wearing one of his trademark linen suits, walking away from the viewer with his head down. It hangs in the brasserie today.

The dining room at Langan's Brasserie; Laura Knight's painting selected by Peter Langan for the entrance; David Hockney's drawing from 1984 of business partners Peter Langan, actor Michael Caine and chef Richard Shepherd used in the brasserie menu

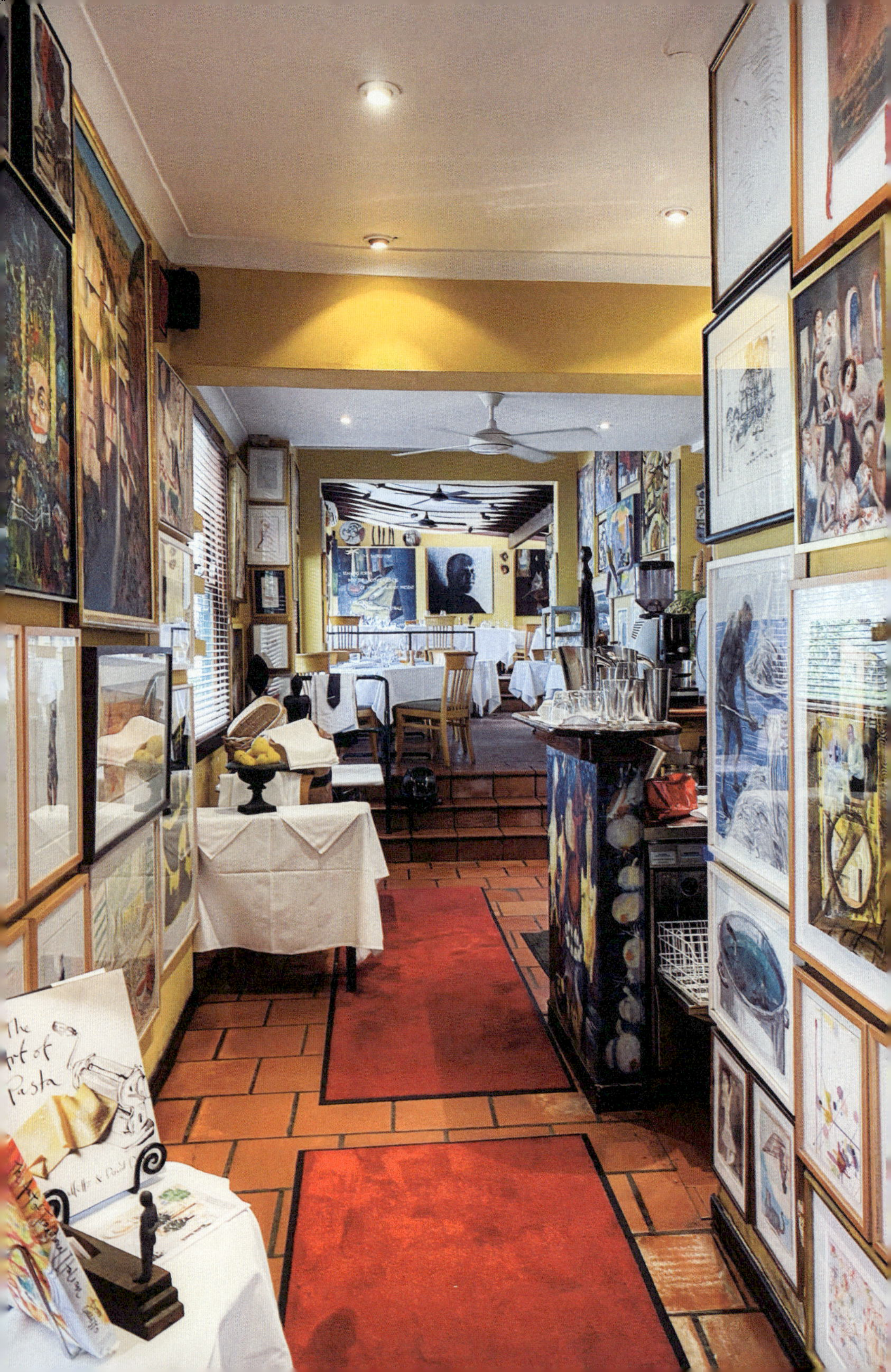

Lucio's

"We leave the restaurant fulfilled in a complete sense rather than full in a sense that is basic."
— John Beard

If an art restaurant can be reduced to a shorthand, then this is how the direction of the Lucio's art collection is outlined. In 1984, the celebrated Australian artist Sidney Nolan visited the restaurant and sketched one of his Ned Kelly figures on a table docket. The gesture was in exchange for a supper he enjoyed in the casual Ligurian establishment in Sydney's bohemian Paddington area. The proprietor, Lucio Galletto, was so touched and honoured by the presentation of the work, that he had it framed in gold leaf and displayed in pride of place in his restaurant. "I saw it as a good omen that an artist like Sidney Nolan would want to make something just for me," says Galletto. The sketch hangs in the same spot as it has for 36 years, like icons hang in corners of rooms to bless spaces for the religiously devout. Nolan, too, was moved by the enshrining of the sketch and subsequently kept coming back for meals, asking for paper of varying sizes to draw on and gift to the chef.

This episode ignited Galletto's fervour to acquire art by living Australian artists, and he asked several of them who were his regular diners to make works for him to display. He was subtle about it in the first few years, but then as Lucio's played host to more gallerists, collectors and artists, they would ask him if he would like a piece to hang in the trattoria. The artist Euan Macleod tells of stories of artists such as Tim Storrier ("he's trouble") who fought over specific spaces and walls, or Michael Johnson and Salvatore Zofrea who both wanted the same spot for their paintings and had to settle for a curatorial shared custody by swapping walls every six months. For over three decades, this resulted in plates, paintings, menus and more recently cookbooks featuring new works of the most significant modern and contemporary artists of Australia being made for Lucio. Since opening, the restaurant has been the destination for many distinguished members of Sydney's cultural elite and Australian artistic aristocracy. They all come for the food and the comprehensive survey of the nation's modern art, which ironically began with the depiction of the country's popular bushranger outlaw figure.

So far, so good in terms of art restaurant creation myths. However, Galletto's first exposure to artists came from further afield: his Italian motherland. The Gallettos were restaurateurs in Bocca di Magra, a beachside village in Liguria. They understood there was a link between food and art for certain kinds of diners and established a gallery to attract more visitors to the village and the family restaurant. It began as a seasonal project, but soon attracted artists from all around Europe. This instilled an interest in art and architecture in the young Lucio, and he recalls a Damascene moment when a Miró exhibition was staged in the gallery next to the restaurant in the early 1970s: "When I saw these artists coming to the village for their exhibition, they looked very different from the local people. They were wearing different clothes, haircuts, and my mother would comment 'look at those strange people', but I found them fascinating. To me, they were a window to the world beyond. I wanted to know what the world was like outside our small village." He went on to study architecture and then as a young man "ran away for love" to Australia, following a blonde, bronzed Australian woman, Sally White, in 1975. She wandered into his village in a Kombi van, as he likes to recall, and it was storybook love at first sight. The expanse of the Australian landscape and its progressive society appealed to him early on, in addition to it offering an easier environment for his entrepreneurialism. The country "was full of new ideas" and he enjoyed "the openness of the mind as well as [his] association with the artists". Australia facilitated creativity and the revelling in the joy of unaccountability that comes with being physically and ideologically so far away. Australian artists have captured this freedom in their work in the 20th century; Galletto through his cooking and his art collecting.

The site of Lucio's was a happy coincidence and possibly imbued it with good luck in terms of being an artists' restaurant: the building once housed both a restaurant and the Hungry Horse Gallery decades before Galletto's arrival. The grand Victorian edifice with a balcony of white corrugated iron and yellow plaster walls is on the corner of Windsor Street and Elizabeth Street in Paddington, an area with a high concentration of galleries and an insalubrious, bohemian past. Artists would visit the galleries and dine in the bistro, inaugurating a relationship between art and food in the location.

The shorthand of this is depicted in a now famous 1963 photograph by David Mist of Frank Hodgkinson, Stanislaus Rapotec, Charles Reddington, William Rose, Carl Plate, Colin Lanceley, John Olsen, Leonard Hessing, Robert Klippel, John Coburn, Robert Hughes and Emanuel Raft posing in between the cast-iron pattern of the balcony: a roll-call of some of the most significant 20th-century Australian artists and certainly one of the most significant art critics of the 20th century.

Lucio's became an artists' restaurant from the moment the poet Geoffrey Dutton, who dined there regularly, invited John Olsen to lunch with him. The artist was so impressed that on his next visit he brought the young emerging artist Tim Storrier. Then Charles Blackman came in with the other contemporaries. There was a prandial indoctrination with older generation artists introducing their younger counterparts to Lucio's. "When the artists started to visit, they all would notice the Nolan hung in pride of place, and they realised first I love art, and second I take good care of their work," Galletto recalls.

The Nolan sketch must have been a talisman because the artists just kept coming. Luke Sciberras began to visit as a young art student – as a guest of a dealer – and instantly was drawn to Galletto's warmth, wisdom and congeniality. Over three decades later, he still eats there weekly and Lucio owns a portrait of the artist sketched at Table One by Ben Quilty, who was in turn introduced to the restaurant by Sciberras. Artists go to Lucio's to meet other artists, "as though gathering under a salient old tree or at a meaningful place in a loved garden", he says. "I cannot think of any other place I've known where so many creative people have been instinctively drawn." For decades Galletto collected friendships as much as artworks, ensuring his restaurant became a preferred space for them to meet and explore ideas and debate their practices. Many of the most prestigious gatherings were hosted at Lucio's, such as an annual Academy artists' lunch and dinners after the Archibald Prize awards. The artists captured Galletto's imagination as a young child and he associated them with showing people new ways of looking at the world through their work. Now he could also look at cooking in a new light in his kitchen.

Lucio sees his cooking as a creative practice: "I grew up in the family restaurant learning the saying 'the eye wants its share'. When we prepare a dish, we think about the full experience of the dish." He is a designer of experiences. And when he had his own restaurant, he wanted to welcome artists, who were as important as celebrities, politicians or businessmen. Galletto loves and reveres artists not because he is part of the art world or the industry – he has never bought a single piece of art from a gallery – but because they teach him how to see and combine ingredients to produce experiences through his dishes.

John Olsen and Galletto formed a particular bond. "John was one of the first people that understood my view on food and cooking," he says. "We were on the same wavelength, that same approach to conviviality and cooking." The artist ineffably understands the philosophy of food and maintains he even taught the chef how to perfect his garlic pasta. Galletto wrote a cookbook based on the most traditional recipes and decorated it with specially commissioned works by the Lucio's artists. His dream project was always to combine "art and food". According to artist John Beard, dining in Lucio's is "a confirmation of structure and purpose that has evolved from experience and an understanding of the past". Galletto takes tradition and cooking skills from Italy and "magically fuses [them] with new ideas (respectfully muted when appropriate) to give definition to our own contemporary palate". Like the artists take techniques and traditions from European art, the chef imports Italian traditions of cooking but infuses them with Australian freedom and light. The food of his restaurant was an opportunity for Galletto to remain connected to his homeland and to interpret "taste" as an open and comforting experience for diners.

There is a beauty in the simplicity of the everyday for the chef and he is drawn to artworks that portray simple ingredients and still lifes of food, which is reflected in what's on the walls. Ingredients, foodstuffs and tables of meals have held a place in art since ancient times. In Renaissance art, this genre emphasised the joyful side of searching for ingredients and the labour of preparing food by focusing on feasts and luscious plates of meat, fish, vegetables and fruit. "A lot of people think Italian food is 'ugly'. I've seen it described as ugly. Not even a bean soup is ugly if you look at it correctly," Galletto maintains. The Australian "feeling of being" comes out in terms of mixed artists and styles in the collection, but all works recount and depict the Australian quotidian in a formalism of purity, light and use of colour. Ned Kelly's famous last words, "such is life", take on a different meaning in Lucio's. Olsen, who has been dining, observing and contributing to the growth of the collection for decades, says the art in Lucio's is "essentially and uniquely Australian". It demands close observation to understand the methods and aesthetic approach to this being "Australian" art, summed up in the following explanation on perspective: "Sid [Nolan] could understand that Australia is just very, very different from a European experience." The immensity is received and interpreted, "just because you live there. For example, there are oak trees and other trees which are symmetrical, whereas the Australian eucalyptus tree is asymmetrical, and it seems to spread all over the place." These eccentricities and aberrations on perspective are strewn across the restaurant walls – watercolours of squid, plates of salad, offcuts of lamb. Sciberras, who has given Galletto more than 20 works over the years to include subject matter "related to food and the creatures we cook, octopus, hare, fish of various varieties, plucked poultry, baccalà, pigs", says each piece has a story of a meal associated with it. Dining among the artworks slows the diner down to experience this "sense of place" and take in the full extent of how the senses are stimulated.

Nolan's Ned Kelly ignites an art restaurant endeavour worthy of its European originators. By the 20th century, the historical view of Kelly as a lovable rogue, a Robin Hood figure, had wavered, but there remains an enduring romance and fondness for the outlaw anti-authoritarian, the eternal rebel. Nolan's Ned Kelly series is significant in the history of Australian art; the square-headed figure is both Modernist in terms of being minimalist, stark, angular, but also integrated into the Australian landscape, combining man and nature. Nolan often worked on disposable paper and cardboard, using quick-drying materials, having begun his artistic journey as a graphic designer of adverts and signage. In this respect the sketch on the docket is not just a scrap or doodle, but artistic synecdoche in terms of the drawing standing for a wider tradition of Australian Modernism. Lucio's art collection of 20th-century Australian art was sanctioned by Nolan through the gesture of this drawing.

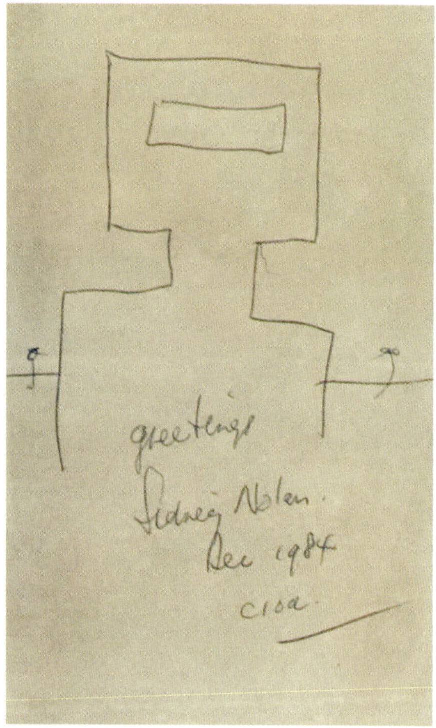

The collection is a mosaic of the Australian quotidian that emits and diffuses food memories and happiness, but it is also a register of accomplishments in styles and techniques that Australian artists experimented with, arguably since Nolan interpreted his version of Modernist painting in the mid-20th century. There are key names that have participated in past artistic movements and battles of the "isms": Sydney 9, the Antipodeans, plus more contemporary artists who have won the Archibald Prize – six in the collection to be precise. One winner, Gary Shead, painted a portrait of Galletto in 2009, *The Soffritto of Lucio*, which now hangs in the Australian National Portrait Gallery in Canberra. The image features Galletto surrounded by figures he has fed and loved in an amalgamation of the Ligurian and Australian landscape. The art-collecting chef is commemorated as a national treasure.

There is also a playfulness in the collection, a celebration of life. John Beard believes this is the result of the "light in Australia and the colour and the youth of the country and the energy, and it comes through apparent in the work". Lucio's array of art is built on "an optimism" explored in the food-related and Australian landscape subjects. They are not abstract or conceptual works, but depict subjects relating to dining in an accessible, celebratory manner. There is enough complexity in the make-up of the everyday and how artists see this and place it on canvas that there is no need to divert attention away from what is before the eyes. The restaurant presents a survey of modern Australian art, while diners tuck into handkerchief cuttlefish pasta.

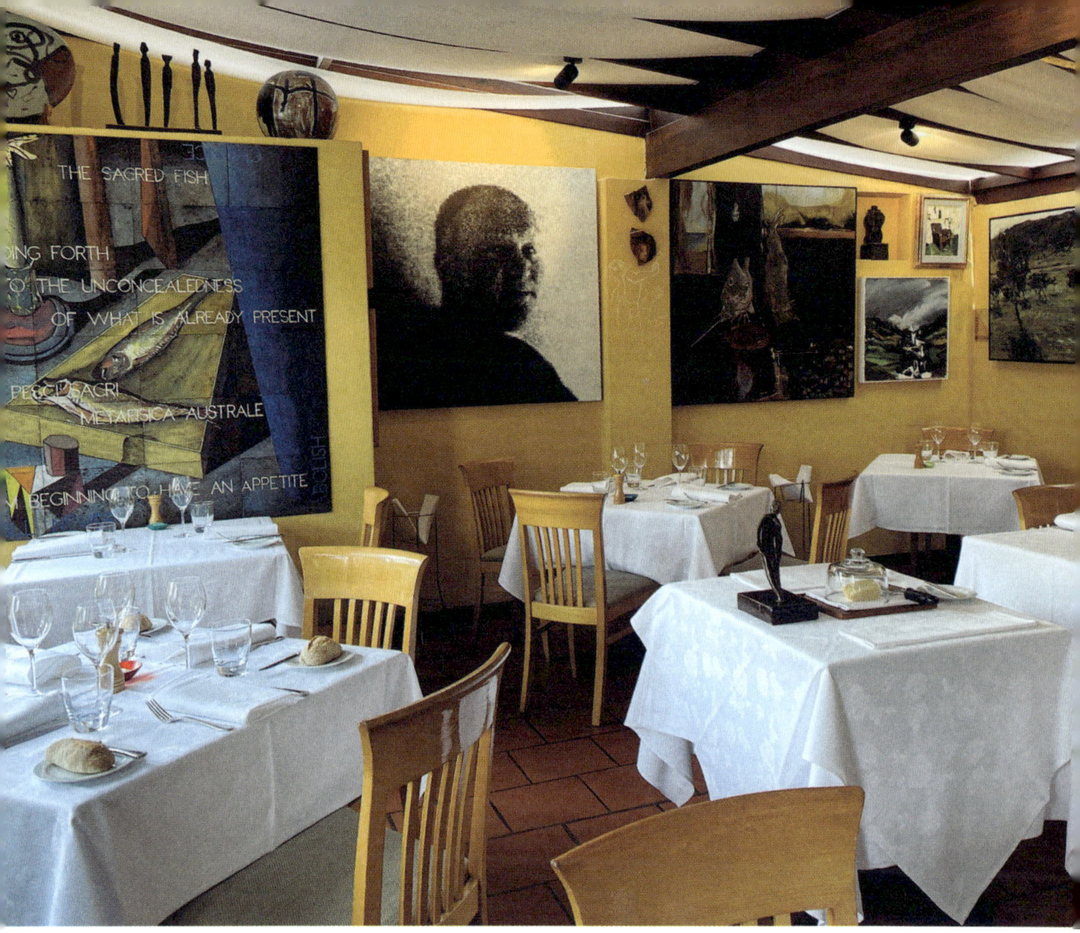

The walls are a compendium of artists' testaments and responses to Lucio's importance to their sense of community, and significantly how they see Lucio himself as a creative in terms of his cooking and the restaurant. Sciberras says Lucio's and the regular dining in the restaurant "broadened his understanding of what it is to be a painter", of what is alive and fresh and the animism in the landscape: "We share a passion for the delectable sexiness of our crafts and their rewards." He thinks there is an ongoing collaboration between the artists and the chef. "Certainly, Lucio and his restaurant are a culture in crucible form. It is a wholly unique experience (entirely addictive) to dine in a haven of the world's finest food and wine and swaddled in the cream fat of Australia's most loved artists." Galletto is a chef who learns from artists and then feeds everybody else, and Lucio's is an art restaurant that has its own art scene or could be its own art movement. As Sciberras says: "Lucio's is like a body memory, a familiar face and a touchstone in my life. A journalist once asked me 'how do you want to die?' I answered that I want to die laughing at Table One at Lucio's."

Works and artists in the Lucio's collection

—

Tim Storrier is the most colourful of the Lucio's artists, regularly involved in altercations and animated behaviour. He has insisted his trademark elongated canvas of a linear wildfire in the bush never leaves its space above the restaurant windows, and he regularly likes to dine under it.

—

John Beard is a representational artist who often paints portraits in a faded way. His portrait of Lucio in the restaurant is oversized and features his head in close-up like a psychological study.

—

Charles Blackman was a figurative artist who founded the Antipodeans movement, which rallied against the influence of American Abstract Expressionism in Australian art in the 1950s. He is known for his *Alice in Wonderland* and *Schoolgirl* series – charming graphic design works of fancy and fantasy.

—

Imants Tillers's multi-panelled piece, one of the largest in the restaurant, depicts a table with the artist's characteristic philosophically poetic phrases overlaying the composition: "METAFISICA AUSTRALE" references the mystery of the dining ritual and ends with "I AM BEGINNING TO HAVE AN APPETITE". The work is a reminder of how the mystical and metaphysical are also a part of food and dining rituals.

—

Euan Macleod creates moody landscapes reminiscent of Anselm Kiefer, though his biggest influence is Frank Auerbach. Macleod's landscapes convey the unknowable, sublime feeling of expansive space and there is a self-referential artist at an easel observing and controlling nature.

—

John Olsen, Australia's oldest and most celebrated living artist, has several pieces in the restaurant. His drip painting of earthy food tones is museum-quality, and his work is often inspired by the chemistry and cooking of food. Also of note are two female nude drawings, which are rare for this abstract artist.

The entrance to the restaurant with its saturated gallery walls; Sidney Nolan's 1984 sketch of Ned Kelly on one of the restaurant's order dockets; the dining room at Lucio's Sydney

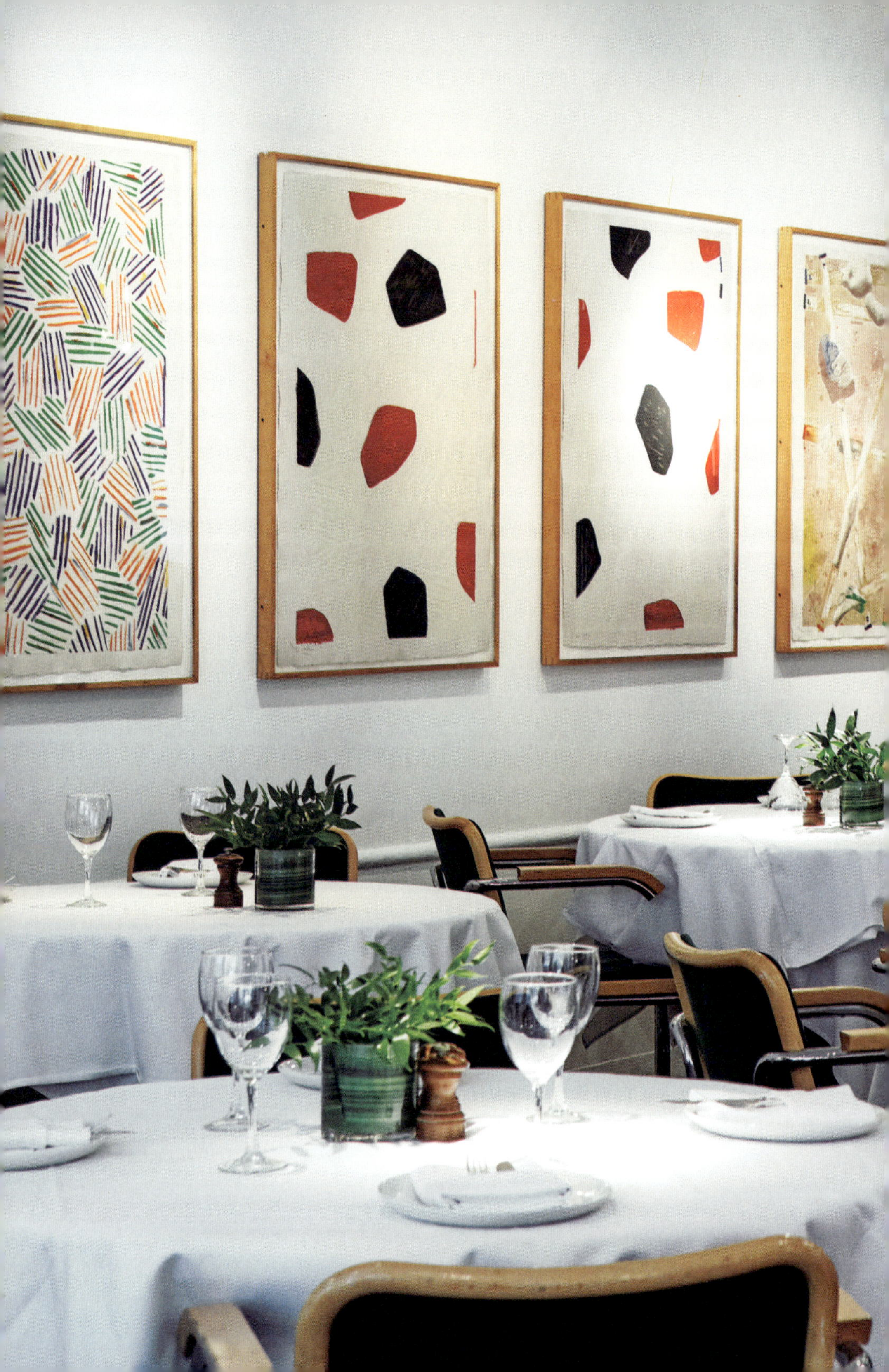

Michael's

SANTA MONICA AND NEW YORK

"Dining partners, regardless of gender, social standing, or the years they've lived, should be chosen for their ability to eat – and drink! – with the right mixture of abandon and restraint. They should enjoy food, and look upon its preparation and its dégustation as one of the human arts."
– M.F.K. Fisher

Michael McCarty is the man who invented the modern restaurant in America in the 1980s by breaking with its formal, serious, European archetype. In its place, he threw a party. At home. With art. By creating his eponymous restaurant in Santa Monica in 1979, fine dining would now take place in a relaxed, slightly louche environment, surrounded by attractive, tanned friends and modern art around the table, dry Californian "Cab Sauv", Davidoffs unfurling in the evening light and ferns swaying in the breeze on the patio. Michael's would be an extension of his home on a Friday night. McCarty's *bon vivant* flair and gregarious approach to hospitality realises food writer M.F.K. Fisher's maxim: "Since we must live to eat let us do it with both grace and gusto." With so much vivacity, in fact, that the restaurateur once angrily hung up the phone on Fisher when she called to reserve a table, thinking she was a restaurant critic, and he hated restaurant critics. Such was the success of his first restaurant in Santa Monica that McCarty was able to replicate this "SoCal" insouciance bicoastally, establishing Michael's in New York City a decade later in 1989. The Californian exploration of luminosity and a fresh approach to making – be it art or cuisine – was exported East. Central to McCarty's concoction and culinary philosophy of restaurants was displaying art, which he collected for decades, rotating works between home and his establishments' walls, the two interchangeable for him. He wanted to "expand the definition of the restaurant" and capture the spirit and climate of California "the same way the artists tried to do it". The artists ranged from Richard Diebenkorn to David Hockney, Helen Frankenthaler to John Cage, Frank Stella and Jasper Johns. They broke with tradition and reinterpreted Modernism before them, and McCarty broke with the culinary tradition of restaurant dining before him. By collecting and displaying the art on the walls, he signals he too is avant-garde, creating a new era of restaurateuring.

Both establishments have been important to American restaurant history of the past four decades and, within that history, tell a story of how chefs interested in art collect works and share their taste with their patrons, and through this build a scene to attract groups from certain fields or like-minded people. The art displayed in the Michael's restaurants becomes a conduit for Californian aesthetics and mood. McCarty could identify with artists who went out to California to explore freedom and possibility, and sent their discoveries back to the East Coast and beyond. Possibly the culinary equivalent of a blithe Hockney painting: all greens and blues and violets on the plate. The "primary colour of California is blue", McCarty says, and since there's "no such thing as blue food", the most important colour in all his recipes is green. Every single dish served must have some green on it – at the very least chives or a sprig of parsley. It is his interpretation of the "light and space" in his cooking.

McCarty chose Los Angeles, the "full metal jacket" and "crazy city" that "didn't start until '65, culturally speaking", as the place to set up his first restaurant. This signalled a new world order in terms of eschewing the conservative culinary traditions and dining settings of the East Coast and even developments in northern California. His first location was a bright, airy Santa Monica street off the main promenade, and at the time was credited with inaugurating the new craze for California cuisine. This meant fresh, young American reinterpretations of traditional and revered French dishes, served in a purpose-built open space that blended indoor-outdoor dining with a plant-filled patio and wall-to-wall and ceiling glass, striking, oversized, fresh flower arrangements and bright spotlights over the tables. The last of these caused much consternation among the locals: why would you have lights on in *daylight* on the *West Coast*? As former chef John Sedlar recalls: "Michael's was a very magical place... it was brash, and he was sassy, and he had modern art and great wine. It was a party. It was youthful. Everything was European up until that time, and this was something *Californian*." McCarty saw himself as a "wheeler-dealer" as much as a chef, taking what he had learned from the French and transporting it to the West Coast in the prosperous, yuppie 1980s, when restaurants were growing in popularity and becoming cultural markers for those who wanted to signal their good taste and success. His own creative act was to reinterpret French restaurant tradition to fit a new American context. For McCarty, "The best part is the theatre of it all: throwing a party every night, getting the mix of the crowd, having a 'club' where everybody is having a big time, putting people together and, best of all... good eats and drinks!" He regarded Michael's as an artistic happening, sensual and spectacular, suggesting it could hold its own in relation to other forms of cultural production.

McCarty claims he was the restaurateur who introduced so many of the elements now taken for granted in modern restaurants: the jazz soundtrack, the white space, the large white plates, spotlights, contemporary art on the walls. Design details experienced by most diners in countless restaurants since the 1980s, often going unnoticed and unregistered. He even had Knoll leather and chrome chairs, and recalls being challenged on this: "You have *office chairs* in a restaurant!" His reply: "Well, yeah, I think you'll find those cost over $2,000 each." However, in a restaurant, these touches acquire extra meaning because

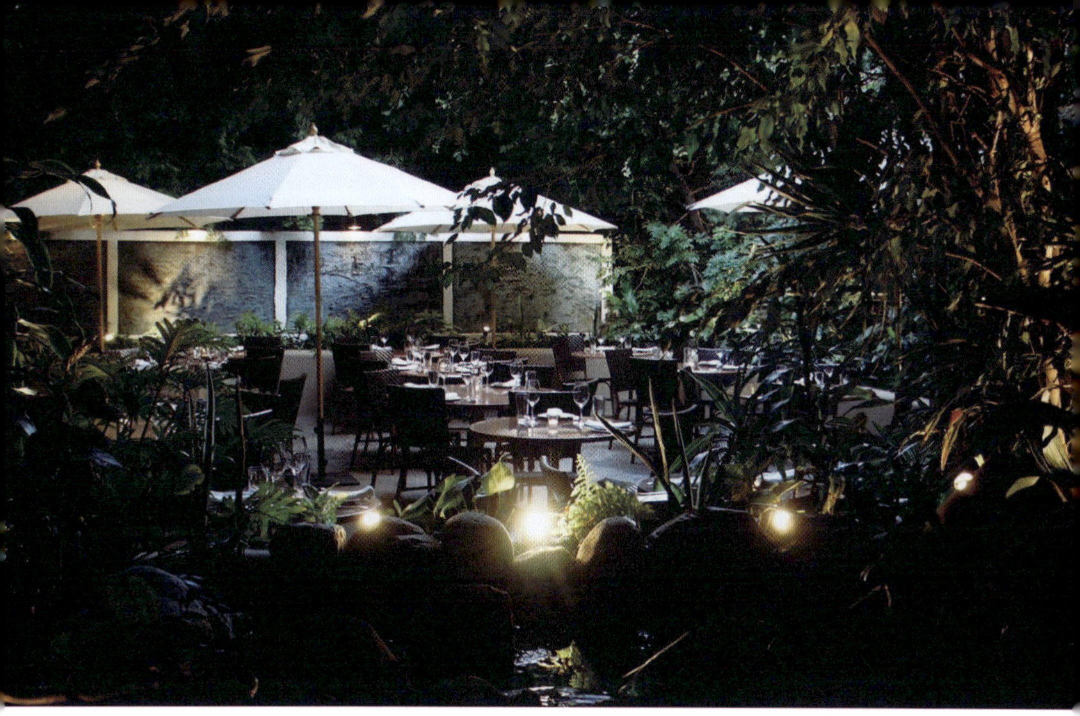

they mark good taste and construct an environment to facilitate the pleasure and enjoyment that is promised to diners. The individual satisfaction that takes place when we eat is sidelined, and community bonds are formed and fostered instead. Visiting a restaurant, according to McCarty, should be "like you are going to somebody's house to eat", and be a relaxed, casual and comfortable affair. This belief was formed from his childhood in an upper New York State household that regularly threw dinner parties in surroundings filled with art. His parents encouraged the young Michael to participate in cooking for and entertaining their guests, sharpening his skills as a gregarious host from an early age. In many ways, this plucky precociousness carried over to his approach to hospitality.

The chef spent his youth touring the culinary meccas of Europe in Italy and France, and he enrolled on the Cordon Bleu course. These formative experiences gave him an understanding of tradition and his place in it as a chef, but also how this tradition existed to be disrupted. McCarty's mantra became "green, crunchy and acidic" to counter the "brown, sweet and mushy". He transplanted these ideas into his kitchen, inviting a series of long-haired, "drug-addled", upstart American chefs to cook in his restaurant. Each was encouraged to improve on and rework dishes on the menu. Ken Frank, Mark Peel, Billy Pflug, Nancy Silverton, Jonathan Waxman, Kazuto Matsusaka, Gordon Naccarato and Sally Clarke were all alumni who went on to multiply the McCarty formula in other establishments in the United States and United Kingdom. He blurred "the line between employer and employee, partying with his crew after hours" and living a rock-star lifestyle, as expected of chefs who were creative and artistic. "It's a party!" – one of his most used phrases.

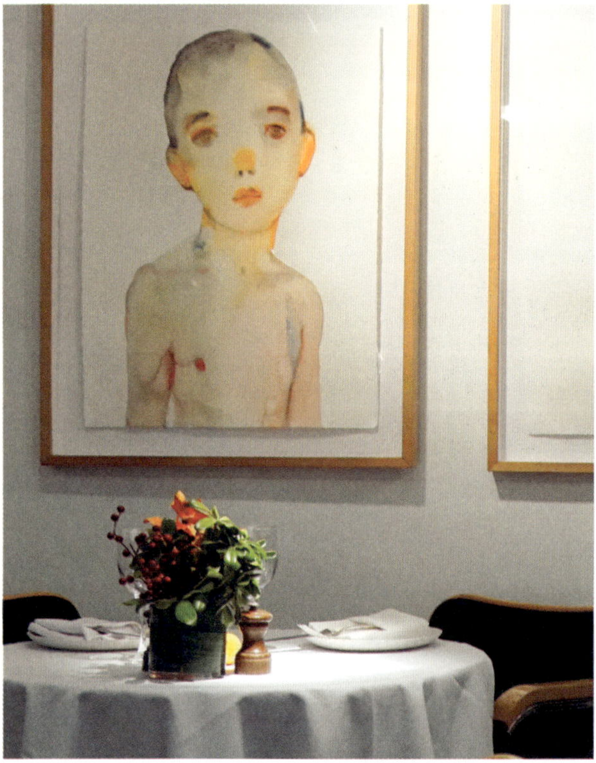

And then there was the art scene. When McCarty arrived in southern California in the 1970s, the artistic landscape of Santa Monica and Venice Beach was residual, fading in the influence of the Ferus Gallery and its associated artists and collectors. Ferus was infamous in the 1960s for its coterie of handsome, often womanising, hippie, beatnik artists such as Edward Kienholtz, Ed Ruscha, Ed Moses, Alan Light, Billy Al Bengston, Robert Irwin and John Altoon: artists who exploited Los Angeles's lack of artistic reputation and history to work in their own aesthetics of irreverence and experimentation. Eventually, in McCarty's own words, "they got old, the art got old". By the late 1970s, the West Coast was disregarded as a cultural backwater by the art world in New York. Man Ray, who lived in Hollywood for 10 years, dismissed it as "a real desert", somewhere you ended up rather than chose to go to.

When the 24-year-old McCarty planned his new restaurant in the late 1970s, he approached various galleries in Los Angeles to lend him art to display on his walls. The answer he heard the most was: "Beat it, kid." By the time he established his eponymous venue on 3rd Street, he had befriended Peter Goulds, the founder of the famed L.A. Louver gallery, established in 1975 to promote iconoclastic artists working in Los Angeles to international acclaim. Fortunately for McCarty, Goulds understood the potential reach of displaying art in an unusual space outside of the gallery circuit, like a restaurant, and agreed to the loans. As a result of this partnership, McCarty began to collect L.A. Louver art too. Goulds originally came to Los Angeles lured, like so many other creatives before him, by the promise of the film industry, but became a gallerist instead. He imported the best of British figurative painting from the London School to the West Coast, with a specific emphasis on Hockney, the pivotal artist in the McCarty collection. The first piece McCarty acquired was Hockney's lithograph *Wind,* from 1973, a work featuring four drawings blowing in the wind and a street sign pointing towards "Melrose Avenue". The chef wanted the piece because it contains a pun: Melrose Avenue was "Restaurant Row" in the 1970s. Since the 1980s, Hockney has been a regular in Michael's, not least because he could smoke on the garden patio – McCarty takes pride in the fact that the restaurant was one of the last places diners could smoke in public in LA before the smoking ban in 2007. He was also proud that a guest could be sitting next to the artist whose work was on the wall above them. This created a buzz and curiosity about the restaurant. Goulds was instrumental in ensuring a steady supply of artists' visits to Michael's for business meetings and entertainment. The gallery attracted some of the biggest British and American names of the 1970s, including John Cage and Bruce Nauman, boosting Los Angeles's credibility for artistic innovation and re-establishing an art scene. And when they all needed to conduct business over lunch, or host dinners after shows, they went to Michael's.

Santa Monica began to shed its tired associations with the art of the 1960s, and by the 1970s and 1980s southern California had become a serious location for writers, artists, critics and academics to live and work. Michael's Santa Monica benefited from this change in the cultural mood and the growth of a new community. It became a watering hole for creatives and intellectuals attracted to the liberal Californian lifestyle of possibility and pioneering ideology – as well as the physical attributes of the West Coast: the sun, the ocean, the terrain, the light, the beautiful healthy bodies. According to historian Michael Friedman, McCarty became "very attached to the whole art scene... The hippie thing had ended. The disco thing hadn't quite started yet. So there's this period of time where it's, like, who are the edgy people? Well, they're the artists." McCarty aligned the culinary as an art form, non-conformist, free and expressive. "Michael's, that space was just so thought-out and so slick, and yet it had this huge patio in the middle of it," continues Friedman. "It had all this amazing art on the walls. It was filled with art. It was filled with light." The combination proved to be irresistible,

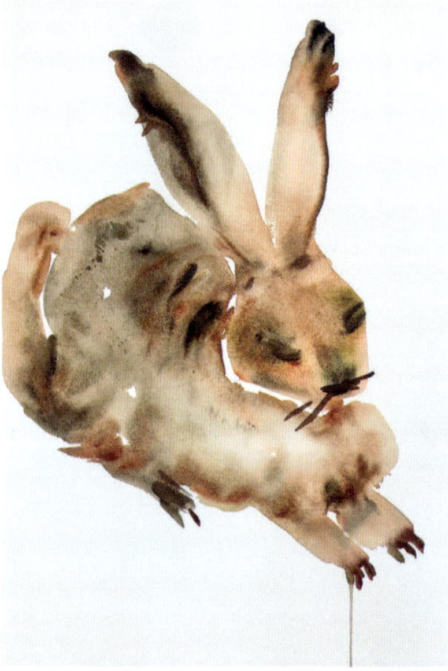

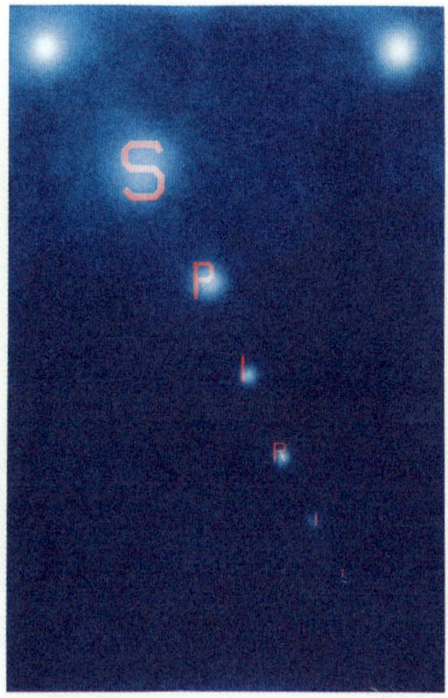

and, according to Sally Clarke, the "pieces he chose were so eye-catching it was as important as the food". The works were "always selected for their inherent beauty". That simple. McCarty consistently explains to his waiters: "When you place the plates down on the table, what's the first thing everybody does? Everybody looks at everybody else's plate… then they look at the walls, they see the art, then they look at the plants… it's all about initiating sensory pleasure around them. That's how it starts." The art was tied to his hospitality – art at home and art in the restaurant – but McCarty also accommodated the artistic community through his style of hospitality. He became part of the same social circles, connected to and connecting patrons. He was a maverick when it came to rewriting the rules of the American restaurant, as the artists were forgers of a new visual aesthetic.

The artistic momentum of southern California gathered pace and other galleries arrived on the scene, which the young chef associated himself with. The respected gallery Gemini G.E.L.'s owner, Stanley Grinstein, lived five minutes away from the restaurant in an imposing Spanish-Californian house, and as a result, any British artists, including David Hockney, or East Coast artists, including James Rosenquist, Jasper Johns and Roy Lichtenstein, who came to the West Coast to work on editions for the gallery stayed in the gallerist's house and would go to Michael's for lunch and dinner. Gemini G.E.L.

transformed printmaking into an important medium and was responsible for several iconic large-scale prints, including the largest Robert Rauschenberg self-portrait, of 1967, and others from Claes Oldenburg, Ellsworth Kelly and Richard Serra. The visiting artists began to mix with their local counterparts, such as Jonathan Borofsky, Vija Celmins, Sam Francis, Bruce Nauman, Ken Price and Ed Ruscha. Most of the gallery opening dinners and parties took place at Michael's and the restaurateur began to collect works from artists he befriended. That is why there is an emphasis on works on paper in his collection, coupled with the practicalities of displaying art in restaurants. McCarty recalls how in the first year he hung paintings by Hockney and Diebenkorn, until 12 months later there was red wine and duck sauce splashed on them. Then his wife, Kim McCarty, also an artist, said: "We can't do this anymore. We're going to ruin all this stuff." They replaced the paintings with watercolours, drawings, prints – everything protected behind glass.

Meanwhile, in 1989 on the East Coast, McCarty's first attempt at securing West 55th Street – sought-after for its quintessential SoCal property feature, an outdoor patio – failed. He tried again and eventually established his second restaurant in a strategic position in the heart of Midtown Manhattan, and began attracting the scions of the advertising, music, publishing, literary and movie industries, and their followers. The timing was right. By the late 1980s there was an established buzz in the public mind and media around chefs, as well as the beginning of a creative period for innovation in the restaurant industry. Friedman again: "After the Seventies and Studio 54, people just finally woke up from that cocaine age and said, 'What are we going to do now?' Restaurants became the place where people would go, and that was the evening. It wasn't going to a club anymore. That was over and it was done. People were just looking for something new, and there were people who wanted to understand the personalities behind the food." McCarty lived the life his restaurant persona projected. He stopped cooking and remained front of house to mix with his diners and patrons. Michael's New York quickly became a "nexus of publishing people, television people, agents and assorted bullshit artists", according to long-standing regular Gil Schwartz. "Remarkably, the same people are frequenting it today." The restaurant built a reputation as the place to be seen for members of the publishing and media industries, "a cross between a peacock farm and a high-school cafeteria".

Through his restaurants, McCarty has integrated himself in a developing time of the art world in Los Angeles and New York. He still collects art but will not take the piece unless he meets the artist, upholding his reputation as chef-collector. He has maintained friendships with Tony Berlant, Ed Moses, David Hockney, Richard Diebenkorn and Sam Francis. He has met every artist in his collection, except Duchamp – having to settle for Alexina Sattler, the artist's widow, who would regularly dine in the restaurant, to prove his point. Both Michael's restaurants retain their appeal as a time capsule in terms of the art restaurant being as significant an outlet of cultural production as any other form. There is a romance and nostalgia that still lingers in Michael's Californian free-spiritedness. The patio with its plants and dining style of candles lit on early evenings mean the light and mood refer to a sublime, oceanic ambience, and the artists and patrons that frequented it in the 1980s and 1990s.

McCarty wrote himself into American restaurant history and ensured his links to the art world and collecting were included in that "party" narrative. The pioneering entrepreneurialism is matched by the artists on the walls of both restaurants who were drawn to the promise of the liberal lifestyle of the West Coast where the atmosphere and climate were explored in the pursuit of pleasure, and where celebrations, gatherings and dining with friends were not just an ephemeral pastime, but key to discovering sensuality and the experience of being in a particular environment. His version of aesthetic dining is also "good for you".

Works and artists in the Michael's collection

Santa Monica

—

A selection of works from David Hockney's *Weather Series* reflect the light and airiness of southern California. Hockney became fascinated with weather, using the 19th-century Japanese *ukiyo-e* woodblock prints by Hokusai, as well as Monet, as a starting point to depict shifts and changes in atmosphere and light. One piece, *Wind*, depicts paper blowing in the wind and a street sign for Melrose Avenue, both there but elsewhere.

—

Dennis Hopper's photography documenting the social change and creative energy of the 1960s is quintessentially Californian in its subject matter and access to countercultures. It is coterie art for a coterie place. Perhaps the restaurateur feels an affinity with the subject matter, given the raucous and wild behaviour of his early years with his chefs.

—

Charles Garabedian, an Armenian-American figurative artist, represented by L.A. Louver, was known for his paintings and drawings referencing classical Greek and Chinese imagery. The pieces are sexual, sensual and celebrate the sybaritic, meaning they work in the restaurant setting.

—

There is a Robert Graham frieze depicting the female form in long, languorous varied positions in the patio dining area among the foliage. Sensual, healthy bodies in the SoCal light and warm air keep guests company.

—

Early watercolours by Kim McCarty, Michael's wife, further build the links between the art, the household, the couple and the restaurant. She has had over 20 solo shows since the early 1990s, in addition to participating in more than 42 group exhibitions, and is known for her ethereal, monochromatic, wet-on-wet portraits.

New York

—

Jasper Johns works from his *Scent* series – abstract, primary colour lines, bright and repetitive, mesmerising in their fresh jubilance.

—

The collection also features works from Johns's *0 Through 9* series. This was part of the artist's investigation into pure form, foregrounding the image for focus in the present moment.

—

John Cage swapped California for New York. The restaurant collection includes line drawings that introduce moments of meditation and calm into a buzzing atmosphere.

Jasper Johns' *Untitled 1972* in the main dining room of the New York restaurant; David Hockney and Kim McCarty's *The Man in the Red Suit* in New York; Kim McCarty in New York; a watercolour rabbit by Kim McCarty; a painting displayed in Michael's

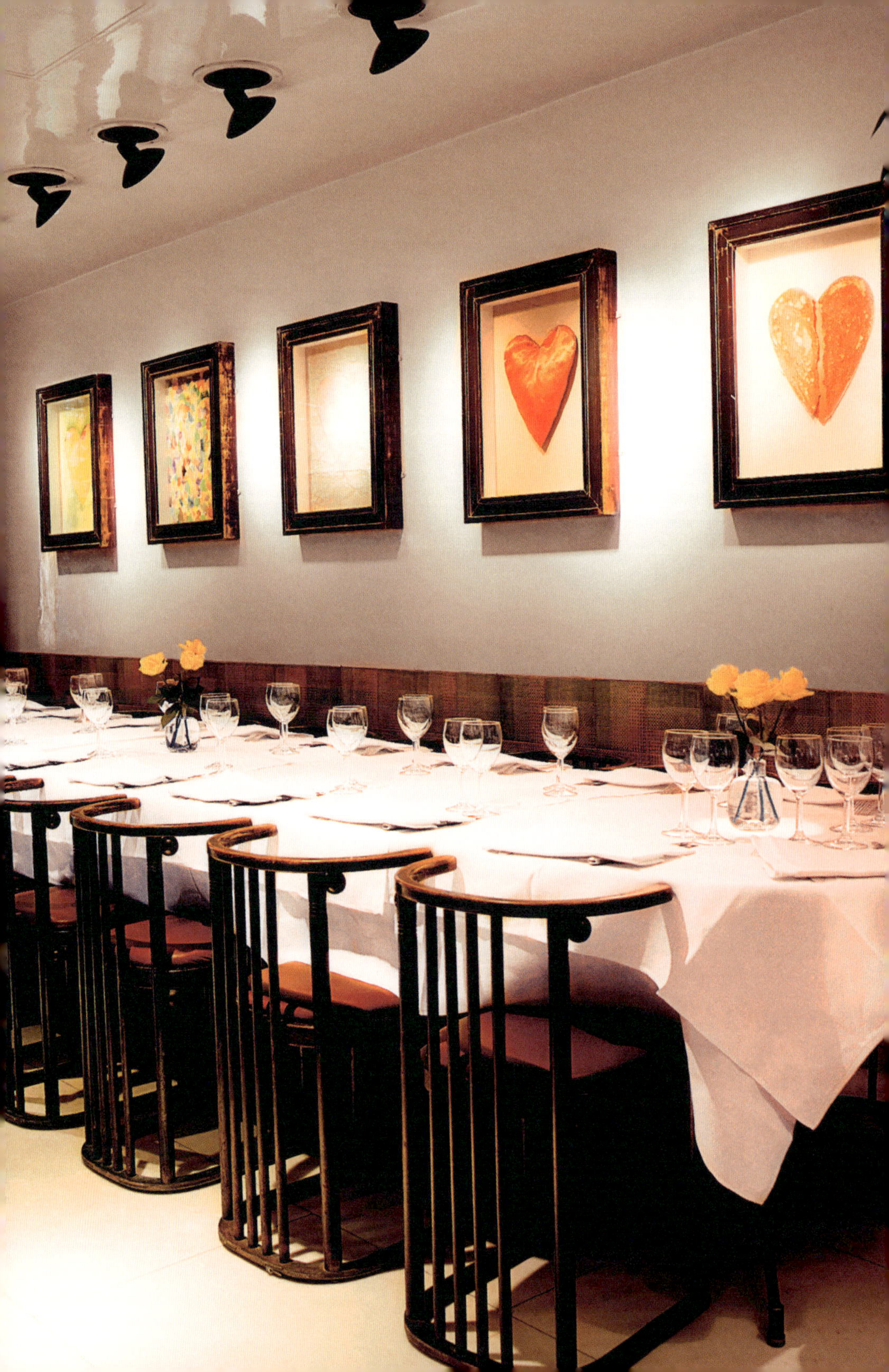

Mr Chow

"Difficult, expensive and heavy is good."
— Michael Chow

Five red plush hearts hang in box-frames along the wall over the tables of the Mr Chow Chinese restaurant in London. They are bold, dramatic and have probably added pleasure to a fair few date nights over the years. They look obvious, even clichéd in terms of being perfectly symmetrical, red and cuddly. They are, of course, works of American Pop artist Jim Dine, a shape and colour that reoccurs throughout his œuvre. Befittingly, Mr Chow opened its doors on Valentine's Day in 1968. The curiously different restaurant in affluent Knightsbridge invited Mick Jagger and Marianne Faithfull as its first guests. Until that point in the capital, Chinese cuisine, Cantonese in particular, had been offered by immigrants in areas including Chinatown and in modest café-style venues in the East End. With the arrival of Mr Chow, glass noodles and scallion pancakes were suddenly served with flair and aplomb in this sleek, mirrored bijoux space with its lacquered panels, Josef Hoffmann Art Deco circular chairs and white tableclothed tables overseen by jolly waiters in dinner jackets. Art would also play a role in what made Mr Chow a success.

Michael Chow – or "M" as he expects to be called – has led a life in a series of contrasts that have formed his view on how restaurant "artistic projects" should be designed as "a controlled accident". Contradictions that include sharing a bedsit with two other Chinese students as a refugee in south London in 1963, to eventually purchasing the home of a Getty heiress for $70m in Beverly Hills in 2019. From arriving alone at art school as a young unknown man to later on dating Patti Smith, and eventually marrying not one, but two international models, Grace Coddington and Tina Chow. Or from taking a gamble on setting up one upmarket Chinese restaurant in West London to then scaling up the formula to incorporate nine global establishments in premium locations, such as Beverly Hills and Miami Beach.

In the late 1960s, trattorias had become popular and widespread throughout West London. A group of Italian waiters immigrating from Italy after the Second World War were responsible for a quiet food revolution in the city. The fountainhead of these trattorias was Alvaro's, established by Alvaro Maccioni, a style of restaurant just as much a part of the Swinging Sixties as Mary Quant's miniskirts and David Bailey's monochrome photographs. These eateries were places for innovation in cooking: fresh products imported from Italy, staff who were first-generation émigrés and understood how to make diners feel like they were part of the family, and, most importantly, late opening hours to quench the new thirst for nightlife in the capital. Today, such family-run trattorias may seem tired or generic, but at that time they offered an exotic escape from post-war, drab London, which coincided with the hedonistic optimism of the 1960s. The artist and interior designer Enzo Apicella was the progenitor of this modern trattoria design – clean interiors, shiny tiles on floors and walls, and statement art and decor, in addition to the import of the tradition of the friendly and cheery Italian waiter – that spread through many now historic restaurants, La Trattoria Terrazza, La Famiglia, Aretusa and Meridiana.

Amidst this Italianate influence on prandial London, Mr Chow was opened in partnership with Sandro Tobi, who had run Alvaro's, at 151 Knightsbridge. The idea was to offer a design-conscious, modern trattoria, but to serve high-end Peking cuisine to more selective West End patrons. M recalls how he decided against employing his fellow countrymen as waiters because "the sophistication and subtlety of the Chinese" in terms of hospitality "would be lost" on Western audiences. Instead, he would give the West a "Chinese trattoria" that elevated his home country's food, which in Britain was at the time widely considered the "lowest of the low". The difference between "customers" versus "clients", M says, is "one you get to charge one dollar more". The restaurant and its dining experience would be a way for him to show Western audiences the imperial and noble traditions of Chinese culture and rituals. The first restaurants known to mankind opened during the Song Dynasty (900-1100) – almost seven centuries earlier than the Western establishments we are more familiar with from post-revolutionary Paris. Peking cuisine had more than 3,000 years to evolve and innovate its dishes and methods. Devised in the Forbidden City, and perfected over three dynasties, it was much more than sloppy chop suey. But it was also more than just reworking Peking duck and chow mein. The restaurant was Chow's chance to recreate the concept of Chinese food and demonstrate it rightfully had an equivalence with high-end, luxurious Western culture. If it was suitable for emperors in the old country, it would be acceptable to London's burgeoning cultural and celebrity scenes. Art collecting, and using works as trophies and signals of good taste, would be instrumental to this.

Some of M's views on the restaurant may now seem dated ("don't bore the audience"), but he has lasted for over five decades in the industry, still active, still opening new venues, such as his most recent Las Vegas Chow in 2016. His restaurants have hosted legendary parties, celebrations and gatherings in the past four decades. An iconic black-and-white photo from 23 April 1985 features David Hockney, Julian Schnabel, Andy Warhol, Alex Katz, Keith Haring, Jean-Michel Basquiat, Robert Mapplethorpe, Larry Rivers, Nam June Paik, Jenny Holzer, Barbara Kruger, Sol LeWitt and Tom Wesselmann – a catalogue or *Who's Who* of contemporary art at the time. The 1960s in London saw the integration of the arts and cultural sectors, be it film, art, music, architecture, sports or photography. The old class barriers were breaking down and, according to M: "Here you have truly a cultural revolution that made us completely free and creative. We were young and we ruled the world – the most exciting time." He may have been a casualty of Mao's Cultural Revolution, having lost his family as a young boy and his social status by emigrating to a new country, but he benefited from the cultural revolution happening in his new homeland.

In some respects, his friendships with artists have mirrored the development of modern and contemporary British and American art, enacted through a succession of portraits of him painted by everyone from Peter Blake to Urs Fischer. Chow is an artist himself, and the portraits are evidence of his standing with fellow practitioners. In the 1960s he socialised with Pop artists such as Blake and Richard Hamilton, as well as members of The Rolling Stones and The Beatles. By the 1980s, art had become commercial and enterprising, the commodity model that is still prevalent today. Artists such as Keith Haring, Jean-Michel Basquiat and Julian Schnabel were willing participants in this system, revelling in their new-found wealth and celebrity status, with publicists and journalists following them from bars to restaurants to parties to inflate their egos. Many of them would flock to Mr Chow in New York to cavort with superstars such as Madonna and David Bowie.

Michael Chow's story is not *exactly* a rags-to-riches one – he was always in riches. He just took a detour to Britain to attend boarding school, then enrolled in Saint Martin's School of Art to study painting. Upon graduation he shared a modest bedsit with two other impecunious artists. This led to his working in a hair salon, then meeting influential people such as Joseph Ettedgui and Vidal Sassoon, and eventually establishing his eponymous restaurant and taking his place again among the privileged, befriending and mixing with successful artists, pop stars, fashion icons and actors of the 1970s and 1980s. *Paradise Chicken* lost and regained. In some ways, his *making it back* was important and unfinished business, given his family history. M grew up in an artistic and theatrical family. His father, Zhou Xinfang, was one of China's greatest opera stars in the 1940s and 1950s and became director of the Peking Opera. The young M was surrounded by art, poetry and music through feasts and dinners, giving him a sense of occasion and magic in the commensality of dining and making it extraordinary. Zhou was imprisoned and executed by Mao – M never saw him again after he left China – but his father and the ideals he represented remained inspirational throughout his son's life.

M's creative upbringing and training as an artist stood him in good stead to justify his belief of being a tastemaker who could fashion aesthetic synergies in his vision of hospitality. He was not going to let a new homeland stand in his

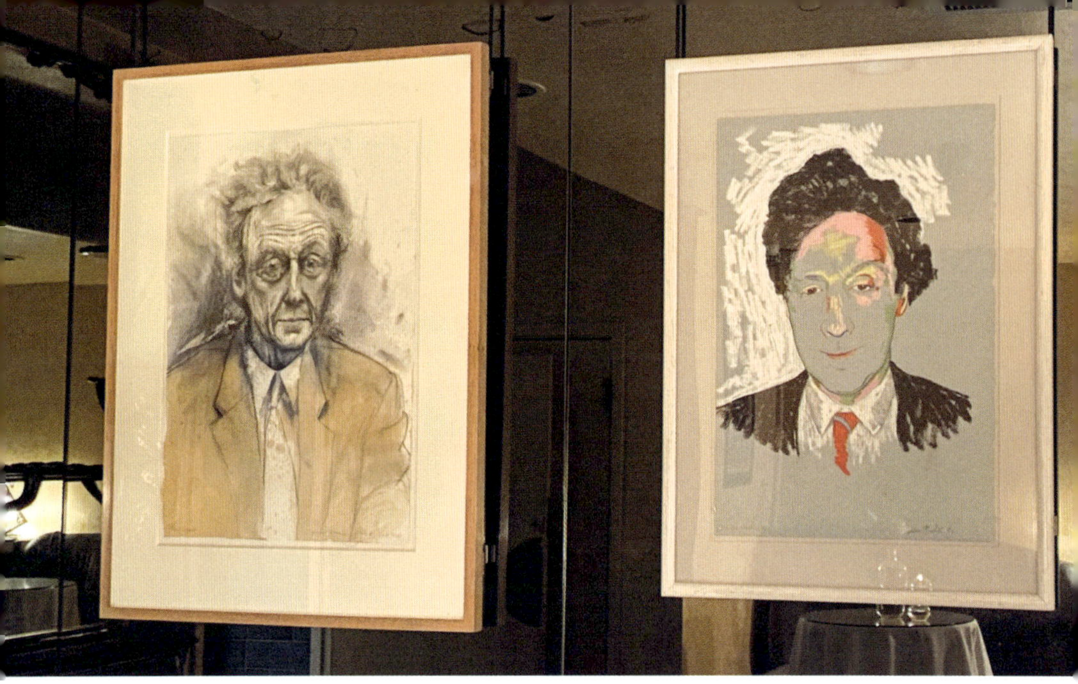

way. Nor was he going to let the West speak for him and his culture. He remains indignant about how Chinese culture has been misrepresented and misunderstood for decades in the UK and the US.

The Knightsbridge restaurant initially had five artists in its collection: Peter Blake, David Hockney, Patrick Caulfield, Jim Dine and Richard Smith. M commissioned works and "paid them exactly the same amount through food". He and Blake first met through the artist Richard Lin. Blake was sharing a flat with Richard Smith and M, Lin and another artist shared one across the road. The group became friends and held dinners together. When M began to plan the opening of his restaurant, he asked Blake if he would paint a portrait of him. The only stipulation was "nothing ethnic, no chinoiserie racism". Blake responded with the painting *Frisco and Lorenzo Wong and Wildman Michael Chow* (1966), depicting the pride, leadership and entrepreneurial zest of M combined with made-up figures from the artist's repertoire of wrestlers. Chow is presented as a yellow wrestler-manager flanked by two half-Chinese, half-Italian wrestlers/bodyguards. It is an amalgamation of Blake's work and Chow's ego that melds the restaurateur into a Pop icon fit for the changing times of the Sixties. Chow wanted to subvert expectations of Chinese immigrants in London: "That's why I wear glasses, not to look so Asian!" This resulted in an eating down exchange, which Blake proudly still draws upon – unlike Jim Dine, who "used his up in the first two weeks" as a result of all the parties he'd throw in Chow's, as Blake likes to retell: "They were halcyon days. I went up to London to the Royal College to give tutorials. In those days you could live on a couple of days' teaching." Blake used credit he had at Mr Chow to take all his students and associates – one of whom was the musician Ian Dury – out to lunch. He recalls: "We had appreciated everything so much, coming into the art world in the period just after the war. Everything seemed possible." Including a high-end Chinese trattoria.

M then commissioned more work for the restaurant and for his personal collection. Artists ranging from Andy Warhol, Keith Haring and David Bailey to Julian Schnabel all produced portraits of Chow. They reflect the changing face of the sitter – as a Mod in the late Sixties; long-haired and louche in the Seventies; corporate and clipped in the Eighties; and into the more respectable businessman and socialite of the Nineties. Schnabel's vast oil portrait from 1985, made up of broken painted plates, comes into focus only when taken in from some distance. In 1986, Haring painted a portrait of Chow as a huge green prawn in a bowl of noodles – his favourite dish at Mr Chow. Artists have also been invited to contribute to the restaurant's Artist Book, which includes doodles, messages and works of art from Jean-Michel Basquiat, Andy Warhol and Jasper Johns, among others. "Sometimes you had three or four artists [at work simultaneously]," recalls Chow. "Everybody was having a great time. It was like a jazz session with improvisation. There was lots of energy there." As the collection grew, so did the artists' competitiveness, says Chow, as each contributor strove to produce something new and different in the pages beyond a doodle and autograph. His Artist Book collection includes Eduardo Paolozzi, Ed Ruscha, Allen Jones, Larry Rivers, Richard Hamilton, Jasper Johns, Dieter Roth, Joe Tilson, Patrick Caulfield, Jean-Michel Basquiat, Richard Prince, David Hockney, Anthony Caro, Georg Baselitz, Dennis Hopper, Jeff Koons, Julian Schnabel, Damien Hirst, Donald Baechler, Howard Hodgkin, Keith Haring, Urs Fischer, Peter Blake, Ian Dury, Francis Bacon, George Condo, Andy Warhol and Cy Twombly. M is uninterested in the art market; he has never sold a work, preferring to bolster a collection that reinforces his taste, and extends this to his family, also involved in the restaurants.

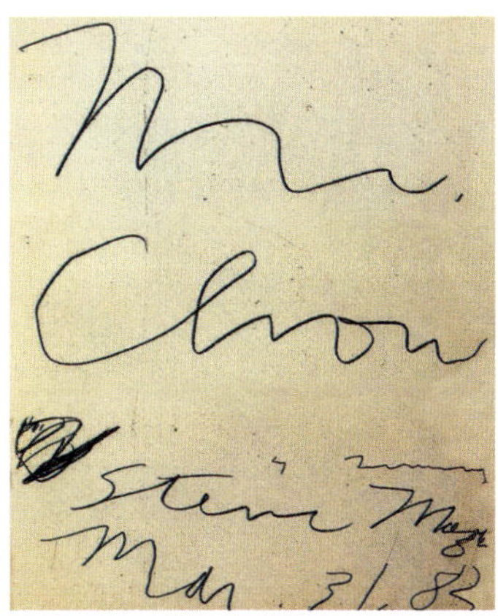

The commissioned artists have also painted members of his family, including his latest child with his fourth wife in 2019, who acquired his first piece of art at one month old, "the youngest art collector ever!" The portraits hang throughout his restaurants, and in addition to being trophies, they are symbols of the solidarity and ease M feels in his relationships with these artists.

He began his collection by charming the artists around him, but then became successful enough to commission them to produce works for his collection. He wanted to own *them* – to *own* Warhol and Basquiat and even channel them into the restaurant experience, in the decor, in the details, in the ambience, in the mythology. Ed Ruscha made a food painting in 1973 in his trademark bold capitals ("MR CHOW") using oyster sauce, bean paste, red cabbage and egg yolk; this is now reproduced on the matchboxes the restaurant offers guests at reception. Of all his artists, M says, "Cy Twombly is my god." He drew the restaurant logo that adorns the plates in all the Chow venues: "The chicest motherfucking logo on the planet."

The art in his establishments is integrated into the environment in a similar way as it is in his favourite restaurant in the world, the Kronenhalle. The restaurant should be "ego translated into emotional energy", according to M. It is a fusion between him seeing himself as a tastemaker and attempting to elicit an excitement and sensory pleasure in his diners. Mr Chow was the "first 'design' restaurant'" in London, according to designer and restaurateur Terence Conran. It was unprecedented even though it was a small space. Maintaining the cosy trattoria layout, it was planned to the very last detail in terms of symmetry, colour scheme and ambience. Chow used artworks "successfully and dramatically". This would come from his childhood and exposure to opera. Chinese opera was a *gesamtkunstwerk*, combining visual art with staging dialogue and music a thousand years before Bayreuth. The art in the dining space produced an energy and excitement, and jostled for the diners' attention as much as their companions did. When M speaks about his restaurants, he uses poetic phrases and metaphysical concepts deftly and confidently: "My restaurants must be all art and orchestration." The restaurant must be like a theatrical or religious ceremony, elevated to a spiritual level with the requisite accoutrements for ritual. Artists are priests in his establishments. The dining service is a performance, with staff poised to make the diner feel like they are being revered; the maître d' "must look you in the eye". A successful restaurant also depends on the audience communicating back to indicate they participate in the ritual and receive the tastemaking. This is why the restaurant is "a noble concept", M says; the dining climaxes every night, like the magic of the theatre.

Restaurants augment feelings of fantasy and escapism as much as they ground diners in a particular time and setting. This paradox of dining captures the enduring popularity and fascination with restaurants associated with a particular scene. M argues they must have a vision and produce a transcendental moment, "changing by not changing". The restaurant is elevated to the metaphysical and "every detail is a universe". The utter enjoyment and pleasure of dining with others as well as the sensual experience of eating "builds the energy of the restaurant into the moment", and "Mr Chow is a place where all arts meet. Every night is a performance."

Works and artists in the Mr Chow collection

—

The Three Peking Ducks (1969), by Clive Barker, are silver on bronze, and continue to glint in the front window of Mr Chow as though on a conveyor belt. They are cast from real ducks. Cheap Asian restaurants often display plastic dishes to entice diners; here they are silver. Chow is making a statement on quality.

—

Andy Warhol autographed a pair of chopstick covers and a silver serving spoon in 1985, and Chow collected them as artworks and replicated them throughout his restaurants. The originals are in the Andy Warhol Museum in Pittsburgh.

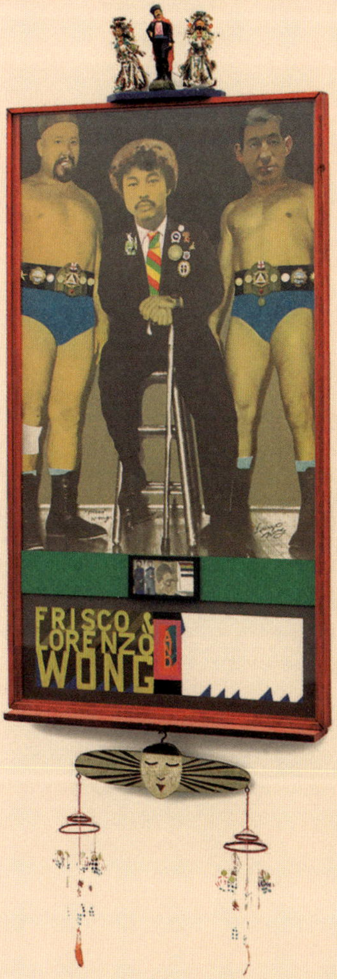

Works by Jim Dine displayed over dining tables; the bar at Mr Chow; "Mr Chow" scribble by Cy Twombly; *Frisco and Lorenzo Wong and Wildman Michael Chow* by Peter Blake

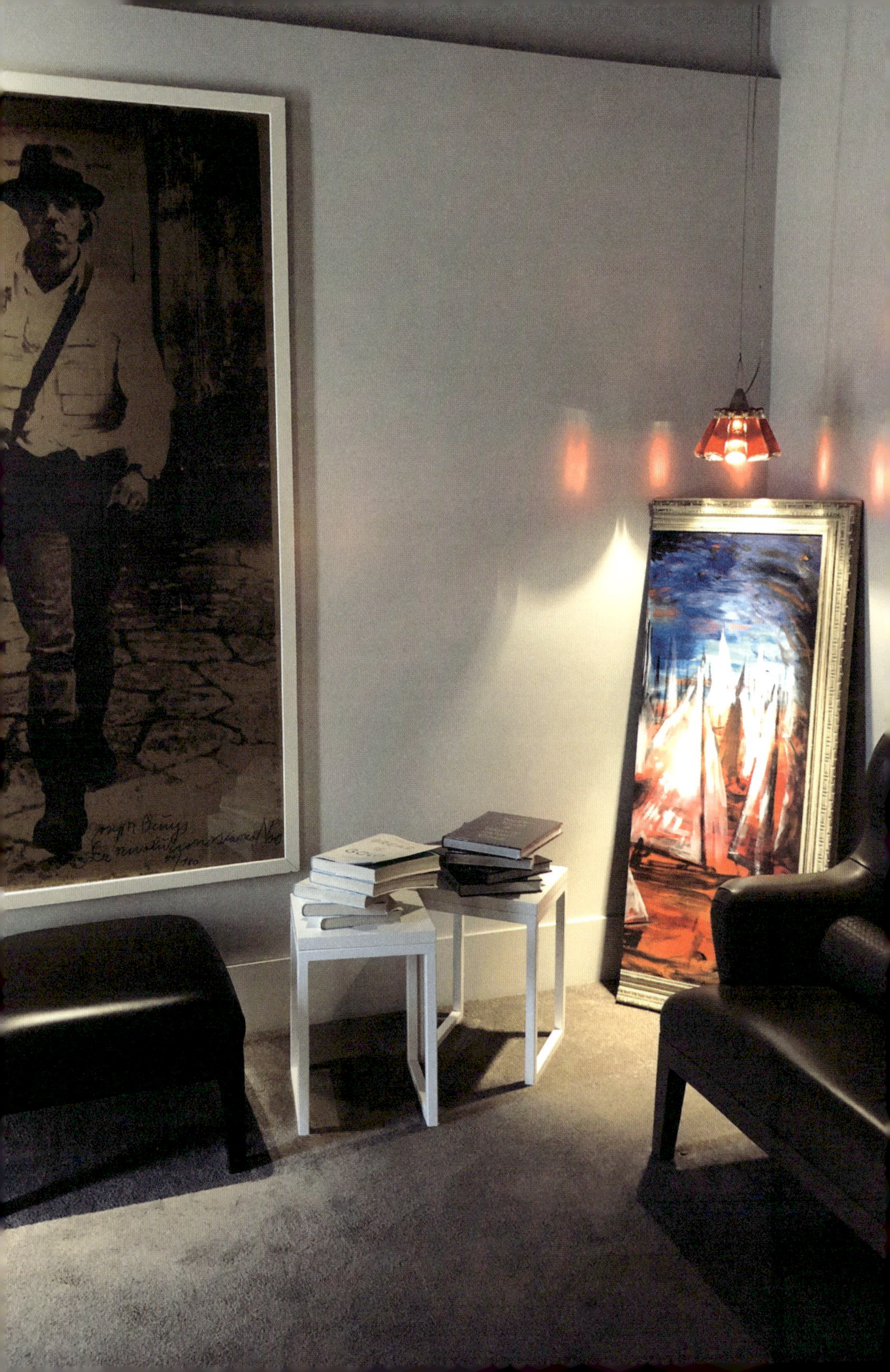

Osteria Francescana

"Even the act of peeling a potato can be an artistic act if it is consciously done."
— Joseph Beuys

If ever there was a chef who could deftly navigate the complexities overlooked by the rest of us regarding food and its relationship to creativity, taste and dining traditions, Massimo Bottura is that person. His zest for innovation, ability to conceptualise and clear refusal to stick within one discipline in the pursuit of realising his culinary vision – "the noise in my head" – spills out throughout the contemporary Italian cuisine he remakes. This dynamic and dissonant chef is overtly conscious of his place in history and within the tradition of Italian cooking. Furthermore, he is aware of his effect on it – "bringing the best of the past into the future" – by innovating, ensuring his dishes and restaurant experiences remain thrilling and extraordinary. Underpinning these endeavours is Bottura's involvement with contemporary art, his "sharing ideas with artists", "feeding them" as much as they "feed him". In this constant state of flux that is his vision, which began in the cosy Modenese kitchen and is now a gastronomic enterprise with a global reach, his obsession with art provides another platform for him to carry out his conceptual culinary experiments. Very few chefs are afforded the privilege of referring to their work as art. But Bottura brings an unusual ability to think like an artist to his cooking. However, it does not mean he claims to be an artist; this status is reserved for aesthetic practitioners he admires and respects for their liberty – people from whom he can learn. Instead, he regards himself as "an artisan"; he must combine ingredients, timing and presentation in the making of the products to incorporate the traditions of the recipes. Artists "have total freedom to make and output, whereas the chef must fulfil certain constraints – food must be nutritious, healthy, taste good", he states. Thinking about the art pieces he owns inspires Bottura to construct the dishes in the kitchen. Here aesthetic taste is translated into literal taste. Food is art in terms of conceptual aesthetics: the intentions and rationale behind the execution of the recipes is as important – arguably more important – than the plate itself. And Osteria Francescana is the art restaurant that most overtly aligns art and cooking to elevate modest ingredients and processes to something extraordinary. As the chef writes in his cookbook: "Art reminds you to keep a small window open for everyday poetry, and when that happens, the most mundane object turns to gold."

As early as the 1990s, the original Osteria on Calle Rosa had already been drawing in artists who had studios in the neighbouring streets. Bottura took over in 1995, and as the artists became more established in the area and their numbers grew, art dealers, gallerists and others from the industry began to visit the eatery. Emilio Mazzoli ran a space on the same street and used the Osteria to entertain, and with this came American, Italian and European photographers and painters. The two struck up a friendship. Mazzoli is credited with persuading Bottura to "pay his dues" to the regional classic dishes. The gallerist requested a classic *tagliatelle al ragu* when he first arrived to dine. He was told it was too simple a dish for Osteria Francescana to offer. The gallerist replied: "You think you can drive a Ferrari without learning first how to use the indicators and brakes?" Bottura explains this opened his eyes and helped him to understand the parallel with the Italian Transavanguardia movement that Mazzoli and critic Achille Oliva supported, with artists including Enzo Cucchi, Mimmo Paladino and Sandro Chia. This Italian version of Neo-Expressionism departed from conceptual art to evoke a joy and emotion in its execution. Its art produced new images, and Bottura wanted to try the same philosophy in his recipes – to deconstruct and rebuild elements of dining taken for granted or overlooked when the focus is on the faithful, unwavering execution of traditional methods.

At times, artists influence the chef's thinking and working by unlocking ways to adapt and experiment with traditional cooking, and to translate it onto the plate. For instance, in 2014 he created "beautiful, psychedelic spin-painted veal, not flame grilled", the meat cooked *sous vide*, blasted with ash and attacked by several coloured sauces. He used colour "like Damien Hirst in his spin paintings". When the artist heard about the dish, he was so impressed he sent the chef one of his spin paintings. Giuliano Della Casa introduced Bottura to more interdisciplinary possibilities for art through his own poem-painting works and intellectual ideas. The latter thanked him by asking him to illustrate the menus for the restaurant. The artist and chef have also operated an informal eat down policy where they trade food for work – including a Tortellini Table from 1968, featuring a gold tortellini on top. Since that time, artists, critics and collectors, "too many to be named, filled the restaurant with their words, ideas and dreams," says Bottura. "We fed them, and they fed us. The exchange brought unlimited energy and stimulus to Osteria Francescana". He is an art restaurant chef who does not collect just for enjoyment of the art – he collects for the artistic practices and concepts that he will convert into dishes.

Bottura was not a stranger to art, having grown up with the 19th-century "classic provincial, upper middle-class art" that decorated the family house outside of Modena. He met his wife, Lara Gilmore, in New York when they both worked in a SoHo restaurant, and as she was also painting at the time, she introduced him to the artists of the Sensation generation in the UK: Chris Ofili, Sam Taylor-Wood and Gillian Wearing, among others. That began his life as a collector, and years later they rotate works between their personal collection and the restaurant, "moving paintings and sculptures around like ingredients on a plate. With each addition, our walls began to speak." He insists the only way to collect art is "instinct", but also stresses the importance of reading, studying and looking at as much of it as you can, as contemporary art constantly changes and moves on, so there is no other way to keep track of what is significant. In the case of Ugo Rondinone, he says he waited 15 years to purchase a piece by the artist. The collection is disparate and contemporary, and the acquisitions are characterised by social, political and cultural historical references, underpinned by his irreverent sense of humour and bolstered by his personal relationships with the artists.

For instance, one of the earliest pieces he acquired was Maurizio Cattelan's *Tourists*, which features three stuffed Venetian pigeons and was part of an installation showcased at the 1997 Venice Biennale. It appealed to Bottura's brazen approach to modern Italian culture. He says the artist "broke all the rules; from high in the rafters of the Italian Pavilion, hundreds of taxidermy pigeons were looking down and pooping on the artwork of a previous generation". When Cattelan was informed it was purchased to be installed in a high-end restaurant, he came to Modena to "see who this crazy guy was, buying dead pigeons", and the pair struck up a friendship that continues to this day. The work now travels between the original Francescana, the couple's home in Modena and their second Francescana in their villa, Casa Maria Luigia.

Osteria Francescana is in a 15th-century Emilian home, on a typically quiet and cobbled Modenese lane. One could easily walk by and not notice it if it weren't for the congregation of diners outside, speaking in different languages and decibels, taking photos of the doorbell, peeking into the kitchen windows, waiting to fulfil reservations that typically take a minimum of six months in advance to secure. They fly in from all over the world, a reminder that despite the charming and traditional appearance of the Osteria in this part of the city, it is a bucket-list destination for international consumers of luxury experiences. The home features just three dining rooms with a total of 24 tables and the original wooden beams. The interiors are pared back, clean and contemporary, with thick white linen tablecloths and minimally delicate cutlery and crockery, ensuring the focus remains on details of the arrangements on the dishes and art on the walls. In June 2020, after Italy lifted its national lockdown in the global pandemic, and coinciding with the restaurant's 25th anniversary, Gilmore and Bottura rehung works when they reopened to celebrate the hope that comes with the "eternal spring". The Osteria was updated with upbeat Murakami cartoons, Hirst's butterflies... and a multicoloured floral carpet.

There are three things that are untouchable in Italy, according to Bottura: the Pope, football and grandmothers' cooking. The former two he leaves alone, but the last he dismantles. He describes the Damascene moment when an artwork

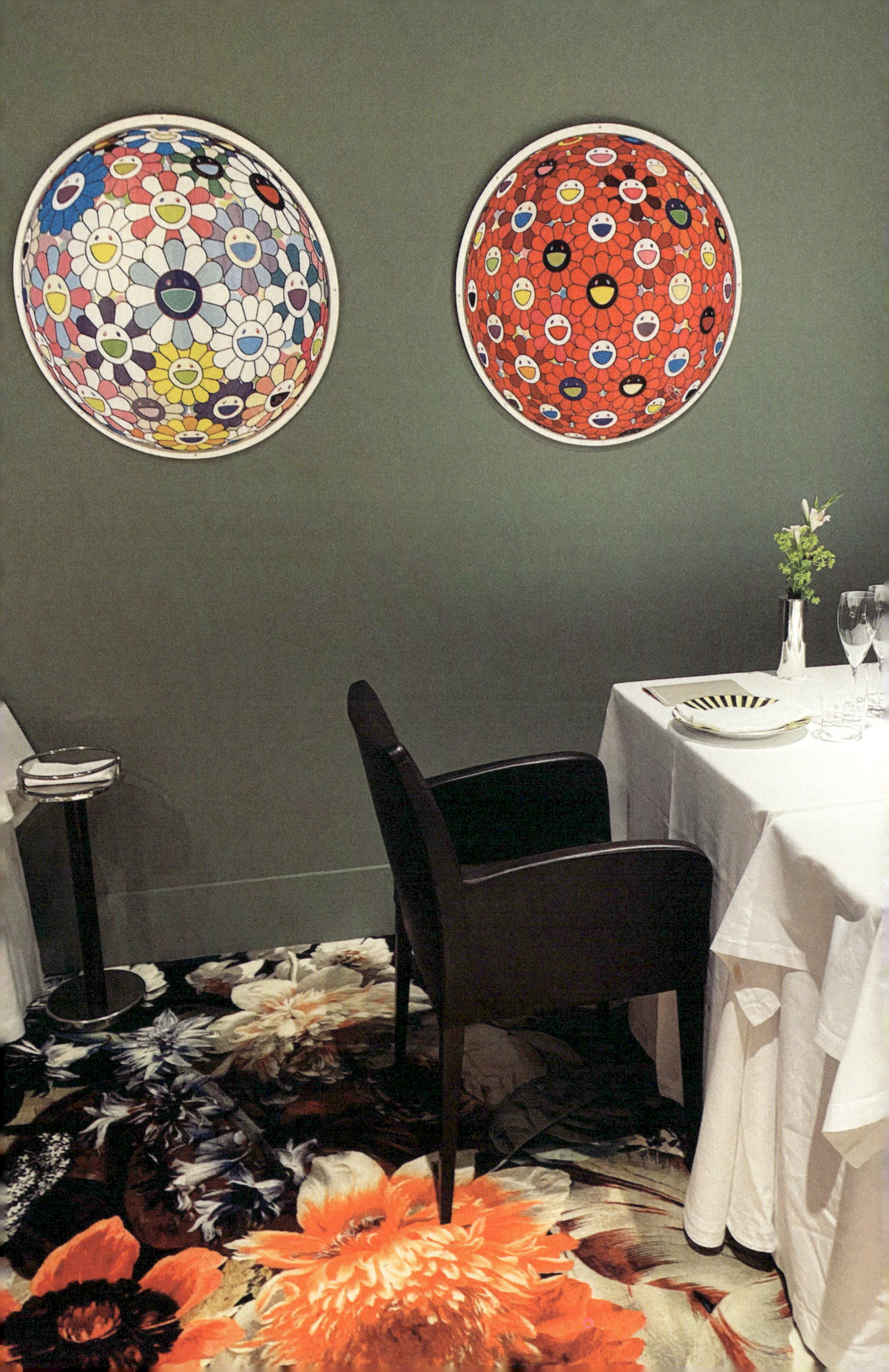

helped him to understand how he would reconstitute Nona's dishes and the feelings transmitted: Ai Weiwei's *Dropping a Han Dynasty Urn* (1995). He recalls initially being baffled as to why the artist would break a 2,000-year-old artefact. "Why break thousands of years of history in an instant? Suddenly, I understood. Ai Weiwei's destructive gesture was actually a constructive one. A beginning." From then on, he would "break, transform, create", he would build a new tradition filtered through a contemporary mind, recreating emotions "in edible form". There can be no creativity without constraints, and it is a renegotiation of these controls and what is produced within those rules that progresses innovation. For the chef, the art does not just hang on the restaurant walls, it stimulates and makes his whole creative process possible.

Similarly, Lucio Fontana is also an influential artist for Bottura, because he is "the perfect expression of the northern Italian mind... with a simple gesture he tells you everything... The act of breaking the pictorial surface was the moment of creation."

The artist searched for the fourth dimension "beyond the picture frame and into the unknown, and his imagination took him to infinity". Certainly, Osteria Francescana's gastronomy pushes limits and deconstructs expectations of ingredients, presentation of food and order of consumption. "Was it too much to ask flavour to travel beyond territorial border or push a recipe across space or time? We could try," Fontana reflects.

A number of his dishes are directly inspired by contemporary art. *Camouflage*, with its custard of *foie gras*, dark chocolate and espresso foam, comes from a conversation between Picasso and Gertrude Stein, as a camouflaged truck rolled past them on Boulevard Raspail in 1914. Picasso, who had never seen camouflage before, cried: "Yes, it is we who made it, that is Cubism!" This is one of the 18 dishes from the tasting menu that the lucky 28 people dining there will taste in the Osteria. Bottura's dishes are constantly evolving and they pass through many phases in terms of appearance – from complicated and intricate pinches and dollops of ingredients, to complete minimalism and self-effacement of a culinary hand. He explains this is the same way an artist will change phases of production throughout their career. There is a series of recipes based on Alighiero e Boetti's notion of *immagine e somiglianza* (image and likeness). The artist's fascination with duplication and concern with multiplication inspired the dishes for the chef. Bottura studied the effects of reproduction and multiplicity of individual ingredients through varying temperatures and in different textures to come up with more combinations, applying "Boettian duality to a razor clam".

Just as the artists deploy irony in the works to argue their philosophy of breaking and rearranging tradition, Bottura does the same thing in his cooking. He conveys the metaphor of the past and future, tradition and innovation, to the dining experience. A chef and his restaurant must find their place in the world. "We had never considered art a decoration, but a way of expanding beyond our physical confines, letting us see beyond the medieval city of Modena while remaining within it," he says. The experience of dining at Osteria Francescana is to be steeped in tradition but to also lose that certainty in a pleasurable way because the process is never fixed. "Our kitchen is never finished or fixed, but in a continuous process of exploration, evolution and change." Joseph Beuys is also one of the most important artists for Bottura's culinary project because the artist revealed parallels between his creative process and his own work in the kitchen. Beuys once declared: "Process is never finished."

The irony of the dishes, like in the artworks, is part of the chef's system of giving with one hand but taking away with the other. *BURNT*, a jet-black dish of squid broth and cuttlefish ink, makes the diner wonder where the food begins and the plate ends, while *Oops, I Dropped the Lemon Tart* presents the dessert as a fragmented, sloppy mess of crust and custard. This is uncomfortable comfort food. The art is familiarly unfamiliar, such as a Dan Colen work of chewing gum spat out and stuck on the canvas in the entry hall to the dining rooms. Diners are bombarded by the stimuli, visual and taste, and must attempt to balance the intellectual and the emotional. This tension keeps their senses on edge and heightens the experience of tasting and looking at the food and art. It is a form of sensory bombardment, albeit using premium ingredients. Bottura thinks in synesthetic terms, "cross-pollinating" and "tasting" his "creativity". It can become difficult to keep up with the concepts, the energy and the many influences on his œuvre, how pieces fall into place during the dining. But he charts his course through it because art is both "a landscape of ideas" and his "muse", constantly updating his culinary development. The artworks are like "the Hansel and Gretel breadcrumbs", according to Lara Gilmore. They are "little clues that lead our guests to understanding or not understanding or being pleasantly confused". It may be a world-class restaurant with every honour and culinary award on the planet, but she maintains: "Things may not be exactly as they seem."

If Osteria Francescana broke with local tradition to explore "the fourth dimension", it also turned a provincial town into a global landmark for gastronomes and food critics. The restaurant collection contains a Gavin Turk sculpture of a rubbish bag, confounding many well-heeled diners through the years who took its *trompe-l'œil* illusion literally and wondered why such an establishment would forget a bag of rubbish in the corridor. The work is characteristic of Bottura's humorous taste in art, but like all artworks that acquire new meanings from the context in which they are displayed, it also serves as a reminder of the luxury consumption, excess and wealth that the restaurant has

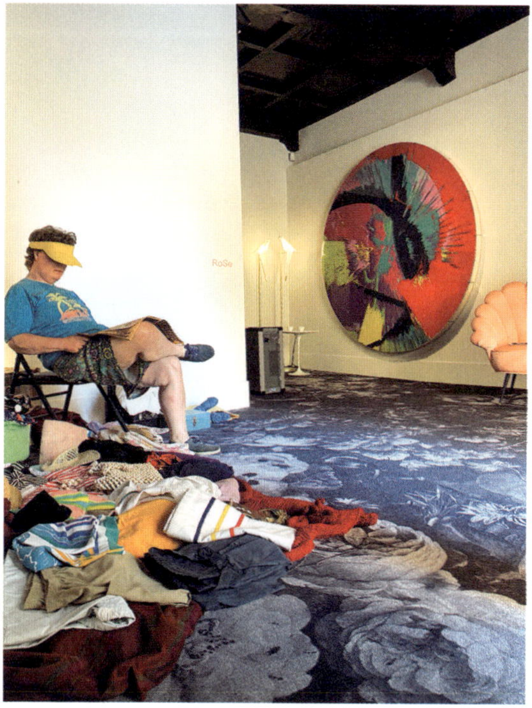

come to represent. After the rehang in 2020, guests enter the reception to be greeted by a rotund, oblivious flea-market seller, Rose, wearing a faded Florida T-shirt, shorts and flip flops. She reads a gossip magazine and strewn across the floor are old shoes, records, bric-à-brac and other junk. She is a Duane Hanson sculpture and she too is a *trompe-l'œil* for confused diners to follow their "breadcrumbs" into the restaurant.

Osteria Francescana has topped the esteemed and peer-reviewed World's 50 Best Restaurants list twice, and has comfortably sat in the top five for almost a decade. This prize has been criticised for being too Western-focused, with critics and chefs judging from New York and London, but the accolade directly contributes to the never-ending waiting list for tables.

The astronomical rise of Bottura's brand as a super-chef in the past decade coincided with the rise in luxury consumption by newly affluent classes on a global level. It now encompasses high-end experiences such as the couple's Casa Maria Luigia inn, collaborations with the likes of Gucci, as well as the *noblesse oblige* that is the requisite accompaniment to a solid public platform, through Bottura's Refretto Felix and Bread is Gold philanthropic projects. The appeal to the emotions of his dining and culinary projects, and the transmission of these, led to calls from Italian politicians to make the chef the Culture Minister, plus claims that Bottura is the sixth artist of the Transavanguardia movement. These achievements are far advanced from cooking tortellini in his Nona's Modenese kitchen, yet his interest in the tradition of the ingredient is not just the luxury of fine quality – he seeks out the origins and acknowledges the supply chain, thinking about where food comes from, about the producers and their craft, the economics of their knowledge and expertise. It's conscious eating and appreciation of the miniscule, the complement, the morsel. This philosophy is connected to contemporary developments in luxury food consumerism and cultural consumption. French sociologists Luc Boltanski and Arnaud Esquerre argue this "economy of enrichment" can offer an explanation for the economic sociology of luxury. To sustain the luxury food industry, and all its producers, farmers and artisans, and differentiate it from normal or mass-produced food, it is essential to highlight the complex narratives around a dish's past, its origin, how it was produced, where it came from, who produced it. Every ingredient and component should have an origin and a stated purpose – as though it were a piece in an art collection.

However, this does not detract from the experiencing of simple enjoyment and pleasure from the object or its authenticity. Bottura is respectful of the modest origins of Italian cuisine. His taste – both in art and in ingredients – mitigates empty and ephemeral consumption. Just like his beloved artists, he is taking his place in the history of innovation, after all. And for the discerning diner participating in aesthetic eating among the art, it should allow them to appreciate the complexities and synthesis of these concepts of taste, ingredients and sensual stimuli. If anything, Osteria Francescana and the role of art in his restaurant ennobles the quotidian and elevates what in an ordinary context may seem straightforward; the modest loaf of bread or sprig of asparagus is given centre stage in his composition of dining. The fact that guests wait for years for a table or jump on a plane from Tokyo for dinner and then fly back the next day, is testament to how his passion and conviction have been so well-presented and communicated to his diners that he has legions of followers internationally. Food is "the transfer of emotion in edible bites", he says, and the art is the extra ingredient that enables him to replicate excellence and turn modest, simple local ingredients into experiences of art and poetry, or even "gold".

Works and artists in the Osteria Francescana collection

—

Francesco Vezzoli's *La Vie en Rose*, a series of 19 embroidered photographs depicting Edith Piaf with a range of melodramatic and bathetic facial expressions. The work combines the power and dominance of the diva with the delicacy of needlework. Vezzoli was an early adopter of embroidery in the 1990s at Central Saint Martins art school. Carlo Benvenuto's *Table and glass* and Mario Schifano's *World Map* have also helped to define Osteria Francescana's unique style with their poetic interpretations.

—

Ceal Floyer's minimalist *Paper and Ink*, made with a box of 20 scholastic coloured markers and watercolour paper. Bottura has often explained how he tries to see the world anew, without preconceptions and set ideas – the way children do.

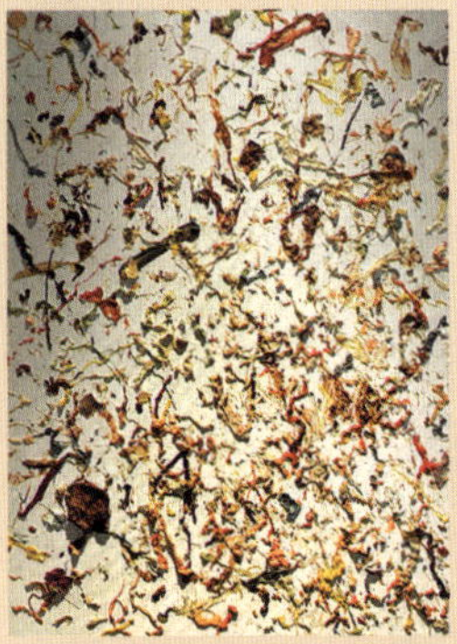

—

Jonathan Borofsky's *Half a Sailboat Painting* – literally half a painting – reflects the chef's picaresque way of keeping his diners alert and aware of what they eat by interrupting what is assumed. In response to this work, Bottura created his "Half a Cheesecake" dessert, where half of the dish is missing.

—

World Map by Mario Schifano is, as its title suggests, a world map, but created in bright colours that blend and bleed into each other. The piece is fitting for a restaurant that has attracted diners from across the planet, and its execution is a reminder of the sensuality and raw processing that is involved in dining.

—

A series of Icelandic landscapes by Olafur Eliasson speak about nature, land and how it is the foundation for raw ingredients – in the artworks and in his kitchen.

Works by Joseph Beuys and Jonathan Borofsky; Francesco Vezzoli's series, Takashi Murakami's *Flower Ball* prints; Damien Hirst's *Beautiful Sonic Disco of Love and Hate at the Gate of Hell Painting with Wicked Pools of Glorious Massimo Bottura Colour and Psychedelic Spin Painted Veal, Not Flame Grilled*, 2007 alongside Duane Hanson's bronze statue *Rose* in the entrance; a canvas covered with colourful chewing gum by Dan Colen

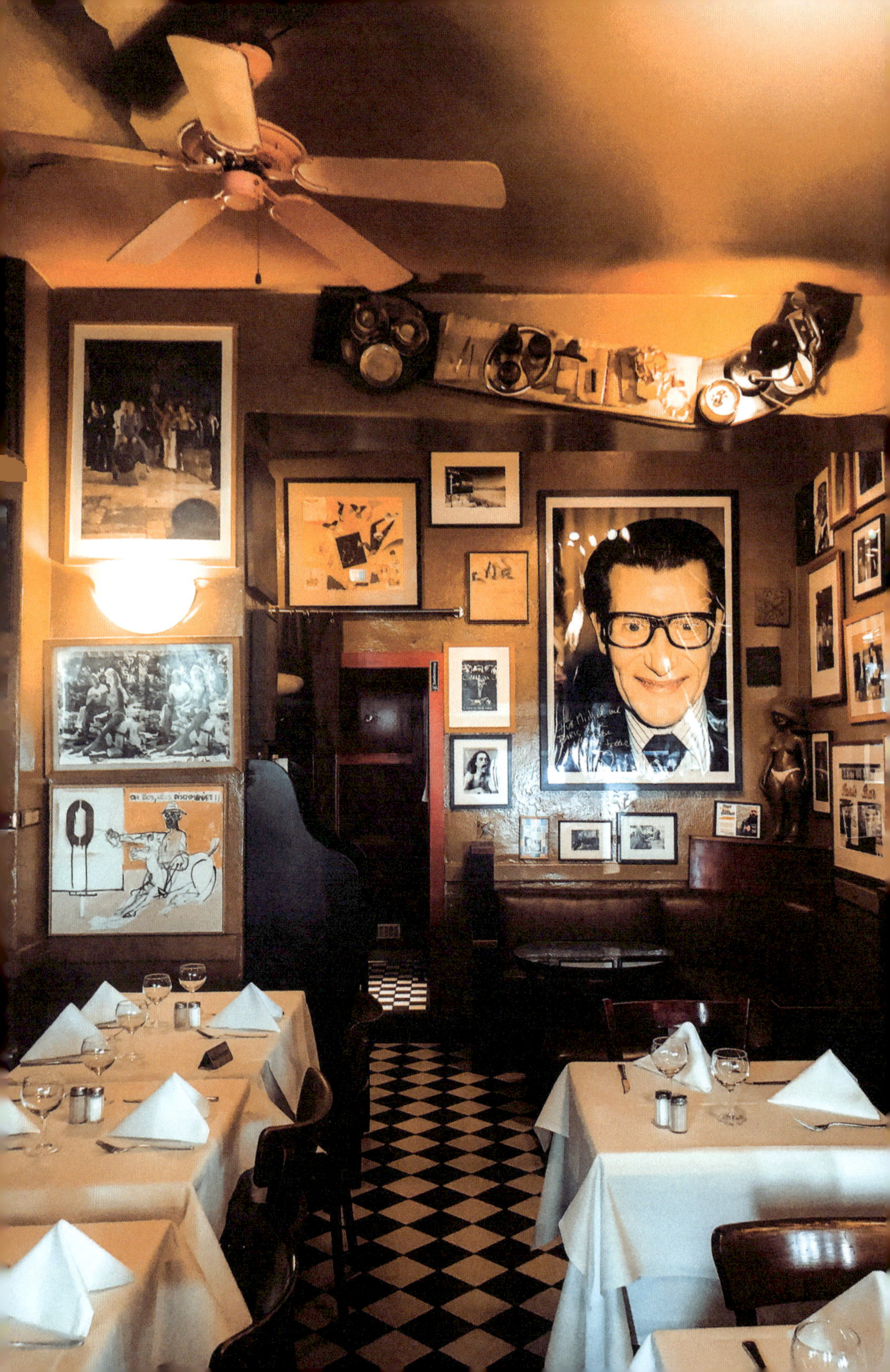

Paris Bar

"There must be a certain type of client in the restaurant as well, the poor are boring, the rich are boring, and the worst are the people in between!"
— Michel Würthle

The Paris Bar on a bustling Saturday night is pure Berlin when the performance of dining is in full swing: air kisses, champagne flowing, raucous laughter, gorging on rich meat, and, occasionally, sneakily peering around the room at other tables to decide if any of their diners are more important or look like they are having a better time. Sitting at a back-corner table, the art restaurant's louche, charismatic proprietor, Michel Würthle, observes: "When it's dark and we have many guests it actually looks like a web." He has been trapping and spinning narratives and stories about his patrons and the social changes in the city for the past four decades. The Paris Bar is the quintessential bohemian Berliner restaurant, evoking Weimar decadence and part-punk irreverence, and consummately celebrity driven. The celebrities, however, are counterculture stars of the arts and creative industries, intellectuals that megastars from the United States wanted to be like and younger *arrivistes* in the city wanted to paint and write like. They all mixed and cavorted at the Paris Bar, and this hedonistic hullaballoo is reflected and refracted on the walls of the brasserie, with every square inch covered with paintings, drawings, photographs, sketches and barfly paraphernalia. Each piece is unlike the one next to it in size and composition, but each is a memento of a relationship, an artistic endeavour, an in-joke, a rude anecdote about one of the patrons. This adds to the interior being confidently retro with its monochrome tiled floor, Parisian brasserie furniture and starched tablecloths, but yet to decide which era exactly it represents.

Contrary to the constant serving of anecdotes about badly behaved artists and stroppy Hollywood stars boisterously squabbling away on any given night, the Paris Bar in Charlottenburg is best to visit in its off-duty moments, as though you walked through the looking glass into the oversized Daniel Richter painting of the interior that hangs in the restaurant – a painting of a painting by Martin Kippenberger. It is ideal to go, say, in the midday heat of a Berlin summer for a daydreamy, languorous experience, to spend ample time scanning the walls for a hidden Alexander Kosolapov parody or a Sarah Lucas self-portrait. The brasserie was established out of this spirit of protest: in 1950, in the early years of the Cold War, a disgruntled French army officer, frustrated with German food, convinced a former French armed forces canteen cook to set up a traditional French brasserie in the heart of West Berlin. Finally, he would be able to enjoy his onion soup and *moules et frites* in the manner to which he was accustomed in the motherland. The Paris Bar's generic name suggests it was "founded by someone very provincial", according to Würthle. But its founder was irritable and independent and wanted Berlin to be elsewhere, or wanted a small corner of "elsewhere" to be transported into bleak Berlin. From that moment on, the venue turned its back on the sprawling yet divided city around it, fostering its own creative and intellectual culture within its walls.

That community has been frequenting the same location on Kantstrasse since 1962. Würthle took over with fellow artist Reinald Nohal in 1977 and sought to elevate the bistro as a place for creatives and cultural patrons to visit, providing escape and an exciting alternative in the then-depressed city. Like his fellow art restaurateurs Paul Roux and Michael Chow, Würthle painted and took photographs, having trained as an artist. This created an affinity with artists and gallerists – Sigmar Polke nicknamed him "the talking *Mozartkugel*" – who were part of his milieu, attracting his friends and fellow artists from subcultural Berlin. They renovated the restaurant, keeping the feel of a French brasserie but changing the decoration. "Back then the bar was full of decorative crabs, fishing nets and little Eiffel Towers," recalls Würthle. "We decided to hang contemporary art on the walls." The first work was from his friend the Neo-Expressionist Markus Lüpertz, followed by the mixed-media and food painter Dieter Roth and figurative painter Ina Barfuss. Commercial galleries were rare in Berlin in the late 1970s, thus the artists were keen to show their work in a public place.

The collection became an invitation and a signal, and since then, the Paris Bar has hosted actors, artists and intellectuals, forming the backdrop to moments of cultural history, the effects of the "industry of anecdote". People from film, art, media, publishing and journalism all came to dine – too many to recount, according to Würthle: "In retrospect, the names of people who have made it are picked out and remembered. The others just disappear." New German Cinema pioneer Rainer Werner Fassbinder was a regular, disappearing into the bathroom on a frequent basis. "I was always wondering what they were doing in the bathrooms! I was thinking: it's not possible that they fuck every half hour again and again. Nobody is that potent," says Würthle. Celebrities made it a point to stop at the restaurant when they visited Berlin for the film festival or music and art events. It was the scene of a famous, booze-addled Iggy Pop interview for *Rolling Stone* in 1979. The restaurant became part of that story and photographic history. It became a mixture of counterculture and established culture in the 1970s and 1980s. West Berlin celebrities, unknown elsewhere, would sit next to American stars, perhaps Madonna or often Peter Gabriel. American pop stars, European intelligentsia, idealistic art students, tourists… all wanted to be part of the narrative that the Paris Bar – as historic and successful restaurants do – presented.

The brasserie itself is simple and modest in layout: black-and-white checked floor, tobacco-stain-coloured walls, white linen tablecloths on the small tables, bistro chairs, a small bar in the middle of the space. The hang suggests a developing collection, not like art restaurants that plan their interior design around particular pieces. Instead, works of all shapes, sizes and media clamour for wall space, a visual cacophony by some standards, but also authentic and organic in terms of mood boards or bobby-pinned selections of sentimental objects. In what other dining environment would you find an image with a woman performing oral sex on a man (a popular table) with images of Freud hung above it, or an oversized signed portrait of a grinning Yves Saint Laurent? This "ever-evolving patchwork" incorporates the swapping, selling and changing of art from Würthle's own collection and from his artist friends. The walls are conversations and exchanges of ideas, they are bawdy laughter, the telling of sexual jokes, the performing of story punchlines by the peacocks at each dining party's table.

The first time Würthle met Martin Kippenberger, in 1979, they had a stare-off for half an hour, like dogs sniffing round each other before they decide if the other is a friend or foe. Instead of fighting, the restaurateur asked the artist if he would hang black-and-white early works in the bar. "I told him he could eat and drink here for the rest of his life, in exchange for a few pieces," he recalls. "He told me we had a deal – but I would only get two pieces for it. We shook hands, and that was it." Kippenberger and Würthle agreed on the ultimate eating down exchange: the artist would grow and curate the art collection and keep an open tab in perpetuity. Würthle understood the cult of Kippenberger, and that his insalubrious personality and inebriated antics would suffice to recoup the costs, given he had so many followers in the art world. The artist, as a master of ceremonies, would use the venue to entertain the cultural intelligentsia. He would give impromptu speeches, make promises to hire diners as studio assistants, insult those he disliked, sing in the bar. Alcohol was an instrument to him, according to friend and art dealer Gisela Capitain. He drank to excess, but it was always socially – he never worked under the influence of alcohol or drugs. The brasserie was also an extension of his studio space – literally, as he would draw and make works at his table when not drunkenly performing for diners. The gallerist Christian Nagel remembers the artist "wanted to be Picasso, Beuys and Warhol at the same time", and the conflict led him to have a love/hate relationship with the art scene, a total disgust of the art market, but also a desire to be in the centre of it all.

The Paris Bar became an alternative gallery space for Kippenberger. He would include his own works and also showcase artists he respected and believed did not have the recognition they deserved. This was especially true of female artists such as Louise Lawler, Laurie Simmons, Barbara Ess and Zoe Leonard.

"I am a woman too!" he once proclaimed in an interview. Kippenberger was the ringleader of the restaurant, known for his rumbustious bad behaviour (imagine if he had dined and drank with Peter Langan), and an irreverence and mockery of his own work, the art world, celebrities, politicos and even cooking. Würthle used the artist as bait to draw creatives into something more meaningful than transactional dining. "I was never in favour of fun," he says, "always excess. Just excess." The restaurant was an exchange of ideas, influences and debates at a time when artistic and creative identities and structures were in flux. The proximity to Berlin's University of the Arts meant a steady supply of art students visiting for access to gallerists, actors, theatre directors and influential people. This curiosity extended to a list of international artists who enrolled on the DAAD Akademischer Austauschdienst (German Academic Exchange Service), which invited artists, musicians and filmmakers to live and work in Berlin for a year. From 1964 more than 1,000 artists, ranging from Richard Hamilton, Jannis Kounellis and Marina Abramovi to Nan Goldin, came to the city. Among them was Damien Hirst, in 1993.

The restaurant art collection was informed by the same spirit of rebellion and irreverence as the Paris Bar's establishment, according to Würthle. Both artist and restaurateur were motivated by the neglect and disdain shown towards contemporary art. Kippenberger's sister, Susanna, recalls: "The German art set of the 1980s was convinced that humour didn't belong in art. For them, it meant lack of seriousness. In their eyes any art that used humour was irrelevant." This may be the reason Kippenberger had only two museum solo exhibitions in Germany during his lifetime (Darmstadt and Mönchengladbach), whereas he had dozens in the United States. The exchange between the two became mutually beneficial, as Kippenberger was building his reputation and body of work as a dexterous contemporary artist, and the Paris Bar was his stage. He even held festivals in the restaurant around his shows in the NGBK Gallery (and smuggled in his father's 60th birthday party as a happening). He was prolific, producing works every day – sketches, paintings, drawings, artist's books – no matter how drunk he got the night before (answer: completely). Once a year he would check into a health clinic in Innsbruck, and he would always return rejuvenated, "fit, with a good tan to boot", and then start all over again. The artist ensured the bar became the most talked-about venue in Berlin. It also invigorated the myth of the artists' restaurant, placing the Paris Bar on a par with Max's Kansas City or the Kronenhalle.

The Paris Bar was immortalised in a sober way too, by the artist making a large-scale painting of the interior to display in the restaurant. His first version, created in 1993, was exhibited in a retrospective at the Centre Pompidou and sold for £636,000 in 2007. "Now what?" Würthle asked when he lost it.

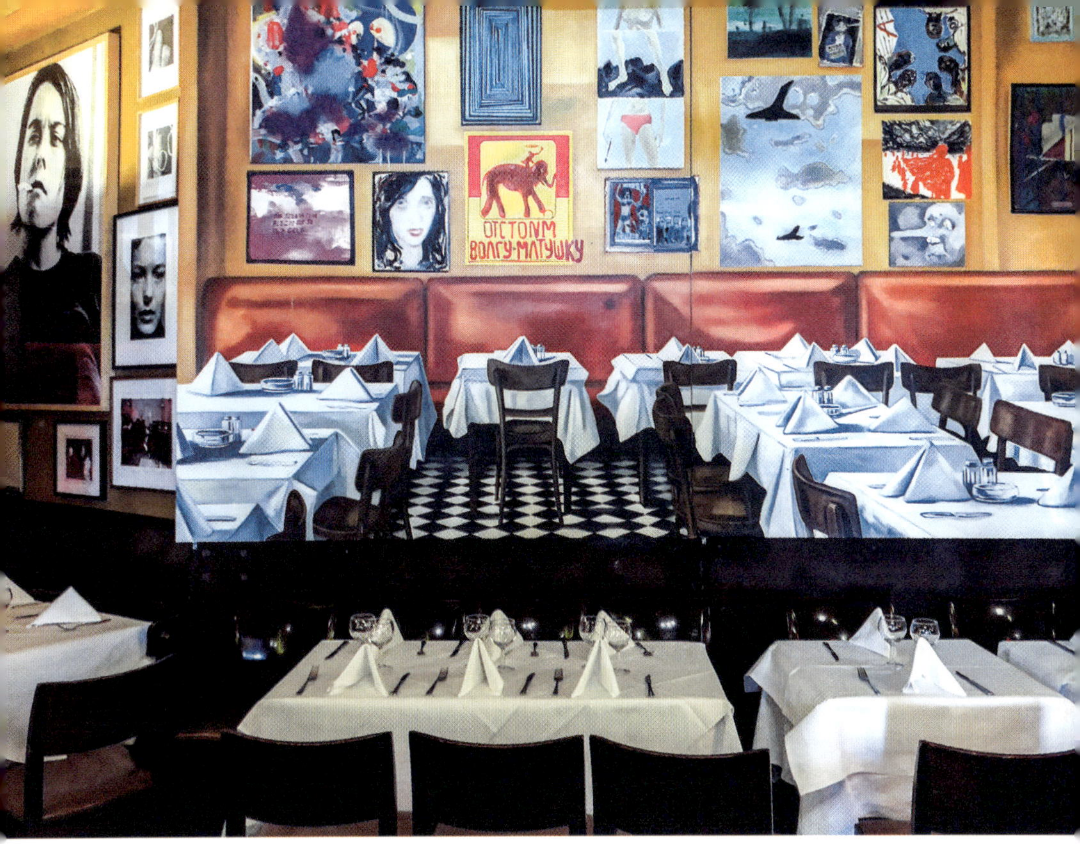

Kippenberger then produced a second one the same year to hang in the same spot. Like a painting of a cabinet of curiosities or a royal collection of images by Old Masters, it works on many levels of circular reflexivity: a restaurant art collection is captured in an artwork by a sought-after artist and displayed in that same restaurant for diners to observe and eat under. The second work was sold at auction in 2009 for £2.3m to help to settle a tax bill for the proprietor, also providing a realistic estimate of eating down possibilities. There is now a version of the Kippenberger painting by Richter in its place. The original clearly appealed to the artistic imaginations. The contemporary German artist Christian Jankowski, a patron of the Paris Bar throughout his art school days and later on when he became an established practitioner, created a work based on this "construction plot" of the figure of the artist (*The Legend of the Artist and Other Construction Sites*) in 2016. He used the Paris Bar as the backdrop, and the performance of Kippenberger's artistic persona was essential to making the mythology. Jankowski reproduced the Richter that was a reproduction of the Kippenberger representational painting of the interior.

Kippenberger, the conductor of the Paris Bar's synthesising philosophy, and his artistic practice help to make sense of the unruly, visually chaotic, mixed aesthetic experience of the art restaurant. All befitting a city undergoing identity changes and coming to terms with its history – the war, the wall, its avant-garde and countercultures. Kippenberger claimed in 1990 that "although by now everybody knows that I'm the one that covered the eighties", museums did not buy his work and thus he had "no time to wait" – "I like for it to reach the public, making it accessible to more than a handful of people after the exhibition, after the coming-into-the-world. I make my work public by other means: by books, publications of any kind, posters, action… museums equal antiquity rubbish." He would always carry a stack of invitation cards and invite drunkards, children, random people he encountered on the street back to the Paris Bar. Restaurants must have held some special significance in Kippenberger's imagination, given that he also eventually invested in one – the Capri – in Venice Beach, California, in the mid-1990s, a few years before he died. "Capri" was an emblem of kitsch for him, having made his *Capri* car series some years before to argue the place of mass-produced, commodified products in an artistic context.

The Paris Bar never purported to be underground, which is an irreverent part of the narrative that befits modern Berlin. It flaunted its celebrity status, it was *outré* and brash, yet members of subcultures and many other outsiders also wanted to frequent it. Early on in Kippenberger's curation of the art collection, a patron slit a work by the artist in reaction to its subject matter. Another time, one of the ox heads by Damien Hirst generated outrage, and Würthle recalls a diner shouting: "What is this shit? How am I supposed to eat next to this?" Eventually, the tastes in art changed in Berlin, and "the mainstream decided to say 'yes' to everything. Suddenly there was a general consensus of acceptance. It has always been like that and will continue being that way." The avant-garde just becomes "garde", artists make money and become brands, protests calm down. The Paris Bar as an art restaurant provided a backdrop for the meaning of counterculture to be redrawn, but the counterculture needed the mainstream to exist in the first place. Today, the artworks remain behind as reminders of this time when Berlin was reconstructing its meaning and identity.

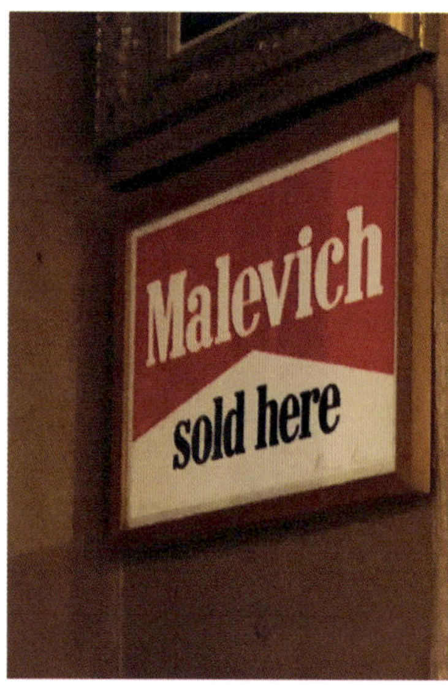

Works and artists in the Paris Bar collection

—

In 2012, all 100-plus works from the Paris Bar were taken down for six weeks and exhibited in the Haubrokshow Gallery, which seems superfluous if the art restaurant is a sufficient alternative to the gallery space. In their place, the gallery sent the same number of artworks by Christopher Williams for the duration of the show.

—

Nikolai Makarov donated a series of paintings to the restaurant. He says: "As soon as I step into the Paris Bar the waiter brings me three things: a beer to calm me down, a Fernet-Branca for the stomach and an espresso to keep me awake. I don't order them, they just come to me. I've come regularly since 1980, back when if you wanted to be a part of the Berlin art scene, you had to come to the Paris Bar. Most people from the old guard have moved on or passed away, but I sometimes still bump into Markus Lüpertz. It's no longer just artists, but also musicians, designers and actors, bourgeois Charlottenburgers who live around the corner... and, of course, visiting celebrities. I once saw Pierce Brosnan here – I knew he'd bought one of my paintings, so I wanted to say hello. When I showed him a book here with my art in it, he randomly opened it on the middle page and exclaimed: 'This is my painting. You did this?' My favourite place is on the sofas near the toilet. That way I can say 'hi' to people, because everyone uses the bathroom. I usually know around one-third of the guests in the room. I couldn't even dream about not coming here. Yes, the atmosphere has changed, but it's still fantastic – it's cult."

—

Sarah Lucas's self-portrait, *Fighting Fire with Fire* (1996), is one of the artist's best-known works, in which she is seen drawing on a cigarette with furrowed brow, androgynous in appearance, with short hair and nondescript T-shirt. It is a large piece and dominates the back wall in the bar. In the series, she is making a statement about her masculine appearance and artistic persona; in this placement, she is stating she is also one of the boys and can drink and smoke them under the table. The cigarette is a weapon, it is phallic, it is a symbol of rebellion.

—

Ever since a businessman made an offer to Paul Roux to buy the Colombe d'Or in the 1980s, art restaurant histories have been littered with tales of brash visitors wanting to purchase works in their collections. The Hollywood actress Dakota Johnson reputedly tried to buy Angus Fairhurst's neon *Stand Still and Rot*. When she was told it was not for sale, she insisted that it's "always a matter of price". She was flatly rejected by Herr Würthle.

The dining room of the Paris Bar with its explosion of works on the walls; Daniel Richter's painting of Kippenberger's painting of the internal space of the Paris Bar; a gallery view of various works

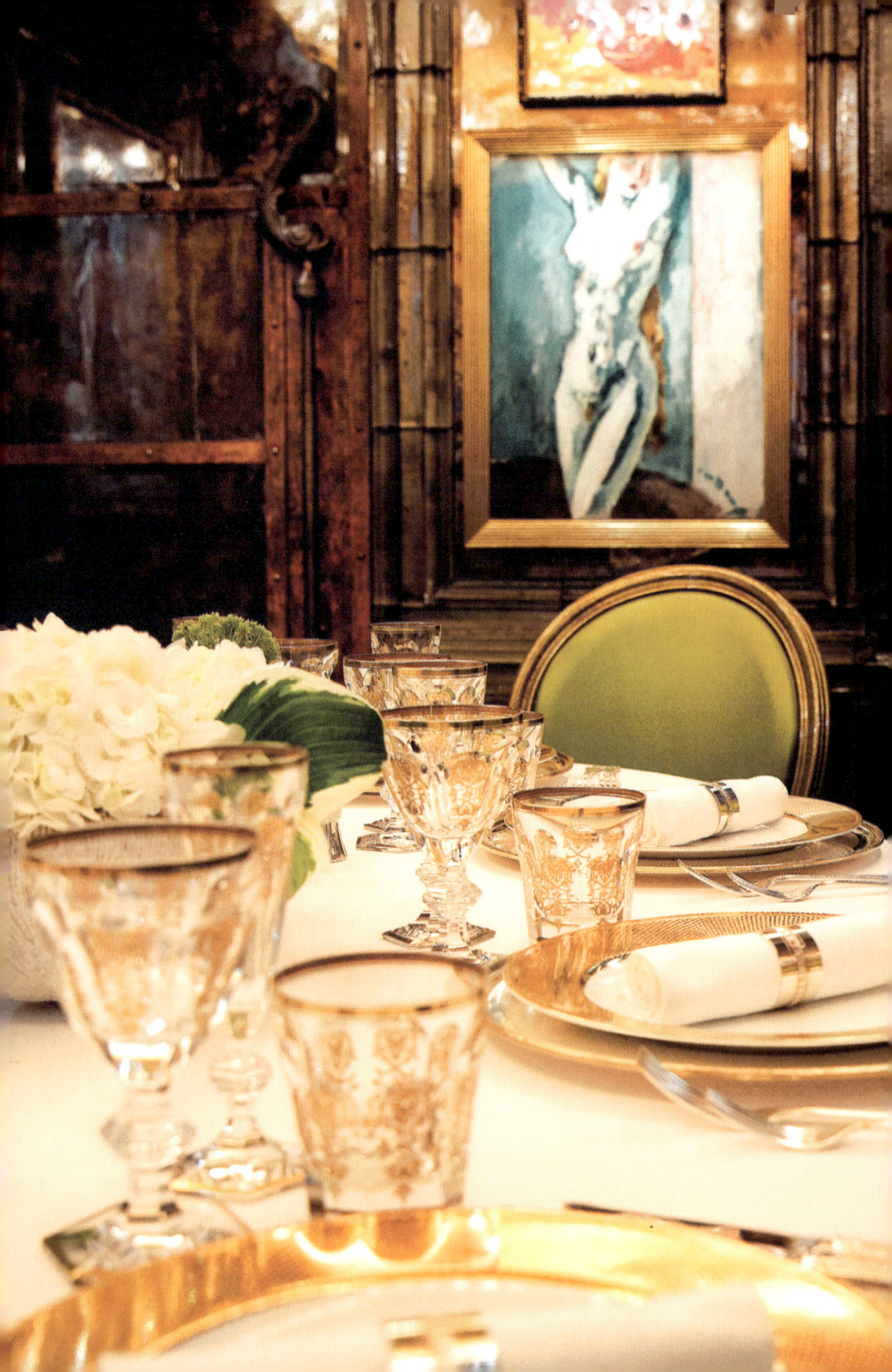

Scott's

"Without the assistance of eating and drinking, the most sparkling wit would be as heavy as a bad soufflé, and the brightest talent as dull as a looking-glass on a foggy day."
— Alexis Soyer

As the fifth oldest restaurant in London, Scott's has had its fair share of moments participating in popular, political and cultural history. It is the fabled birthplace of James Bond's signature tipple, the Vesper Martini; the IRA bombed it twice during the Troubles in 1975; and it has been the site of countless celebrity sightings and their *outré* antics in tabloid press stories from the 1990s to the present. And in the restaurant today, works by the Young British Artists, such as Damien Hirst, Tracey Emin, Fiona Rae and Mark Quinn, among others, introduce a stimulating and iconoclastic moment of art history. The art that hangs on its walls is now global in terms of its creators' marketability and demand, denoting the worldwide reach that British versions of luxury have achieved. The collection enriches an historical restaurant by matching the success and wealth of these artists in recent decades with the success and wealth of the clientele of Scott's. Often the two overlap. Compared with Italian equivalents, British luxury is known for being understated, unassuming, even self-effacing. Within the context of art history, the Young British Artists were known for being irreverent, rebellious, even lacking in talent. This makes Scott's an art restaurant where the art is associated with being a reward of material and social achievement and a trophy of success. This group of artists are successful and go to Scott's, their collectors are successful and go to Scott's, and as such, Scott's is a restaurant to showcase *having made it*, and the implied good taste that comes along with that. Dining in this art restaurant is both a prize for and exercise in good taste, as defined by a group of people who are entrepreneurial, wealthy but also interested in the provocation that the art provides. The YBAs were brats, but they were businesspeople too, enjoying the same material trappings and social climbing as their collectors and admirers.

The original restaurant dates back to 1851, when it was established as an oyster warehouse by John Scott in Haymarket on Coventry Street, on the former site of the Trocadero. This was the year of the Great Exhibition in London, and the era of bourgeois dining habits changing as a result of industrialisation, the spread of the leisure classes and the acceleration of restaurant culture in London and its rival, Paris. Scott's is an example of these 19th-century modern restaurants, where newly affluent middle-class diners could realise their desires for new social experiences and novelty in cuisine, to explore fine dining married with fine service. In many ways, this history continues in terms of what Scott's signifies for the London restaurant scene today. Its purpose fits the function of what a classic, sophisticated restaurant should do – it should reward, it should allow the exploration and refinement of taste and the celebration of this with peers. Historically, in these classic restaurants, upper-class diners looked for examples of good taste to follow and how to behave in terms of projecting and demonstrating refinement in the restaurant space. "Taste begins where appetite ends," according to critic Bernard Berenson. Scott's evolved as an elegant response to the bourgeois demand for social gathering places that revelled in good taste. In recent times it has become the canteen of London as a global city of wealth and luxury, yet its development is tied to the history of restaurant evolution in Europe.

It expanded and moved to its current site on Mayfair's Mount Street in 1967 and since then has been a steady purveyor of Mayfair indulgence. This was also the year its serendipitous connection and subsequent interweaving with the art world began. Robert Fraser – "groovy Bob" – the infamous art dealer of Swinging Sixties London, lived on the third floor above the restaurant at number 20. He was a friend of The Beatles and recommended they commission Peter Blake to design their *Sgt. Pepper's* album cover. Groovy Bob was also a stalwart confidant and sidekick of the Rolling Stones. The infamous photograph of him being handcuffed with Mick Jagger in 1967 in the back of a police van was made into a work of art by Richard Hamilton, *Swingeing London 67*. He was a social connector who brought artists and other creatives together, and he used Scott's downstairs for many of these meetings.

Scott's has its place in the family tree of London restaurants that shared the same key individuals who held a similar vision of hospitality and belief that a fine-dining establishment is enhanced by the addition of quality artwork, more than just background decor. The collector and celebrity chef Mark Hix began his career at Scott's in 2005, when it was in the Corbin and King stable of restaurants. He knew many YBA artists of his generation and was tasked with curating the collection, so he approached his friends to make works for the restaurant. He says this "makes all the difference. Every piece has got a story rather than it being just going out shopping for art." Hix went to Michael Landy's studio in 2006 when the artist was working on his *H.2.N.Y.* series and asked him to create a piece for the spot it still hangs in today. *Suicide Carriage Breaks Down on the Way to Drown Itself in Maillols' the River Whilst Metallic Sculpture is Set Ablaze* is an homage to Jean Tinguely (an artist found in the Kronenhalle and Colombe d'Or collections) and depicts one of the sculptor's auto-destructive "meta-machines". Landy recalls agreeing the exchange details with Hix: "I said, 'Well, how am I supposed to come up with an idea of how many [meals]? I've never done this before.'" The artist knew a few of his fellow ex-Goldsmiths students were involved in building the collection, including Gary Hume. "I said, 'Well, how many meals is he getting?' And Hix said, 'He's getting 103 sittings a year.' I said, 'Well, I want 104.' Anything to get one over Gary Hume."

Next to Landy's piece, Hume's *Bouquet* is an oversized mural of three flowers that resemble Margaret Thatcher's trademark rounded coiffure (or bouquet of carnations for those who refuse to see it), rendered in his trademark lacquered industrial paint and basic, bold shapes. Hume made the piece because Hix asked him as a friend, describing it as "a sort of Margaret Thatcher-stroke-wealthy lady". He says: "I thought it'd be quite nice for the wealthy ladies with their hair, which is sort of gone now, to see pictures of themselves." He originally misjudged the space, and the work that he made in his New York studio was too small. Realising his mistake, he added three panels to it, much like an altarpiece – "an altarpiece to Thatcherism". The artist still goes back to the restaurant and reflects on the work. He says he looks at it differently every time, and wonders why he painted it that way, why he made it in that size. And, of course, he occasionally sees "women with their hair sat up under the painting, which is just thrilling to me".

Hume's work is not the only reference to the former prime minister. Keith Coventry's *Grand Hotel* in the entrance is political, possibly undermining Thatcher, but the fact it does this among commercially successful artworks commissioned for this restaurant also acknowledges the power and capitalism of 1980s and early 1990s Britain.

The art acquired is from the late 1990s and early 2000s, and is emblematic of the best of breed among commercial British artists – artistic brands and trophies the Scott's patrons would want to collect, the social scene they would want to be a part of, and the artists they would want to know. Anecdotes of *outré* behaviour and tabloid shots of YBAs bouncing off the walls and stumbling onto Mount Street would have enhanced the reputations of artists and restaurant alike. For Scott's, cultivating this particular art collection demonstrates a specifically British version of taste: as British as the menu, as British as Mayfair. Damien Hirst's *Hortensia*, a diamond on a black background, can be read as a reference to owning blue-chip art, and displaying the trophy in the heart of Mayfair. But there are other levels of meaning to this and all the works in their particular place in this collection, not least as a bit of restaurant folklore: Ian Fleming, a regular patron, first used the phrase "shaken not stirred" in Scott's, in a passage in 1956's *Diamonds are Forever*, the novel's plot being about diamond smuggling.

Scott's was sold to the Caprice group in 2007, to which it currently belongs, and Richard Caring has continued his own interpretation of the art restaurant, fostering his own relationship with the artists. The interior is opulent, yet simple

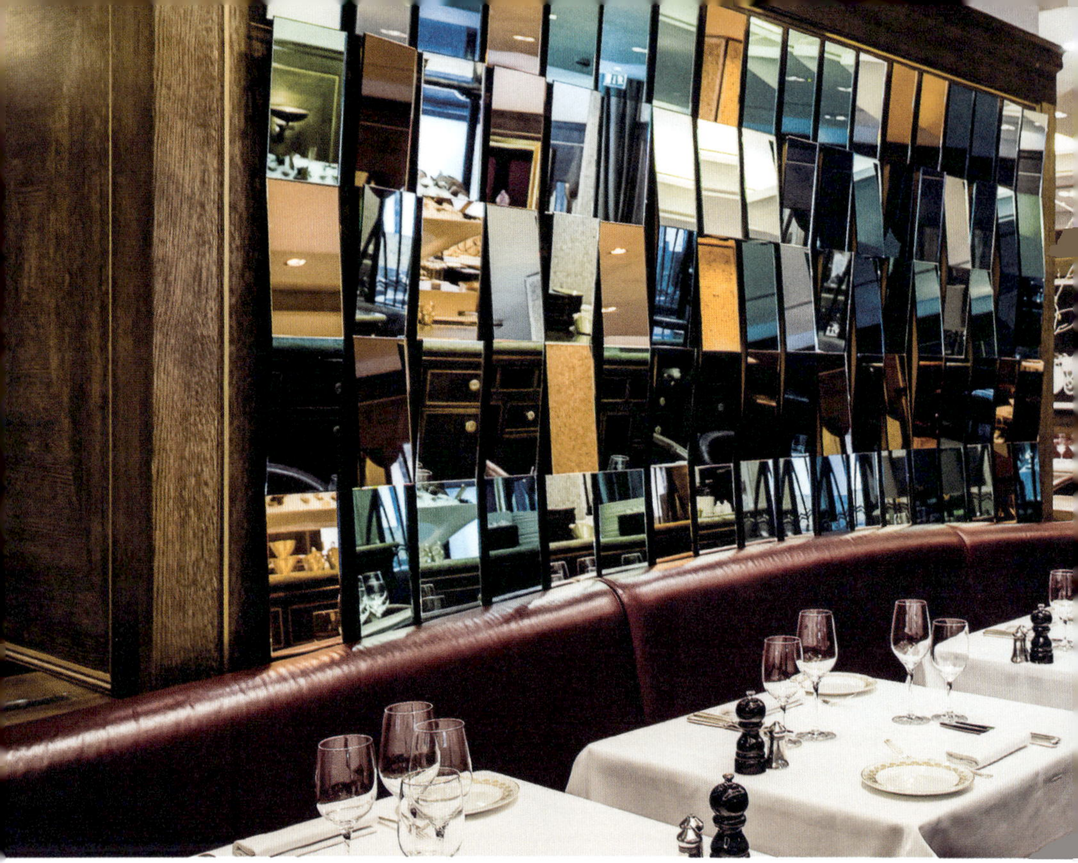

compared with other establishments in the Caprice Holdings portfolio: "classic" in the context of the contemporary restaurant scene in London. Its historical credentials are updated for what today's discerning diners want to project. And there is meritocracy at work – anyone from any socioeconomic background is welcome, as long as they have made money and can dine here. Scott's no longer keeps VIP tables. However, as a gesture to how turbo-charged Mayfair has become as an international centre for art collecting, it recently added the Platinum Arowana room, a private dining space seating up to eight people at £200 per head, with an illuminated agate floor, rose-gold panelled walls, Lalique crystal lighting and a collection of museum-quality Modern artworks that include Renoir's *Nu debout*, Chagall's *La Danse* and Pissarro's *Portrait du Peintre Ludovic Piette Avec Son Chapeau Rond*. (Also Émile Bernard, Kees van Dongen, Louis Valtat, Louis Roy, Serge Férat and Henri Manguin.) Caring went to two Impressionist and Modern art auctions at Christie's and Sotheby's to buy works he liked for this room, which is a time capsule of bourgeois good taste in art of a previous generation. The result is a condensed, expedited aesthetic eating experiment, and scintillates like a lab-grown diamond.

In some respects, Scott's is furnishing the same fundamental tenets of leisure-class dining as it was in 1851. From the mid-19th century, the same

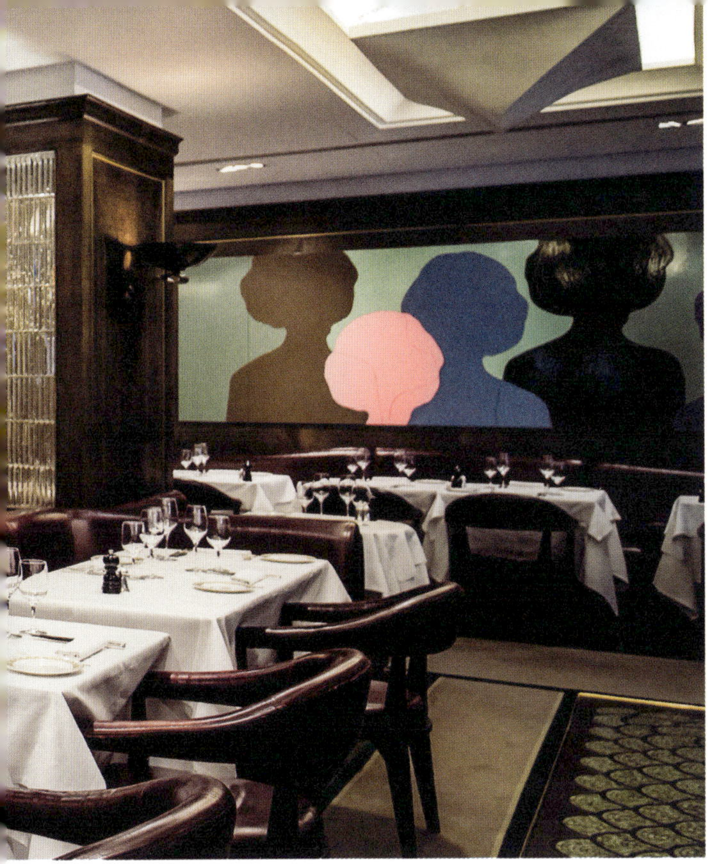

period the modern restaurant was established in Paris and London, the private act of eating was taken out of the home and into the public sphere. It was especially sought-after by emerging wealthy clientele who went to restaurants to demonstrate they had taste and also to learn about notions of new taste. The fact that Scott's has remained in business for so long is testament to this historical phenomenon. The leisure classes were international in what they consumed, they constantly took in new influences, cultures, foods and literature, and aspired to be mobile. Taste was not fixed. It was always in pursuit of what was considered good and superior.

The inclusion of a YBA-centred art collection in Scott's is playful provocation, given the artists often had a propensity for pushing the boundaries of decency and good taste, using shocking, pornographic or violent imagery. However, this collection furnishes a paradox because these same artists who strove to shock audiences are now established and wealthy – just the type of clientele Scott's seeks to attract. "I've made a lot of money and whenever I celebrate, I always celebrate with food." There is a delightful postmodernism at play with the breakdown of high and low culture, a flouting of expectations, a rejection of good bourgeois taste – albeit in a bourgeois way. It keeps the restaurant from becoming staid and too gold-plated. Today, it also celebrates affluent

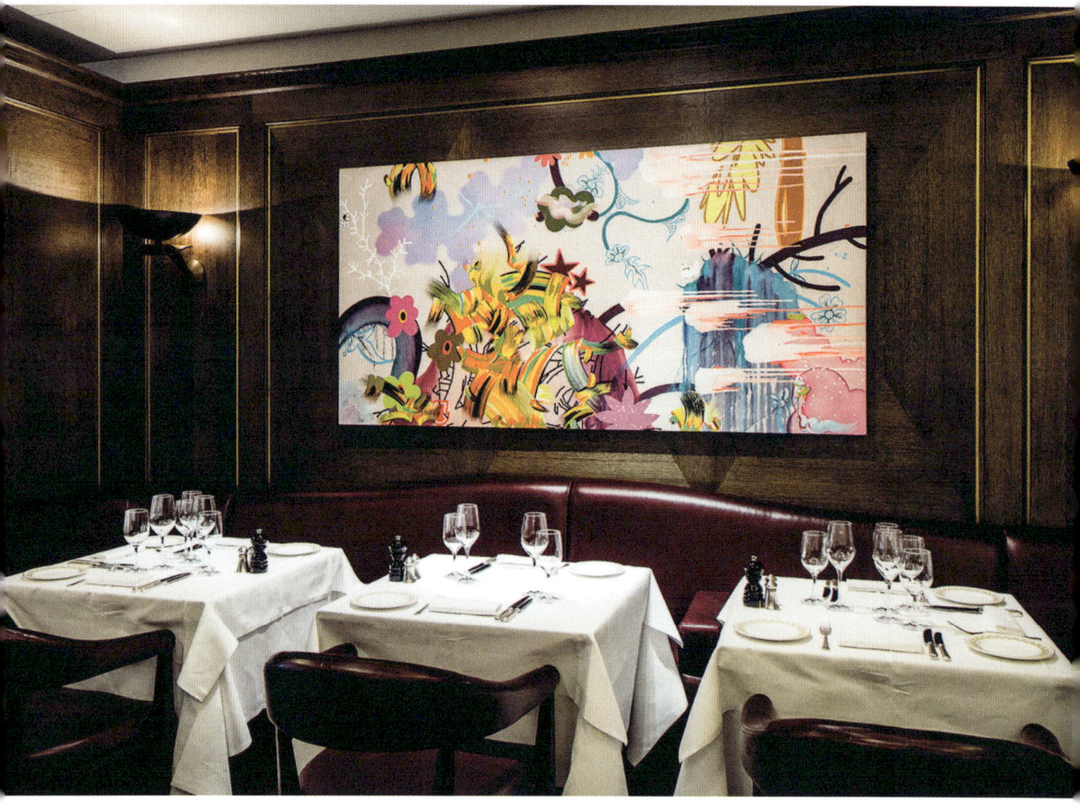

taste and what it means to dine in a comfortable, opulent but not ostentatious environment. Scott's is not over the top. The quality of the taste is accessible and levels anybody from whatever background. All are accepted and take their place in the dining rituals and history of the leisure classes before them. Scott's is a bellwether of the social and economic success of the capital – if Scott's is OK, London is OK.

Works and artists in the Scott's collection

—

Upon entering the restaurant, diners encounter Tim Noble and Sue Webster's *Spinning Heads in Reverse*, two spot-lit black glass vases on plinths. They feature curved stems which upon closer inspection are formed as the imprint of the artists' profiles. In this context, this gestalt playfulness serves as a reminder of how dining is not all it first appears, but part of a magic and playful celebration.

—

Martin Creed's pen-on-paper series, *Work No. 469*, guides guests down the stairs to the private dining room. The more than 100 framed pieces of paper with meticulously and methodically applied markers in rainbow colours are welcoming, accessible and visually sensual.

—

Tracey Emin's *But I Didn't Go to Bed, I Stayed up All Night + Cried* is a small, intimate confession with a rosette that the artist admits amuses her to know is hanging in the restaurant.

—

There is a work by Keith Coventry, *Silhouette of the Grand Hotel*, which is a reference to the assassination attempt by the IRA on Margaret Thatcher at the Conservative Party Conference in 1984. It is deceptively simple – white paint on the canvas with delicate brushstrokes to indicate the shape of the building.

—

A *Black Headed Gull* by Polly Morgan is listlessly draped over a perch under a glass dome next to the entrance. The artist is renowned for her taxidermy of small, delicate animals. In this art restaurant context, the gull takes on extra meaning, given that gulls' eggs are a delicacy, that cooking is as much a science as it is an art, and that what diners eat on the plate once lived and breathed.

The Platinum Arowana Room, a private dining space with paintings by Marc Chagall, Joan Miró and Kees van Dongen; the Scott's dining room featuring Gary Hume's work displayed in the background; Fiona Rae's work above some dining tables

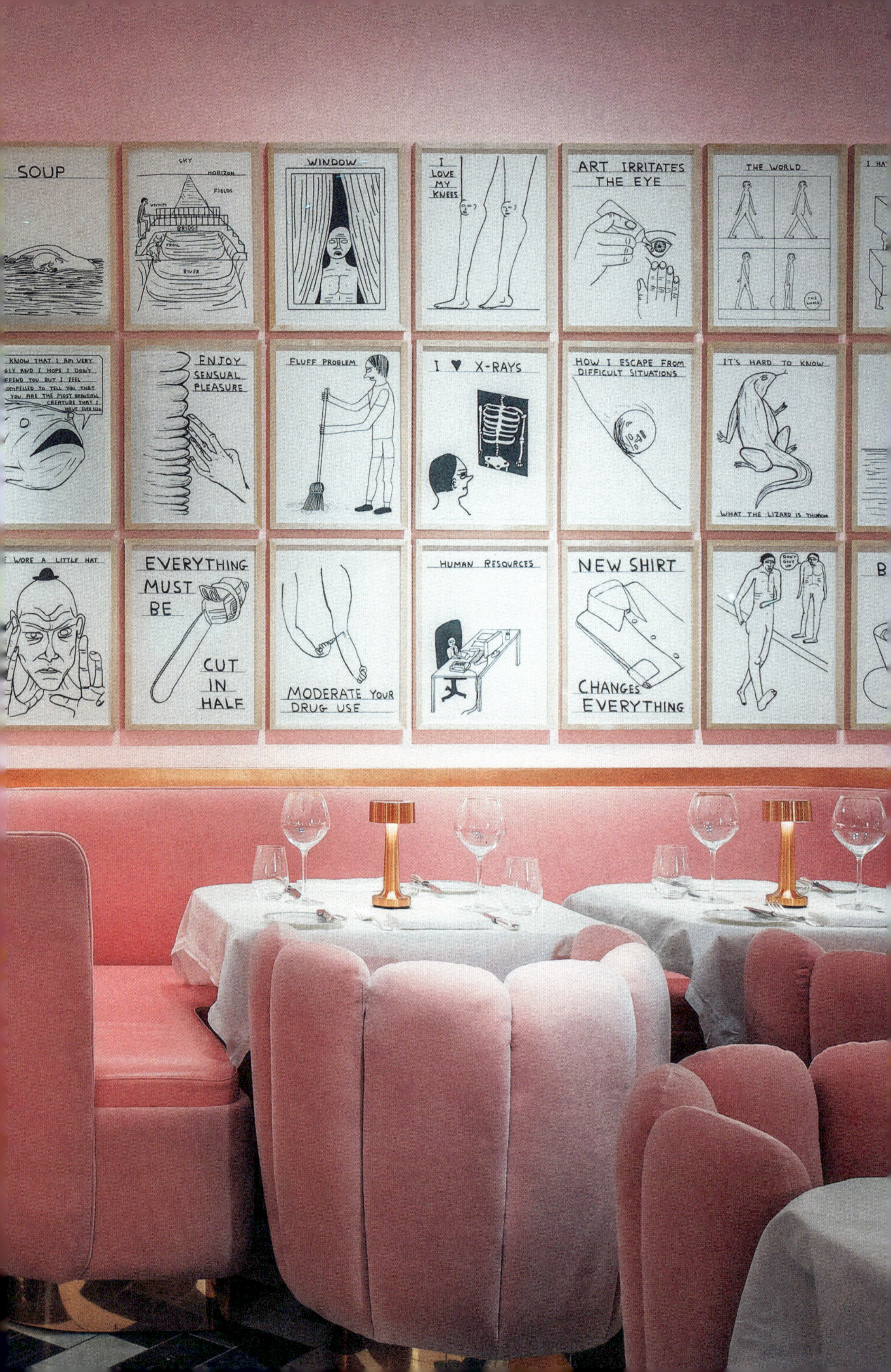
SOUP
WINDOW
I LOVE MY KNEES
ART IRRITATES THE EYE
THE WORLD
ENJOY SENSUAL PLEASURE
FLUFF PROBLEM
I ♥ X-RAYS
HOW I ESCAPE FROM DIFFICULT SITUATIONS
IT'S HARD TO KNOW
EVERYTHING MUST BE CUT IN HALF
MODERATE YOUR DRUG USE
HUMAN RESOURCES
NEW SHIRT CHANGES EVERYTHING

Sketch

"People who do not accept the new, grow old very quickly."
— Auguste Escoffier

Enter the elegant and stately townhouse at 9 Conduit Street with a hop, skip and a step over hopscotch markings in the corridor, and you will be greeted by a portrait of the monarch with her eyes closed, before being, in turn, blinded by glaring neon letters on a black wall (JOUEZ!), cuddled and caressed by a pink-velvet parlour room, and dizzied and disorientated by a partially sunken bar where you stand above the bartenders. And eventually you will use the bathroom, which requires navigating around and entering a giant egg-sculpture pod on a platform straight from a science-fiction film set.

The seasoned French restaurateur, Mourad Mazouz, launched Sketch in London in 2002, alongside French Michelin-starred chef Pierre Gagnaire, as an immersive experience to combine the appreciation of food, art and music. In Mazouz's own words, his purpose was "to create the impossible" for a restaurant: "A magical place for our diners to enjoy – a destination which can be explored and enjoyed by many different people." Mazouz thinks of Sketch "like a flower": the cuisine, the art, the decor, the location are all petals, and he is in the middle, as the connector. "Everything I have done here, I have done for others, not myself," he says. And in a city where the hospitality industry is incessantly competitive, Sketch is able to remain relevant and unique as a result of the whole endeavour being infused with art and design, and every detail saturated with thoughts on how that particular facet contributes to the greater whole of a glimmering dining experience. The restaurant, its mood and effect on the diner must become "a fairy tale" – escapism through taste and sensory play.

The 18th-century building in Mayfair's Conduit Street, converted into a neoclassical townhouse in the 1950s, was purchased in 1999. Originally designed by James Wyatt in 1779, it has a solid historical pedigree, having housed the suffragettes, served as Christian Dior's atelier, and finally becoming the headquarters of the Royal Institute of British Architects. Mazouz had other successful creative restaurants under his belt in the city – Momo and the Double Club in collaboration with Fondazione Prada, designed by Carsten Höller – as well as internationally. From the outset, he covered his bases, both in terms of purveying exceptional cuisine and introducing contemporary art. Sketch would be a restaurant "conceived by artists", complete with artists' events, talks and exhibitions to ensure art and food came together to continuously delight – and provoke. Mazouz commissions artists to make pieces, but never with specific instructions beyond a brief asking them to transform the space into an experience where his customers will be bombarded with images and colours that will require their senses to be in perpetual motion and receptive. He seeks a "beautiful collision of art and design, humour and finesse", believing art has the power to reveal and show them works that "confront them". He wants his diners to find pleasure in Sketch, but he wants them to be active in this pursuit, to laugh and to think. The restaurant has undergone various transformations in design and decor, in addition to changing art displays, so it is almost a gallery space with a full-service Michelin-starred restaurant attached.

In its 20-year history, Sketch has hosted more than 50 exhibitions. A series of moving-image art included works by John Baldessari, Jonas Mekas, Sylvie Fleury and Carsten Nicolai. To mark its 10th anniversary in 2012, Turner Prize-winning Martin Creed was invited to redesign the gallery dining room with an installation to disorientate and disrupt the dining service. Under strict instructions to ensure no two objects or details used would be the same, just as no two dinner seatings are the same in terms of how they are experienced, he installed *Work No. 1347*, composed of 96 types of marble (similar to his *Scotsman Steps* commission in Edinburgh in 2011), with 1,347 individual, varying, mis-matched pieces of furniture, cutlery, crockery and tableware. Creed wanted to exhibit his work in a "hostile environment" to militate against the "cosseting" conditions of the "precious" art gallery; "Art becomes less self-conscious when people are doing other things around it; when the work is just backdrop," he says. This is a live and liveable form of art, a living among art, and suggests the barriers of the gallery and the restaurant are dismantled by the art restaurant.

From top to bottom, the three floors of the townhouse are an explosion and reconfiguration of decorative arts and design. Paris-based designer and sculptor Noé Duchaufour-Lawrance created the bathrooms that have gone down in social media history, and several other international designers were commissioned for signature pieces, which are featured throughout. Crucially, in A.A. Gill's words, this "ululatingly sublime" restaurant has remained a favourite of the critics. Marina O'Loughlin called it a "camply *outré*" combination of Mae West and Barbara Cartland. Longevity and staying power are essential for a London luxury restaurant, and Sketch has remained a curiosity and popular in this continuously innovating city. It may offer the visual experience of the art and design, it may be quirky, incomprehensible and engaging, but it has never compromised on taste, either artistic or culinary. Pierre Gagnaire "is the Picasso of cuisine for me", according to its proprietor. Both factors are present on an equal plane. Gagnaire is also an art collector and has been known to travel to museums and art fairs to look at art and respond to pieces by creating new dishes.

In 2014, Mazouz commissioned David Shrigley to rework the interior of the gallery. In addition to being an admired and notable visual artist in the UK, he

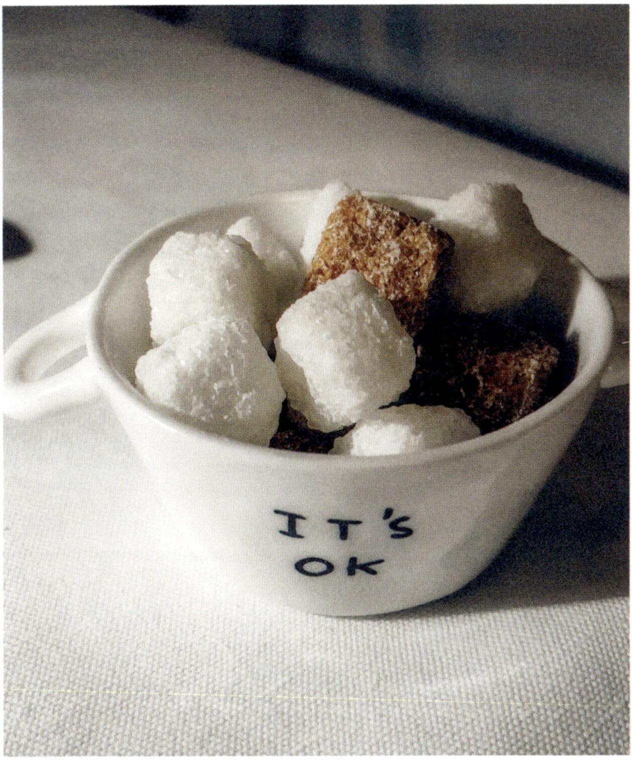

began his career as a graphic artist, and this complements Sketch's blurring of boundaries between art and design, demonstrating that it is not the discipline that matters, it is the overall effect the aesthetic has on the diner. Shrigley made 239 of his signature line drawings that contain pithy, witty and irreverent observations on modern life. His work has earned him a large fan base, as he is able to convey, in simple terms, truths – often poetic – that are known to all. Here, his thought-provoking satirical and morbid comments on everyday situations and human interactions ensure the dining experience is not taken for granted – and the art is certainly more than background.

Mazouz understood Shrigley "was the right artist for the gallery when he suggested the dining table itself be thought of as an extended exhibition space, a platform for presentation of his new work and our chef Pierre Gagnaire". The artist says he was interested in the project because he is constantly learning from placing art in unusual settings: "The dining table is an intimate space where you might be looking at the walls, but this is also an exhibition and you get to see all the bits and bobs, and it reveals itself the more cake you eat, and I like that. And the more tea you drink, it reveals itself again." The table is a space of interaction with teacups, plates, the teapot – prosaic objects in one respect, but vessels of dining rites in another. Tea and its intricate system of order and control has sacred significance for ceremonies in the Far East, while being a platform for etiquette and civilised table manners that govern behaviour in the West. Shrigley interprets this transcendental significance in his own way, seeing the table as "a sculpture", and it means diners "discover things in an intimate way in an intimate exhibition". He elevates the objects to the status of artwork. The table draws its diners together and reveals the magic of the everyday through the prandial rituals.

The Shrigley commission includes ceramic tableware with his distinctive economical drawings and acerbic messages to house Gagnaire's haute cuisine. For example, a cruet set that states "dust", "nothing" and "dirt". The artist says this is "the first artwork that I have made that can go in the dishwasher. It will be very clean artwork. Clean artwork is good artwork, in my opinion." True to his style, the drawings on the walls continue these dry, wry and metaphysical musings on all aspects of urban life. The messages include slogans and statements such as "CRUISE SHIP VULGARITY"; "STICK YOUR SYNTHETIC BURGER UP YOUR ARSE"; "I LOVE YOU TO A CERTAIN EXTENT"; "GOD WANTS TO SEE YOUR SKETCHBOOK"; "I'M DISTORTED"; and "DON'T STOP SHAVING".

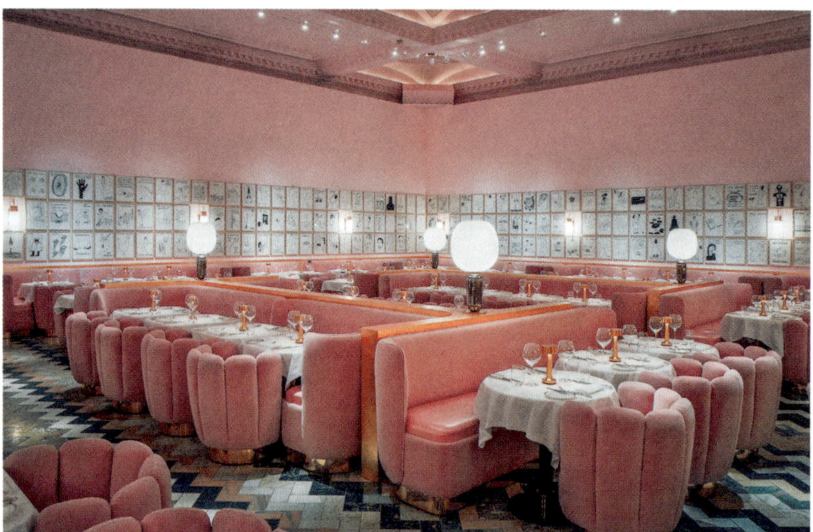

At the same time, the gallery was refurbished by Paris-based architect and designer India Mahdavi. Given the activity in Shrigley's work, the space needed to provide an uncomplicated and bright backdrop. The result is a fresh, direct, brasserie-style setting, complete with brass fixtures and plush velvet furniture. Mahdavi chose pink as the main colour for the furniture and walls – a colour associated with frivolity, impracticality and excess – as the foundation for Shrigley's profound messages and philosophies. The architect believes pink is a "mood" and "flag" because it conveys both "strength and fragility". Shrigley also uses it in his works – "straight out of the tube", making them "blobs" – "because human bodies are sort of pink". To be surrounded by so much of the colour detracts from its associations of weakness and cuteness, redirecting it into an empowering and overwhelming feeling of presence.

In early 2018, the artist updated the dining room and replaced the drawings with 91 "painted works" (he does not like to refer to them as "paintings"), arranged in rows to envelop the gallery. The intention, he says, is for diners to counter the "banality of everyday life" with the humour and wisdom of his works. The new pieces include messages such as "GREY HAIR IS OK", "BEGETTING" and "WE CANNOT SURVIVE WITHOUT STRUCTURE". If Freud argued jokes and humour were an outlet for what was forbidden or masked aggression in society, then Shrigley's one-liners deliver poetic slaps, jabs and uppercuts in the same way. They are complementary to a space where guests go to relieve urges and satisfy desires. It may be pink, but it is not prissy. For the discerning patron, there is a free play of the senses when they eat, when they look at the art, when they read the witticisms.

When sitting down to eat, we take in the conversation with our companions, but our mind wanders and thinks about other things at the same time. The art in Sketch enhances this, and ensures dining is not complacent and mindless: "ART IRRITATES THE EYE". The lived experience of dining in Sketch is to eat in an art installation. The food is carefully and beautifully presented on Shrigley's crockery. As time progresses, you drink, you eat and converse with others at the table just like any other dining experience. However, unlike any other dining experience, your eyes glance around the room and fall upon the artist's images and phrases, which inevitably disrupt your thoughts unconsciously or even consciously – some induce a chuckle, some are puzzling and require you to look more, and some are simply visually pleasing in terms of shape and composition on the page. This is the art restaurant coaxing and seducing you into engagement, ensuring its place in the dining ritual is not taken for granted. "I am going somewhere" – this dining ritual demands participation from its patrons.

Ultimately, Sketch is art restaurant pronoia – a psychological phenomenon or state of mind where you believe and behave as though the environment seeks

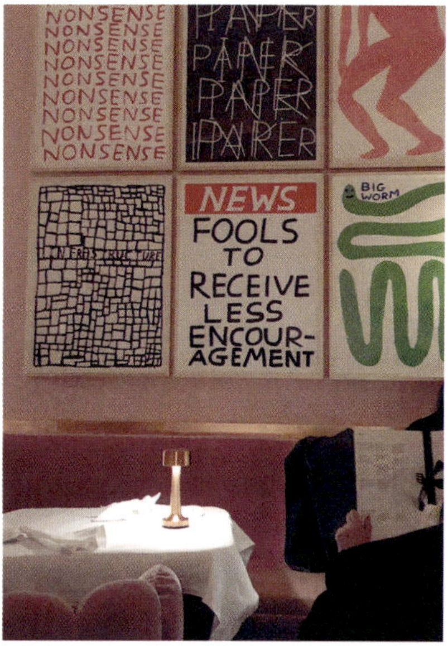

to do you good. Here, the pronoia of the artworks and interior is engineered to encourage and support the diner's sense of discernment and free play. The interiors conspire to promote sensory proliferation and enjoyment. The physical location of the restaurant and its palimpsest history is the starting point for creating the dining space. For Mazouz, space is "a concept", as opposed to a location. Space is like soil, "where ideas grow out of it at different stages and times". Sketch is "the triple dream", launching a centre or destination place for food, art and music. Claude Lévêque's neon *Jouez!* work makes the exploration an imperative.

The enduring appeal and success of Sketch is partially due to how it is integrated into the international art scene. It is an example of a collaborative art restaurant, meaning it is set up from the outset to feature art as much as the cuisine. The restaurant is not restricted by boundaries and in its interdisciplinary presentation of art and design, it also furnishes the eating element of the dining experience. It expands the exhibition space to mean more than just the gallery wall – the art is around the diners, in front of the diners, above and below the diners. As Mazouz says: "When I do restaurants, people say to me as they leave, 'Thank you, we have been away for two hours.'" As its name implies, Sketch is unfinished, constantly transforming and evolving. In this respect, the assortment of art, design, decor and space is in constant flux, and will not settle: "THE END".

Works and artists in the Sketch collection

—

Chris Levine has exhibited at Sketch. The light artist created an electromagnetic light show through the gallery that is based on the sacred geometry of Pythagoras, a form of vibrating projection that requires the observer to place their attention to see it, thus becoming one with the work. In the Glade section of the restaurant, his *Red Laser Pods* are a permanent installation, ensuring the art is not just a passive background or wallpaper.

—

Upstairs in the formal, Michelin-starred dining space, guests encounter the plush interior of designer Gahban O'Keeffe, punctuated by pieces from French-Chinese artist Zan Jbai.

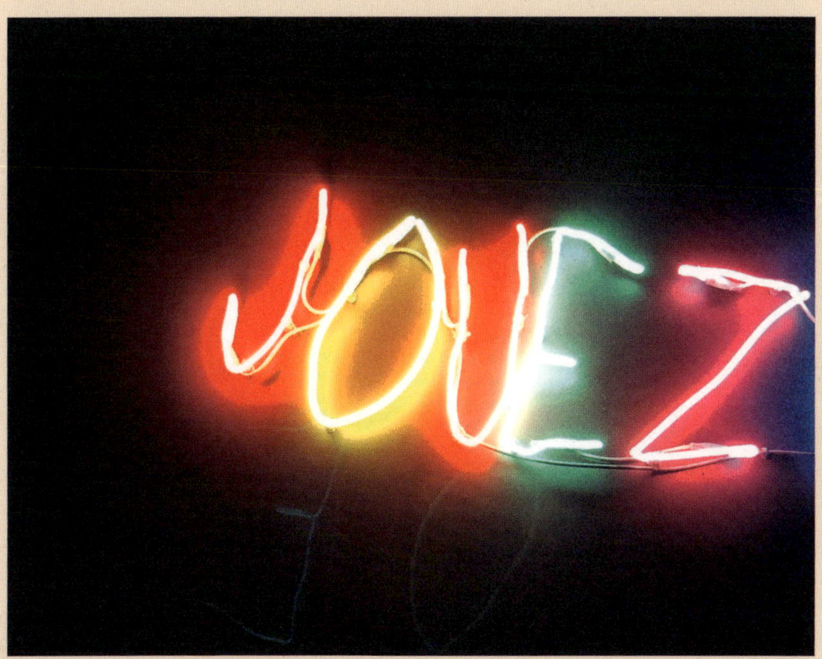

David Shrigley's drawings in the gallery of Sketch; the artist's tableware; the gallery room; the first edition of Shrigley's graphic works in colour, which were replaced in 2018; Claude Lévêque's neon and playful *Jouez!*

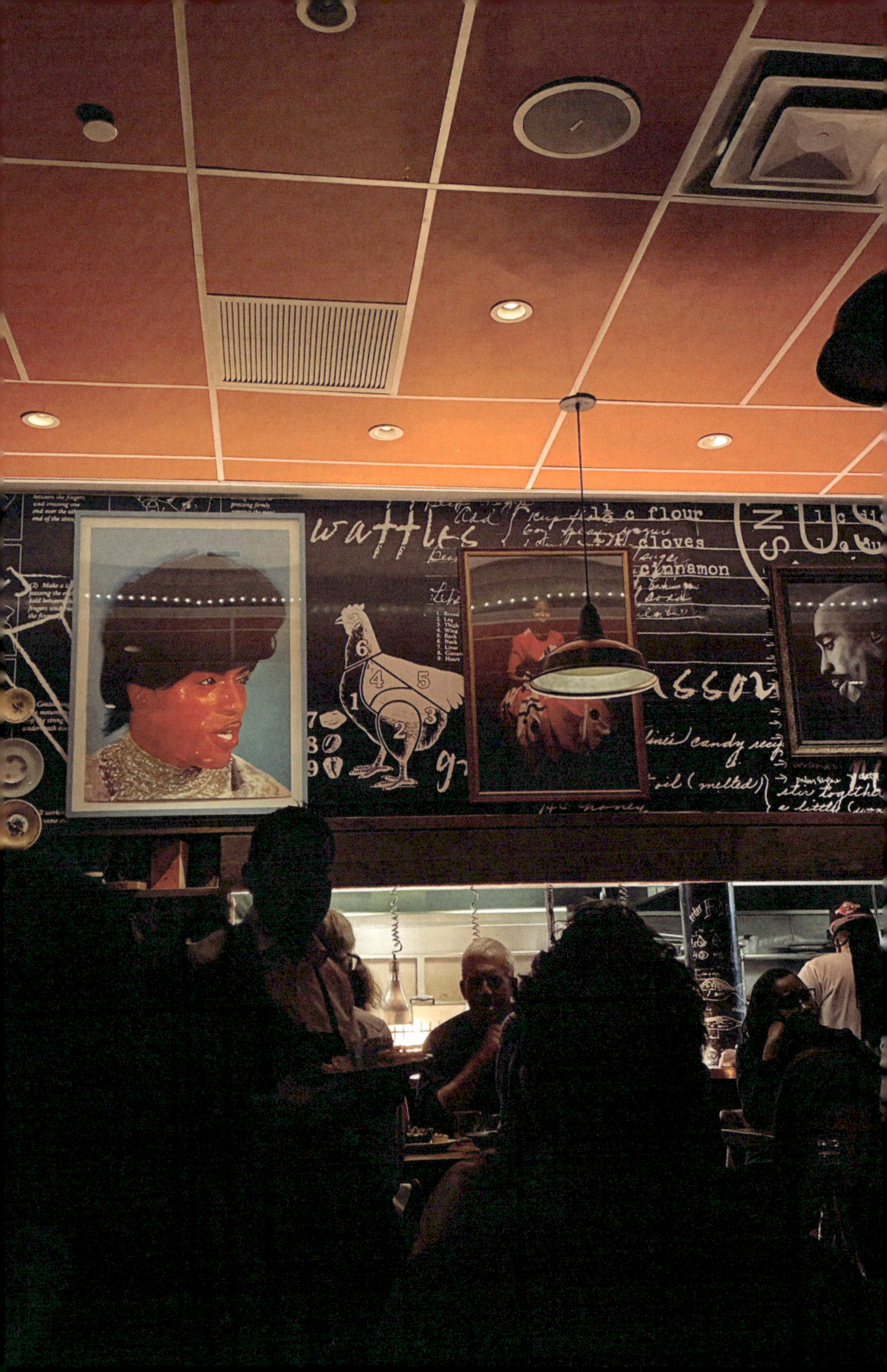
waffles
flour
cloves
cinnamon
oil (melted)

Red Rooster

NEW YORK

"Black cooking is the engine of what we commonly understand to be American food. And if you want to understand the culture and history of the United States, you need to understand Black cooks and Black food."
— Marcus Samuelsson

Nobody forgets their first time at the Red Rooster in Harlem. Nobody forgets the buzzing atmosphere, the animated conversation with their dining companions, the feeling of being full and satiated, and of course the art that surrounds them during the meal. Paintings of proud hip hop stars, photographs of poised, voguing men, images of elderly ladies in immaculate patterned frocks. This mash-up, the mixing of influences, textures and elements, is an invitation from Marcus Samuelsson into the African American experience of a thriving Harlem culture. For him, art, music and food all belong in the same space and come together to celebrate and educate diners about Harlem through his taste, but also, for a short while, to make them feel and see what is around them as an artist would see it. The contemporary artist Sanford Biggers says the restaurant encourages the level of "synaesthesia" that "all of us creatives want to be operating on". At the Red Rooster, this is extended to diners. It takes a certain auteur to bring together elements from different cultures and societies, be they ingredients, patterns, colours, influences, stories, and Samuelsson deftly mixes Swedish contemporary artists with spices from Africa and recipes from the creole Caribbean. Each element has its own history and original position but becomes part of a greater whole in the Red Rooster to present an identity formed by a new community that attracts new diners. It integrates the locals with "internationals and downtowners", as Biggers says. Through the chef's visual and literal taste, and the role of art in the experience, all diners will receive "the love, the respect, the history and the homage" to this singular part of New York in a morsel. The art is shorthand for the wider culture of Harlem and comes out in different forms of expression in this art restaurant.

Samuelsson's own life journey is an extraordinary assemblage of events and influences. Having survived tuberculosis as a child in his native Ethiopia, he was adopted by a nurse in Addis Ababa and taken to Sweden. He moved to New York in 1994 and worked in various restaurants, including in the Twin Towers, eventually becoming the head chef at Aquavit. Several of his former colleagues dying on 9/11 made him realise he could not "just cook for the one per cent". He knew he wanted to create his own restaurant in Harlem to contribute to the area's heritage and take his place within that history. He spent the next eight years embedding himself in the neighbourhood, attending church services

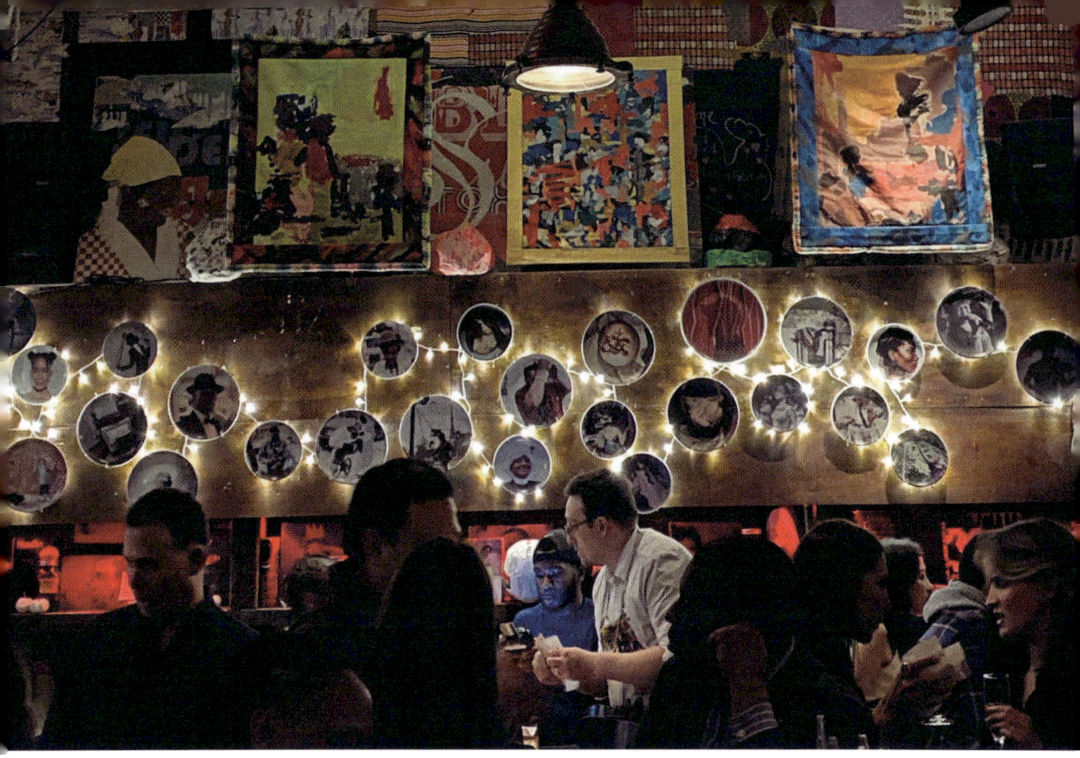

and community events, and eating at Sylvia's, a Southern soul food institution comfort-feeding locals since 1962. Samuelsson's move to New York coincided with the arrival in the city of other cultural figures such as Thelma Golden, the director of the highly respected Studio Museum. It was there that he met Biggers and they all became friends, supporting one another in terms of how each one worked with the diaspora story in their respective fields. Much like an artistic or creative movement, they contributed to and influenced each other's projects. Samuelsson is the culinary component of this movement, James Baldwin was the novelist, contemporary artists including Lorna Simpson and Julie Mehretu were part of the art element, and Golden a cultural leader. Ultimately, this group of creative individuals became a remix, an update, of the Harlem Renaissance. Something "not far-fetched", according to Biggers, as the group consider themselves "custodians of a rich legacy" in Harlem. Samuelsson furthers this when he says: "We all work in the similar space where we try to express a Black experience through an artistic movement." The Harlem Renaissance not only advanced Black artists and culture in America at a time when this ethnic group was attempting to forge and express its own identity, it also attracted and imported new audiences to Harlem itself. It is not enough to export the culture of Harlem to connoisseurs of different cultural productions, it has to be experienced in the location itself, and the Red Rooster delivers this in one dinner reservation.

Samuelsson understands his place in local history and the duty that comes with restoring the "dialogue of hospitality". The restaurant is located on the site of what was Ginny's speakeasy in the 1920s. There is a sense of responsibility and respect for local history, which has welcomed many from other cultures, and Samuelsson wants to play his part in this diaspora. From the Cotton Club, the legendary jazz venue that defied prohibition laws and Jim Crow segregation in the 1920s and 1930s, and the Apollo Theatre, which has showcased Black music and performing arts since the 1930s, including Bessie Smith and Count Basie, to, more recently, the Studio Museum, dedicated to art and artists of African descent, with resident artists such as Kehinde Wiley and Njideka Akunyili Crosby, and the National Black Theatre, which stages and produces award-winning theatre devoted to the Black experience. The Red Rooster takes its place in this roster of significant cultural institutions in the neighbourhood by exhibiting art by local African American artists and those who have settled in Harlem. For Golden, the Red Rooster is the "museum kitchen" of the institution she has been directing for more than 30 years, showcasing art from the African diaspora. Samuelsson wanted to create something "to inspire and aspire", and metrics for success are based not just on how busy the restaurant is, but on the community it fosters and the artists it supports. Local resident and renowned artist Faith Ringgold says: "The Red Rooster is a Harlem landmark. We used to go there, back in the day, to eat their delicious soul food and to see the stars." It was the scene to be seen. "Just name them: Dinah, Sugar Ray, Josephine, Ella, Billie, Dizzy, Cab, Malcolm, Zora, Rommie and Jacob. They were all at the Red Rooster." Samuelsson's taste and synthesis of influences through his art restaurant adds an extra layer to the local history.

Through his friendship with Golden, the restaurateur realised the importance of visual art and how it contributes to the cultural story. Golden says the local community has always been interested in culture and is open to receiving new ideas and influences. The expression of creativity is everywhere in Harlem, in how locals dress, how they present themselves and speak, in social bonds, in the dining rituals. The connection of food and art, according to Samuelsson, is a lived metaphor for this "multi-level of expression where hospitality food and service is the core, the base, but with that, when you deal with Black culture, the core of it is the African wave and the diaspora, and that has to be expressed in multi-levels". By being in the Red Rooster, eating his food surrounded by the art, you feel and think like an artist. The art is "the force of expression" that not only changes the narrative but gives the narrative opportunity to sink in at a different level. As he says, in order to "design something with people who may or may not have had a full understanding of a multi-layered Black experience, there's no point in arguing with architects, so it's better to draw it out yourself". In this way he *painted out* the restaurant.

He began displaying his collection with more representational, figurative art, including Lorna Simpson and Mickalene Thomas. This evolved as he collected

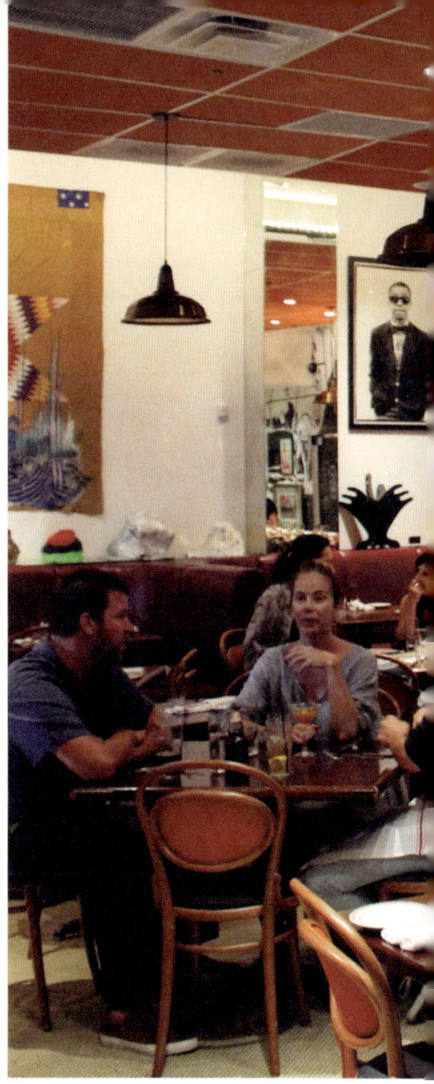

abstract African American artists such as Theaster Gates and Rashid Johnson. The progression became educational for visitors to the restaurant who may not have had an extensive knowledge of art. The display is curated to feature well-known historical artists alongside emerging and independent practitioners, like Miss Leah did in Dooky Chase, whom Samuelsson acknowledges as an inspiration. The chef's model of collecting for the restaurant is not to show trophy pieces or conceptual works, rather he feels he has a duty of care towards his diners and the local artist community by guiding the former through relatable, accessible works and preserving the artistic integrity of the latter. Faith Ringgold, an artistic fixture and figure in Harlem, hangs five of her visual story quilts in the restaurant, which combine narrative with textiles as sculpture. She also takes her place in the history of quilt-making in America, citing the importance of how they were practical necessities to keep slaves warm in the 19th century, and are now the most "portable artworks". She herself mashes up visual storytelling, combining acrylic painting, embroidery and writing in her pieces. Having lived in Harlem all her life, the multifaceted way of interpreting these experiences comes out in her work, dealing with communities, families, storytelling. It is honest yet exuberant.

Samuelsson is drawn to quilts because their seemingly ordinary origins hold a significant place in the history of the United States. He commissioned Biggers to create more of them for the restaurant because of this history and how quilting traditionally belonged to the domestic sphere, like cooking. The artist's *Flying Lotus #14* (2012) hangs in the main dining area, and pays tribute to folk art and heritage crafts, despite being displayed in a busy, vibrant environment. The work interrupts this contemporary scene, but also takes its rightful place among the different voices in the history of this community as a reminder of the past. In post-bellum United States, women's slave labour was associated with spinning, weaving and textile production. As the craft developed and emancipation and the Civil War began, the labourers integrated symbols and codes of communication into the abolition efforts and campaigns. Quilts were used along the Underground Railroad in the South as

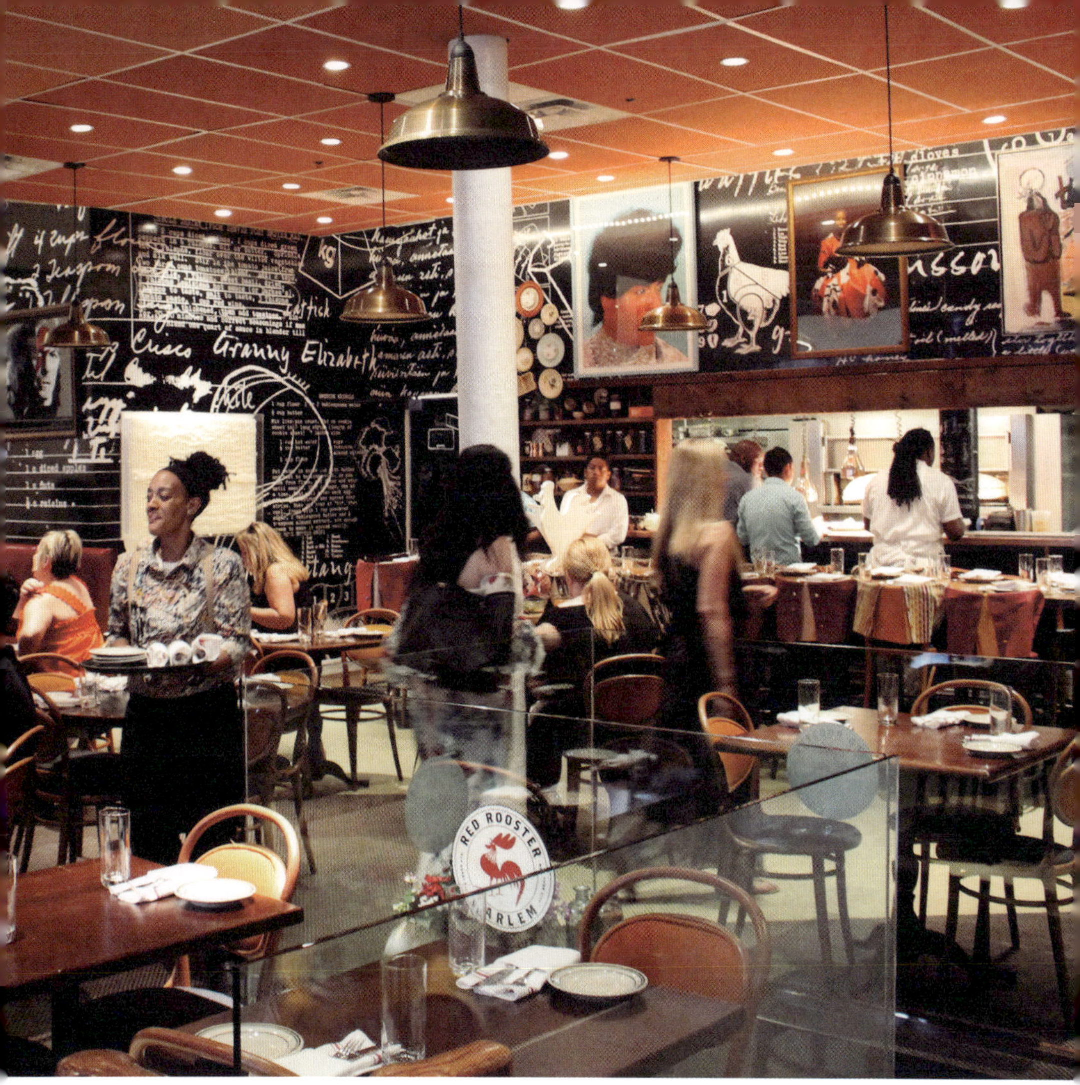

signals for escaped slaves to know when there was food available in particular houses, or when and where they could find shelter. Samuelsson was fascinated by this history and wanted to honour it through the commission, even though he admits "99 per cent of the people coming here have no clue about this". Also, since Biggers mixes cultures and people "just like a chef", the work complements his own œuvre in the kitchen.

The Red Rooster's collection is a compendium of other art restaurant collectors' motivations. It contains private pieces that belong to Samuelsson, works lent from commercial galleries and from institutions such as the Studio Museum, pieces acquired from emerging artists outside of the gallery system, and philanthropic acquisitions from disadvantaged communities. The chef always painted on the side, further aligning him with the creative community, and says he trusts artists to speak the truth about their particular period in time.

He never trusted official voices or politicians, because "as a Black man, what they present to you is not reality". The stories from the artists have always been "much more truthful or told from an experience that related to me. So what I learned about urban America from artists was, for me, more informative than going to CNN." As a young man in Sweden, he first read about Jean-Michel Basquiat, a "dynamic Black artist doing something different", and suddenly realised what it meant to be an artist. "I've always gone to artists and artisans to understand the world, whether that's music or through paintings," he says. They assemble a reality that he can process. "One of the blessings about being Black is that you know that whatever is out there is not factual. So you go and search for your own information, and you go to these voices, whatever the different medium."

Samuelsson began to display art in the Red Rooster because it means an individual is recognised – they have a voice. There are also commercial advantages, because the restaurant creates a marketplace for the artists, recommending and sponsoring them the same way galleries do. It also mimics cultural institutions by creating a dialogue with the artistic community. Samuelsson works with artists who have been part of the Studio Museum by having solo shows there or whose art is in the permanent collection, such as Sanford Biggers, Lorna Simpson and Mark Bradford. He also incubates emerging local artists, such as Nick Low and Brandon Cox, giving them an exhibition space that may otherwise be challenging to obtain. Samuelsson has a particular interest in encouraging ex-offenders and prison inmates to show work in the restaurant. There is also an artists' programme at the Red Rooster with artists' talks and lectures, to which the media and journalists are invited to learn about the work. "It's deep-tissue involvement," he says. This restaurant is full service: it nurtures the creation of the art, displays and showcases its products to attract new talent, and then does it all over again, day after day, breakfast, lunch and dinner.

The chef hopes surrounding the dining space with art removes some of the barriers that someone interested in art might find in a gallery. "It's not a traditional space, so it opens up the conversation – you can ask straightforward questions," he explains. "People have to have dinner anyway – how often do you do that while you meet an artist who can share their vision and passion with other people?" Biggers supports this: "When I'm in the Red Rooster, it is not uncommon at all for me to speak to 90-year-old women who have been quilting all of their lives, because I've been doing these paintings on quilts. I might not run into them at the museum, but I will run into them at the restaurant." These are "intersections of people" that form a common identity when they are in the restaurant. As an endeavour, the Red Rooster is an investment in the local community because it promotes Harlem's distinct heritage in a bustling, evolving metropolis. Samuelsson is a well-respected figure among locals; people stop him on the street, offer their advice about his recipes or ask him for advice on job hunting, or just shake his hand in appreciation.

If a restaurant is a universe in itself, with its own order and system of rules for how communities build identities, the Red Rooster takes the ingredients of this historical array, mashes them up and feeds them to diners. "Just like in the days of Langston Hughes, Harlem is a dizzying mixture of joy and pain: the weary blues, swing and boogie all rolled into one," writes Samuelsson. It is a restaurant experience comfortable with being multisensory, in fact flaunting it, because anybody interested in art and creativity, as well as good food, will seek this sensory freefall in an art restaurant like the Red Rooster. "Even if you're a visual artist," Biggers says, "you do want to engage people's sense of poetry. And you want them to basically hear sounds as they're looking at your colours. It sounds very romantic, but I think we all want some degree of that to happen." By placing art in the restaurant, in addition to his mixing of influences, histories and ingredients, Samuelsson creates a reality where diners experience their environment differently, more sensitively, more heightened, more creatively. They will see that history, reality, narratives are not as straightforward as they seem, they are multifaceted and thus enriching. Restaurants are their own singular, inspiring space, according to Golden, "a microcosm of the experience of Harlem itself", and the Red Rooster serves this to its patrons while welcoming artists, making them feel they belong and can thrive here. As Ringgold insists: "Marcus has brought the Red Rooster back to life. Me and my art are at home at the Red Rooster and in Harlem where I was born. Go see."

Works and artists in the Red Rooster collection

—

There is a series of photographs by Gordon Parks from the 1950s of the African American community: strong, confident figures of Black culture. The images are street scenes and group portraits of urban life.

—

Pontus Höök, an artist with a similar cultural background to Samuelsson, moved from Sweden to New York in the 1990s. He features a series of 17 photographs of local diners in the restaurant itself, all in their Sunday best, celebrating the tradition of family lunches after church, as well as the creative flair and pride in appearance of this community. "I had seen the photographs of Harlem in its glory days, stylish men in bespoke suits, women so well dressed that they'd put the models in *Vogue* to shame," says Höök. "I knew that Harlemites loved to dance, to pray, and to eat." The black-and-white images are timeless, with the sitters staring into the camera, and show the influence of Richard Avedon's colloquial portraits of mainstream United States. The Red Rooster is an art restaurant that depicts and celebrates the very diners who form part of the tradition.

—

A portrait of Little Richard by Mark Leckey, in the artist's trademark hyperreal, technicolour style, shines with a glittery, metallic, shimmering overlay. It hangs above the kitchen, making him look like he is melting in the heat.

—

Diners are greeted by a squatting young woman with an afro, holding a spray-paint can. This is Harlem-based graphic artist Nick Low's avatar, a funky figure in retro 1980s sneakers who presides like a doorman over guests who enter. Her clothing is multicoloured, her face and skin are left unfinished; the Red Rooster welcomes liminal identities.

—

Romare Bearden's collage of a jazz band depicts the members in full play. Bearden was born in Charlotte, North Carolina, and moved to Harlem when he was a teenager, bringing with him his deep South spiritualism to the blues and jazz music and culture of the neighbourhood.

—

Ebony Patterson's photograph of marching women in a parade holding banners celebrates her Jamaican ancestry. The artist works in various media and uses photography and printmaking as a way of documenting her culture.

—

A black-and-white photograph of Run-DMC by Janette Beckman, an artist who started by working with magazines such as *The Face* and *Melody Maker*, hangs in the dining space. Samuelsson talks about how music is also an important influence on his aesthetic – it helps him to fuse together the other elements.

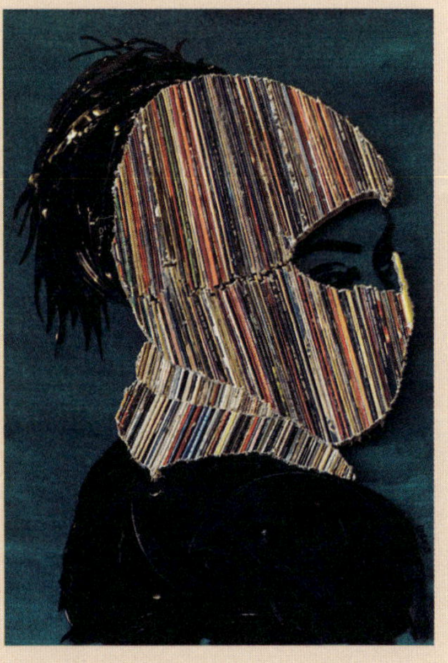

Marcus Lecky's *Little Richard*; Faith Ringgold's works above the dining table; *Flying Lotus #14* by Sanford Biggers in the main dining room; Nick Low's graffiti art

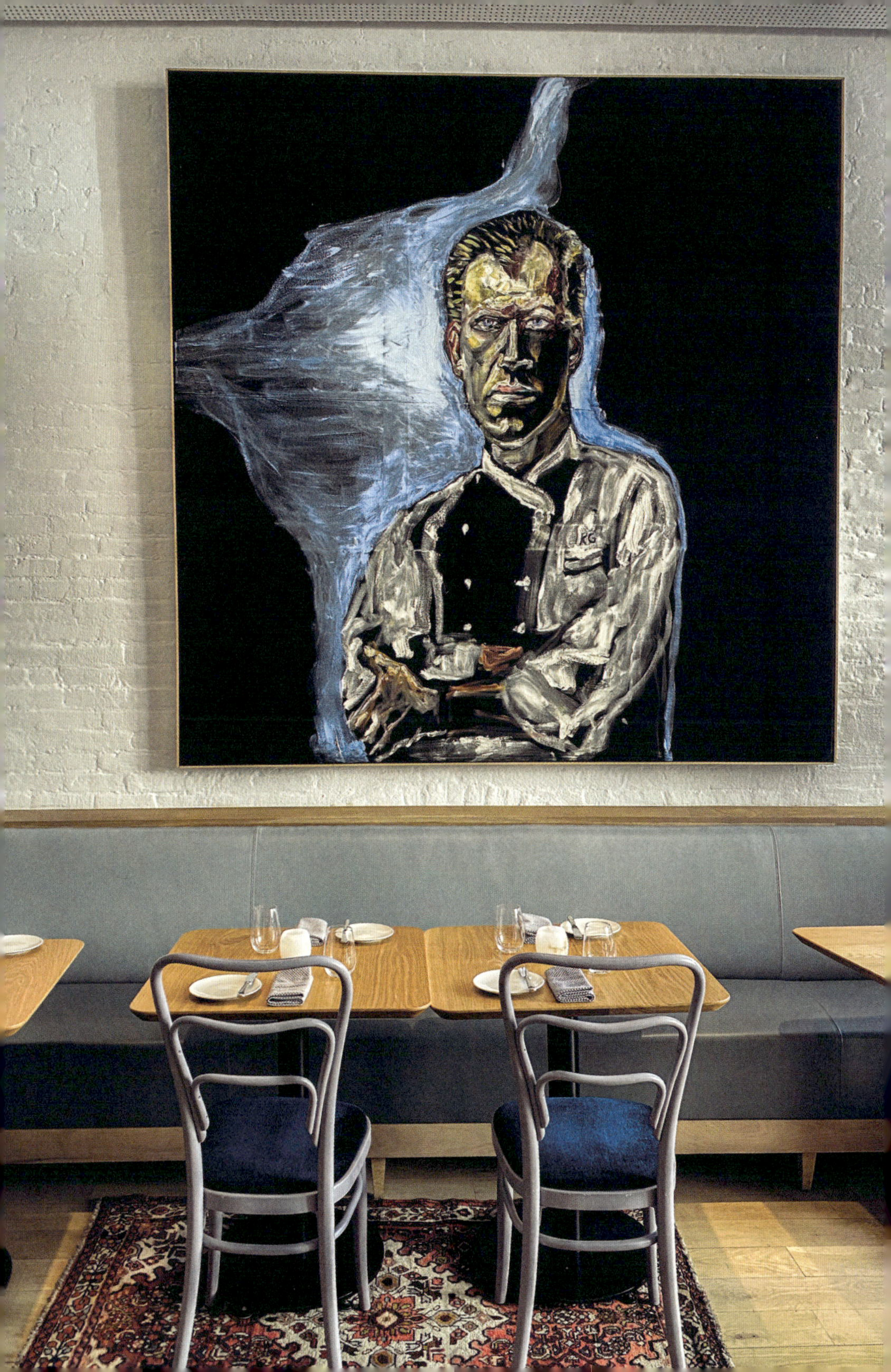

Wallsé

"Be not afraid of being called unfashionable."
— Adolf Loos

"He calls me at 5pm in the evening and asks me for a table," says the Austrian chef and restaurateur Kurt Gutenbrunner of Wallsé in New York City. "I tell him it's Valentine's Day, I don't have a table, *I can't do it*." No matter the restaurant, no matter the caller, no matter the reason, in this city, the rules of reservations are unshakeable. Even if that person calling is Julian Schnabel. Wallsé, the bijoux-sized restaurant in the West Village of Manhattan on the corner of 11th and Washington, is in a heritage building dating from 1890. It has only 15 tables, but makes up for its lack of size in quality and attention to detail in terms of how each facet of the dining process is acquired and presented for guests. Aside from its pristine cooking (traditional Austrian cuisine with an East Coast overlay), the restaurant is characterised by a clean interior punctuated by art from Martin Kippenberger, Hermann Nitsch, Albert Oehlen and... Julian Schnabel. The last of these is a neighbour and close friend of the chef. Over the 20 years the establishment has been in existence, the pair have developed a friendship and shared views on art and food, and they have explored contemporary art connected to Austria and Germany. Pairing this with the Michelin-starred menu of exquisitely crafted dishes and ingredients, Wallsé takes its patrons on an intelligent conversation about expression and emotion in the dining ritual that prevents it from being a novelty venue. Instead, it becomes an art restaurant where the chef allows an artist to roam free throughout the dining area and kitchen.

Wallsé was founded on Gutenbrunner's distinctive interior design and architectural taste regarding Viennese Modernism and cuisine. This also involved Schnabel, his "restaurant curator", displaying pieces of his own abstract work and other artists relevant to the Neo-Expressionist aesthetic the chef promotes. In fact, Schnabel was integral to the success of the experiment. "I just let him do whatever he wants," the chef says, with a shrug of the shoulders and a smirk. The artist's dexterity and ability to glide between media reinforces his status as an auteur – one who can even extend his artistic practice into a restaurant.

Gutenbrunner's Austrian upbringing instilled an early interest in art and architecture. His native country has ample examples of leading modern design and aesthetic innovation from the late 19th and early 20th centuries. Adolf Loos, the chef's biggest influence, was the design diluent to counter the dominance of Art Nouveau that remained in Europe. He promoted minimalism and functionality in interiors, so as to eliminate ornate excess and focus on the human actions and interactions in the space. Gutenbrunner asked the contemporary architect

Constantin Wickenburg to design his restaurant on the Viennese architect's thesis of clean lines and, importantly, the concept of the cube. Wallsé is in fact a cube, and it pays tribute to Loos's use of this shape in architecture and interiors, as well as referencing white cube spaces of art galleries, given the inclusion of contemporary art. The effect is to isolate emotions involved in feeling when dining and when in the company of others. There is also a reference to Loos's Café Museum of 1899 where the architect shocked Viennese society by inviting them to take their *sachertorte* in a purist, stripped back space of open light, large windows and dark lines to encourage the dynamism that comes when people meet. The café quickly became an artists' and intellectuals' eatery with important figures from the Successionist movement including Oskar Kokoschka, Gustav Klimt and Egon Schiele, and writers and composers such as Robert Musil, Georg Trakl, Otto Wagner, Hermann Broch and Alban Berg. The aesthetic was so different from the plush, luxurious interiors the Viennese were accustomed to that it became known as "Café Nihilism".

The chef's love of this minimalist, stark Austrian art and design – and particularly chair design – serendipitously led him to Renée Price and Ronald Lauder, director and founder of the Neue Galerie in 2000. As Gutenbrunner was putting together the finishing touches for the restaurant, he wanted to remain faithful to Loos's philosophy of confident simplicity and forthright functionality. Loos designed the iconic Thonet chairs for his Café Museum. They featured curved beechwood backs and woven cane seats. Loos declared they "represent the spirit of the age". Gutenbrunner ordered the same chairs directly from the original manufacturer in Austria: "We didn't buy the chairs in Czechoslovakia or in South Carolina, we bought them in Vienna, constantly insisting that they must come from Vienna." The cost was high, but so is authenticity. Then the CEO of Thonet alerted Lauder to this other New Yorker purchasing the same chairs as he had: "I don't know what's going on in New York, but there was a young guy here who bought all the chairs and bar stools as you did… for 30 years we haven't sold a single chair in the US and now everybody is buying them." Lauder contacted the young chef, and it resulted in an invitation to operate Café Sabarsky at the Neue Galerie. This elevated and set a new standard for the museum café internationally, making it a destination, rather than an afterthought to an exhibition visit.

The restaurant must be a *gesamtkunstwerk* for diners, according to Gutenbrunner, and he engineers such an all-encompassing experience: "Food, wine, architecture, art; all together these things make a happy house. Then, if you have happy people visiting your house, I believe you have a wonderful and successful restaurant." Loos argued that architecture "arouses sentiments in man" and it was the architect's work to focus these. Gutenbrunner activates the same feeling through

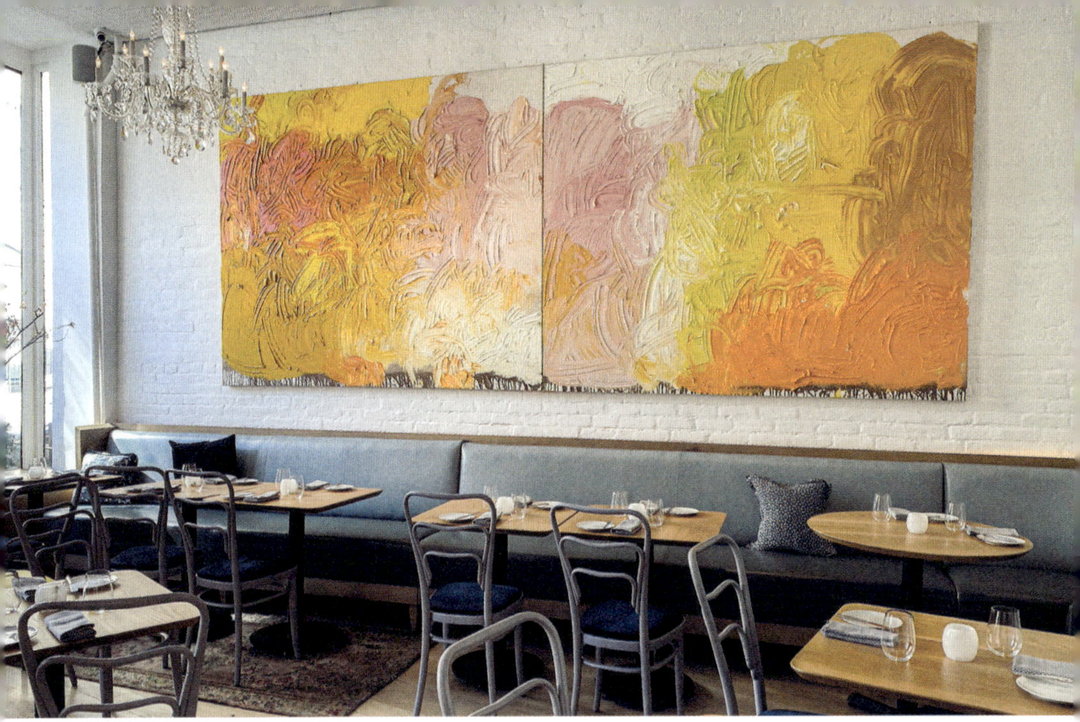

the restaurant, suggesting a perfect diorama of an internal world, with its daily theatre of dining-ritual performances. In turn, the artworks are not ornament but a way to isolate and channel emotions through their Neo-Expressionist abstractions that reinforce the pleasure of eating. "If you are the hospitality industry, in the hospitality business, I think that this is what you have to be able to give to your customers," he says. It is a space for pleasure, for enjoyment of the senses with others. "Why are people going out? Because they want to have a good time, they want to be in an environment… They could say, 'Hey, this is my living room… it could be my living room, and I'm going to have a good time with my friends or family, and my private chef is there.' This is probably the reason why we are here for 20 years."

Wallsé is a neighbourhood restaurant, but this particular locale contains some of the most expensive, stealthily wealthy real estate in the world. It is the home of residents successful in whatever field they are in, from finance to media, or even the arts. Among these, Lou Reed and Laurie Anderson lived a few blocks away and regularly took their meals at Wallsé. Once you cut your bohemian teeth in the East Village, then grow up and old, you migrate to the West Village. Wallsé is unassuming and hence intimate. It is the kind of restaurant where regulars meet those in their circles and their friends and remain undiscovered by the outside world. Gutenbrunner is most "happy being around other creative people, cooking for them and making them happy. I think they go hand in hand." His contribution to creativity and the artists' scene is through his cooking. "Over the years my love of food and art has helped me to build many friendships, which has furthered my passion for the art world," he says. Lou Reed "was a very, very,

very good friend", and his persona and presence still infuses the restaurant, from the framed photograph in the entrance to the soundtrack of his music and that of his contemporaries. He always ate at the same corner table and behaved discreetly, observing the street from the windowed walls. Gutenbrunner likes to think of Wallsé as "a little bit Mozart and a little bit Lou Reed. You have to have a little classic, you have to be a little rock star, and then you put this together and you create a mix. I tried to create a mix in this area."

The restaurant is also testament to how New York City has evolved: the gentrification of a previously insalubrious neighbourhood now houses the avant-garde who settle down here once they are successful and make their fortune. The West Village was originally a rough and run-down part of the city in the 1970s and 1980s, with a high crime rate, poor accommodation, drug dealing, transvestite prostitution and warehouse labourers. Yet this was also a part of New York that adhered to the principle of *Stadluft macht frei* – urban air makes you free – attracting bohemians, artists, musicians, writers and general outsiders. Locals were always tolerant and welcoming of others, be they immigrants or progressives. "Cuisine cannot exist without the free and fair movement of ingredients, ideas and people," the chef René Redzepi writes. "Deliciousness is an undeniable benefit of immigration. When people move around, food gets better." Thus, an authentic Viennese bistro, established by a first-generation immigrant, tucked away at the end of one of the West Village streets, is a continuation of this tradition. But

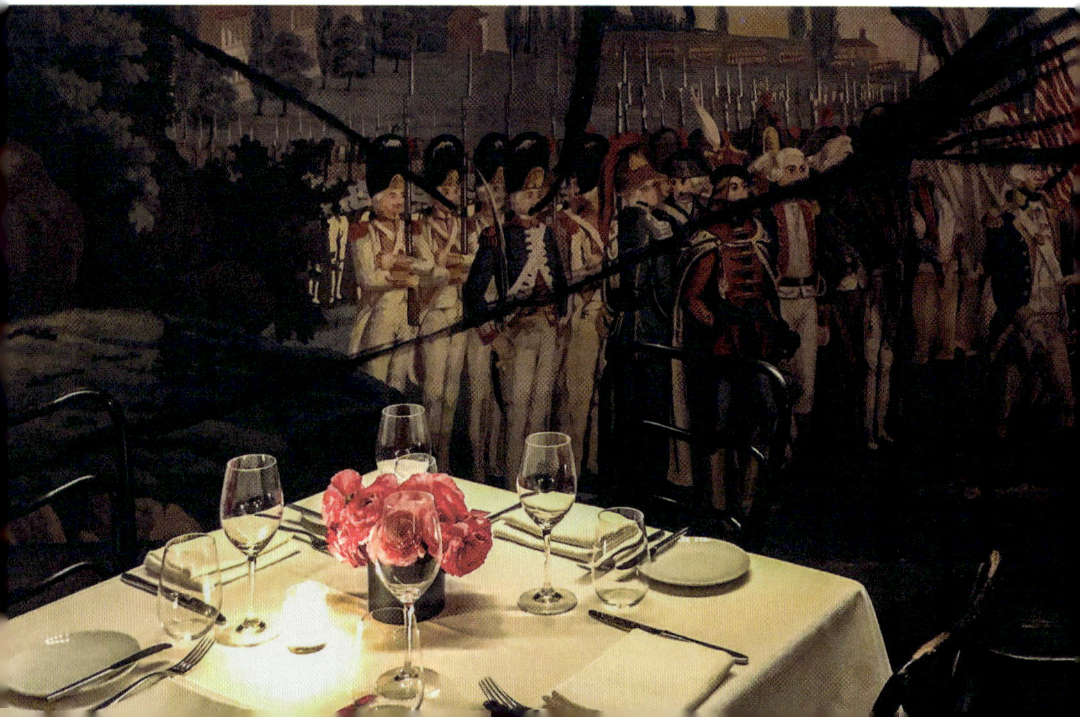

as often happens with pioneers of gentrification, they are first met with resistance: "Twenty years ago, out here in the far West Village with the transvestites, everybody thought I'm a little out of my mind," says Gutenbrunner. For the chef, however, there was another reason to come to the area: the markets and warehouses that stored imported foodstuffs. Gutenbrunner "based [my] cuisine on products I love. I buy a lot from the markets here, have a strong relationship with the people from whom I buy my fish, my meat, my produce." The urban thinker Daniel Sennett writes of the West Village, "form will emerge from the way people dwell". Inhabitants adjust their activities, "nipping and tucking" to adapt to the neighbourhood they are in. A restaurant described as "local" is particularly relevant in a megalopolis where dwellings are small and restaurants are used for entertaining and meeting friends. This is a European model for eateries in cities.

There is a social and artistic meaning to the restaurant as a place where like-minded people gather and discuss projects and ideas, gossip and further their own thinking, often sparking inspiration. It reinforces identity with a particular community and belonging to a group. The restaurant is a symbol of a *scene*, which seldom just exists, but is made by people who join and congregate there. At Wallsé, this was created by the charismatic presence of Schnabel, who has dined here with Gus Van Sant, Dennis Hopper and a host of other artists. As a magnetic artist and now celebrity, Schnabel is surrounded by an entourage and followers, given he was once part of New York's avant-garde mixing with pop stars, art royalty and wealthy collectors by the late 1980s. Some of that associative magic is retained in the restaurant.

Cooking and restaurants with their own scene have been important to Schnabel since he arrived in New York in the late 1970s with a girlfriend and got a job as a cook at Max's Kansas City. Started by Mickey Rustin, it was a favourite venue for Sixties aristocracy: artists, fashion designers and musicians. Rustin had a gift for "curating people", deciding who was in and who was out. Schnabel recalls that Max's Kansas City "was a giant, in the tradition of artists' bars like Le Chat Noir, Moulin Rouge, the Pont-Royal and the Cedar Tavern". He was one of the youngest in the place and it introduced him to many influential artists he admired: "If a person flew to New York, got in a taxi, and their one word of English was 'Max's', they'd be taken to a place where sculptors, rock musicians, movie stars, poets, composers, strippers, groupies, drug dealers, laser artists, lion tamers, acrobats (and their wives, with Yorkshire terriers in their purses) and artists of every aesthetic and sexual persuasion, including painters, even great painters, came to witness each other." It was frequented by Andy Warhol, Carl Andre, Larry Rivers, Robert Rauschenberg, Dan Flavin and Roy Lichtenstein, among others. The artists would cavort with the likes of The Velvet

Underground, Alice Cooper, Allen Ginsberg and William Burroughs. Schnabel says: "Even if they didn't speak, they all came to Max's just to check in, just to make sure that life was still going on and to let people know they were still alive." The proprietor used the eating down model to generate a scene and ensure he retained the "right" artists. He consequently amassed his own art collection. It was during his time as a chef at Max's Kansas City that Schnabel would invite gallerists and art world professionals who were regular clientele to his studio to look at his pieces. Here he met the dazzling wild-child art dealer Mary Boone, who decided on the spot to represent him. "Max's wasn't particularly cosy or friendly," he recalls. "Once you got over the trauma of being there, everything got worse, but you couldn't leave. If you could handle your own questions – why you were there in the first place – maybe you could exist there. For some reason, the uneasiness made me feel at home."

By the 1980s Schnabel had become an art celebrity, a media star. *Artforum* declared he had "reinvented the art world". The decade's capitalism and newly made financiers and businesspeople developed and bought in this part of the city. Schnabel was an artist they collected. He benefited from being in vogue and desirable in the era of Wall Street greed-being-good. He would become recognisable by art world and non-art world alike. The fact he was successful

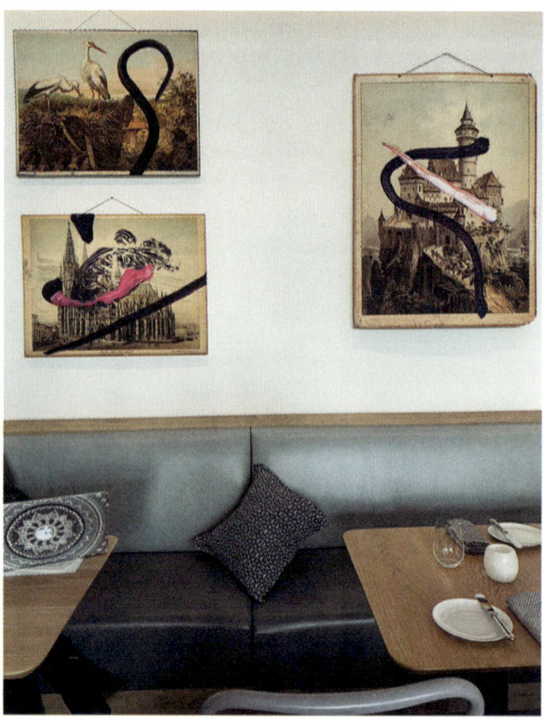

and moved to the same areas of the city as his collectors did, purchasing a whole block to create Palazzo Chupi on West 11th Street, was a sign of what a superstar he became – "the big Opera", as his friend Dennis Hopper referred to him.

One day, Schnabel walked into Wallsé and said, "Kurt, I wanna paint you." The chef replied, "You're kidding, right?" By this time, the artist had become well-known for portraits of actors and celebrities. "He said, 'No, no, no, I want to paint *you*.'" Gutenbrunner ignored the request. "And then one day, he called me up and he says, 'Come down to the studio, the light is right, I want to paint you *today*.'" The chef relented and went to the studio. Schnabel commanded, "Walk around me", and "an hour and a half and a pack of cigarettes later" the portrait was completed. The chef "was so exhausted, I had to go home and lie down". The artist insisted it should be hung in the restaurant. The work is there today, in pride of place in the main dining room, greeting guests as they arrive and wait for tables. It is a trademark Schnabel portrait on black velvet with expressive brushwork in cool colours. The chef is wearing his apron, with his name stitched on it, and holding a cigarette. Gutenbrunner was unable to look at it for months when it was first displayed, finding Schnabel's perspective too intense. This also evidences his preference for his ego to show what it can do in the kitchen rather than in front of house. Schnabel says he painted the chef in gratitude, "because he was nice to my dad who came from Czechoslovakia, he would make him soup with chopped egg noodles and send it over when he was sick".

From that moment on, Gutenbrunner and Schnabel controlled all details in the Wallsé dining experience, from the precision of the cooking to the authenticity of the art curation. It veers between an informality of a collaboration born out of friendship and ease, and the formality of collaboration born out of an art project with aesthetic method and practice. Gutenbrunner says: "The same creativity that one requires to be an artist in many ways is required to be a chef. Whether you express yourself through making films or through painting, or sculpture, the same artistry applies to food and cooking. I never wanted to have just a restaurant, but a space that also reflects my passion for art and its direct correlation to food." The chef admires the artist's "way of seeing" and it influences his cooking. Owning a restaurant is an artistic endeavour because of how Gutenbrunner works as a chef. "I consider my job as being art," he says. "Like a painter goes to the studio and paints, I go to my studio and cook, and I have enormous joy doing this." The chef is sensitive and shy, the artist is the opposite, but the collaboration works.

They discussed the interior of the restaurant and the art to be displayed in it, and when to rotate it. Gutenbrunner is an admirer of Hermann Nitsch, the Austrian multimedia Actionist artist, and collects his work. He wanted to place a piece in the restaurant and "had many conversations with Julian, always about putting a Nitsch in here. Julian always said, 'You don't want to have a big work of red blood in the restaurant,' and I didn't have an argument against that, because of course he was right." It was too jarring and discordant in the space. He then asked Nitsch to paint a new piece specifically for the restaurant, which the artist delivered – in uncharacteristic yellow. Schnabel remained unimpressed. Then Gutenbrunner remembered the concluding scene of Schnabel's 2018 biopic of Vincent van Gogh, *At Eternity's Gate*, after the artist dies and is mourned. The very last image is the warm yet sulphurous yellow that is used throughout the film for the wheat fields, the sunshine and even Willem Dafoe's straw hat. Yellow is warm, inviting, but it is also acidic and expressively burns uncomfortably. "It was my selling point to him," he says. "He couldn't say anything anymore." The piece hangs in the restaurant today.

Schnabel's own piece is from his later series of abstract works, made in 2017. It is large, painted on discarded tarpaulin found in a Mexican fruit market. It is harsh, almost brutal, but the pink calms it down and diverts the aggression into energy and action. Schnabel has an ability to seek out the sublime in his practice, given his fascination with skies, water and surfing. He is concerned with colour and scale, rather than a particular narrative. The restaurant is contained in its compact space, but there are flourishes of escape through these large-scale artworks and the sensory feelings and memory-making the food evokes. This is "affect", that which "arises in the midst of in-between-ness: in the capabilities to act and be acted upon", as explained by Professor Gregory Seigworth. Schnabel's work aims to reproduce these emotional states where people can walk into and be engulfed by the artwork, and transmit that emotion to others, and in turn share with others. And at the very least, because food similarly produces these emotive states for Gutenbrunner, it must immerse the diners in the totality of the dining moment. This playing with internal spaces, moods and emotions is also a reference to Austrian and German Expressionism and the Neo-Expressionism of the artists selected for the restaurant. Even by importing this aesthetic, Gutenbrunner updates it for a New York audience.

"We overcame the ornament," said Adolf Loos in 1908, and in this same aesthetic philosophy, the artworks in Wallsé are not merely abstractions and decor. When paired with Schnabel's artistic practice and ability to see and invoke overarching emotions of experiences, in a restaurant they are markers of sensory pleasure and can evoke raw feeling, ineffable but no less intense. Eating heightens the senses and by extension emotions, and in this respect the abstract works are essential elements in an aesthetic dining experience. And because Schnabel is so proficient in producing these total moods and effects, his curation of the artworks in the restaurant are another version of his artistic and directorial vision, with diners as viewers and participants.

Works and artists in the Wallsé collection

—

A selection of Martin Kippenberger drawings including a sketch on notepaper from the Hotel Royal in Vienna. Kippenberger wanted to make his art autobiographical and works on paper are immediate, off the cuff, suggesting they were made at the time the artist was living his precarious life.

—

A photograph of Lou Reed by Dennis Hopper. Hopper met Schnabel in 1986 when the artist held his first exhibition in New York. The actor, a self-proclaimed "gallery bum", moved to New York to hone his method-acting skills, and became involved in the city's neo-Dada and Expressionist art movements and happenings.

—

Mixed-media works by Albert Oehlen, a German contemporary artist concerned with cranking up representation of moods and emotions through colour to the point where it becomes uncomfortable, hysterical.

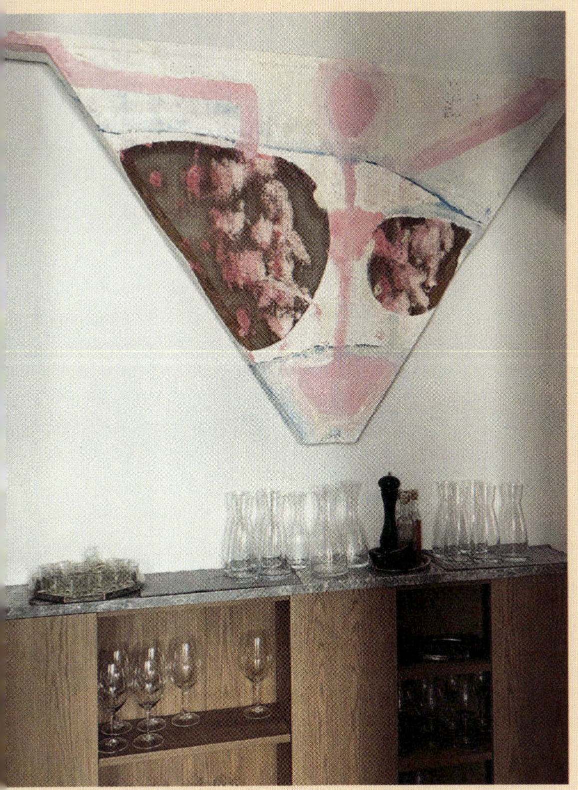

The portrait of chef Kurt Gutenbrunner painted by Julian Schnabel; Hermann Nitsch's abstract work in the recent rehang; a dining table in the restaurant; works by Julian Schnabel; Chuck Manion's painting hangs over a cabinet

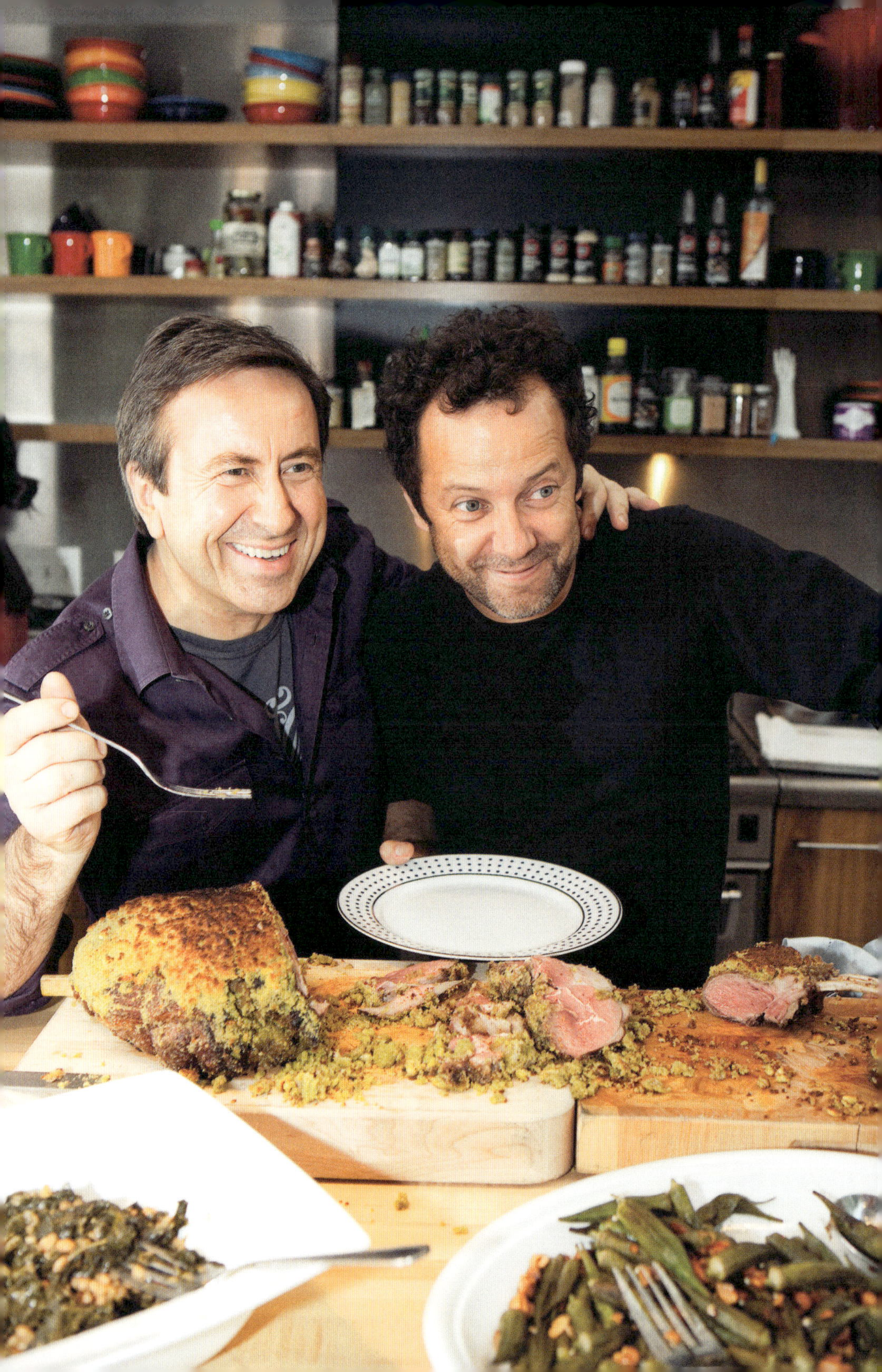

Bar Boulud and beyond

"I build a painting by putting little marks together—some look like hot dogs, some like doughnuts."
— Chuck Close

In the history of accoutrements used in dining, the tablecloth can trace its origins back to Byzantium. Double-weave damask textile techniques were developed in Damascus and then exported to Europe. This produced myriad variations and resulted in the white cloth that now universally enshrouds dining tables. In some cultures, especially in the Far East, the less pristine the tablecloth – displaying stains, spills, smears and smells with pride – the more evidence it is of a successful gathering. In the Middle Ages, the tablecloth symbolised brotherhood and suggested diners belonged to the same group. When noblemen held feasts, extending the tablecloth to guests signalled this inclusion. If the cloth held such meaning throughout history, this significance also carried through to New York City in 1998, at Daniel Boulud's eponymous restaurant, Bar Boulud. There, in a centrepiece created by the chef's friend, the renowned Brazilian artist Vik Muniz, hang 32 framed photographs of tablecloths stained by red wine. The work is emblematic of a long-term and ongoing collaboration between the artist and chef. Muniz and Boulud both think artistically and act artistically through their making. The artist says: "Chefs are artists who make things you must consume fast. Artists and chefs usually get along well because they think in very similar ways." They fashion the small ingredients, components, materials into a greater whole, into something grander for viewers and diners, then replicate the process through other works, other dining settings. They provoke the senses, isolating how patrons think and feel about food and art – the experiential model of an art restaurant.

Boulud has known Muniz for over two decades. They met at a party in the artist's Brooklyn studio, and after discussing his lifelong curiosity about how fine art can relate to fine cuisine, the chef mentioned he was considering incorporating art into a new restaurant he was building, Bar Boulud, throughout a long, narrow brick-lined space, framed by curved arches. He wanted to include something that would be a talking point, encourage thought and enhance the dining experience for his patrons. "Vik had a theory that after every great gathering, what remained on the table were wine stains, thereby marking the engaging conversation and enjoyment that was had around the table," Boulud recalls. Words are real; what is uttered at the dinner seating is not ephemeral, it builds collective memory, shared experience, a sense of being with others. And if these are exchanges of sensory pleasure, so much the better. Muniz thus

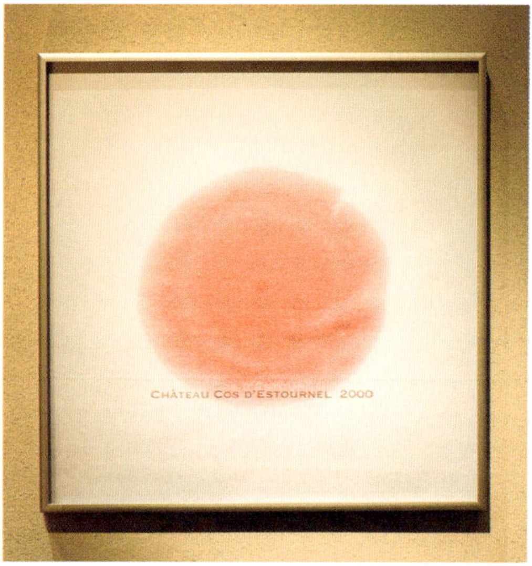

wanted something to mark this tradition of the table. He "ruminated over a subject that is heavily loaded with rules, structures and cultural significance: wine", placing "this loaded symbol in an almost hostile context" and viewing it in its "most detestable role: the stain – the one thing about wine that people find annoying". Muniz threw two parties with dozens of friends. He brought in 85 bottles of well-regarded vintages from world-class winemakers including Domain Dujac, Gevrey Chambertin and Bonnes-Mares. The chef prepared a meal, spread the tablecloth, laid the table. The usual dining conditions prevailed: animated conversation, embraces, rollicking laughter, debates and storytelling. This resulted in 25 different wine stains both intentionally and accidentally produced on the tablecloth. Each vintage resulted in a different shade of red. Muniz wanted to "propose a kind of erudition of stains, postulating that the stain of an exceptional Bordeaux can be appreciated as much as its bouquet, its taste". The chef was impressed with the result and hung the tablecloths around the restaurant, producing something that is part Rorschach test, part abstract watercolour, underpinned by a dry-cleaning headache. Although the works were made in response to a commission, for Muniz, the project also fed back into his practice, as an example of "a good-humoured commentary" using wine stains to "re-examine the minute details of decontextualization" and noting the "perceptive consequences of presenting things outside of their normal, expected setting". This way, the art restaurant in its live state of enacting the meal became an annex of the artist's studio to pair up, to experiment, to reconfigure.

The pair struck up a friendship, which has resulted in a number of collaborations over the years, in permanent spaces and pop-ups, and at dinner parties and happenings. Muniz is the chef's go-to artist when he needs something artistic, and Boulud is Muniz's go-to when he needs something culinary. Thus, since Boulud is a chef who considers his process artistic, and Muniz uses food and perishables in his practice, this model of art restaurant is situational in the sense that an art restaurant experience is created when the two work together. It can be concrete like at Bar Boulud, but it also expands to encompass the history of the pair's decades-long collaboration. The artist explains his process as being similar to a chef's because "creation, execution and exhibition are entirely simultaneous". For the diner, this produces an effect that feels real, because the intention of the artist and chef is to evoke emotions and moods during dining. Each is fascinated by the other's practice and their alliance has resulted in many memorable dinners that people want to be a part of for their notion of inclusivity and art world cachet, but also for the multisensory pleasure these gatherings evoke on an individual, experiential level.

Their collaboration is another model of an art restaurant because it excites and attracts followers who are interested in the cult of both the artist and the chef, and provokes an ethos. The social anthropologist Gregory Bateson defined this ethos as "a force of collectivity brought together when like-minded groups gather", often to celebrate or to participate in a social ritual. These rituals have a binding hold over participants, they produce a fervour and ossify through time. Muniz reveres dining as ritualistic because of his Catholic upbringing and his studying the Old Masters. Of the Christian sacraments, the Eucharist is the most significant: "I read it. I look at it. Why do you have to take it in? Why do you take in a symbol that's already so strong?" he wonders. We are "fetishistic" about what we ingest, "so the idea that you eat to get the spirit of something, you have to consume it orally, I find this… fascinating". The Last Supper is a recurring theme in Muniz's work. When people gather to eat together, this ethos, or *le partage du sensible* – the distribution of the sensible – orchestrates "perception, sensorial culture, affective intensities", according to Bateson. Despite dining at its immediate level being bodily and animalistic, satiating individualistic hunger, in a setting with others this becomes curtailed and people become tremendously obedient and orderly in terms of their behaviour and participation in ritual, and in turn are rewarded by sensorial stimulation. Muniz is not fazed by throwing dinners with Boulud – from intimate post-gallery gatherings to their own quasi-religious apotheosis of their partnership in St. John the Divine in Manhattan, to seat 650 diners in the cathedral, in 2016.

Boulud and art collecting

Boulud hails from the same lineage of boundary-breaking chefs as Pierre Gagnaire, Grant Achatz and Ferran Adrià – all of whom believe artists and chefs "have always had a symbiotic relationship". He cut his teeth in Roger Vergé's Michelin-starred classic restaurant, Moulin de Mougins, which was constantly surrounded by great artists from L'école de Nice. Vergé collected their works, including those of the Nouveau Réalisme sculptor César Baldaccini, Arman, the French-American artist who painted traces and residues of objects, and Théo Tobiasse, the Expressionist figurative painter. The dexterity with which his mentor moved between media left an impression on young Boulud: "While I could not afford their work at the time, I appreciated being exposed to their craft as they often drew inspiration from the culinary world, sharing in that same passion for creation." This set the connection for him between art and cooking through sharing taste.

The restaurant in Mougins, purveyor of *cuisine de soleil,* attracted many from the art world, including Leo Castelli, the famous dealer who was at the forefront of Surrealist, abstract and Pop art. He would lunch daily with a different artist in tow. Boulud remembers "a party that was held in his honour where the greatest concentration of living contemporary American artists came to celebrate the most renowned gallery owner in the world. The cluster of artists – from Willem de Kooning to Jasper Johns, Frank Stella, James Rosenquist, Jeff Koons and many more – left me with a desire to showcase their craft and collect art." They came to his restaurant and befriended the chef. He in turn became close to a few of them, visiting their studios, listening to their plans. Boulud remembers the first time he went to visit Rosenquist's studio, "armed with a few burgers" – his DB burger is the Platonic archetype of burgers – and it became a regular occurrence: "We would sit, talk and eat burgers together and he would show me his art."

Vik Muniz and cooking

If Boulud began to collect art to enrich his cooking practices, Muniz collected food to construct his art. The artist made his name with a series of works using foodstuffs to reproduce homages to Old Master paintings and then photographing them. This practice encompasses both the ephemerality of the materials and the perpetuity of archiving them. There's a peanut butter Mona Lisa and a chocolate sauce Last Supper triptych. "If you're taking a picture of chocolate," Muniz says, "or if you take a picture of honey, immediately you will sense the material – and once you sense the material, you will sense its activities, its properties, its taste, and you will know it's haptic." He minimises the primacy of the eye and vision as the way into experiencing an artwork and in its place elevates touch and taste. "Probably what I've been doing for the past 25 years is searching for the largest number of ways to say exactly the same thing, which is *look at this*. When you look at things harder and carefully, immediately they become magical, they inspire that kind of thinking that evokes sound, taste and scent." He is arguing for a more embodied visuality of art and using foodstuffs as material triggers this response. It complements aesthetic dining because this is total sensorial engagement: "For some weird reason, I find that whenever I'm eating something, I'm so close to my senses and also I'm doing something essential for my being." This shows "there can be a science of the particular as a stairway to the universal", in the words of the philosopher Michel Onfray. "Food is an argument that can penetrate the real... a stratagem for the construction of the self as a coherent work of art." Our memories are visceral, processed and felt in the body, and if cooking is artistic, it contributes to the creation of a sense of self. Muniz recalls watching his Brazilian grandmother cook with traditional methods using firewood. He would help her in the kitchen, and he became aware of process through the culinary action: "It's always about process – I may have worked with all kinds of materials, but the fact is that materials put you into different processes." Each material demands its own treatment. "If you do something with chocolate, or if you do something with diamonds, or if you do something with garbage, you make it work differently every time. So I am not interested in the end result as much as I am interested in how you get there." Muniz teases it out by working with different and varied materials, ranging from chocolate and honey to diamonds and dust, to adjust and measure and monitor their transformation.

There is also a suggestion that when the artist and chef have this tacit understanding and deftness in creating a dining mood through their gatherings, they investigate and arrange for diners to find their way through it. Representation may be illusion, yet executed in a considered way, it will isolate how perception is active and requires application when one looks at the work. In Muniz's practice, seemingly mundane materials become art because they are planned and assembled to produce an effect, and then to engage taste. "Relationships between senses are very important for any artist," he says. "When artists connect with chefs, I think these things are underlying the conversations." Just like cooking assembles materials to produce a dish. Both rework and transform the ingredients into something more, something extraordinary, something different that uses perception to be processed and appreciated.

Muniz has hosted many talked-about, spectacular dinners throughout his career. He has also been involved in the restaurant industry in the past decade.

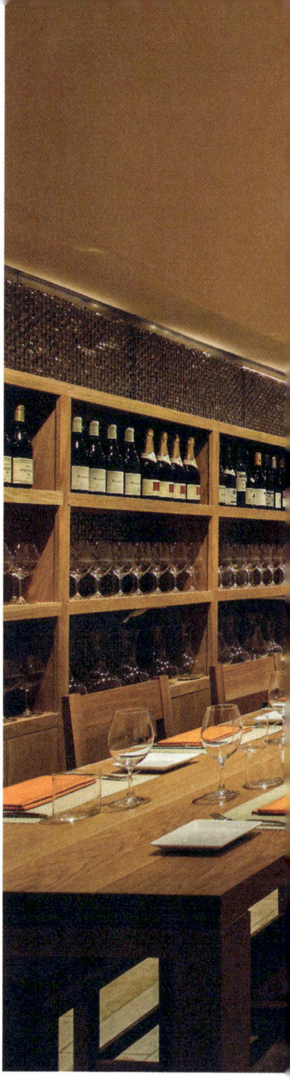

In 2016 he established Casa Camolese in Rio, a modern architectural restaurant featuring photographs of his chocolate Old Masters series. Osteria Francescana's Massimo Bottura asked him to contribute works to the chef's Refettorio Felix in the megalopolis, serving meals to poor and disadvantaged members of the community. He sent a Last Supper in chocolate sauce, linking this restaurant to medieval alms house histories decorated with frescoed murals. He goes holy, he goes haute-luxe. Most recently he collaborated with champagne house Ruinart to produce a series of works that link to the *terroir* and the meal Daniel Boulud and Michel Troisgros concocted. The artist went to Reims, walked the vineyards and created works that were the result of his residency. All of these dinners are cultural markers, but they also form part of Muniz's enquiry into process and materials. Ultimately, for him a restaurant is akin to a museum – if visitors go to the latter to ritualise a visual experience, in a restaurant "the whole experience has been ritualised; the fact it comes in courses means you understand a little bit of the ceremony".

When artists collaborate with chefs

Muniz and Boulud harmoniously work together on projects because the act of cooking involves artistic qualities that provoke certain emotions and sustain moods. Both are fascinated by each other's disciplines and maintain a mutual respect and exploration. The artist and chef also have something in common in terms of materiality and making, assembling ingredients to create a greater whole. Muniz says: "Gastronomy is truly the only art that encompasses all the senses at once." Food – acquiring, assembling and eating – moves beyond just being a biological necessity for sustenance, and this way it can take on an artistic quality. Cooking is not even conceptual art, because it is tied to materiality and the body. It needs the senses to function, and it synthesises all five of them. Muniz says chefs help him to understand "the value of an experience that transcends the boundaries of my professional practice". He explores through the analogy of another discipline: "A great chef, and a great artist, is a curious seeker of new experiences, a person deeply involved with the world he lives in and the people he shares this world with." Both try to capture this and replicate it in dining experiences.

Boulud commissions other artists for works in his restaurants – for example, in his New York formal restaurant, DANIEL, he wanted something modern

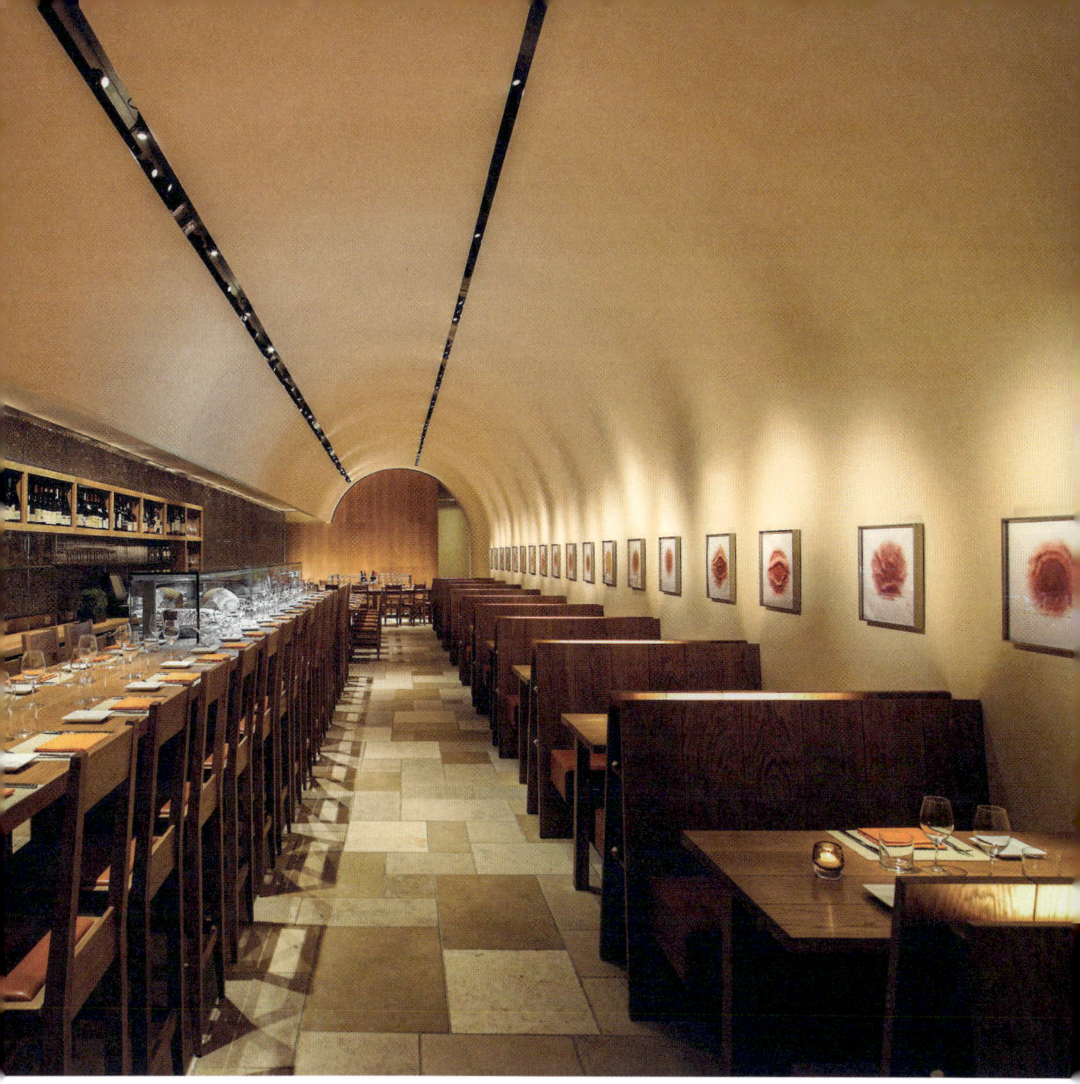

and classic, and "inspired by *Las Meninas* from Diego Velázquez, Manolo Valdés studied the dining room and created beautiful collages of his work that have an aesthetic that is both contemporary and timeless". But he and Muniz continue to explore how food highlights the senses, transforms, brings together. There is a meeting of minds when they host events. "We've had occasions to create moments together," Boulud says. They share an understanding of process and synthesis, but through the effect it elicits in the diner/viewer. Although Boulud recognises he has created iconic dishes which were "inspiration from Old Masters", he does not consider himself an artist, but is willing to learn from the process of art. The dishes "were like art to me – it's a reflection of art on the endeavour". It's not art as food on the plate. The expression is about the production, the historical reference and the look. "Although I can be artistic in my own way, as chefs, what we create on a plate is ephemeral, while an artist's work is made to sustain time," he says. The paradox of the ephemeral – the food – rendered to portray the eternal – the Old Masters – is why Muniz's work and Boulud's cooking have an affinity. For his part, Muniz says: "The only way you can feel all the senses at the same time is in a meal." They are not so much talking at cross purposes as just showing and making rather than explaining. "You can spend a career as an artist focusing on one specific sense, but you can never develop any real knowledge if you don't nourish your experience to encompass the entire spectrum of sensations." It is not an accident that the artist uses a food-related description – eating is restorative and involves the full set of senses. In some ways the sensory hierarchy can be inverted to make taste the synthesising force: "Taste is a complex sense that connects to all other senses simultaneously. It's very subjective, very personal and very instinctive."

Ethos and how it plays into taste is abstract in one way – but there are concrete elements and doing, perceiving and affective intensities, affordances and uses of feelings. "Culture," Muniz believes, "is at its most fundamental built upon and determined by taste." Belonging together and choosing the same taste binds communities, from small in-crowds to nations. This ethos contains "a definite tone of appropriate behaviour as a definite set of sentiments towards the rest of the world". Like a dinner, a happening, those in that gathering form a kinship – even if temporary for that sitting – but feel and believe that they are a part of a greater whole. This "emotional background" may be the reason artists' dinners are so desirable, and invitations are so sought-after year after year. This art restaurant, the situational art restaurant, immerses its diners in an experience so extraordinary they want to come back for more.

Boulud and Muniz: meals and artworks

—

Because the Boulud Sud is a purveyor of Mediterranean *cuisine de soleil*, Muniz references Van Gogh, Matisse and Cézanne's work from Provence, but because nothing is as it seems for the artist, the composition is made of fragments of images from his *Pictures of Magazines* series.

—

Boulud and Muniz hosted a dinner together at the opening of a Francis Bacon exhibition in Sarasota, prior to which the artist discovered the Ringling Circus Museum, which he went to before the dinner for inspiration. "Vik was more excited about that museum" than the official opening, Boulud says.

—

Boulud hosted a dinner in St. Stephen's Cathedral on the Upper East Side for 800 Brazilian diners to honour his artist friend, where he made traditional Brazilian fish *moqueca* – and had Muniz secretly whisper to him that it was even better than what is served at home.

—

The artist surprised the chef by making a life-sized mosaic of him at the 72nd Street subway station on New York's Upper East Side. Boulud is depicted holding a shopping bag from the market, and the work suggests he is part of the furniture of the city.

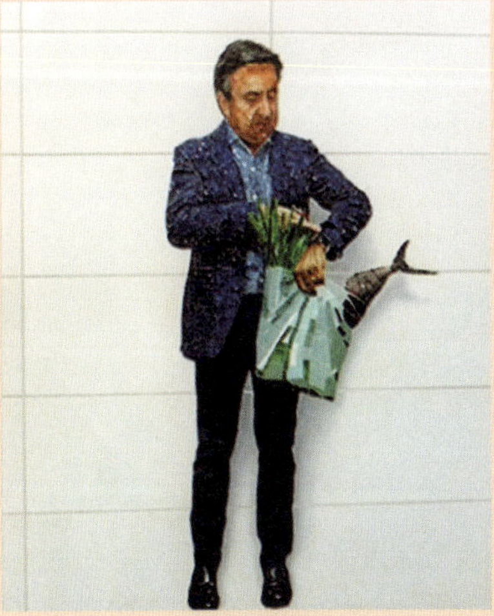

Daniel Boulud and Vik Muniz at one of their countless collaboration dinners; a wine stain that inspired the decades-long collaboration; the tablecloth canvases along the wall of Bar Boulud; Muniz's subway art

Interviews

These interviews were conducted by Christina Makris and Tim Marlow between July 2018 and March 2020 in London, New York, Berlin, Sydney, Rio de Janeiro, and Provence. It was an immense pleasure to aesthetically dine and drink with the artists, eat under their artworks, explore matters of taste, find parallels between art and cooking and, of course, recall memorable restaurant experiences – the interviews themselves being an enduring example of that.

Ai Weiwei

— with Tim Marlow

What prompted you to take on the vineyard commission at Château la Coste? The materials used, such as stones from Marseille, and references to your father's history are particularly interesting.

Château la Coste was founded by my friend Paddy [McKillen], who asked me to do an installation there. I initially hesitated, though he continued to insist, and I felt sorry that I was unable to give him an immediate answer. The reason for my hesitation was because I can't start a work without first convincing myself. It is not just that a work has to relate to my aesthetic judgement or my understanding of craftsmanship, it must also offer opportunities to learn and become involved.

I finally saw the site, where there were already many existing artworks, some very well known. They stand out as sculptures with their own integrity, which is what I chose to avoid with my work. Paddy was very sincere, and I could sense he would execute my humble idea precisely. I decided to create a road to connect the original Roman path to a new one – so that my work reflects the history of the land.

What is the connection between gustatory taste and aesthetic taste?

Aesthetic taste is related to all our sensitivities, such as our taste for food and sex, or taste for peace or war. There is no aesthetic taste without ordinary feelings.

Is it important to display artworks in a restaurant, as Massimo Bottura has done with your *Dropping a Han Dynasty Urn* in one of his?

It is very important to hang artworks, or the carcass of a cow, as long as it is not poisonous.

Is there a connection between art and food in terms of process and tradition, recipes or rituals?

Rituals and recipes in relation to art are no different from anything else humans have made for presentation, though they are often restricted by time, place and the human condition. I have been to all kinds of dinners and banquets, but nothing was as memorable as eating in a refugee camp. They would chop some garlic and tomatoes and cook them with olive oil in a frying pan – often just a piece of aluminium foil completely blackened from use – then use their hands and bread to eat because there were no forks or napkins. It was the most delicious food I have ever had, and the most gracious invitation I ever received, because they had nothing but were generous enough to share their food. Sharing is the most important thing about possession.

Are the relationships between food and wine universal or culturally specific?

Nothing is universal. The word "universal" only comes into use after the Industrial Revolution, this kind of Bauhaus-style brutal interpretation of our human condition. Very often, the further you go, the poorer the area, the better the food becomes. It has fewer ingredients but is more real and vibrant, served in rustic restaurants without courtesy.

Antony Gormley

— with Tim Marlow

I try to acknowledge the space of the human body as a zone of transformation. For my sculpture *Bed* (1980–1981), made from 600 loaves of Mother's Pride bread, I ate my own body's volume of bread to carve out the two spaces where a figure might have lain. The works *Natural Selection*, *One Apple* and *Fruits of the Earth* contain fruits, vegetables and wine, sealed in lead.

I have always thought of the body less as a subject defined by appearance than as a place that life flows through. A place where the winding course of the internal digestive tract is a river. Food is the way in which the landscape that surrounds us is internalised – it flows through us to become landscape again. The relationship between our internal biome and the wider biosphere is something we are only just beginning to realise and celebrate.

Eating is a form of sculpture. If Michelangelo, in his Neoplatonic mode, was trying to impress mind onto matter, surely eating – the reverse process of turning matter into mind – is a sculptural action. Art and food are the bookends of life. They are sustenance: we need food to maintain the body. Once the body is maintained, what celebrates the joy of being alive?

Bringing art and food together in the same place is a good idea. Of course, El Bulli, Noma and countless other restaurants have raised the calorie to the level of the symphony. The broadening of everyone's culinary palates and the explosion of fusion cooking have made eating itself into an aesthetic adventure. Creative minds need creative fuelling. It's not surprising that the lively architectural practice of Richard Rogers gave birth to Ruth Rogers's and Rose Gray's River Café in London, or that Olafur Eliasson has given priority to integrating food production with his environmental and aesthetic concerns.

The collective bonding and shared enjoyment of eating together has to be at the foundation of any collective endeavour. In our modest way at my studio the daily lunch is a time when individual friendships and collective celebrations happen. The delight we take in the greenest of leaves, the bright colours of flowers, the smells and textures of pulses, vegetables, fruits and berries, are a fundamental part of our enjoyment when eating them. How the colours and forms of the food on our plates are arranged evokes the same pleasure we get from a painted still life. The rituals of the preparation, presentation and social sharing of food are fundamental to any society. The workplace and restaurant are places where the closeness of domestic sharing becomes public.

In my childhood household all our meals were preceded by grace. That element of thanksgiving and recognition of privilege in some sense has now been subsumed into the rituals of presentation itself. The appreciation of the time and care that has gone into the growing, gathering and preparation of the food is acknowledged in that short moment of silence.

As we become more and more aware of the fragility of the biosphere, the ritual aspect of shared food becomes more precious. If, as it has to, provisioning becomes more and more local, so the growers and locations of that food become more known, and the act of eating becomes embedded into relations with people, season and place.

It's not surprising that Iwan and Manuela Wirth have put so much effort into the restaurant at their Somerset gallery, that Delfina Entrecanales has always put shared dining front-and-centre at her foundation, or that

Mario Cristiani of Galleria Continua travels the world with cheese, sausages and truffles gathered from the oak forests of Tuscany. Rarely does he arrive without a second suitcase entirely filled with these emissaries of locally grown food. Mario understands the relationship between the stomach and the imagination.

It's an old story but one that still needs to be told: the tastebuds of Britain were opened by the pain of the partition of India and Pakistan. Since the 1950s our palates have been exposed to Indian and then South Asian cooking, followed by that of Africa via the West Indies. This has broadened our appreciation and stimulated a taste for travel. It's now hard to think of London without its Korean, Japanese, Thai, Indian, Ethiopian, Caribbean, Mexican, Brazilian, Spanish, Italian and French restaurants. But now all those tastes have migrated to the spice drawer in all our kitchens.

The ambience of wherever you choose to eat makes a huge difference to your enjoyment and even the taste of the food. Extremely polarised examples of context might be the delight of eating outside a Tuscan villa under spreading vines, with open views onto vineyards, olive groves, hilltop towns and cypress trees, versus the experience I had at a famous fish restaurant in central Madrid, where the salted turbot was paraded around the room like a heraldic shield. The room was entirely surrounded in dark red drapes. This was pretty well my parents' idea about dining-room decor: floor-to-ceiling red damask curtains and wood panelling, with a serving hatch through which the meals were delivered. The Tuscan hillside ambience could be the model: where art gives you a sense of not just what you are eating but also where you are.

What are the grandest experiences of art in restaurants? I suppose the most famous would be Rothko's paintings for The Four Seasons restaurant in New York, which he intended to make people cry into their soup but were never installed. It would have been the equivalent of my family drapes – dining as if in a funeral parlour. Ivor Braka's pot-pourri of British art at the Gunton Arms in Norfolk goes so well with the smoky atmosphere of the pub: Tracey Emin and Lucian Freud mixed in with the venison and black pudding. As far as I know, the artistic equivalent of the Tuscan countryside – bright, light and energetic – is still to be achieved!

Beatriz Milhazes

— with Christina Makris and Tim Marlow

Christina Makris: what is different when your works are hanging in a restaurant rather than in a gallery?

A restaurant is a public space and people are there to enjoy a meal, relax or celebrate some special date; they don't go expecting to look at art. The art in a restaurant then invades people's lives. This fact gives an interesting approach to it. The public could see the works as in a gallery space but could also just live with them as part of an interior, and this would make them enjoy the space more. I'm often positive about such combinations of art and life.

CM: how did your work come to the Gunton Arms?

Ivor Braka made a good selection in my three works there: two screenprints, which have an ornamented, baroque, intense circular composition, and one collage with a variety of cut-out materials creating a geometric, optical surface. There is a strange but good communication between my work and the architecture of the restaurant.

Tim Marlow: have you been involved in any other restaurant projects?

In 2005 I worked on a major project called *Guanabara* for the restaurant on the seventh level of Tate Modern. I developed a very large mural for the two walls that face two gigantic glass façades with beautiful views of London. It was a special opportunity to invite the museum's visitors to have a different experience of living with art.

TM: what is the connection between art and food in terms of the senses we use to experience and process them?

Art is about an intelligence of the senses. Food is what keeps us alive but at the same time has this profound sense of culture, taste, feeling and beauty. Art and food can share similar worlds but differently. The ultimate difference is that if you eat something poisonous, you are going to die, while in art you can experience the poison and never die – in fact you live.

© Beatriz Milhazes. Photo: Vicente de Paulo. Courtesy of White Cube

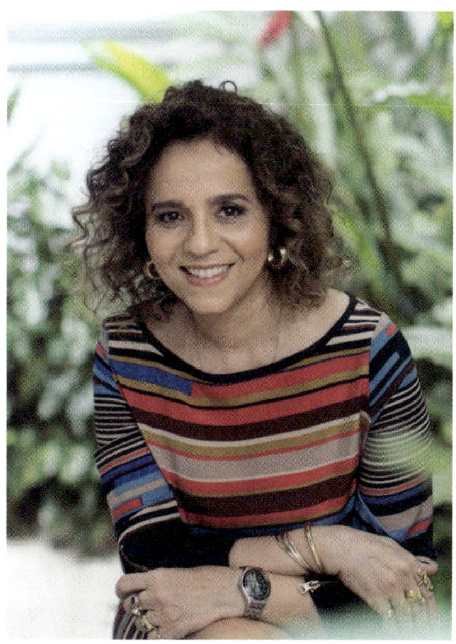

Bill Jacklin

— with Christina Makris

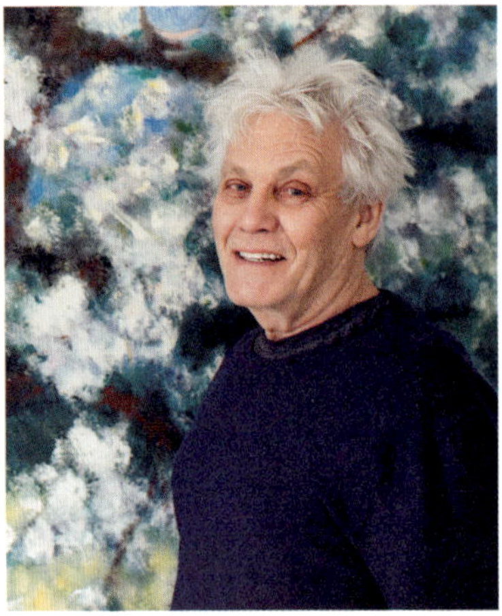

Bill Jacklin

How did The Ivy commission come to you?

Peter Blake, who taught me at the Royal College of Art and was a great mentor to me, used to go to The Ivy and eat down his bill. He would always invite artists with him, and we would go together and be seen together. Then Chris Corbin asked me if I would make a piece for the restaurant in 1992. Everybody who is aware of my work, either from New York or London, knows I like to paint people in places, *in situ*, especially collections of people all doing the same thing. I like collectives of motley groups. So for this commission, it of course had to be a live scene in The Ivy on a typical night with people gathered together to dine. I am glad to see the work is still in the restaurant. Tastes and fashions change and The Ivy changed hands, so it's good to see it is still there.

It is an artwork of the artwork that is the restaurant. The same thing happened in the Paris Bar in Berlin – for which Martin Kippenberger painted a scene set in the restaurant. The proprietor then had to sell the work to settle a tax bill, but asked a younger artist to paint a copy of the Kippenberger for the restaurant.

That's a great story. In my Ivy picture you can see the Allen Jones work in the top right-hand corner, which I think is still there. You can see some of my friends: my dealer Pierre Levai on the left, the photographer Abe Frajndlich straight ahead and my wife. Jeremy King is somewhere in the piece, as is Jesus [Adorno] waiting tables.

Did you make the work from memory or on site?

I ask my friends to pose for me and I place them in compositions. I would go to The Ivy and sit for days and days sketching people I saw around me, some of them reflected in the mirrors.

Mirrors are very important to the theatre of dining spaces. Maxim's was responsible for the first modern innovation in the restaurant, by placing mirrors in which customers could people-watch. In this case, you imply the restaurant was the laboratory for your work.

The Ivy is good like that because people always go there pretending that they don't want to be noticed or that they are dining there to be anonymous, when they know they are being observed by everybody around them.

So they go there to be publicly anonymous or to show they pretend they are not being noticed...

That's part of the allure of The Ivy – it always was for me and it's what I like to paint. You go there for the presence of people who behave like characters in a play. Al Hirschfeld, the caricaturist who drew scenes from city life for *The New Yorker*, was an inspiration to me for that painting. I met him in the early 2000s right before he died, when he was in his 90s. He said he wanted to caricature a mirror image of what he saw in New York society. I am doing the same thing with my work and the Ivy piece – it's a reflection of itself, a reflection of a reflection.

Was there something different about The Ivy that led to it becoming an artists' restaurant?

Allen Jones, Peter Blake, that generation, and my generation of RCA artists would all go there, mainly, of course, because we had credit. When times were good you would visit and host a bigger table or group and treat your friends, who were usually other artists. It was a way to share in the success. (Peter still has credit there; he often reminds me.) That's what happens with these artists' restaurants – they become associated with specific groups of people. There's the Odeon in New York, or Orsino's, which used to be a pub in Notting Hill that David Hockney visited all the time, as well as teddy boys and not very salubrious types. There was also Lucian Freud in The Wolseley: everybody would know which table was his and he'd go to the same one, which always struck me as strange because he was so keen on not being noticed or bothered or observed. So why go back to the same restaurant time and time again?

It's a conscious tactic of many restaurant proprietors, from Colombe d'Or in Saint-Paul-de-Vence to Lucio's in Sydney, to invite artists and encourage them to bring their colleagues and friends. Have you ever eaten under your own work?

I try not to! But, of course, I will visit with friends and sit by it and look at it out of the corner of my eye during the meal and conversations. Always there, in the corner of my eye.

When you go back and see the work, do you ever notice things that you could have done differently?

Yes – the more you look at your work as an artist, sometimes the more these things come to you.

Do you believe there is a connection between art and dining in terms of taste; aesthetic taste and gustatory taste? Why is it that restaurateurs find it important to add good art to their spaces? What does it symbolise, or what does it do for the diner?

The connection is important because such an array of people will look at your artwork, not just those who'd go to a museum. In a museum, they are prepared to encounter art. Looking at art in different spaces, especially something as everyday as the restaurant, is important. And, as I say, I like to paint scenes and groups of people from daily life, so a work in a restaurant reflects this belief of mine, and I think that's what that piece is about.

Conrad Shawcross

— with Tim Marlow

How did you approach the context of the place for the commission you completed recently at Château la Coste?

I went there on a number of occasions to meet Paddy [McKillen] and tour the site. Paddy is a man of few words in some ways, who keeps his cards close to his chest, but he has a specific eye, and, over time, I realised what his direction was. One thing he was interested in was the idea of immersion, the experience of entering into something, or the finding of a strange object in a remote or unexpected place. He was very keen on keeping my work high up the mountain so that people might stumble upon it among the trees and hills. He wanted to create discoveries in the landscape.

Clearly place and landscape, that idea of *terroir* – taste linked to the land and the vineyard – are incorporated into Louison, the restaurant at Château la Coste. Does that concept resonate with you and how you approached your work there?

I love constraints on a project and working within them. As a believer of the freedom found in constraints, knowing a context is really helpful in making the work. I believe there is a neutral subservient space for art to exist in, but the landscape of la Coste pushed me to make four- to five-metre works. I took it to another level and even featured engineering techniques to respond to that challenge of the space. I had to consult existing studies to escalate the piece to this level, to ensure it would be structurally sound, but also to show the expanding history of the tetrahedron theme.

How are sculpture and architecture in dialogue with each other in this landscape?

It's such an incredible endeavour. The courage of it is extraordinary. There's a Richard Rogers cantilever structure above mine over the valley, there's the Oscar Niemeyer pavilion. Norman Foster was here talking about building his viewing pavilion, and then there are ancient ruins of a Gaul settlement at the top of the estate. The fact that Paddy and his sister Mara are in charge means it is still a family-run operation, so it feels very genuine. My family is also in hospitality, so I see this sincerity, and I think that's rare.

One of the things that struck me about la Coste is how non-hierarchical it is – it's a collective, or an assemblage, of sculpture, architecture, food, wine and art. Your taste is synthesised in different ways, but you don't feel art is an appendage to a restaurant tacked on to a gallery. It feels very integrated and it's a sensory experience. It resonates with my experience of your work.

The collection is extraordinary and that comes through having a real relationship with artists. Paddy is really good friends with Tracey Emin, for instance; he is very personable and just knows everyone by name, and everyone works so hard for him. One of the best things about him is he is so down to earth. He will eat with his staff: construction workers, diggers, fabricators. I would come in covered in mud and dirt, grimy as hell, and we'd sit down and have a steak and red wine and I wouldn't feel embarrassed. There was a lovely lack of rules and hierarchies.

There is a dress code in Claridge's!

I was enjoying living like a coal miner. It was very hands-on to work on the installation. Because of the pandemic travel bans, I couldn't get all my studio team out, so I had to train local guys, and as the kitchen at la Coste was closed, it made sense to train the kitchen staff. Some of them quit after a few days... They said they valued their hands too much. I enjoyed going on site and lifting these 250-kilo planks one by one in the June heat with my Argentinian kitchen workers, Diego and Marco. I found I became more directorial in my approach.

It's like being a master chef in the kitchen.

It isn't as satisfying as doing the groundwork and preparation yourself. Out there I didn't have a choice but to do the work, and we just mucked in. It reminded me of being a child and trying to move the wardrobe from one side of my room to the other just to see what it looked like. I was an only child, so started using levers and pulleys and managed to move it across the floor on my own; my mum came in and wondered how I'd done it. That sense of resourcefulness, of trying to work out how to do things on your own, was very exhilarating.

Would it interest you to take on the design of a space where people eat, where people become embedded into the concept of the space? Restaurants use art in intriguing ways.

In the Louison restaurant at la Coste, the [Louise] Bourgeois lovemaking couple trespass into the functional objects and they help to make the experience immersive. I love the idea of dealing with everything in totality from an architectural point of view. I'm working on a pop-up opera festival project where we are going to do just that and I'm conceiving everything for it.

On the subject of artists and food, I am very suspicious of artists who can't cook. If you are unsure about an artist, you should ask them to cook for you. It's different for people who don't cook, but people who can't cook, that's really suspicious.

Let's explore that a little bit further. Because in whatever practice, it should be about knowing how to put things together.

Yes – it's the same as with a painting, or at least a well-proportioned sculpture, in terms of using a material palette. Presentation is a different thing and not the most important thing about cooking; it's best not to get involved in that. Timing, juxtaposition, the proportions of ingredients and imagination in how you put things together are important. And I've always cooked for my staff. We always take turns.

Do you have a signature dish? Your art is expansive but there are elements we can recognise.

Venison stew.

I am curious about the notion of taste for you. Do you think about taste or cultural taste in your work?

Taste feels a little bit linked to fashion. The fear I have with work is that you end up somewhere where it dates badly. I hope with my work I am dealing with found geographies that have a lasting stability.

Damien Hirst

— with Tim Marlow

Do you remember the first time that art in a restaurant had an impact on you?

Yeah. I got sacked for stealing movie posters from a posh one in Leeds, called Flying Pizza, where I used to wash up. I was always into restaurants, and this was a place with Ferraris parked outside and where movie stars would go. The allure of all that always appealed to me – the status aspect of it, and the great food.

Is that what you think art does in restaurants, reinforces status?

When I had no money, I would always take… sorry, I'm eating a KitKat… I'd take girls to posh restaurants and have to add up what they were ordering so I had enough to pay for it. So it was risky. They would've been happy to go to KFC, but I wouldn't.

Why?

I don't know. Restaurants are like art without the evidence. If somebody says, "Do you remember that meal we had 15 years ago in that little place," and you go, "Oh yeah, wasn't that amazing?" The memory is incredibly powerful, but there's nothing left. That always seemed to be this great thing that occurred with food, and it was really like art. I wanted experiences like that, I suppose, when I was taking girls out for dinner.

So, art is experiential in a restaurant, and in addition to taste? There is aesthetic and physical taste of course.

There's a piece from the early 1990s in my show *End of a Century* at the moment, a butcher's shop window in formaldehyde called *Shut Up and Eat Your Fucking Dinner*. "Shut up and eat your dinner" was what my mum would say if I'd say "this chicken used to be running around in a field" when we were eating. I remember thinking you can aestheticise things, but the bottom line is, shut up and eat your dinner. If you don't eat, you die, so there's that fundamental thing, and then it gets completely aestheticised into this grand experience. I remember going to Marco Pierre White's restaurant in the 1990s and it was the first time I ever thought about the texture of mashed potatoes – it was perfect. It was an unbelievable experience.

The funny thing is, when I opened Pharmacy, my first restaurant, I believed that it would be around forever and my art might not be – that there was a good chance my art was going to end up in a dusty basement or disappear in a museum and get lost. Even if you suck off the head of Tate gallery, he might get replenished by someone else. I eventually realised that you've got much more chance in a museum; all my forays into restaurants have failed.

You talk about immortality, but did you want to make an environment with Pharmacy that was comparable with the conditions in which you show your own art?

I guess. I genuinely believe that anything done incredibly well is art if it takes things out of the ordinary and into this other realm. You can have a bacon sandwich that you remember years later.

What were the circumstances that led you to open Pharmacy?

I knew about art in restaurants, and good restaurants – the Colombe d'Or and the Rothkos in The Four Seasons. A restaurant that really interested me early on was Gordon Matta-Clark's FOOD in New York, where artists would cook. Donald Judd did one week, and the food was shit. Then when I was in New York in the 1990s, Rirkrit Tiravanija was doing exhibitions where you could go in and cook noodles for everyone, and I hung out a little bit with Felix Gonzalez-Torres who did the sweets that you could eat: John Lennon eating Yoko's apple. All that stuff appealed to me. I'm really into installation and the idea of creating an environment, and I wanted to make art that was alive. There's also a lot of feeding in my installations: flies feed off a head and you've got to feed them sugar water and feed the maggots every day, replenishing the lifecycle. When I was doing the butterfly pieces and things with live animals, restaurants seemed like a really good place to fill with those. And I thought, if you design the pots and pans and salt pots and knives and forks and the menus, then you have living things in it – it seemed like the perfect installation. Maybe that's why I thought it would last forever, because when people were coming and paying and shaking my hand, or there on a date... that always appealed to me. It's connected to love in that way and to money; all the ingredients I was interested in in terms of art, including art on the walls, but it couldn't just be that. A restaurant was a living thing, the furthest away from the gallery you could get, which was merely a room for dead artists if you weren't careful.

What about the process of cooking and its parallels with art?

I've always cooked. After my dad left when I was 12, we didn't have money for anything and my mum worked from very early to late, so I'd cook for my brother and sister, and I remember there'd be like one tomato. I'd just say, how can I make a meal out of these ingredients? A lot of my art came out of that experience, I think. I don't like wasting art.

There seems to be some kind of symbiosis between artists and restaurants.

I think the chefs want to be seen to be painters, but the proof of their great meals is always getting eaten. They've got no catalogue raisonné. Marco Pierre White's big frustration, also I suppose Jamie Oliver's, was they had the artist's ego to say, "It's me, me, me, I'm cooking the food", but they can't cook in 10 restaurants at once. Whereas artists want that kind of transience, I think, because it can be pretty alarming when somebody goes "I've got this painting you made 10 years ago" that you wish had disappeared. We all deteriorate. It'd be nice if art did the same thing.

So artists and chefs sort of meet in the middle. In order for the chef to feel like an artist, they have to hang around with one, and the artist wants to feel like there's an impermanence to what they're doing and that they don't give a fuck. A collector once said to Sarah Lucas: "This artwork you sold me is decaying." She said: "Well, you can give me the work back, but you're not getting your money back." I think that's a little bit like what happens in a restaurant.

That idea of authenticity is interesting. Some people presume that every part of an artwork is made by the named artist, which has never been the case with a lot of art.

When Marco's in the kitchen, the food tastes better. The thing that always gets me is architects don't build their own houses. So, if you can, farm it out and make it, you know?

You don't paint every one of your own spot paintings, do you?

I made the first 10, but I always think the idea is more important than the actual thing. Everybody said, "I want one painted by you", and they're not interested in the quality.

Pharmacy 1 exists from 1997 to 2003. It closes down, and you get the artworks back. Then you work again with Marco to set up Pharmacy 2 at Newport Street. It's kind of an evolved version.

Pharmacy seemed like a really big success because we sold the contents for £20 million or whatever it was, but it always felt like a failure because I was striving for a restaurant that goes on and on like a living entity. With the museum, it made sense to have another stab at Pharmacy. I failed again because... it's very hard to make money in restaurants. Unless you're weighing the tuna and shit like that. And, also, if the chefs are any good, they go: "I don't care that lobster's not in season. Get it from Iceland." In the end I was losing £900,000 a year.

Why do you think the Colombe d'Or has survived so long?

There's not a lot of competition in the area. It's a classic and had a lot of that celebrity. It's in Provence with those great ingredients – great lamb, herbs, spices.

And what about the art? The fact that Picasso was there. It's like being in history.

Yeah. I suppose art's fragile, and in a restaurant, it doesn't feel like that – it feels open and like it's out there to be experienced.

Philip Johnson told me Rothko pulled his paintings from The Four Seasons because he couldn't bear them just being a backdrop for the chatter of the idle rich. Whereas your view is that the art feels more alive. You don't see a restaurant as being hierarchically inferior to a gallery.

No, it's better. I don't want to appeal to people who art appeals to. I want the art to be able to get your attention while you're busy, art that you can't walk past, so a busy restaurant is a good place to have a challenging piece of art in.

You've done three restaurants, including The Quay in Devon, which all lost money. Does that preclude you doing it again?

No. With the first Pharmacy I said to my partner Matthew Freud, "I'm not doing this for the money." He said, "Neither am I." I was like, "We're fucked." The only way I'd do one again is if I was doing it with somebody who was.

What's the most successful installation of a particular work of yours in a restaurant?

The guy at Da Ivo in Venice has a drawing on the wall I did on a napkin of a skull, and I quite like that.

David Bailey

— with Tim Marlow

You went to Langan's; were you part of that scene?

I went there a lot – but I'm not sure I was part of the scene. I mean, I wasn't lying on the floor with Peter Langan or anything like that...

And what defined it?
The artists that went there?

Well, it was like La Coupole meets an East End pub. People behaved so badly.

And there was art on the walls.

I had some pieces on the walls as well. I really liked going there.

Odin's was the precursor to Langan's, and also an artists' restaurant. How was it different?

Odin's was much more reserved and tried to be posher. Langan's was a bit more like La Coupole. It was "Society". La Coupole had two sections to it – one posh side with linen tablecloths and another with paper tablecloths that was cheaper, so the artists obviously used to just go to the cheap side and eat, and of course doodle on the paper tablecloths. It wasn't a snobbery thing; it was just a division of those who were artists and those who were not. Peter's idea was to replicate this type of French-style brasserie in London.

Did it make a difference that there was art on the walls?

It wasn't so much the art, it was that the artists were all his mates. He was an odd bloke, but I liked him. He was profiled in the media a lot in the 1980s and said in one interview that I was his best friend. I said to him: "Can you not say that?" I knew it would get me into a lot of trouble.

Did you go to other art restaurants, such as Mr Chow?

I know Michael Chow really well. He was a great mate of mine. He still is. Now he's a billionaire. He's done it all: restaurants, art, even made recipes and a canned food range. He has a 100m^2 house I think.

Was Mr Chow a mould-breaking restaurant for the rest of London?

Like La Trattoria Terrazza in the 1960s, I guess. It was the place to be seen and impossible to get into unless you knew somebody. Full of beautiful people.

Where else have you had work displayed in a restaurant?

Michael Chow loved my work. I photographed him many times. Soon after he opened, he put up an exhibition of my work and they all got stolen two weeks later.

You had photographs in Le Caprice too?

Those were all purchases and commissions. I would rather restaurateurs buy works and that's that, rather than exchanging for food because some of that process can get a bit dodgy.

David Hockney

— Interview with Tim Marlow

I met Peter Langan through Patrick Proctor. It was called Odin restaurant. This was in the Sixties. We used to go four or five times a week; we could even go after the opera. I remember a bottle of Gewürztraminer was about £4 then. He always liked pictures and artists. He'd buy pictures at sales, paying not that much money, but they were always interesting. He did a picnic for me at Glyndebourne for the first night of The Rake's Progress. It was midsummer night, 21 June 1975. It was fantastic – he'd put up a big table with the best smoked salmon, large lobsters and hams that were delicious. It was supposed to be for 35 people but he took 125 bottles of champagne, and none went back. When the opera ended around 9.30pm, the table was still up with a lot of food on it, so I invited the singers and orchestra. We watched the setting sun and then the moon came up and cast shadows on the lawn. I knew the opera would be a success – and it was – and then we had a bus to take us back to London and he had buckets on the bus to pee in or be sick. When we got back to Odin restaurant, there were waiters with more champagne at about 3am. I had done a drawing on his menu for the picnic and he had written on it: "An evening of excess." It really was. I think everyone there will always remember it. Peter was a very generous spirit, who loved champagne. I did quite a few drawings of him. Then he opened the brasserie [Langan's] in Swallow Street, which was a success from the start. I went there a lot in those days, my hearing was better. If a drunk came into the restaurant, Peter would sit them down with himself and pour champagne out for them. He was a great character and his death was tragic.

David Shrigley

— with Christina Makris

Why did you accept the commission to make art for Sketch? What is it about art in a restaurant that makes it a different type of project?

Well, as we know, the context is half the work; it informs the work. So if you haven't made art in a restaurant before, you have to take that opportunity in order to make something different. I want to learn about something different every time and see the work through somebody else's eyes. I'm the type of artist who will kind of do anything and everything. I seem to be invited to do things because my work is close to craft of course – it's words and pictures, and a lot of it is conceptualism – and there is comedy in what I do which makes it digestible, and it's quite recognisable.

What does it feel like to eat surrounded by your art? Do you say, "Oh, I did that one when I was in that mood or that moment"?

I guess the work gets made in a compressed, set period of time when I have to complete it. Often you finish the art, and you look at it and say "that's a good one", or "that's a bad one", and the good ones disappear. But I like that. I don't remember making all the pieces here, so it's quite nice looking at them with a fresh eye. Then you think, "Hmm, I used a lot of that light magenta", or "Oh, there's another picture of a rabbit, maybe I should lay off them". It's quite rabbit-heavy here.

Your art is full of witty one-liners or poetic statements that make you chuckle. Is the humour an interruption to the aesthetic moment?

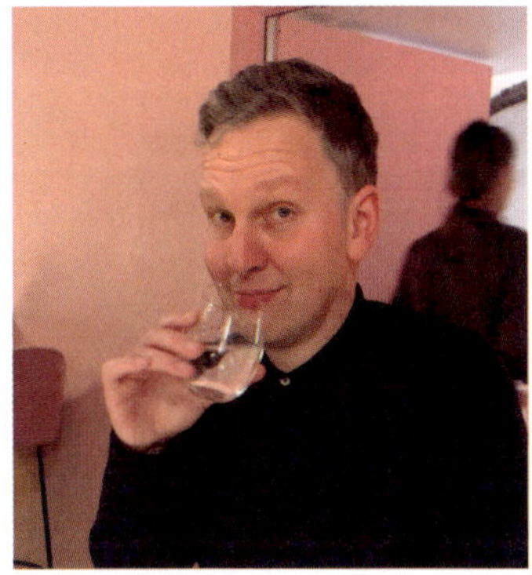

David Shrigley. Photo by author. Courtesy of David Shrigley and Stephen Friedman Gallery, London

I tend to make statements and figure out what they mean afterwards. Like a joke, I guess. You just tell it, and then try to decide whether if it was funny. That's a bad strategy, but it is the way I operate. You drink and when you come to the end it says "forget about it" in the bottom of the cup. I don't really know what I meant by that. And it's really only by creating the cup and having hundreds upon thousands of people looking at it, suddenly it's a work in progress. I've realised that all work is that, in that my own understanding of it will change. It might have seemed amusing when I did it, but now I can't actually remember what I intended. It just being here is an opportunity for it to ferment and change or acquire meaning. It's funny but not that funny. A joke a comedian tells is delivered in real time, but this is different, and I am not resistant to people acknowledging or identifying comedy in my work. It has a propositional nature to it, so it's not a definitive statement. I have the option of doing this and nobody has ever told me not to. So I continue. "It's OK", "It's not OK" – I suppose that can refer to sugar, but then again...

They are jokes, but also poetic. You say you do it without knowing how it will be received. Poetry is taking words out of the normal order. "Sugar" is repositioned to mean something else. And this is a powerful thing for a dining context. You are with friends, laughing, conversing, dining, but the art is in the back of your mind. Then you look up and it hits you. Do you hate it when people tell you what your works mean?

What I've come to realise is that when I have a conversation, when I am interviewed, or invited to talk, I never think about it until the moment itself. That's totally problematic because people paraphrase me. But this is a time when I have to talk about the work and think about it. So I am interested, always, to be told or shown what it means.

When art restaurants are operational, that is what is engineered – we behave differently in front of artworks because we are looking at them in a different way than we would in a gallery. Also, there is something about seeing art in an unusual context, in a space like a restaurant. Is there something democratic or accessible about this?

It's probably less democratic, given the nature of this restaurant. The art is an added bonus to dining here and this is a regulated space. Anyone can go to Stephen Friedman Gallery and get in, as long as you behave yourself, but this is the inner sanctum. I just go back to the context: there are other facets of seeing art here because people are in the way, you are drunk, you are crazy full of sugar if you're having the afternoon tea, which affects how you see it. And then there's the interventional art on the table with the teacups, plates and the teapot. My idea originally was that it was an installation on the table, a sculpture. You might be looking at the walls, but the dining table is also an exhibition, and it reveals itself the more cake you eat – I like that. So you discover things in an intimate way in an intimate exhibition.

This is an exquisite restaurant. Tell me a bit about the role of graphic art and design. Is there a hierarchy between the forms? Is there crossover between art and design?

I think the "other" art world is something that is not sanctioned by the state, it doesn't have public funding, etc. In that sense there is a hierarchy, and the other art world is DIY; it's neither good nor bad.

You have visited other artists' restaurants and art restaurants. Are there any that stand out?

I went to Noma to interview René Redzepi, and we were talking about art and food, but the restaurant was closed. Everybody kept asking me, "How was the food? What did you eat?" and he basically just gave me some Marmite, but it was the best Marmite I've ever had. I also went to the Paris Bar one time – with an artist who will go unnamed. He had made some art for it and the deal was that he would have a tab and invite people. He continuously said: "Come and have more champagne." There were loads of us there, and when the bill came it was like, "oh, shit". He had to talk to the owner and the owner said: "Ah, that's ok – just give me another painting."

Gary Hume

— with Christina Makris

How did the commission for *Bouquet* in Scott's came about?

Mark Hix is a friend of mine and was the head waiter at the time. They were refurbishing Scott's, and he had the idea of displaying art in there, so he approached me. And then I took measurements and went off and made it in New York. I was thinking about how Scott's had been bombed by the IRA many years before, because it was a big Tory political hangout in its previous iteration, so I painted a sort of Margaret Thatcher/wealthy lady, because I thought it'd be quite nice for the wealthy ladies with their hair, which is sort of gone now (the hair), to see pictures of themselves. So, I painted it, and then I was thinking, it doesn't feel right. I rechecked my measurements, and I'd done it too short. Fuck, man, what do I do? So, I added the two bits on the side.

Of course, when you look closely there are two side panels to it – like an altarpiece.

Yes, that was really fortuitous, because it made it into a fake little altarpiece...

To Thatcherism?

Yeah, to Thatcherism. Ladies who lunch. And that was it. I sent it off to the restaurant.

Did you ever think about the connection between food and art, or what it is to eat in the company of good art? We use aesthetic taste to kind of describe and appreciate art.

Well, I've got a lot of friends who are chefs, and there is a real connection between chefs and artists. When we were all younger, we'd go out to the restaurants, and when the chefs finished their shifts, the artists were still there. We also work very hard to make things hoping that all their little nuances are going to be appreciated, so there's an affinity. We sort of understand each other.

And then, of course, these places can become fantastic time capsules, both an imagined period for us to look back on and think how wonderful it all was, whatever it was really like, and a snapshot of a cultural history. From the Paris Bar in Berlin, which is all fags, booze, sex and artists enjoying getting out of the East and into the West, to the Colombe d'Or, which represents an incredible, self-assured, relaxed state of mind. I did do a whole restaurant, actually, in Pollen Street, with weaves and wallpaper – everything. I thought it looked really, really great, but it lasted for only about six months and then shut down. That was the absolute opposite: all promise and no action.

Is there something about displaying art outside of the gallery, not just for those who love art and are in the art world? People going to Michael McCarty's restaurant in New York and realising that they're eating under Hockneys; seeing museum-quality works in non-museum settings?

Well, it's hard for me to tell. I think it's very interesting when an artist does an installation, like Michael Craig-Martin did with that short-lived restaurant Ambrose for Corbin and King, and I did with the other short-lived one. I don't know whether it's democratic or not. Basically, the things that you make get bought, occasionally by a museum, or go to private places, so what intrigues me most is to go back to a restaurant, and actually see a painting over a course of many years and remember what it was that made me want to paint it; being surprised that I no longer paint like that and wondering what made that happen. It's like having a little space in your studio with a table and food being prepared for you, to go and re-look at something. But really, you'd have to ask the patrons of the restaurant whether it's just a vibe that they enjoy, you know, at Scott's. It does look beautiful in there, and so I don't know whether it's a relaxing sensibility of wealth and privilege that is so appealing, or whatever the fuck art's supposed to do when you actually do look at it. I mean, I do occasionally see women with their hair up sat under the painting, which is just thrilling to me. Whether the person they're having lunch with opposite actually goes, "Oh my God Moira, look, you are in the painting."

Art in restaurants is on the one level very aesthetic; you eat, you do all that visual, Kantian discernment stuff, but then each work also has a history, or an inside joke, or more meaning. I guess restaurants are a viable cultural output, not just a place to go and eat; things happen in them.

Most of this is sort of to do with friendships, too. Occasionally, I go to Scott's alone and it's lovely to look up from my book and see things that I like. I'll go, "Oh, there you still are, crikey. You were made a long time ago." Or, "Oh my God, that still looks rubbish." There's that sense of intimacy with the work that makes you feel less alone.

Yes, it is like renting an artwork for a while. My favourite work in the Kronenhalle in Zurich is a Soutine, a decapitated duck (it's really violent), and I just love it and I feel like it's mine when I'm sitting there. And next time you go back, it will still be there.

And when the restaurants close down, of course, they don't have time to have a history, so you don't know them in that way. But it would be very sad if [Richard] Caring decided he wants to get rid of it all, it'll feel like something's happened. Although all institutions go in the end, and there will be a moment of, "There used to be a great restaurant here and you saw these great works."

I have talked to their team and I'm hoping it's going to stay.

My friend Thomas Grünfeld has a very standard kind of coffee shop in Cologne, with a rule that says no telephones or laptops – he's sort of cross all the time in a friendly way. But he hangs works that he either borrows or gets from friends, so sitting in this rather ordinary place, you suddenly go: "Christ, that's interesting, what the fuck's that?"

I think it's a different way of spending time with an artwork. When they are placed in the dining ritual it changes the normal experience of sitting and eating, because of the way art is hallowed. We look at artworks differently from any other object in our field of vision.

Always. Well, if you ever have a dinner in one of the galleries in a museum, you do put yourself away for a moment while you acclimatise to what you're looking at.

John Beard

— with Christina Makris

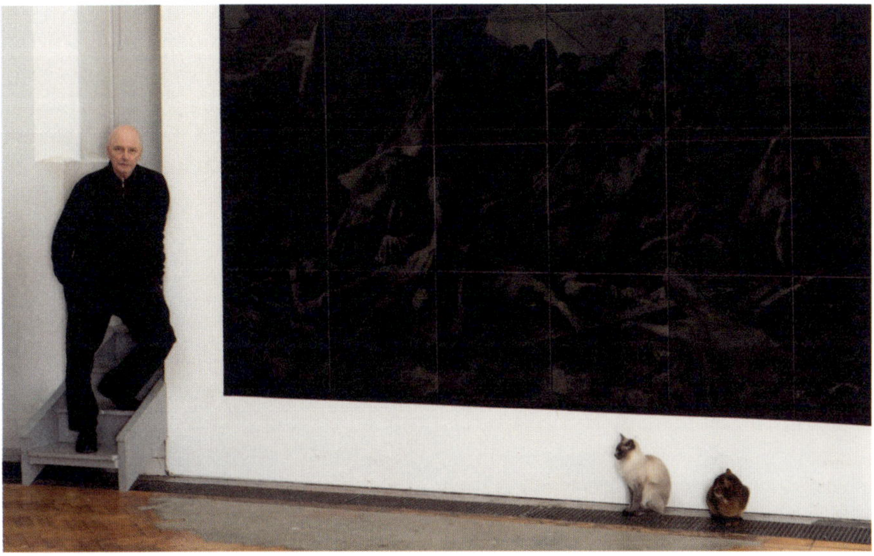

John Beard with his 1 to 4 scale version of *The Raft of the Medusa*.
Courtesy of Dominik Mersch Gallery

How did you become part of Lucio's art restaurant scene?

I was introduced to Lucio's early on in my career when I had an exhibition in a leading gallery in Sydney. They took me there for dinner and I saw Lucio had some art on the walls. The rest is history – art history. I have, in fact, introduced two or three artists who I think are exceptional, such as Imants Tillers and Hillary May, to Lucio's, who are very grateful. Quite often he would say to me: "So-and-so has brought me this work, what do you think?" It may not have been to my taste, but I would never comment on the quality of the work objectively or subjectively. I would only say to him: "I think it's wonderful that you're able to do this because it celebrates this amazing relationship you have with generosity and ideas and stuff." You're all dealing with stuff. Food is a bit like stuff.

On a restaurant menu, not everything is to your taste. You don't fancy everything, but it works. I guess it could be similar with the art.

Yes. There are works in his restaurant of different standards, but you don't go there because he's got the best art, you go because it's a place that's filled with love and inspiration, and Lucio is very proud of that. He always wants to have lunches with lots of artists. A lot of politicians and media people also go to Lucio's. It's interesting that the place is full of politicians, who are very good at telling lies, and then all these artists who try their very best to stick as close to the truth as they can.

The way the collection began with a Ned Kelly sketch on a docket is fantastic. Lucio told me that all his pieces were given to him by the artists. He's never paid for them.

Absolutely true. And he never says: "You owe me a picture now, I'd like you to do this." He asked me if I would do some illustrations for one of his cookbooks he wrote, but he's never specific and money was never discussed.

Do you think there's an element of democratisation in placing art in restaurants? More people go to restaurants than to galleries.

I think art can be seen and placed in a multitude of contexts, or at different times demands different sorts of looking. And when you have a beautiful dish, you don't want to gobble it up and talk about something else; I think it deserves your focus. A lot of my work is first and foremost about this: if there's any chance at all that it's going to be a worthwhile experience, you have to give it time. You feel with lots of young people, where is that focus? There is incredible focus on the screen, but what else is happening? I once wanted to see what would happen if I made paintings from looking at the television screen rather than from being with someone in the real world. I think the more different contexts that we see things in, the better.

We know that something happens to our cognition when we look at art, and there's something more when we add the aesthetic experience to the dining ritual. Château la Coste has a Louise Bourgeois couple hanging over the main dining table. How wonderful to eat under that for hours with those close to you.

There's certainly a dialogue. I go on my own to Lucio's and don't feel alone, not because I know the waiters and Lucio, but because I'm surrounded by all these connections when I look at the works – I know the artists, so that makes it very welcoming. I love that conversation between what's on your plate and the work. Often when I'm on my own, I actually enjoy the food a lot more because you're bringing in so many different sensations, your receptivity is fully charged. The last time we were there with Imants Tillers, who's a very well-established Australian artist, I said to Lucio, we want to sit under our paintings.

What is it like to eat under your artwork?

It's better when we're sitting with our backs to it. People come up and Lucio will say, "Oh, that's John, he painted this." You have a little bit of that, which I don't really want. But I guess it's gratifying and there's a warmth about it when you have this thing that you made behind you. It's particularly nice when you're with somebody else who's in that same position. I think it makes you drink more wine.

That's probably a good effect. So it isn't a case of you looking at it and thinking I should've done that?

You always do that. And the thing is, with a work in Lucio's, I probably see it more often than other works because they are in museums, or not always out. Some of them I'll never see again. It's always a little daunting seeing something you did a long time ago, but I'll be very honest, most of the time when I look back at things I did 10, 20, or 30 years ago, I think, "that's not bad". Whereas at the time, things are close to you and you need time to reflect upon them. There's continuity of having something at Lucio's because we go there every two or three weeks.

Lucio's collection is authentic and organic and, of course, Australian – because all the artists are. Do you look at the art and think, this is an Australian way of seeing?

I would say yes. Of course, there are some works in there that perhaps don't celebrate happiness, but are about sadness or much darker, but on the whole, it's a pretty optimistic body of ideas. I don't think if you walked into a European restaurant or even one in Japan, you'd find that. I'm not saying that they're necessarily lighter or have less valuable purpose, but there's something overall that distinctively tells you that they're Australian. Is there a frivolity? Yes, there's a playfulness, a celebration of life. The light in Australia and the colour and the youth of the country and the energy. Lucio hasn't many really complex conceptual works, and not much minimalism. It's what he's liked in the artists, but if he knew more artists, he'd have a much broader collection.

So you are actively introducing artists? That goes back to the origins of the restaurant as well: John Olsen would go there then bring other artists, so it becomes a backdrop to this cultural exchange and these discussions and ideas.

And growth in that sense, in opening up and learning from both sides. And then you enjoy the food, which you also learn things from.

It's wonderful for a restaurant to take on an educating role like that. Why do you think bodily taste is usually considered the lowest of the senses, when we experience everything through our bodies and dining is the most potent, literal, basic reminder that we have bodies?

The most famous restaurant in Australia for a while was Berowra Waters Inn on a creek outside Sydney. You could only go by boat or by plane, landing right on the river. Gay Bilson was the chef. I had my wedding reception there, which was absolutely amazing. There was purée, there was venison. I don't know what she'd done with the beetroot, but the colours were like out of a painting, and she said, we're not going to serve the dinner until the light's gone because I want people to be looking at the food not the view.

John Olsen

— with Christina Makris

I went to Lucio's yesterday for supper and sat by your painting, the smaller one with the brown hues on the main wall, which was very enjoyable. When did you first go to the restaurant?

Many years ago, there was a hotel opposite what is now Lucio's on the corner, and the artists always met there. It was kind of a watering hole. And Lucio's was a French restaurant called the Hungry Horse, which we used to gravitate towards. Then Lucio came and took over, and we liked him, and in no time he began to extend the building to what it is now. So that is the beginning. He was most generous with those of us who really couldn't afford very much. And in lieu of, well, debts he exchanged food for paintings.

That's a classic eating down system that operated at the Colombe d'Or and the Kronenhalle, and actually at Poilâne, the baker.

Really?

More for sketches. I quite like the idea of simple sketches for bread. Of course, in the history of aesthetics, taste is usually the lowest of the senses. It's not as privileged as sound or sight.

That depends on who you are.

Yes, tell me.

Well, in actual fact, taste is more important than looking.

Is there a connection between food and art, or eating and looking at and appreciating art?

Yes. What art's like is a style, and, you see, Lucio is superb at making people welcome and feel special. He's a master at it, but there's nothing forced about it, because that's just the way he is.

There are studies in anthropology that say dining together creates community and kinship. To add the aesthetic experience to that environment makes it an exercise in discernment. Would you agree?

Yeah, I think so. You see, food also has a memory. It incorporates a style. And when you're in, say, Lucio's restaurant, it's a fast trip to Italy; his cuisine is really built on the foundation of where he was brought up. I think that really good food has a sense of place, and I guess I'm speaking as a traditionalist, but we go to a restaurant not so much as a fashion thing, but because it's a passport to, in Lucio's case, Italy. As an artist, I like a sense of place.

You make annual New Year sketches and drawings for Lucio. How many years has that been going on for?

Oh, as long as the restaurant's been going. Since 1986.

I think it's pretty astonishing that from Sidney Nolan's off-the-table sketch of Ned Kelly is born this collection, which I see as a mosaic or a survey of very significant modern Australian art. You can actually have a crash course in Australian art while you have a meal there.

I like your idea of crash.

Yes. It does hit you. Would you say that Australian artists of the 20th century very consciously turned their backs on the styles and techniques of Europe, and decided to explore and interpret their own? Even a still life that is produced here feels different to me. It's pretty ineffable.

Yeah, it is difficult. Sid Nolan was very good at that; he could understand that Australia is just very, very different from a European experience. For example, there are oaks and other trees which are symmetrical, whereas the Australian eucalyptus tree is asymmetrical, and it seems to spread all over the place.

It's a different programming, isn't it?

One is based on symmetry. That's the European, English. But the Australian experience is like a dog's hind leg.

I'm here, far away from London, negotiating different time zones, and it's pretty liberating. I can imagine that could translate to a sense of possibility. It's primarily that I feel very unaccountable while I'm here, because I am 12 hours ahead of everybody, and it's a wonderful feeling.

It reduces paranoia.

Yes, maybe.

Because they can't get at you.

I guess if you're an artist, if you go and train in Europe, or have shows there, and then come back, it must translate somehow into the way you make your work.

It does. I lived in Spain and Paris for three years, and it did have a very big influence on me, but I had to return here, and it's all different. It has to, or should, turn into an Australian experience. Certainly, it has European antecedents.

I should think it would have to be that way, because you have to honour the time and place that you're in.

Yes. Sense of place is vital.

And you can't fake that. You can't fudge it.

You've got to experience it as you're experiencing it. For example, we've recently had these bush fires, but we've always had monstrous bush fires right from early colonial days. So what is a shock to a European is, for us, seasonal. I don't know if you've seen the papers this morning: the extraordinary rain clouds up in northern Australia? They've had 100 millimetres in 24 hours. The whole place is like a vast lake.

It's astonishing. I've been here for over a week now, and it's helped me to start to appreciate what I see as Australian art in a different way. Lucio's has a lot of paintings where the subject matter is food and still lifes – quotidian, if you like. But it's incorrect to compare these with still lifes by an artist in Spain.

It's different. I'm so glad you came to Australia.

Julian Schnabel

— with Christina Makris and Tim Marlow

Christina Makris: How did your project in Wallsé come about?

I wouldn't call it a project. It came about naturally. The velvet painting of Kurt, I gave him. He was very nice to my father, who was from Czechoslovakia, so they were both Europeans, and he took care of my dad until he died. My dad loved being European with Kurt and vice versa. Kurt would send him noodle soup made from egg that he would slice up. The Martin Kippenberger belongs to me, so do the Albert Oehlen paintings that were there and the big painting of the upside-down chandelier by my brother-in-law, Alejandro Garmendia – a Basque painter who was a contemporary of Albert. Kurt owns a few Kippenbergers and drawings and little paintings of Alejandro's. He owns the Baselitz drawing. The Dennis Hopper photos are mine. Most of the stuff is mine.

Tim Marlow: Do you just rotate the paintings?

All the stuff has been there for years, and in general it has been me rotating them when I feel like it. Kurt is an excellent chef. The food is good, and I wanted Kurt to feel like his was a place where people would like to be. Lou, Laurie and I lived up the block. I wanted to help Kurt because he made it so very nice for us there.

TM: So it was your idea to put in the art? Or did he know about the art?

I don't think he knew too much about it. He knew who I was. I just wanted to help him make the place successful. But it's nice when you see really good art in an excellent restaurant. At the Kronenthaler, for example, I was there after a show and looking at this old guy at another table who's looking at me. I say, "It's Joan Miró, he can tell that I'm an artist the way he's staring at me." So I write "to Joan Miró" in a catalogue and I give it to him, and sit down to eat. Then my friend said, "I don't think that's Joan Miró." I said, "Of course it is." There were about 14 people at his table speaking Swiss German, and I figured he had a big family. Anyway, I asked the waiter: "Who's that over there? Don't make it obvious I'm asking." He said, "That's a doctor, Frederick Wilty." It was his 84th birthday and he just gave a wing for dentistry to the Zurich University. So I took the catalogue back and I crossed out Joan Miró's name and I wrote, "To Frederick Wilty on your 84th birthday." This was 1982.

TM: Are the Colombe d'Or and the Kronenhalle the places that everyone tries to copy in Europe, whereas in America, is it Max's Kansas City that everybody is trying to ape? Or are people doing new things?

It's a different world now. Those places don't exist anymore. But it's always good to put paintings in unlikely places, and it's nice if they get it right. When I redesigned the Gramercy Park Hotel, the idea was to have an authentic place that had real stuff in it. I hung a Cy Twombly painting and an Andy Warhol *Rorschach* painting, as well as my painting *The Teddy Bears Picnic.* When Aby Rosen took over, he changed some of the art around. I still have some work there. My son Vito and Jeff Zalaznick also put art in the restaurant Carbone, which belongs to Major Food Group. It adds another aspect of life to a restaurant.

TM: What happened to Max's in the end? Did they try to revive it?

They tried, but Mickey Ruskin died, and it didn't work. Bands played there on the second floor: Iggy Pop, Sid Vicious. Obviously, there's a tradition in trading art for food if you look at the Colombe d'Or. It has to do with the people who run these places.

TM: It was artists and musicians that predominantly hung out at Max's Kansas City, rather than, say, writers?

Not true, but I predominately knew artists. Brice Marden was there, David Diazo. Neil Williams, David Budd, all sorts of artists. Bill de Kooning. William Burroughs, who knew Budd, because David was married to a circus acrobat from The Flying Wallendas. It seemed like I was the youngest artist in there at the time. There were people like John Chamberlain and Larry Poons. Larry thought that I was related to "Arthur Schnabel", so he used to give me a ride home sometimes – I'd be out until four o'clock in the morning until it closed. Mickey had been a lawyer, but he always had on a red crew-neck sweater, a tailored light-blue shirt and a T-shirt with his collar stuck in the back of his sweater. He had one gold tooth and kind of looked like Alice Cooper, but his hair was shorter. Mickey had immense fame and style. He befriended many artists and they followed him to restaurants that he opened. He gave me a cooking job at the Ocean Club some years later, even though it was against his policy because I had been a customer.

TM: Does the fact that you worked as a chef have any bearing on how you might install art in restaurants?

No, I always like to eat, and I met people who have restaurants. It's nice when they take care of you and feed you. When I was living in Milan between 1977 and 1978, I had paint on my clothes and people would give me something to eat if I gave them paintings or drawings. I liked the idea that you could make something and give it to somebody, and you didn't need money. It's very different from later, when you have money and you don't need to do that. In the US, they know who Abraham Lincoln is, but in Italy, they know who Caravaggio is. They know the artists: regular people who know that's their culture. I went to an eyeglass store once and the woman asked me if I was a student. I said I was a painter and she said there's an art collector who lives right next door. His name is Giuseppe Panza di Biumo, would you like to see his collection? I knew who he was. He had the biggest collection of late 20th-century art in the world. Ultimately, it went to MoCA in Los Angeles. I said, "Yeah." I get a phone call one day: "Hello, this is Giuseppe Panza di Biumo, would you like to go to Varese with me?" "Absolutely."

Maggi Hambling

— with Christina Makris and Tim Marlow

My memory of the old Ivy is the big Howard Hodgkin print, a Patrick Caulfield and Michael Craig-Martin's clock. Then the [former] restaurant owners bought two of my George Melly paintings, *George Always I* and *II*. *George Always II* still hangs in the club. And then Fernando [Peire] asked me to produce a painting for this long wall here, so we are sitting now under this wall of champagne.

Christina Makris: Oh, it's a wall of champagne?

Can't you see the bubbles, Madam?

Tim Marlow: Was the starting point for this the effect of champagne, or were you playing with paint in the abstract?

I'd been doing the *Wall of Water* series, which was shown in the National Gallery, so I especially made this painting this size, because none of those others were at all proportioned for this wall.

TM: You haven't done other walls of champagne, you just did this for The Ivy?

It's the only one, and it is on loan...

CM: So there's no eating down model, whereas there used to be with the previous proprietors?

Yes, it was wonderful. No money changed hands. And one got quite a nice tab. Have you ordered? I always have the same thing.

TM: I'll have the shepherd's pie, thank you.

Waitress: Madam, your steak tartare – a large, right?

Big, yes, big. Thank you.

TM: Does it alter your experience of the work of art, seeing it hanging above a restaurant table?

Of course it's nice to walk in and see one's painting on the wall, because it is a public collection, for the people who can afford to eat here. And I love the fact that the portrait of my great and much missed friend, George Melly, hangs in the club at The Ivy. When they had both the pictures, George and I sat underneath. It's very nice to see him, always there. I miss him so much.

TM: It's like he's here with you.

Yes. In a way.

TM: For you and George, and many other artists, was this one of the restaurants that you all came to? I quite like the idea that there seem to be obvious affinities between art and food and artists and restaurants. One theory is that artists often spend long hours in the studio and then go out and socialise with their peers in restaurants – that's the Parisian model. As a successful mature artist, are there still restaurants where you meet up with other artists, or has that scene gone?

If I had to do an interview for something like *Lunch With the FT*, I'd come here and have the steak tartare, and here we are today.

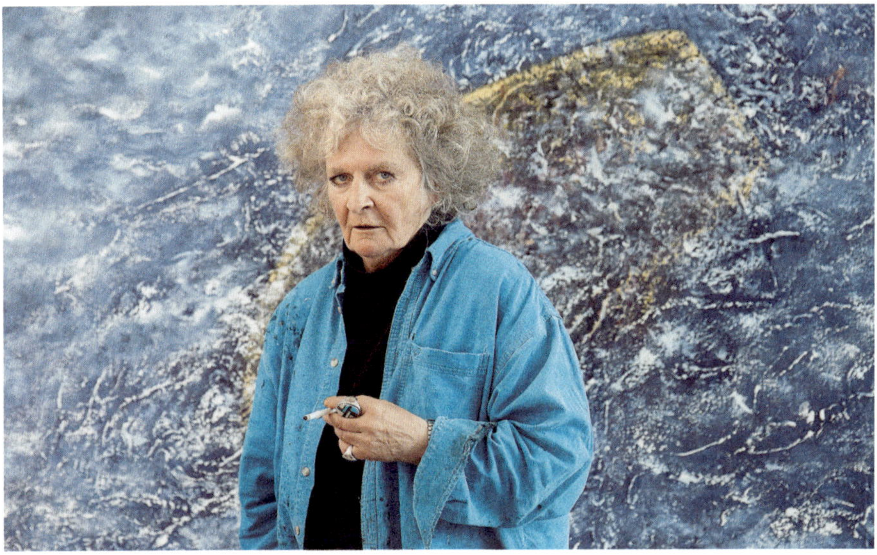

Maggi Hambling in her studio, 2016. © Luke Walker.
Courtesy of Marlborough Gallery London

TM: I love the fact you eat steak tartare, because if you have the ingredients and make it yourself, it must be like mixing paint.

I seldom mix paint. I put it on, and it mixes itself in the painting. I like things pure. But I don't know that I really mixed with many other artists. I mean, Sarah Lucas is a great friend, but we meet in Suffolk. Not many of my friends are artists!

CM: When did you first visit The Ivy?

I'd eaten here several times before they came to me [about the paintings]. It turned out that I have the same birthday as Sebastian Horsley, through whom I met Sarah Lucas at The Colony. We became great friends, and it was Sebastian who suggested those boys came along to my studio.

CM: And why is it that The Ivy has always had a reputation for attracting the cultural establishment?

Well, they come here to see stars and celeb-spot, and all that.

TM: Yeah, and celebrities in the broadest sense across the arts. They want art celebrities as much as anyone, don't they? Was the cultural establishment always here?

CM: The Ivy began as a restaurant for actors, and then there became a following.

TM: But if you look at somewhere like Joe Allen's in London, it started off being for actors and never went beyond that. Whereas this has become a place where architects, painters and artists come. It must have something to do with what's on the walls.

It is incredible at the Colombe d'Or, isn't it, to look across at a Matisse? When I ate there and it was time for pudding, my friend Tory said, "I just want something simple, an apple." And, of course, they couldn't produce just an apple, thank you very much. It came inside a draw-string bag, like money does in a pantomime. I started mine first and was chewing away, and said, "The food here is so extraordinary you can even eat the string." And she said, "I don't think so." Out of my mouth came yards of real string which I'd attempted to eat, thinking it must be edible. Anyone want a chip? Chips are always very tempting.

CM: Do you think there is a connection between art and food? What do artworks placed in a dining context do?

Well, of course, if there's a gap in the conversation, one can have a bit of a conversation with a piece of artwork, can't one?

CM: It's saved a lot of bad dates. Is there an element of access for people who might not be interested in the art – a middle-class meritocratic aspect to art in restaurants?

TM: You confer status with it.

Well, The Ivy is known for the quality of its drink and its food, isn't it? I think it's good in this new restaurant that there is such a variety of works of art; there's no sort of high style about it. In so many places, there's an awful suite of prints of China or something, and nobody can tell if it is wallpaper – you don't take any notice. But everything here is different from everything else, and so you do take notice. And that's another sign of quality.

TM: I was always quite sympathetic to Mark Rothko pulling the Seagram murals. To some, there would be a guilt involved in somehow compromising their art by putting it in such a space. But clearly you don't have any?

No. No.

TM: You don't care?

I mean, essentially, a restaurant is about pleasure, isn't it? You feel with friends a sort of warmth, and you're eating wonderful things.

CM: It's a sensual experience.

Exactly. Sensuality. Some art is more sensual than others. Of course, we don't need to go there at the moment.

TM: If you're in a museum collection, you often have to accept where the curators hang you, and with whom. Does the level of quality of the artists here matter?

I think The Ivy has always set a very high standard with its art. I would say this is first division art, wouldn't you?

TM: I would, and with the best restaurants, that's the thing that they have.

Michael Craig-Martin

— with Christina Makris and Tim Marlow

Christina Makris: How did you come to have work in The Ivy?

I was very, very lucky. I met Jeremy [King] and Chris [Corbin] through the art dealer Leslie Waddington, who ate at Le Caprice every day and always had the best table. Very often I was invited to have lunch with them. I loved the restaurant then, it was so much like a New York restaurant, and the only one at the time that felt unlike any other, with the long black and chrome bar. It was chic in an American way. Then they took over The Ivy and really wanted to have art there. There was work by Joe Tilson and Allen Jones. Patrick Caulfield did the beautiful window downstairs, Paolozzi did the staircase – it doesn't get better. It captured a moment. That was the first time I remember in London when there was an association of having good, identifiable art in restaurants. People would say, "that's a Bridget Riley, that's a Patrick Caulfield", which was unusual. They asked me to do a painting for downstairs, and on the basis of that I got credit. I wasn't paid. My whole life at that time in the 1990s was incredible, unbelievable. I certainly could not afford to go to The Ivy, but I came at least once every week or two, often with two, three, four, five guests, and had champagne and ate fabulously, and then just signed the bill. I never knew how much credit I had – nobody ever mentioned it. I love the eating and drinking down and obviously we won't tell the taxman, but it was the context. There's a certain level of design and food and a certain level of artists that it would attract or repel. Of course, King and Corbin were interested in art; they knew about it and thought about it. When they asked me to do the clock, there were all these stained-glass windows downstairs, so I used stained glass and included a knife and fork as a play on that. Of course, that increased my credit again, so I was able to continue living in the manner to which I had become accustomed.

TM: Without stating the obvious, the clock was functional. And with its references to dining and that nod towards Patrick, it fitted with your artistic practice – it mixed anything.

Well, I wanted it to be mine, and I am not the same kind of artist as Patrick. His window looked like nothing from the outside – you needed to see it from the inside, and it's beautiful. Whereas mine had to be beautiful and readable from the outside, and to have light on the inside. This tiny room it's in is like a cupboard, so all you had to do was put a light in it to illuminate the whole space.

TM: You have made art for different contexts. Are there specific things in the context of art in restaurants, or art that mediates your journey into a restaurant, that differ from others?

If I'm asked to do something for a specific place, I always make work as particular to that place as I can. The little painting I had here was in two parts, because the wall had a break in it, so it fit that space.

CM: Can you talk about the interiors you did for St Alban, which was a much more expansive proposition in terms of an artist creating work for a restaurant?

It was a disaster, in my view, that it failed. There

were things about it that were good and things that were odd. The architect Mike Smith was good, very minimalist. But it was a corner restaurant in the wrong part of town. On the other side of the street, you are in Mayfair, but this side was in Leicester Square – it is looking grander today than it did 10 or 12 years ago. They said something wonderful to Mike and me: that they wanted the restaurant to look like the first-class dining room on an Italian steam ship in the 1950s. Isn't that a great idea?

TM: Which would have art in it?

Yes, and elegant furniture. I did all the art, the furniture, the walls. It opened the same week as Scott's, which was much more upmarket and glamorous and got all the praise; all the reviews were a comparison of the two, so it didn't start well. And if you went in and it was not full, it would seem very empty. There are some rooms like that – this room was so low and so big. There were beautiful banquettes. I suggested carpeting for sound. It was the best restaurant in that you could sit six to eight people at a table, and everybody could hear everybody else, but you wouldn't hear the next table. It was the ultimate dining pleasure.

TM: The original Four Seasons was terrible for sound, and so is The Wolseley.

Many restaurants in London are glamorous in every other way, but the sound is terrible. And the St Alban also opened during the time of the banking crisis.

CM: So expense accounts couldn't pay for it. What happened to the art?

Everything was destroyed because it was built into the fabric of the building. I did images across all the windows and along the walls. There were floor-to-ceiling line drawings. I thought it would be like The Ivy with people standing outside looking in at people eating. It's been six things since then.

TM: Did the art draw criticism?

Very little attention was paid to it, and I always felt it was partly my fault that the art didn't work – that there was too much of me in it. There was no guidance about what they wanted or how much I should do. If you opened a restaurant like that today, it would have been a success. It was before its time.

TM: It's still radical to have an artist do the total installation. Damien did it with the Pharmacy and that worked – people's criticism of it was the food. An artist working with an architect to design a restaurant interior is not the conventional model; the restaurateur usually commissions artists to do specific works.

It's a very interesting model. The greatest tragedy about the St Alban failing is that it was a very daring project from the word go. No marble, no oak, no mirrors, no wood panelling – very chic in a different kind of way – and to have the artist and the architect come in from the first day and design the furniture, china, all the glass, all the spaces.

TM: Do you think restaurants are not radical enough? Is it too much when artists co-design them?

I don't think the restaurant would have succeeded either way, and I don't think I was the reason it failed. It may have been that it was too much.

CM: It's a competitive industry. Creative chefs and entrepreneurs can have everything in place and still there are external economic factors that lead to its failing.

TM: What art does is bring a different context, and a different feeling. And if the food is at a certain standard, it becomes a place where you want to be.

It indicates that you are in a glamorous place, and one at that social level at which this art sits.

CM: Can you think of artists' restaurants as cultural markers?

There's a kind you get on the continent which is truly an artists' restaurant; where artists meet and the walls are covered in art because they have given work and it's an honour to have their art on the walls. Such as the Paris Bar or the Kronenhalle. The Ivy was never used by artists – you needed to be wealthy to do that. Most of the artists eating there had given work.

TM: So before you got to the level of being invited to make work for The Ivy, were there any restaurants that you felt compelled to go to because other artists were there?

Not in London. In New York there was Max's Kansas City. That was my first experience of what it meant to be an artists' restaurant. All my friends were there; we were going at a very young age and glamorous people were there – it was a way of mixing. And there was very good art: I think a Judd, and there were Warhols. I suspect artists lent things.

CM: We are looking at different models of collectors, with Mark Hix, Marcus Samuelsson, it's a system.

You're absolutely right. The understanding of the uses of art to enhance the ambience and give it an identity attracts a certain kind of person. There is a much greater understanding of how all that works today than 20 or 30 years ago.

CM: We're back to taste and discernment – it's a differentiator.

I always assumed there are people who find it very attractive, who would not normally be in a world where they are dining in a room with a Damien Hirst; that would be aspirational. It's like renting a car you can't afford. It gives you that sense you are a part of a context that may be grander than you, which is a lovely thing about restaurants.

TM: This returns art to its function. So much art in the past was made for the wealthy to adorn their houses. The museum, as we all know, is a 19-century invention. So the idea that putting a work of art in a restaurant contaminates it, that we should see it in a pure white box, is merely an interlude of 150 to 200 years.

I like the idea of having art in a public place, where people haven't made a special effort to see it. You decide to go to a museum. I think it's nice to put art in a park or a restaurant where people who do not seek that context find themselves in it.

TM: You repudiate the notion that displaying art in restaurants demeans it?

It obviously has a decorative function, but I don't think it's the only one. It's hard to tell. For people who go to that restaurant and become regulars, part of their pleasure is to see what is on the walls now.

TM: A few years ago, I asked you what the most substantial change in art in the UK had been, and you said scale. Is the shift in people's attitudes to restaurants or art in restaurants also the result of expanded taste, or is London just lagging behind New York?

I came from America where there was a restaurant culture at every price range. Even when we were students, we spent a lot of time in restaurants. Cafés, mainly, and you had a pizza. When I first came to London in the 1960s this culture did not exist. There were three Italian bistros and two expensive French restaurants, and nothing else. Now everywhere you look there are restaurants. It's more than just scale, it's a transformation of taste.

TM: There are interesting parallels between the shifting role of visual culture in Britain and the rise of eating culture.

There is an aspect of sensuality. There is a deep Puritanism in Britain, and in the 1990s in London there was a sense of overcoming certain reservations on how to behave, eat, live; a feeling that it was all right to eat and live voluptuously. Now you can go and eat really well in London. At every level the demand of the audience and what they eat has risen astronomically. And if the art is this good, it signals that you will expect the same quality of food.

CM: Mark Hix told me that Bridget Riley is an important artist for him, as are you. There are three ingredients in art that he likes: colour, form, and also time and place.

He was the YBA restaurateur. He and Fergus [Henderson]. It's interesting that with that generation of artists who have those two restaurants – incredibly different in many ways – the food culture grew with the art culture.

TM: Fergus doesn't have art in St John.

Whereas Fergus's was the restaurant artists went to, to show they were artists.

CM: Trevor Gulliver says there's a hidden painted-over Banksy in St John on one of the white walls.

That's a wonderful story. We can all say that!

TM: Mark talks about three elements in good cooking, and often in your work there are three elements...

Mark is very clever because he liked artists; he understood and learnt. He's not trying to make his cooking look like art, but a certain simplicity and clarity is a very clever thing to have taken.

CM: That is back to the confidence and synthesising that a tastemaker brings to unite the two.

TM: In your work, the interplay between line, form and colour, the classic three elements of any artwork, is what makes the piece. Presumably, there's a direct parallel with a lot of Mark's cooking.

The individual elements merge together but there's a lot that's separated. What I always tried to do was keep the things separate so you can focus on one or the other – you can look at the colour, the line, the form and the subject – and yet the work is made up of the conjunction of all of them. It's deconstructing and reconstructing.

CM: Which I think Mark would be quite happy about, because his ingredients each have an origin – it happens to be British.

But there is a very clear definition of what you are having. Sometimes you have a dish where you don't know what's in it, but not with Mark. Jeppe Hein in Denmark is amazing. I knew him for a while. He was restaurant crazy. He really went into it in a big way. He poured every penny he had into it.

TM: The other model is Ferran Adrià. He's invited to Documenta, he writes books, the art world loves him.

I know people in the other arts, and they often prefer the art world as a social world to that of the cinema or theatre or literature. We have the most exciting world.

Michael Landy

— with Christina Makris and Tim Marlow

Tim Marlow: Can you tell us how the Scott's commission came about?

Mark Hix came out to my studio when I was making all those *H.2.N.Y.* drawings and asked if I wanted to put a piece of work in Scott's, which they were refurbishing. He said, "It's like an exchange: we get the artwork, on a loan, and then you get a certain amount of sittings, plus alcohol." I knew Gary Hume was doing it, we're both ex-Goldsmiths students, so I said, "How many meals is he getting?" Mark said, "103 sittings a year." I said, "Well, I want 104." Anything to get one over Gary Hume.

TM: So, you knew who the other artists were and that mattered?

Well, I knew Gary Hume was going to be my next-door neighbour because his artwork is literally next to mine, and that he was making it a certain size, specifically for that space. So I just made mine the same size. He's my good pal, Gary is.

TM: And it fits with what you were working on at the time?

Yeah. It's called *H.2.N.Y. Suicide Carriage, 2005*, and it's 122 x 304 centimetres.

TM: That body of work came from an event that happened in the Museum of Modern Art in New York and it's been shown in other museums. How was it seeing it in Scott's? Did that context change its meaning?

It was more that's the body of work I was making at the time. So I thought that's what should go into Scott's. I think Gary's kind of work was

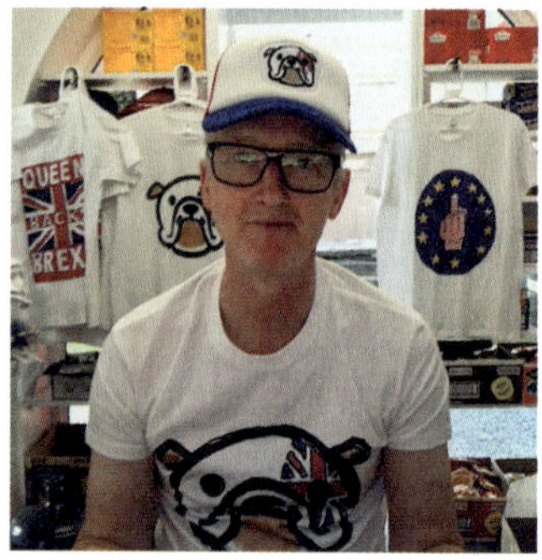

Michael Landy

specific to Scott's. Are you going to speak to Gary as well? Just tell him I got one more meal than him. That's all I'm really interested in.

TM: Were Mark Hix's restaurants in general an interesting context for your generation of British artists?

Well, we drank with Mark and had a nice time with Mark. So it felt all very connected really. And he would acquire work – he bought several drawings of mine. He's still got one in his restaurant in Smithfield Market. I thought it was just a nice exchange, a convivial, pleasant thing. We'd have my mom's 70th at Scott's. It had nice associations.

TM: Do you feel affinities as an artist with that world of chefs and restaurateurs?

No. I remember I once tried to draw Mark's portrait, and he turned up on his Vespa and within five minutes was asleep. So I put a backwards baseball cap on his head and tried to draw him like that. But he's got quite a big head. I gave up in the end. I thought, obviously his thing is much more nocturnal. I mean, I need to remain reasonably sober to make artwork. I can't then have a busy social life. It's one or the other. I've got to get up in the morning and the dog expects me to take it for a walk.

TM: There's a strong tradition, particularly in the 20th century, of artists doing what you did at Scott's, eating down off the work they've given to the restaurant. Would you have done it if it had been a restaurant you didn't actually like the associations of?

No. I mean, I didn't know anything about Scott's, so it was Mark, really. I like Mark, I have a connection with him. I'm pretty sure we went to his for Christmas one year. Not that we ever talked about art in great depth or anything. I was going to do something for his space in Brewer Street, treating his body like slices of meat; a kinetic kind of ceiling piece, hanging, with bits of Mark, but he would have to be naked. And then I was going to take bits of him that we could eat. That obviously never happened.

TM: Why not?

Christina Makris: He didn't want to get naked?

I'm sure he'd probably love to get naked. But, I don't know, just one of those ideas that I had that never materialised.

CM: There's a kinetic Tinguely machine in the Colombe d'Or.

Is that the one that breaks plates?

CM: It's not very kinetic...

Most of them aren't any longer, because they need to conserve them.

CM: Maybe he traded his art for food as well.

You know, if you ever see a black-and-white picture of Tinguely, he's always at a table drinking and smoking...

TM: Do you think art adds anything to a restaurant?

Oh, I'm sure. I don't know what though, apart from the obvious things.

TM: Such as?

That it's cultured somehow. They're not showing reproductions are they? They're showing original artworks.

TM: When you were at art school, or when you decided you were interested in becoming an artist, did the old myth of the artist in the café (usually French) ever chime with you?

I actually wanted to be a textile designer, because I remember someone nailing some daffodils onto a board on my foundation course, and I thought, I don't know... because I'm working class, I wanted to get a job at the end of it. It was only because I worked out that I was going to become completely unemployable that I became an artist. I was actually very reluctant.

Peter Blake

— with Christina Makris and Tim Marlow

Tim Marlow: Was the Colombe d'Or work a commission? Or did you just go to a great restaurant, eat great food and make great drawings?

We spent a holiday there, the girls swam and we didn't move from the hotel. My knees were worse then. We didn't even get to the Foundation Maeght. But I'd been often before. I always draw on holiday. There are drawings on tour with Ian Dury. I draw all the time. But I've never shown them before. So it goes back to 1945 and comes up to the day before the show opened, I did a drawing of Chrissy and cut out the date before the show opened.

TM: What did you make of the art in the Colombe?

There are some great things. I don't much like the Sean Scully, but I like the Calder.

TM: When you were first involved in making art for restaurants, did you know about the Colombe d'Or?

The very first time was when I was a student at Gravesend School of Art. One of the first coffee bars was called El Sombrero in Gravesend, and I helped to do a mural there. That would have been in 1948. A friend of ours started the coffee bar and students painted the mural.

TM: Did you use the eating down model and get free coffee?

Probably! [My work in restaurants] has never been commissioned, it's been more acquired, so I can't put dates on it. In San Lorenzo on Beauchamp Place, Lorenzo bought *Babe Rainbow* in 1967 and some early prints, and they are still there. Le Caprice had a photograph by David Bailey of me. And on the way down to the gents are my wood engravings of a side show, and on the way to the ladies are the etching portfolio, *James Joyce in Paris*.

TM: Did they discuss acquiring them with you?

At that point, Chris [Corbin] and Jeremy [King] were good friends and I think I ate that down for a while. I'm still eating down the legacy of them, because when they sold everything, they made a stipulation that anyone that was eating down got a set amount. At Scott's, we still just sign the bill, which is wonderful because it's one of my favourite restaurants.

TM: Do you remember Scott's when it was just a hole in the ground?

Yeah, I do, I went to the earlier one. It was always a fish restaurant. I also went to Sheekey's when Henry Cooper used to go there. If he had a fight the next day, he'd go there and have lunch, and all the food was white because they couldn't fry in that area, so it all had to be boiled. It was very Jewish and boiled, such as fish with potatoes. Of course, now it would be a themed restaurant with a minimalist aesthetic. Sheekey's built its reputation around the theatre, but Scott's interests me as an art idea because it wasn't conceived as an art restaurant, and it wasn't an artists' restaurant. That was very much aimed at the YBAs on the whole. Damien has got a piece there, Gary, Tracey. All of them. Later, they asked me to do something, but we never got round to it.

TM: What about Michael Chow?

He is very interesting. Have you seen the current Bonhams magazine? There's a long article on Richard Lin, who's having an enormous comeback. A while after the Royal College, Dick [Richard] Smith and I had a flat in Chiswick, and across the road was Richard Lin. We were both painting in the front, so I would wave to him, and he was obviously Chinese. He had long black hair and was handsome. Eventually, I went to see his studio. It was the first kind of minimal space I saw. It had nothing, just an easel and a wooden box. That was absolutely it. I became friends with him. Michael was his friend. They were refugees from China, and they had all been to art school by then. Michael lived in the garage of Victor Pasmore's house on the Thames. So I met Michael and he invited us to dinner in his garage. It had a dirt floor and he cooked on a stove and slept on a mattress on the floor. I mean literally a dirt floor. We became friends, and when he opened the restaurant, he started to commission art. Jim Dine ate his down within two weeks, because he was going back to the States and took parties of 20 every night. I'm still eating down because when I finished, Michael said: "Oh, just keep coming, I like it that you come." When he commissioned me, he said: "Don't do anything too ethnic, I don't want any chinoiserie." So I made it as Chinese as I could: it's got glass hanging off it and little Chinese figures. So Michael is the manager of the two wrestlers.

TM: But he had no connection to wrestlers. Is this Peter Blake slightly subverting his request not to make something Chinese?

Yes, that's it. As much chinoiserie as I can throw in there.

TM: Do you think he approaches the relationship between art and restaurants in a significantly different way from other people because he trained as an artist, or is that just one of the things he likes to project?

I think that it probably is different. Chris and Jeremy, the other people who did promote art, never went to art school. Michael was also a sculptor and an architect, so his restaurants have a very architectural approach. Jim Dine made the collage of hearts at Mr Chow and Clive Barker did two Peking ducks in chrome that hang from a chain. Dick Smith actually did an installation upstairs on the right – he made it on the spot. Michael was very aware of art, and me, Clive, Paul Huxley, Dick and maybe John Hoyland were all given a certain amount to eat down at the time.

TM: Did you go to Odin's?

David Hockney and R.B. Kitaj both used the original Odin's a lot – they were eating down there. I didn't particularly. I went a couple of times. And Peter [Langan] just acquired art, he had an eye and commissioned David to do the menu and acquired his works.

TM: Was there a "scene" around Mr Chow and Langan's, or was that a fabrication of the restaurants? And did you artists identify more with one than the other?

Certainly, Langan's, yes. I used Chow's a lot, and when I divorced, my kids would come up to London every two weeks, and we'd have

Sunday lunch there, but there wasn't a group of artists that used it as a meeting place. Patrick Procktor did the big murals upstairs [at Langan's] and David would identify with it.

TM: Did Langan's feel more like The Colony Room, where artists would congregate?

Later they did. When I met Chrissy, we hung out there an awful lot. We'd go to lunch, go home, and then come back for dinner. People like Brian Clarke went, and a lot of galleries used it for aftershow parties. So it was very much an art-scene place.

TM: Why did you go there so often? Did you like the food? Did you like the marriage of food and art? Was Peter just entertainment?

Peter was great. I met Chrissy pretty much through going there, so we had a soft spot for it. And it was just easy to be there. I don't think I ever ate it down there, so it wasn't about that...

TM: A labour of love then? Did you make specific works for specific restaurants?

No. Peter then bought my work for his other restaurants. He came to the drawing show and bought a current piece, but then sadly came back the next day and said: "I'm sorry I've made a mistake, I am going through a divorce and I mustn't buy it." He'd obviously seen his accountant who told him he couldn't buy at this point. Chow's now is packed with stuff. He bought so much. For a long time, any market I had was because Michael bought stuff.

TM: Was work ever sold through restaurants?

I don't think they worked with dealers, but I am certain Michael sold stuff. And he sold a piece about two years ago which set a new market for my work, *Little Lady Luck*. It went for more than anything [my work] ever went for.

TM: Was there a sense of commercial exposure in those restaurants?

No, I wouldn't have thought so.

TM: So, what was the appeal of having art in restaurants, given you can have works in most of the major galleries in the world?

One was asked, and it was flattering that Michael would buy things in auction and put them in the restaurant.

TM: Did it feel part of the legacy of 1960s London?

Yes, pretty much, because it was 1980 when Chrissy and I got together, and it was like a club. The big round table on the left was known as Michael Caine's table. The three owners were Richard Shepherd, Caine and Peter. Richard Hamilton had lots of meetings there with Dieter Roth, and there were always artists on that table.

TM: Do you think Damien Hirst's restaurant felt different because it was an artist who created it?

I think so. It was a new phenomenon. The first few times I tried to book the Pharmacy,

I couldn't get in. There was nothing like that before. Even Michael being an artist wasn't the same. He didn't do the restaurant as an artist, he did it as a restaurateur.

TM: One of the interesting things about Michael is he talks about theatre as performance, and he's quite central; the cult of personality makes him central. Was there a parallel with Langan's – the name of the man above the door?

They were very different in character. Peter was an amazing drunk. I witnessed a night when we were sitting in that front bit and the tables for two were arranged down the middle. Peter came and talked to us, and a little dog three tables along was yapping. Peter dropped to the floor, crawled along and bit the dog. Literally, we saw him do it! So a lot of the legend at Langan's was Peter being drunk and the goings on. He performed, whereas Michael created the space for performance. Peter very rarely ate at Langan's. He introduced us to a wonderful Greek restaurant on Tottenham Court Road that didn't open until 10 at night, so all the croupiers and people of the night went there – low-lifes. It was the best Greek food I ever had. It was a husband and wife, and they had a fat boy and a thin boy. It had a stinking carpet that squelched as you walked across it. If it was cold, they would put an electric heater under the table, and there would always be boxing on the television. At one point he asked me to do a mural for it, but we never got round to it.

TM: Would you have done a boxing mural?

Ancient Greek boxing. But it was tremendous food. The wife used to have a range in the restaurant, and if you had the mezze, you'd have the most incredible food, chips that were hand cut and fried. The best chips. One night it was only Chrissy and me in there, and he came out and chased his wife around with a knife.

TM: So, it was you and Chrissy and Peter sometimes, some prostitutes and Greeks, but it didn't become an art scene?

I can remember various members from the Cambridge Theatre going there.

TM: Were you ever part of The Colony Room Club?

Oh yeah. Very much so. I think later on they had some art behind the bar when the YBAs were using it. I was at the Royal College from 1953 to 1956, so I was using the French Pub and the French Club a lot. Johnny Minton had his last show and a party at the Gargoyle. He put money behind the bar.

TM: Did the French Pub have art in it?

Dodgy photos. They replaced them with photocopies. I have the original photos from there because Michael Hoppen [the photography dealer] bought the lot – I had some Diane Arbus and did a swap with him. They were photographs of French cyclists and boxers. The other place I had some prints in was, the two boys, are they Spanish? They now own Quo Vadis, and a little tapas restaurant off Charlotte Street – the first place I had tapas in London, in the early 1980s. They had my prints in the gentlemen's toilets. They often end up there.

Christina Makris: The Ivy of course also has interesting art.

Yes, it did, and The Ivy was a different matter. MJ Long had done designs for it (I recommended her as the architect) and they actively commissioned works. On the left-hand wall I made a piece with photographs of people who used the old Ivy – Winston Churchill, Olivier. Then on a little shelf in the front there was a red rose that you would give to your lady as you went to dinner, and a box of Black Magic chocolates and a bottle of wine called Olivieri. They are still there – I think the flower was replaced a few times. But that was a commission. I also did a series of Marilyn Monroe pictures, there must have been about 30 that were in the bar. Two are still there.

TM: Langan's came out of Odin's, but it also came out of La Coupole. When your art was commissioned, did it feel part of London, or did it feel part of a bigger commission? Did you feel there was a connection with Paris or to other restaurants?

Yeah, restaurants were changing, weren't they? The idea of La Coupole was new in London. But I suppose there has always been the Café Royal and places like that in London.

TM: But the quality of food changed in the 1960s as well.

Very much. That started with the first trattoria, Terrazza, in Soho behind the French Pub.

TM: Were they Italian immigrants doing Italian cooking?

It became famous and then opened on the King's Road. It was Alvaro [Maccioni] who started the trattoria [in London].

TM: That became very arty. Was there any art in the original?

Oh yes, it would have been [Enzo] Apicella. He's the other very important art figure in art restaurants. He designed the early Pizza Expresses. That would have been all his work, rather like Steinberg cartoons, and in all of the pizza places of that time. He was an Italian living in London.

TM: So, there's an Italian scene, a French scene, a Greek scene, an Irish scene, a Chinese scene. Do you do things in LA or New York?

I went to Los Angeles in 1963. The *Sunday Times* had a commission that offered artists £300 to travel, which you would use on your fare. David [Hockney] went to Egypt and did those beautiful Egyptian drawings and Philip Sutton went to Tahiti. I'd just met Jann Haworth, who needed to go back to LA and I wanted to visit, so I went there. I didn't do anything for restaurants but met Ed Ruscha and that crowd. And Larry Bell – he's such a dude. He's on the *Sgt. Pepper's* cover.

TM: Langan's has been taken over, and while some of the work remains, it has become a bit of a mausoleum. The great Procktor mural went; they painted over it.

I went to the auction when they sold off Peter's collection, and I bought a beautiful Richard Hamilton, the one of the libraries, dedicated to Peter, which I pretend is me.

TM: It's lovely that an artist acquires work from another artist from a restaurant. The Laura Knight is still there, for example. That must be worth a bit.

We went back when one of the galleries had an aftershow there, and it was terrible.

TM: It feels like a monument to something rather than a living thing, I have to say.

I've got the feeling people still go for nostalgia.

TM: It might be bad, but it still stands out in Mayfair now, given everything is so shiny and sushi. We can reclaim Langan's. You are an artist who is very comfortable with art appearing in restaurants and responding to commissions.

I've done a restaurant recently at Paddington Station, at the new back entrance. It's kind of Pop Art and it sticks out. But I have a strange history because at junior art college (I was 13 years old), they told me I should not be a painter and do graphic design instead. I tried for the Royal College as an illustrator, and I got in as a painter. But I had to do national service in the RAF, so I went at the age of 21. I'm a bastard, a rogue in both worlds; I'm misunderstood in the painting world because I'm too graphic. Therefore, I'm comfortable with displaying art in different places.

Polly Morgan

— with Christina Makris

What is different or significant about displaying your work in a restaurant, rather than in a gallery space?

Art and food is a happy marriage. I guess there must be ascetic artists out there who can't be characterised by their overindulgence, but I haven't known one. Restaurants and bars have also always nourished artists, so they are natural places to display their work. Galleries are mostly places of quiet and reverence, restaurants and bars the opposite. It is nice to know art in all climates.

What is it like to go to the Groucho and eat and drink under your work?

It felt such a natural progression from being a regular to being an exhibitor. I suppose it makes places feel more like home when you see your own work and that of your friends.

What does it mean to you to have your work included in an important historical collection such as the Groucho's; to join the ranks of the previous generation of British artists?

It's always a thrill to see my work alongside artists I admire. There is such a long tradition of artists eating and drinking in Soho, and the Groucho especially in recent history. Being able to leave work behind is like marking time – leaving relics of a time gone.

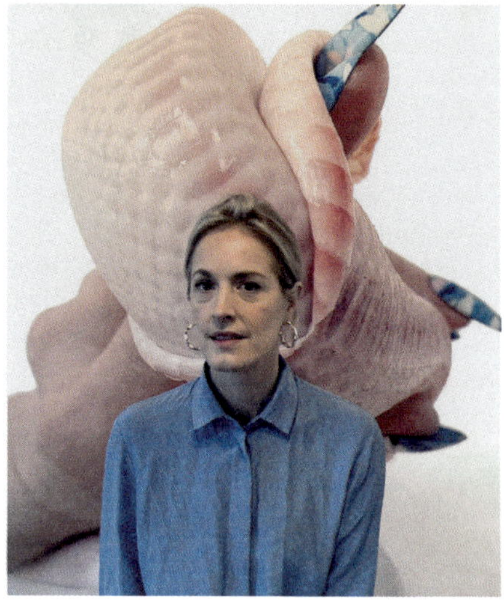

Polly Morgan

Are you involved with any other restaurant commissions or collections (I know you have a piece in Scott's, for example)?

I have long been friends with Mark Hix and have always had work in his restaurants. Art and food have always intermingled in Mark's life and work. Sadly, Hix restaurants have been a Covid casualty, but he is irrepressible and will be back.

Sanford Biggers

— with Christina Makris

Could you tell me about the work you've done with Marcus Samuelsson?

Marcus and I actually go back a couple of decades. We've always really been into the senses and all of the arts – literature, music, fashion, photography, fine art, food and so on – and seeing that as an immersive combined experience. So when he opened the Red Rooster in Harlem, it was a no-brainer that he would have me and Thelma [Golden, director of the Studio Museum] and other creatives there early on in the design phase, just brainstorming about how to make it a comprehensive experience where it's not just the food, but the whole vibe. From the opening day I had one of my larger quilt paintings in the Red Rooster. Over the years he has swapped different paintings in the same place, so it ends up being like a showcase where I can try some things that I don't necessarily send directly to museums or galleries. But my studio's literally a block away, so I could show something there for a few weeks or months and get a response; get a gauge of the reactions, the physics of the work.

So using the restaurant as a lab space to experiment. And what are the reactions that people have had to your work? If they are really into it, do they want to know what they're looking at, or does it just create part of the experience?

Well, I think the Red Rooster is particularly special because Marcus does a lot of experimentation and freestyling to create his cuisine, so it just makes sense that that permeates beyond the kitchen onto the artwork. Even the musicians and DJs there bring flair to the restaurant. And he moves pieces around and invites in other artists, so there's constant flux. If you go, let's say every other month, it's always going to be a new experience.

What is the role of the Red Rooster in the local community as a space to showcase and experience? Why do people love it, do you think?

That's actually an interesting and complicated story. In my humble opinion, I think the Red Rooster really was the beacon, the proof of a concept that you can have a fine-dining experience in Harlem that didn't exclude local Harlem nights, but also invited internationals and downtown people to come and engage. It is very special. In terms of the reaction I've received from my own work, it's ranged over the years. I have business meetings there and we eat under one of my artworks. It's better than me just showing some pictures on an iPad. Just last week I was walking out and a gentleman at the bar stopped my friend and I and said: "Oh, you guys were sitting over there, did you read any of those books? I wrote that book of poetry right there." It was really nice because I was like, "Well, I made that painting." And he said: "I've been looking at that for months." You end up meeting other creatives that you didn't even know about.

You and Marcus and Thelma are from different disciplines, but you're sharing a philosophy. Would you say you could consider the Red Rooster as an artists' restaurant, like the cafés in Paris that welcomed a range of intellectuals and creatives?

Definitely. Probably like a salon in that way.

You might go to The Four Seasons, and of course very important artworks are there, but they don't change. It's not that improvisational, it's more like going to a museum in that sense. Whereas I feel the Red Rooster is almost organic and alive.

And responding to the issues of its time. I see the food as part of the Red Rooster's gathering of ideas and exchange. Is that far-fetched?

No, not at all. It seems very much of the time right now. Artists and musicians know the places where they can go and be treated well, and the Red Rooster has always done that, because of Marcus's great respect for all creatives.

Do you think there is a connection between artists and restaurants?

I think it's synaesthesia – all creatives want to be operating on multisensory levels. If you're a visual artist, you do want to engage people's sense of poetry, and you want them to basically hear sounds as they're looking at your colours. The dining experience is one that has always been able to exploit that. I was living in Rome recently, and you're eating in a beautiful piazza with a fountain and smelling the herbs and the flowers that the wind wafts through, and you're looking at a mosaic, or a marble statue. All your senses are activated and it becomes, for lack of a better word, basically a transcendental dream.

Transcendence is a very loaded term, but it is important because this is how you know that something special is happening; an artwork is extraordinary. I just love the fact that you have these dining traditions in the Red Rooster with families and dates coming in, and it's human, it's quotidian, and it's poetic.

But what Marcus does, which is definitely part of his life philosophy, is to place his restaurants in areas where there is a certain mix of people: a liveliness, a melting pot of ideas and even cultures. He thrives on that and likes the restaurant to be able to absorb that type of energy and give it back, so that everybody feels comfortable and integrated, as opposed to left out.

And you could argue that more people go to restaurants than go to museums.

Absolutely. When I'm in the Red Rooster, it is not uncommon for me to speak to 90-year-old women who have been quilting all of their lives, because I've been doing paintings on quilts. And I might not run into them at a museum, but I will at the Red Rooster – Marcus will introduce me. He changes the way you think you're communicating. Having work in a more quotidian environment does allow for different responses, and you learn from that.

The Studio Museum and the Red Rooster are so closely associated – we've joked that the Red Rooster is basically the canteen of the museum. What is the role that an institution like that plays in the city, and is the Red Rooster part and parcel of that?

I would say Marcus, Thelma and myself

consider ourselves stewards of a rich legacy in Harlem. And that interaction between the museum and the Rooster is really a modern-day version of the Harlem Renaissance. There are these places that are linked to each other. I remember so many openings at the museum where people are meeting up ahead of time at the Red Rooster, going into the show, and then heading right back to the restaurant afterwards. So you have this back and forth, and you're picking up more people along the way, and meeting people at the Rooster who had no idea about the museum, and people at the museum who had no idea about the Rooster, and now they're coming over. There's been a really great synergy between these two places for several years. The three of us have talked about it and there's this great sense of pride that you're actively contributing to the culture beyond just the museum walls and the restaurant walls, but literally on the street – on the thoroughfares between the two.

Tracey Emin

— with Tim Marlow

What is different or significant about encountering art in a restaurant rather than a gallery space?

If it's a favourite restaurant and you always sit at the same table by the same artwork it gives you a feeling of familiarity like it's home. But on the bad side, too many restaurants just choose art for declarative value and the art is unappreciated.

What is it like to visit a restaurant and see your work hanging in it, or eating under it? How involved are you with placing work? I know you created the entire room at 34 but did you specifically request where the neons (*Trust Yourself and I Said Don't Practice on Me*) at the Gunton Arms were sited?

I had nothing to do with The Gunton arms, it was all Ivor Brakka, he's been a long time collector of my work. For 34, I had complete control over it and decided what would go in it and what wouldn't. When Richard Caring first asked me I said no because people might not want to go to a restaurant that was full of my art. So eventually when I agreed to do it, I wanted it to have a classical feel. I heard that there were a few complaints about pubic hair, obviously not in the food but in my artwork. So that's the other problem with art in restaurants, it has to be heavily censored because it has to be palatable.

I am past the point where I will exchange food for art. I now really think if restaurants want my art, they can buy it through the galleries and I get very hurt when the maitre d' doesn't know who I am when my art is hanging up behind her. But I always get a kick seeing my fish fingers drawing by the loo in Scotts.

There seems to be a natural affinity between chefs and artists – do you think the two professions are so close and complementary and if so, why? Mark Hix claims to have taught you to cook. Did he? And how important were his restaurants for London when he began to include art in them?

Fucking liar. I've had great fun with Mark cooking. But yes, he has definitely taught me a few tips. Mark is defiantly an artist's chef. I cannot say that about myself, but a lot of artists are very good cooks because they take a lot of pleasure in using creative ingredients. They like to create beautiful things. Many chefs like Mark Hix and José Pizzaro cook like it's a work of art.

Vik Muniz

— with Christina Makris

Can you talk about your relationship with food and cooking, and with chefs?

Growing up in Brazil, I had a grandmother who was a great cook. She used to cook with firewood, and I used to help her in the kitchen. Chefs and cooks have a very similar practice – it requires putting things together. Relationships between senses are very important for any artist, and I think when artists connect with chefs, these things are underlining conversations. In the 1970s, artists started making some creepy kinds of things inspired by isolation tanks: you smell something, see a light, touch something furry, and then, "Oh, the senses." I always found that so corny and horrible, because if you want to excite all your senses simultaneously, all you have to do is to eat something: it has taste, it has smell, it's visual, it has that noise it makes. Greek salad has a sound, and if it's very fresh, it's music. Also, taste is much more empirical than with visual things. You can actually remember an image. Remembering a taste is very rare. It's very complicated, because the references are more volatile, they are not very defined.

No. There is scholarship that combines food studies with neuroscience and phenomenology and embodiment.

I've been talking to a collector of mine that does something with taste at Columbia University. He can produce taste in your brain; he actually can make something sweet salty, and something salty sweet. Neuroscientists love him. I've been fascinated by taste since I was very little; there was food being cooked and we ate together every day. Sitting together to have a meal is what makes a family.

Yeah, and it makes kinship and community. But taste is often seen as the lowest of the senses because it's animalistic, whereas in aesthetics taste is of the highest order.

I think first you have to make a few case scenarios, to understand this more clearly. Having a dinner in a restaurant involves a lot more factors of experience; like your loved ones, these are all distractions. But if you think about taste from a more scientific perspective, when you make an artwork, you're exteriorising something that exists in your brain, and you're working in this very thin interface between the senses and the intellect, between what's outside and what's inside. Our culture happens in that very thin area, because it's how we understand whatever is outside of us. When you are putting together a meal, it's almost religious – you're putting something inside of you. I think this is what fascinates me the most. It's like a eucharistic thing. Whenever I'm eating, I'm so close to my senses and also doing something so essential for my being, you know?

Yes. Sustenance.

People can live without art, but people cannot live without food. That's why I'm jealous of chefs because of the way it is complete; they can entice every single sense simultaneously.

I do like what you say about taking food into your body.

When I say eucharistic... My parents are very religious, and I'm fascinated by it. I find it funny that Christ is already plenty of symbols, and the ultimate consummation of all of that is when you eat the body of Christ. In anthropology, cannibal people, they eat the warrior; the idea that to get the spirit of something, you have to consume it orally – I find this amazing. And there is a reason why we are so fetishistic about things that we ingest. Japanese food is fetishistic. The guy makes soy sauce, or pickles the same way he has for 200 years. Every single Japanese restaurant I've been to in Tokyo, or Kyoto, I have a meal and I feel like I'm watching a movie. It's an aesthetic experience.

Can you talk more about the link between cooking and your work?

The processes are all part of what you put in your mouth, and when I make a picture, I want people to think of how that was done by looking. I love the fact when you put something in your mouth, the whole process comes through, and it goes beyond the making in the kitchen, into the fields – great food makes you think of the earth it was planted in. I've been fortunate enough, even though we were poor in Brazil, to have sat at the best tables in the world. I get the feeling when you put something in your mouth and, even if it's just a salad, and you go, "Wow, man", your mind goes to another place, you know?

Yes. So it's process, but the process is also a ritual. Something that can be seen as quotidian becomes transcendental. Restaurants are fascinating because that can be misconstrued as everyday: quick, eat, it's done. But if you stop and think of the ceremony of it...

You touched a nerve there, because I always say that museums and galleries are where we ritualise visual experience. Otherwise, it's just like driving and seeing out, or looking at things that appear on the corner of your screen on the computer. When you go to a restaurant, you're there to eat and already the whole experience has been ritualised, and the fact it comes in courses you understand a little bit of the ceremony. And when people subvert it, you also think it's good when they bring dessert first. Crazy! And the subversions sometimes are interesting, sometimes just artistic. I don't like it when it is too artistic.

When a chef places art in his restaurant, there's something there; I'm arguing it has to do with taste and perception, perhaps how we experience pleasure. Pleasure is being in touch with what is our most fundamental programming. We have brains, and through perception I judge that I'm drawn to that object rather than this one, that's all part of it.

There is a difference between real pleasure and just something that feels good. Feeling good has to do with your sensations, comfort, things that you are attracted to. Real pleasure comes when you are experiencing something that feels good, and you're enticed to understand why it feels good. What makes an art image different is that it makes you think about the way you see things. It makes you ask: "What am I looking at? Why am I seeing it this way?"

How did you come to work with Daniel Boulud?

We just hit it off right away. He is one of the people I like the most in the world. He's such a machine. He's very funny, he's a great conversationalist. We cook meals together. He's one of the most accomplished chefs in the world, but at heart, he's an artisan: a cook. And these are the people who I really like, because they know how to make things technically impeccable.

Can we talk about how the wine stains project happened?

A mutual friend said to me: "Daniel wants to talk to you." So I went to the Bar Boulud, and it was a very long space, with curved walls. The ceilings were not very high, and it was very hard to hang anything significant there. He said: "I want something crazy, okay? Something that people don't think about when they are in a wine bar, like a conversation piece." I like wine, but I thought: "What is the thing about wine that people would find annoying? It stains – your carpet, your shirt." That for me is utterly annoying. I get invited to a lot of blind tastings, and the people there are even more annoying than the people in art galleries. You know, the people who know everything about wine. One thing I know about wine and about food is if you know too much about it, you don't know what you're talking about. So I thought wouldn't it be funny if the guy was so good that he could look at a stain and go, "Ooh, that's a Bordeaux..." So I said to Daniel: "Why don't we have small pieces that can run all along the walls, something that repeats, so people will be compelled to look at one then another, like a comic strip, a collection of stains. And they can say, 'Oh, look at this compared to that.'" He loved it. And then I realised how great he was. He was like, "Let's have fun then. I get some people who have really great cellars. Some of them are boring, but they are going to bring good wine. Then you get a bunch of crazy people." At the first meal, I invited David Byrne. It was so much fun. We had two events. We just tasted the wine, and Daniel cooked, and we created this huge collection of stains, which we photographed. I thought that was a really successful partnership, because you couldn't show that anywhere else. It was site specific.

There's a lot that could be read into it. There's a lot of symbolism.

Our biggest dinner was with Creative Time at St. John the Divine. There were 650 people, and Daniel served a Brazilian dish. This was one of the most beautiful things I've ever seen. We have all these really great things that we've done together, but we always have fun doing them.

I love the fact that when he needs something art related, you're the go-to artist, and when you need something culinary, he's the go-to chef.

The way that Daniel does things is very involving and energetic. He's like a star. He's just radiating good vibes and is a very fun guy to be around. There are other chefs who are real characters, such as César Ramirez from Chef's Table. He's Mexican and has this tiny place in the back of a supermarket, but it's one of the top places in New York. His food is Japanese-French, and he's always moody and kind of cranky. But he is great.

He is a character. They say that chefs might not be big speakers, but they speak food.

A lot of artists, especially abstract painters, have a hard time describing what they do, and I think chefs are the same. If they talk about food, they may be a little reticent, but most are very good if you talk about something else. If you talk to César Ramirez about Japan or Mexico, he is wonderful; he rises up and he becomes a person.

Do you have any examples of restaurants around the world that you've been to that might have art incorporated in them, besides the Colombe d'Or?

I would say that El Bulli was something like that, almost to the point of exaggeration. I didn't think I was having a meal, I thought I was in a theatre play or something. I'm not particularly fond of molecular cuisine, I think we've passed that point now, but when it started it was interesting, in terms of trying to find out what your relationship to food is. When I say there is no conceptual food...

It came close.

I have to say that I was challenged by it, in a kind of tasteful, intelligent way.

Do you feel that you and Daniel are engineering this environment for diners to go and experience and test their perception of what happens when you eat?

With Daniel it's different. He did the place in Miami, for instance. We thought let's bring a little bit of the south, it has to be colourful. And it's funny, dialogues happen between the food and what people see. The mosaics you see at Boulud Sud are all kind of broken. It has to do with the fact that with Mediterranean food you don't have to cut too many ingredients. So the mosaics are chopped up like the food. And they're colourful, they're beautiful to look at.

Are there other restaurants in the world, specifically Latin America, that interest you?

The artsiest one is Contramar [in Mexico City]. It doesn't have much art in it, but it's artsy. Rio is not a place where you eat a lot. They always say that São Paulo is a good place to eat, Rio is a good place to drink. For me there are three places in the world that I am a little crazy about: Japan, Italy and Mexico, and coincidentally, they all have extremely rich cultures visually, too.

Acknowledgements

Besides that *other thing*, dining and art are the two most pleasurable activities available to us, so it wasn't a real stretch to undertake research and fieldwork on this project four years ago. As a restaurant brat, my childhood was spent running around these fascinating places, annoying the staff, meddling with the food and hiding where I wasn't supposed to, so restaurants have always been in my blood. Then came the philosophy... then came the art... then it all came together.

I was fortunate to visit many different cities and meet chefs and entrepreneurs for whom this profession and industry is both a calling and a curse. I can't thank them enough for opening up to me about why they do what they do, why their culinary endeavour wouldn't be what it is without the art, and how art speaks to them as chefs and restaurateurs. I hope these stories and essays reveal how magical something as quotidian and prosaic as dining really can be. The artists understand this – I am grateful to all those I spoke to and who gave me their two cents' worth of what dining and restaurants mean to them, why they were captivated by chefs, and what the significance of art and food combined is for them.

None of this would have been possible without the patience and encouragement of my good friends, who at times believed in this more than I did. A list of thanks and gratitude here: Michael Metelits – *il Louche*, you were right (again); Ameera Kawash – from the days of the Gorgons, we knew everything before we knew everything, thanks for supporting a better narrative; Tim Marlow, thank you for the dining, aesthetic and otherwise, as well as all the tough love counter-argumentation. I am grateful to you for your help with access to some of the best creative minds and hands around; Ed Behrens, my fellow *restaurantphile*, the most cool and collected, patient and pertinent editor a girl could ask for; Juan Alvarez, for the reality checks – even the good ones; Hedwig Vollers, for showing me there is joy in the practical; Berber Meindertsma, for unwavering belief in me and this project and reminding me all the time; Danah Sadaawi, for helping me to make connections to all parts of my history; Martina Batovic, for your constant reassurance and giggles; Kimiya Minoukadeh, for your enthusiasm and Socratic method; Alexander Bradford, for your unbounded, rallying cheeriness; the Makris family, yes, mother, I am *still writing* the book; Alyx Wood and Ed Hugo, for keeping the faith and the long positions on my writing portfolio; Hannah Adam Hamshere, for the eternal sunshine of the spotless mind (and body); Frederico Matos, for your academic wisdom; Julia Gallop, for the Pavlovian pop of the cork when I needed a break; Brian Fu, for understanding my project the way an aesthete should; Julia Hobsbawm, for being a cheerleader of me and my projects; Phil Allison and the Cultureshock team, for taking a chance on this hybrid subject, and seeing the potential I did in bringing together art and restaurants.

Bibliography

Allen, Carol, *Leah Chase: Listen, I say Like This*, Pelican Books, 2001

Bachelard, Gaston, *The Poetics of Space*, Beacon Press, Boston, 1994

Bayley, Stephen, *Taste: The Secret Meaning of Things*, Circa Books, 2017

Beriss, David and Sutton, David E., *The Restaurants Book: Ethnographies of Where we Eat*, Berg Publishers, 2007

Bottinelli, Silvia and D'Ayala Valva, Margherita *The Taste of Art: Cooking, Food, and Counterculture in Contemporary Practices*, University of Arkansas, 2017

Bottura, Massimo, *Never Trust a Skinny Italian Chef*, Phaidon, 2014

Brillat-Savarin, Jean Anthelme, *The Physiology of Taste, Or Meditations on Transcendental Gastronomy*, Vintage, 2009

Brillat-Savarin, Jean Anthelme, *The Philosopher in the Kitchen*, Penguin, 1970

Buchet, Martine and Assouline, Prosper, *La Colombe d'Or: Saint Paul de Vence*, Assouline, 2012

Bullard, E. John, Lewis, Richard, Anthony and Tureaud A.P., *Leah Chase: Paintings by Gustave Blache III*, Hudson Hills Press, 2012

Burkhard, Reimschneider, *Kippenberger*, Taschen, 2014

Chow, Michael, *Mr Chow: 50 Years*, Delmonico Prestell, 2018

Dale, David and Galletto, Luico, *Soffritto: A delicious Ligurian Memoir*, Craftsman House, 2008

Fathy, Hassan, *Architecture for the Poor: An Experiment in Rural Egypt*, University of Chicago Press, 2000

Finkelstein, Joanne, *Dining Out: Sociology of Modern Manners*, Polity Press, 1989

Fisher, M.F.K., *The Art of Eating*, Houghton Mifflin Harcourt, 2004

Friedman, Andrew, *Chefs, Drugs and Rock & Roll: How Food Lovers, Free Spirits, Misfits and Wanderers Created a New American Profession*, Harper Collins, 2018

Gallati, Mario, *Mario of the Caprice: An Autobiography*, Hutchinson of London, 1960

Galletto, Lucio, *The Art of Food at Lucio's*, Craftsman House, 1999

Gopnik, Blake, *Warhol*, Ecco, 2020

Gregg, Melissa and Seigworth, Gregory J., *The Affect Theory Reader*, Duke University Press, 2010

Guyer, Paul, *The Cambridge Companion to Kant*, Cambridge University Press, 1992

Heidegger, Martin, *Poetry, Language, Thought*, Harper Perennial, 1975

Hoderich, Ted, *The Oxford Companion to Philosophy*, Oxford University Press, 1995

Howse, Christopher, *Soho in the 80s*, Bloomsbury, 2018

Issa, Rose, *Chant Avedissian: Cairo Stencils*, Saqi, 2006

Ivy, Robert and Hicks, Alistair, *Chateau La Coste: Art and Architecture in Provence*, Merrell, 2020

Kivy, Peter, *De Gustabus*, Oxford University Press, 2015

Korsmeyer, Carolyn, *Making Sense of Taste: Food and Philosophy*, Cornell University Press, 1999

Krass, Leon R., *The Hungry Soul: Eating and the Perfecting of our Nature*, Chicago University Press, 1999

Langan, Peter, *A Life with Food*, Bloomsbury, 1990

Marinetti, Filippo Thommaso, *The Futurist Cookbook*, Penguin, 1989

Martin, Lesley A., *Reflex: Vik Muniz, a Primer*, Aperture Foundation, 2005

Massey, Ian, *Patrick Procktor: Life and Art*, Unicorn Press, 2010

Norberg-Schultz, Christian, *Meaning in Western Architecture*, Rizzoli, 1980

Norton, David Fate and Taylor, Jacqueline, *The Cambridge Companion to Hume*, Cambridge University Press, 2009

Onfray, Michel, *Appetites for Thought: Philosophers and Food*, Reaktion Books, 1989

Ozick, Cynthia, *Art and Ardor*, Plume, 1984

Pallasmaa, Juhani, *The Embodied Image: Imagination and Imagery in Architecture*, Wiley, 2011

Patten, Alice, *The Groucho Club: 30th Anniversary*, Preface Publishing, 2015

Proust, Marcel, *Swann's Way*, Penguin Classics, 2004

Ribbat, Christoph, *In the Restaurant: Society in Four Courses*, Pushkin Press, 2017

Rilke, Ranier Maria, *New Poems*, Copper Canyon Press, 2016

Ryser, Sibylle and Zürcher, Isabel, *Pays de reve: The art of the Kronenhalle Zurich*, Prestel, 2019

Said, Edward, *Homage to a Belly-Dancer*, London Review of Books, 1990

Spang, Rebecca L., *The Invention of the Restaurant*, Harvard Historical Studies, 2000

Spence, Charles, *Gastro Physics: The New Science of Eating*, Penguin, 2017

Sutherland, Alasdair Scott, *The Spaghetti Tree: Mario and Franco and the Trattoria Revolution*, Primavera Books, 2017

Sutton, David, *Remembrance of Repasts: An Anthropology of Food and Memory*, Oxford, 2001

Tallis, Raymond, *Hunger*, Acumen Press, 2008

Tang, David, *Rules for Modern Life: A Connoisseur's Survival Guide*, Penguin, 2016

Telfer, Elizabeth, *Food For Thought: Philosophy & Food*, Routledge, 1996

Visser, Margaret, *The Rituals of Dinner: The Origins, Evolution, Eccentricities and Meaning of Table Manners*, Penguin, 1991

Vyner, Harriet, *Groovy Bob: The Life and Times of Robert Fraser*, Faber, 1999

Walker, John A., *Art and Celebrity*, Pluto Press, 2003

Warhol, Andy, *The Philosophy of Andy Warhol*, Penguin, 2007

Ying, Chris, *You and I Eat the Same: On the Countless Ways Food and Cooking Connect us to One Another*, Artisan, 2018

Index